Joe Jennette
Boxing's Ironman

A Story of Race, Love, &
the 20th Century's Longest Finish Fight

By

Joe Botti

WIN BY KO

Win By KO Publications
Iowa City

Joe Jennette: Boxing's Ironman

A Story of Race, Love, & the 20th Century's Longest Finish Fight

Joe Botti

(ISBN-13): 978-0-9799822-7-9

(hardcover: 55# acid-free alkaline paper)

Includes footnotes, bibliography, and index.

Cover design by Jonathan Slater and Gwyn Snider ©

Manufactured in the United States of America.

Win By KO Publications

Iowa City, Iowa

winbykopublications.com

Dedicated to my children Katrina, Michael, Joshua, and Jenna.

Contents

Acknowledgments

There are many people who helped to make this book a reality. There are those, however, whom without their help this book could not have been possible. My wife Michelle and my children Katrina, Michael, Joshua, and Jenna, they have sacrificed much from my passion for the sport of boxing. My mother Patricia McGinnis-Caputo who works tirelessly on any boxing endeavor I engage in from boxing as an amateur, running a boxing gym, organizing boxing shows, training and managing fighters, to writing this book. My sisters Donna Vaccaro, Robyn Dazza, Patricia Botti, and Kimberly Connallon. My publisher Adam Pollack of Win By KO Publications, Joseph Louis Botti, Robert C. Botti, Clay Moyle, Maria Guerrero-Rosado, Commissioner Lucio Fernandez, Mayor Brian P. Stack, Ben Hawes, William A. Mays, Jessica Rosero, Nick Mastorelli, David Wilcomes, Angelo Palumbino, Denise Del Priore-Villano, JoAnn Flannery-Mostaccio, Jessica Casey, Sabrina Jennette, Vincent Rufino, Mark Rufino, Aldo Martinez Jr., Jonathan Slater, Anthony Borzotta, Joe Borzotta, Tom Hartlieb, Charles Hartlieb, Libero Marotta, Neil Marotta, Henry Naumann, Henry Munker, Theresa Runstadtler, Rich Zampetta, Nicole Palms-Reyes, Paul Hanak, Christopher Crispino, Margaret Barrett, Brian Barrett. Bibliotheque National de France's Daniel Frydman, Francois Wyn, Jean-Michel Dumas, Paola Guayroso, Pascale Guillemin, Elisa Ghennam, and Tatiana Troussevitch. Nancy Jefferson of St. Ann's Church of Hoboken. The British Library's Kathryn Mouncey, Amanda Corp, Debbie Horner, Diane Warden, Jane Walsh, Alison Whittleston and Jim Coyle. Pat Culliton, Larry Shapiro, Mr. Desmons, Union City High School's Jonathan Slater, Adriano "A.G." Garcia, and Anthony Bodiglio. Bob Rooney Sr., Sal Alessi, Jimmy Dupree, Phil Shevak, Abe Torres, Vincent Robles, Hugh Holquin, Carlos Osorio, Leon Ramirez, Robert Fazio, James Sanmartino, John Settembrino, Chuck Wepner, Linda Wepner, Jersey City's Public Library reference staff under John Butler, and the New Jersey Room under Cynthia Harris. Special thanks to Rosemarie Trevelise, Mayor Bruce D. Walter, and Commissioner James Madonna. David E. Toms, my copy-editor for his professional and tireless efforts and sports historian Henry Hascup for his amazing boxing historical knowledge. Last but not least Gregory Speciale, creator of joejennette.com, his knowledge and passion for Joe Jennette is unsurpassed. His inspiration helped make this book a reality. If I left anyone out it was purely unintentional. All French to English periodicals were translated by this author. All photographs in this book came from the collections of JoAnn-Flannery Mostaccio, Gregory Speciale, Ben Hawes, Dave Bergin, Lou Manfra, Denise Del Priore-Villano, and Joe Botti with the exception of the historical marker ceremony photos which were courtesy of Aldo Martinez Jr. Cover design created by Jonathan Slater.

Foreword

During the turn of the twentieth century four gladiators reigned supreme in the ring: Just which of these four fighters was the best is a matter that never was settled.

Of this great foursome Jack Johnson was probably the best boxer, Sam Langford the hardest hitter, and Sam McVea the strongest.

Joe Jennette was the best combination of the three. He was a good hitter, but not a killer like Langford. He was strong, but not as strong as the gigantic McVea, while as a boxer he did not class with Johnson but came close to it.

At strength, boxing ability, and hitting power, Joe Jennette was a combination hard to beat, and he had the additional qualification of being able to eat up punishment. How he could take it. As for courage, stamina, and long-distance fighting ability, he was simply the best.

Joe was a phenomenal athlete. He could have played in any sport today. He was trained by some of the greatest masters in sports history, in sports such as baseball, basketball, boxing, handball, and wrestling. Joe Jennette in my opinion was the Jackie Robinson of boxing.

Jennette transcended the sport by breaking barriers, becoming the first man to fight the injustice of a color line on both sides, black and white, having been born into a biracial family.

On the 100th anniversary of the greatest fight of the century, (Joe Jennette vs. Sam McVea at the Circle of Paris Arena, April 17, 1909) myself and others, including the writer of this book, dedicated the first historical marker in Union City to one of Hudson County's greatest citizens, Joe Jennette.

Gregory Joseph Speciale
Historian/Genealogist
Creator of JoeJennette.com

Do not rejoice over me, my enemy;
When I fall, I will arise;
Micah 7:8

Introduction

On June 15, 1969, Joe Jennette was inducted into New Jersey's Boxing Hall of Fame in its first induction class. Twenty-eight years later, on June 15, 1997, Jennette was inducted into the International Boxing Hall of Fame. The summary of his career in the induction program was less than half a page. The information in the booklet covered the same facts that are frequently mentioned when Jennette has been written about over the years. His battles against Jack Johnson, Sam Langford, Sam McVea, and Georges Carpentier. Very little information has ever been published about the man outside of his battles in the ring with these boxing legends.

In February 1996, students for a local school newspaper in Union City N.J., the *Union Hill Times*, wrote: *Sadly, if nothing else is done, especially in his hometown, in a few years the memory of Joe Jennette will be gone for eternity.*[1]

In 1997, a street rededication ceremony was held in Jennette's honor in his hometown of Union City. Among those in attendance was Jennette's daughter-in-law Angelina Jennette. The street was originally dedicated to Jennette in March of 1933.[2] On April 17, 2009 on the one hundred year anniversary of Jennette's epic battle against Sam McVea, Gregory Speciale, Sabrina Jennette, and I petitioned the city of Union City to place an historical marker at the site of Jennette's home and boxing gym. There was no major media coverage of the event, even though I sent a press release to many media outlets.

In a way, the lack of publicity perfectly mirrored the lack of attention that Jennette's career received during his lifetime. Joe was not the type of person who commanded attention and he did not have a reputation, as did Sam Langford and Jack Johnson, as a womanizer. For this reason Jennette's story was more than likely considered boring.

After Jennette died, an article was written about him by Billy Williams in the September 1958 issue of *The Ring* magazine. Williams described Jennette as: *"quiet, modest, always the gentleman, a fine husband and father..."*[3]

Nat Fleischer, the great boxing historian, said of Jennette: *"Joe was a giant colored fighter of the clean cut type. A gentleman both in and out of the ring, he gained the respect both of his competitors and the public. Joe was never involved in a scandal. He always gave the best that was in him and he was a fighter of high moral character... He was the best heavyweight ever developed in New Jersey."*[4] Fleischer also called Jennette: *"a master strategist."*

Jennette's name was often misspelled and his hometown was also often

---

[1] *Union Hill Times* "Joe Jeannette: The Forgotten Hero" by Kevin Penton & Mike Suarez February, 1996 pg. 7.
[2] *Baltimore Afro-American* April 1, 1933.
[3] *The Ring* September, 1958.
[4] *Black Dynamite "Fighting Furies"* by Nat Fleischer pgs. 190-192.

mistaken as Jersey City and Hoboken. *The Big Book of Boxing* wrote an article on Jennette in 1975 entitled "The Great Black Heavyweight Time Forgot." In the article it was written that: *Jennette could fit no role in his lifetime and his life demonstrates no great lesson for today.[5]*

This common thought on Jennette is disheartening and one that I hope to prove wrong in this book. That a man who was a loyal husband and loving father, who abstained from drinking, smoking, and womanizing, holds no great lessons for today is truly sad. Jennette lived his life combating racism in both his personal life as well as in his quest for an opportunity at fortune and fame in the sport of boxing. His story is one of struggle and perseverance, triumph and tragedy.

Boxing historian Bert Sugar said of Jennette: *"The best place to hide a needle is not in a haystack, but in among other needles. Such was the sad misfortune of Joe Jeannette, a polished, steel-like heavyweight with pinpoint accurate punches, whose name and deeds were well hidden indeed by the exploits of Jack Johnson and Sam Langford for the first decade and a half of the twentieth century. And, not incidentally, denied his rightful place in boxing history by an archaic chastity belt known as the 'color line.' Promulgated by men whose broad minds had changed places with their small waists, the 'color line' was hardly as deep as Pythagoras' theory: It was merely a sheltering line, sheltering white fighters from black, a move based on both bigotry and restraint of trade-holding that incompetent men should be helped to unearned wealth by removing them from head-to-head competition with more gifted performers. And there was no more gifted performer around in his day than Joe Jeannette, called by boxing historian, A.D. Phillips 'one of the ten greatest heavyweights of modern time.' "[6]*

Unfortunately, when Jennette and his wife died so did most of the information on his private life. In this historical narrative, I have done my best to gather as much factual information as possible, to fill in the cracks left by a very quiet and personal man.

Jennette's heritage and nationality was often misreported, whether by accident or on purpose, as Bob Queen describes: *"Jeanette… according to the press reports of the day, was born in various localities and was given just as many varied nationalities. At that time, any act of prowess on the part of a colored man was the cue for the public to find some excuse to say that he wasn't a colored American. In Jeanette's case, it was his name which leaned towards being French. In spite of the fact that he was called an Indian, a West Indian, Dominican, and many other things, he was born just three blocks away from his present business and home."[7]*

In this book you will find that Joe Jennette and Sam McVea's names are spelled different ways in newspaper articles. Unfortunately both of their names were misspelled throughout their careers. In the newspaper articles

---

[5] *The Big Book of Boxing* January 1975 "The Great Black Heavyweight Time Forgot" author unknown pg.26.
[6] "The 100 Greatest Boxers of All-Time" by Bert Randolph Sugar.
[7] *Afro-American* January 25, 1947.

and books I have referenced I have left the spelling of their names as they were written by the authors. You will also find discrepancies in such things as fight outcomes, boxing records, and other name spellings in newspaper articles. Again I have left the articles as the reporters have written them.

In the turn of the twentieth century, boxing rules differed from state to state. Many states, including New York, New Jersey, and Pennsylvania did not render decisions in bouts unless there was a knockout or disqualification. If a bout went the distance it was officially ruled a no-decision bout. However, newspaper reporters would individually or in groups render their own decisions and publish them in the newspapers the following day. Unfortunately, many times reporters differed on the results of a match, much as judges do today. In certain instances reporters favored whichever boxer was the hometown fighter. For the purpose of this book I have decided to use the newspaper decisions- wins, losses, and draws, instead of the technically official no-decisions, simply because the opinions of the reporters greatly influenced the careers of the boxers. Many fighters, managers, and promoters of that time period considered the decisions of the reporters valid, and more importantly, a fighter's career would progress or regress depending on those decisions. Joe Jennette always stated that he lost only nine bouts in his career and the International Boxing Hall of Fame lists Jennette's career record as: 157 bouts, 79 won, 9 lost, 6 draws, 62 no-decisions, 1 no-contest, with 66 knockouts.[8]

For purposes of this book I have used the term "black" instead of "African American" simply because African American was not a common term used at the turn of the twentieth century. The more common terms used to identify African Americans in that time period were Negro, black, and colored, with Negro being the more widely respected. I have decided to use the term black more than any other due to the negative connotations associated with the term Negro from slavery, segregation, and discrimination.

I have tried to be as accurate as possible in regards to boxers' records. Unfortunately it is virtually impossible to know exactly how many fights a boxer participated in at the turn of the twentieth century due to the lack of state boxing commissions' and proper record keeping. Most of what we have to rely on for information comes from newspaper archives. In Joe Jennette's case he is listed as participating in 157 bouts though he himself stated many times that he participated in well over 400 boxing contests.

It is my hope that you will enjoy this book as much as I have enjoyed researching and writing it. I believe we can all learn many great lessons from Joe Jennette's story.

---

[8] International Boxing Hall of Fame

Chapter 1

I dance up and down in my corner waiting for the bell to ring as my black leather boxing shoes with hard leather heels sink deeply into the soft ring padding. The muscles from my neck to my shoulders down my back and abdomen and continuing on down to my thighs and calves are hard yet flexible from my shadow boxing in the dressing room. The warm beads of salty sweat are slowly pushing their way through my pours as they roll down my cinnamon skin. He won't catch me cold. Not tonight, I tell myself.

I look outside the ring and see the crowd that is at least twenty thousand deep, a virtual sea of humanity. The arena is exploding with heavyweight world championship electricity. Camera flash bulbs are popping brightly. Police officers line the apron for security. I look to my right and my eyes focus down on the table at ringside. Sitting at the table in front of the reporters is Nat Fleischer, editor of the storied *Ring Magazine*, and lying on the table in front of him is the ultimate prize.

The gold shines brilliantly while the diamonds and rubies sparkle under the hot glaring ring lights that are strapped to steel girders overhead. The gold-eagle-topped emblem is attached to the leather, red white and blue cloth encased belt. Nat gives me a confident supportive smile, the kind that is conveyed from a fan who has bet his paycheck on his favorite charge. Nat knows tonight is my night. The fans know tonight is my night. I am feeding off of their sizzling electricity. The adrenaline in my veins is being fed by their supportive anticipation. The referee waives us to the center of the ring. We touch gloves and I avoid his eye contact. I will not give him the satisfaction of showing off one of his prepared prefight menacing glares that he has perfected over the years like an academy award winning actor. I also ignore the pompous comments that he needs to exude, not for me but for himself, to build up his own confidence.

I can hear the reporters at ringside saying to each other how impressive I look. My muscles are primed and peaked for the moment. My reflexes perfectly honed in the gym. I return to my corner and turn toward the corner cushions and I make the sign of the cross as I kneel. Please God give me the strength to win, the speed to win, and most of all, the courage to win.

The bell rings and the entire arena fades away. I only see Artha' through a focused tunnel vision and I proceed straight forward as my feet sink into the carpet padded canvas covered floor with each step I take. My feet will be firmly planted for maximum leverage in my punches. I am going to show Artha' who wants this more. I see him quickly turn his left shoulder toward me like a heavy door being slammed shut. I automatically bend my knees in a reflex movement to prepare for a left hook but it is never launched.

Artha' is going to lead with a straight right! I dip down and over to my left and I prepare to drop my left hook on the tip of his jaw just as Artha's right shoulder starts its forward turn.

All of a sudden I stop! What's happening? I can't move. Why aren't my punches coming out? I struggle to free my arms but I cannot move. I am frozen in position! I try to take a deep breath but cannot. The nostrils inside my deviated septum smashed nose are blocked. As I try to inhale a great tightening pain contracts in my chest. Just then I gasp and my eyes snap open. My arms flinch in a defensive reactionary fashion.

Oh my God, I say to myself, I am on my back. What happened? I had my hands up and my chin tucked in. Did Artha's left hook sneak past my high guard? I didn't see the punch if it did. If I was dropped why didn't I hear the thumping of the ring's floorboards that always accompanies a knockdown?

The unseen punch is always the one that under the bright lights causes a boxer's own cerebral lights to violently shut down in an instant like a power outage. I am sweating more and more profusely and I still cannot move my legs. I look to my left and I see a night stand! I look to my right and I see my wife Addie fast asleep. I frantically glance down at my hands and there are no gloves on them. No bandages or tape. My hands are bare!

Addie is awakened by my heavy breathing and sharp flinching movements. She reaches out and caresses my face as she speaks: *"Now, now Joe, you're having another nightmare, darling."* She whispers to me in her soft sleepy voice.

Only boxers know what it's like to have these types of dreams. A police officer dreams of being faced with an armed villain and not being able to shoot his weapon. A boxer dreams of being in a battle and not being able to use his weapons, his hands. I look down again and I do not see the muscular rips in my stomach like the ones I had when I pushed out hundreds of sit-ups a day. Instead I see a rotund, overweight, 66-year-old wrinkled aging body.

I pull myself out of bed and walk down the stairs to the kitchen to compose myself. Its four o'clock in the morning and the only sound is the loud ticking of the coo-coo clock on the kitchen wall. There are no roars of the crowd. There is no golden championship belt waiting at ringside. It was all a dream. Like many I've had before. I pace up and down the hallway several times and then bend over the kitchen faucet to take a drink of cold tap water. As I drink the water, I can still smell the petroleum jelly mixed with leather. How real it seemed. After feeling several ounces of cold water run down my throat, I straighten myself back up. I walk into the living room and pull my scrapbook from the bookshelf. I open the weathered green leather book and I start sifting through the yellowing articles and faded photos of a career and a life that's long since gone. It's a career that lives only in my mind and in the withering pages of my scrapbook, the same scrapbook that I proudly take off of the shelf every time a newspaper

13

reporter knocks on my door. I am not a star in boxing history books like Artha' is. Only occasionally am I mentioned as one of Artha's long ago victims. My career is a voiceless footnote to Artha's megaphone blasting worldwide fame. Artha' was better known to the world as John Arthur "Jack" Johnson, heavyweight champion of the world.

Addie calls me back to bed. *"Joe,"* she said, *"you have a big night tomorrow. Come back to bed, honey."* I listen to my Addie. She always knows what's best for me. She has loyally stood by my side, through a lifetime of glaring looks by ignorant racists both white and black. She has willingly crossed over to feel what all black people are forced to endure simply by being born into this world. I lie back down and close my eyes. There is no noise except the steady ticking of the clock. Later that morning I awoke with an energy I hadn't felt in years. Working at my successful limousine business and training the young boxers in my gym at night is entertaining, but not as exciting as competing myself. Tonight I will be fighting again. Tonight will be exciting. Tonight may be the night I can revive a career that has been suffocating between the dusty, deteriorating pages of a scrapbook.

Chapter 2
Armed Forces Fundraiser
New York City November 1945

The bandages are yellowing and frail as I gently wrap them around my even frailer hands. It has been twenty-three years since I last sat in a dressing room preparing to do battle. I don't know what looks older: the cloth bandages I am wrapping around my hands or the wrinkled, spotted, aging skin that the gauze is covering. It is hard for me to believe that I am 66-years-old. Where did the time go? I watch tiny fabric pieces of the brittle bandages float off into the air as I wrap the gauze around my hand. The tiny threads float off and disappear into nothingness, almost as quickly as my life has floated by.

Several months ago, a small time Manhattan promoter and sports cartoonist named Clem Boddington called me and asked if I would be interested in boxing Jack Johnson in an exhibition bout to raise money for the Liberty Bonds war bond drive. I accepted the invitation, as did Johnson.

It is Tuesday, November 27, 1945 and I am in the makeshift dressing room behind the ballroom stage in the Henry Hudson Hotel.[9] The hotel is located at 356 West 58th street in Manhattan. The boxing ring is set up on the stage. I helped to raise money for our country's soldiers at many events during both the First and Second World Wars. Some of the boxers who performed alongside me included Frankie Nelson, "Kid" Norfolk, Johnny Duff, "Young" Rector, and Frankie Burns.[10]

Tonight's match almost didn't take place. A month prior I was involved in a car accident in Jersey City while driving my limousine for a wedding party. I received a summons to appear in Jersey City's municipal court tonight. Jack Johnson had a court appearance in Manhattan as well. The promoter somehow got both of our court dates rescheduled so the event could take place. Boddington called Jersey City's Mayor Frank Hague, a friend of mine, to have my court date changed. Hague was an avid boxing fan. Hague showed up at the event and had a young man from my hometown with him. Frank told me his name was Billy Musto and he was going to be our next Assemblyman. Unfortunately Clem Boddington wasn't around back in 1909 or 1910 when I was trying desperately to get Johnson back in the ring. Back then nothing fell into place. On the other side of the dressing room in the hotel you could hear his loud boisterous ranting and his crisp English accent. How he got that accent growing up in Galveston, Texas, I'll never know. What I do know is that he loves an audience. The topic of his conversation of course is himself and his greatness. It's kind of comical. I

---

[9] *Philadelphia Tribune* December 15, 1945.
[10] *Hudson Dispatch* July 3, 1958, quote from Frankie Nelson.

never needed or craved the media attention like Artha' did. Could it be that that was my downfall? Is that why Artha' received the shot and not me? All I longed for was a shot at the title and the money that came with it to give my family some of the better things in life. Why else would anyone weave under the manila ropes and sacrifice their life and limb? Is there any other reason? I know of a few all too well.

That deep burning desire that a man with an empty stomach feels when food is far from reach. That hunger pain that overshadows and blocks out all other needs. That desire to satisfy a need that drives a man to desperation. The need to be recognized in a world that doesn't know or even care that he exists. The need to be noticed in a sea of humanity so enormous that he is as invisible as that fabric torn from the piece of gauze that silently floats into nothingness. I wanted this chance for so long. I needed this chance for so long. A chance at redemption.

Those who never bowed under the velvet-covered ropes to step onto the rosined canvas cannot understand the sacrifice or the agreement that one makes with oneself. Tonight may be the night that I lose my hearing from a left hook or a right cross that might pierce my eardrum, leaving me permanently deaf in that ear. Tonight may be the night that I lose my eyesight, and thereby my window to view this world forever, from a well rosined glove, a stitch edged thumb, or razor like glove lace ripping into my cornea. Tonight may be the night my retina gets torn from its base.

Tonight may be the night that a perfectly placed body punch ruptures my spleen, pierces my liver, or bruises my kidney to the point that I urinate dark red blood. Tonight may be the night that fate commands the perfectly timed connection to my temple which sends my skull crashing to the boards, dimming the ring lights forever.

Why does a man risk his health in this sport? Why does a man risk his life? Of course money is without a doubt one of, if not the most important factor. Money, however, can never make a man continue to stand as his head rings with the screaming trumpets of hemorrhaging cerebral concussion. Money can never make a man stand face to face with a finely tuned athlete who has spent months preparing to destroy whoever stands in his path when he knows that on this night he is not nearly in his sharpest form. Yet, there is more. There is much more. There is that burning desire for acceptance, an acceptance that cannot be found outside of the squared circle. An acceptance from everyone present, but really from no one but oneself. A burning desire for immortality. A desire to be proclaimed the world's most dangerous human. To be proclaimed the fiercest pugilist to take a breath. To walk down the street and see the looks that people give you, knowing that they realize they are walking past a living, breathing, Armageddon machine. I was never comfortable speaking or engaging others. I found it so much easier to express myself in the squared circle.

Every leather pusher has the same quest when they first lace on a glove. A shot at the title. A shot at ring immortality. A shot at ring greatness. They all feed off of the cheering fans' electric support.

Here I was finally getting my shot. How ironic. What a twist of fate it is. Thirty-nine years after our last scrap. But this bout will not be in the record books. This bout will not be for the title. This bout will not be for glory and immortality. This bout will do nothing to rewrite the history that is cemented with rebar into the annals of boxing history. Will anyone even remember this event took place ten years from now?

He was the greatest heavyweight champion of all time and the first one of color. He was Jack Johnson. I, Joe Jennette, was nothing but a silent grouping of letters. One of many names listed as opponents of the great Galveston Giant. All I needed was another chance. All I begged for was another chance. All I cried out for was another chance. A chance to face Johnson as an experienced professional. A chance to face Johnson without a thirty-pound weight disadvantage. A chance to face Johnson as a veteran who knew his way around the ring. Not as the green inexperienced novice I was when we met all those years ago. I still get nightmares about it and wake up drenched in sweat as though I have just completed a twenty rounder. It is the same dream over and over. I am screaming at the top of my lungs. Just give me another chance!

If I would have scraped my sepia skin with sandpaper, would I have gotten a title fight? If I had bathed in burning bleach, would I have gotten a title fight? I regretfully denounced my own race when attempting to get a title shot.[11] Fate would be more brutal than all of my matches. The era of the Great White Hope would douse my flame for ring immortality. Does a soul have color? How do they know what color a man's soul is? Was I cursed to live a life that denied me opportunities others could have, because of my skin color? Denied the opportunity by someone that is of my own skin color? Every nightmare always ends the same way. I awake to see the face of Jack Johnson. "Lil" Artha' surrounded by fans. "Lil" Artha' surrounded by newspaper reporters and Joe Jennette left standing in the shadows just as a homeless drunkard lives in the shadows of life in a back alleyway of a city while the bustling activity of life continues to take place all around him. No one hearing me. No one seeing me. No one knowing that I might have beaten Jack and won the title, if only I was given another chance.

Addie, my wife, fought me tooth and nail over this event. She never forgave Johnson for drawing the "color line" against me. She argued with me that Johnson was just using me because he needed me to give himself publicity. She was right, of course, but what difference does it make now. If Jack needed me to get publicity, how far does that mean he has fallen? My

---

[11] 'Boxing' Annual 1914: 'That world's Title by Joe Jeannette pgs. 42-43.

son and daughter were too young to know the frustration we went through trying to get a title shot and a career payday. They just wanted to see me fight. They wanted to see their dad up in the ring again. They were extremely proud of my boxing career. They also knew how important it was to me. In the end, Addie gave in to their pressure, although she refused to acknowledge Johnson's presence at the fundraiser. Just like Johnson refused to acknowledge me throughout my career. I now realize that Jack did not brush me aside because he didn't like me or think I wasn't good enough. It was all business. Why should Jack risk his title against another tough colored fighter when there were so many easy white fighters out there that the public were willing to pay to see him fight?

I was a novice when we first met, still cutting my teeth. I look back and wonder what I could have done differently. I was sent in as a lamb to the slaughter. I was an opponent that was supposed to be a rung on Johnson's ladder to success. A "record padder" for the future champ. A "dead body," as the boxing insiders called it. When an experienced boxer would fight an outclassed opponent with little skills, the ringsiders would say that his manager: *Must have got the shovel and lantern out to dig that guy up!*

Not only was I to lose but I was supposed to be annihilated, fresh meat to be thrown to the hungry young lion. They didn't know what was inside of Joe Jennette. They didn't know the heart and desire that beat inside of me. How I refused to be intimidated by anyone. They would be in for an enormous surprise.

The referee for this event would be another great black boxer that never received the shot at the title he deserved. The great Harry Wills, arguably the best pure heavyweight boxer of his era. Nat Fleischer called Wills: *"A credit to the game and to his race."*[12] Wills was a credit to the human race. Fleischer, to his credit, was one of the earliest supporters of mixed bouts and racial equality in boxing.

I like to think that we black boxers helped to pave the way for our entrance into other professional sports. Black boxers were the pioneers for other black professional athletes. If my peers and I could not reap the benefits of our God-given skills and abilities at least those that came after us were able to do so. When I boxed there were no black professional basketball players, football players, or baseball players. As I sat in my dressing room, my thoughts faded back to my childhood.

---

[12] *Beyond The Ring* by Jeffrey T. Sammons pg. 76.

Chapter 3
The Early Years
New Jersey

I was born in the New Durham, Homestead section of North Bergen, New Jersey, at 349 Paterson Plank Road, in the year 1879. The New Durham section was mostly industrialized and has dated back to the Revolutionary War era. It is located at the bottom of what is now Union and Bergen Turnpikes. The area was home to the Three Pigeon's Tavern in Revolutionary times and it is rumored that General George Washington visited the famous tavern many times before and during the war.

Our home in North Bergen bordered West Hoboken to the southeast, Jersey City to the south, Union Hill to the east, and Secaucus to the west. The area was and still is a bustling immigrant community. At that time the German influence was so great in Union Hill that the local government meetings were held in German. The Irish and Italians would complain that the Germans were trying to change America's language from English to German, an argument that would be repeated as new immigrant groups arrived and settled in the area. Jersey City Height's Central Avenue shopping district was filled with fruit and vegetable stands and tasty bakeries.

This bustling urban area had many German butcher shops and restaurants, Italian Deli's, and Irish Pubs. The aromas of the food shops were fantastic. The biggest industries in the area were the German breweries and the silk embroidery factories. They were scattered all over Union Hill and West Hoboken. One of the largest breweries was owned by William Peter. He was so wealthy that he lived in a home that looked like a castle high up on the top of Union Hill. I wanted a home like that someday. The embroidery shops employed many Armenian immigrants who were skilled in the craft from their home land of Eastern Europe. There were some very foul odors that came from the area dye factories. The worst odor in the area came from the slaughterhouses. There were pig farms to the west, and whenever the wind blew east, the area was engulfed with smells of the slaughtered animals. My mother would tell my brothers and sisters and I not to play in the swamps across the train tracks from our house.[13] We would sneak across anyway and look for turtles to play with. We also loved to burn the cat-tails that grew in the meadow grass.

One of my most vivid memories of childhood was when I lived in New Durham. The freight trains that were loaded with cows, pigs, sheep, and goats would stop not far from my home and sit there overnight waiting to unload their cargo at the slaughterhouses of Secaucus. All night my

---

[13] Interview with JoAnn Flannery-Mostaccio Joe Jennette's great-niece.

brothers, my sisters, and I would hear the animals as they sounded like they were crying for help. I would hold my pillow to my ears but the sound never stopped. All night they would moan, apparently aware of their impending demise.

One night my brother Marshall and I decided to sneak out and let the animals free. We walked down to the train and found that the freight cars were all locked. We tried to pry the doors open. I saw one of the goats staring at me through the louvers, with its dark eyes sparkling in the moonlight. Marshall and I were banging on the lock with a large rock when a train hand must have heard the noise. He came running with a club and chased us from the train yard. I never stopped thinking about that goat being trapped in the freight car, unable to fight his way out, helpless to change his coming fate. I swore at that moment that when I grew up I would help animals. Maybe even become an animal surgeon.[14]

As children in New Durham we spent a lot of time up the hill in the towns of Union Hill and West Hoboken, because New Durham was mostly commercial buildings and farms. In West Hoboken and Union Hill, the trolley cars churned up and down the avenues led by horses clopping their hooves day and night until 1888, when they were powered electrically by Public Service. The noise was so loud that an affluent area resident made a complaint to the local government. He had the horse route moved from Palisade Avenue to Spring Street so he could sleep at night.

The biggest entertainment attractions in the area were burlesque and vaudeville. There were burlesque theaters all over the area. The girls were very pretty and talented. When I was a kid my brothers Marshall and Daniel and I would sneak into the Keystone Theater, which was in the town of West Hoboken. In the hot summer months the theater would leave the side door open and we would sneak in to see all the pretty girls as they prepared to go on stage. My mischievous brothers and I would hide behind the seats in the balcony section as the girls practiced their routines. We would throw bon-bons at the girls and then duck back behind the seats and have a laugh. That was until the manager found us and chased us out.

The Keystone Theater crowd had their own vocabulary. If an act was too clean it was called the "Boston Version," and if the audience was not laughing at the jokes the manager would yell from backstage: *"Bring the asbestos down!"* This signaled the stage crew to bring down the asbestos curtain to get the bombing act off stage quickly. The West Hoboken transfer station was located downtown. Travelers and military personnel transferred from one trolley car to another at the station en route to their destinations.

The Keystone was a vaudeville theater that showcased slapstick acts, song

[14] *'Boxing'* Annual 1914 'That World's Title' by Joe Jeannette pgs. 42-43.

and dance shows, juggling acts, and pantomime. There were three shows a day at the Keystone. The famous magician Harry Houdini performed at both the Roosevelt Theater and the Summit Hippodrome in West Hoboken. Up north at 481-517 Summit Avenue was the Hudson County Consumers Brewery Company which was a huge beer and ale brewery the size of several city blocks. My brothers and I would walk down Hudson Boulevard and watch as the horses would come and go with their wagons filled with barrels of fresh beer.

If my mother Mina, her full name was Sabina Wilhelmina Schultz-Marshall and she was born in 1853 in Bavaria, knew my brothers and I snuck into the vaudeville theaters, oh boy would we have caught a "wuppin." Neither the vaudeville nor the burlesque theaters served alcohol, but still my mother told me that only undesirables frequented these places. With all of the breweries in the area it is no wonder there were so many saloons and bars. My mother constantly warned us of the dangers of drinking: "old John Barleycorn," as she called alcohol.

My mother was a strong German woman proud of her Bavarian heritage and even prouder of her children. Her parents had come from Germany seeking a better life. She had bright pink skin and hazel eyes on her small, five-foot, chunky, solid frame. We had a Coo-Coo clock on the wall in our kitchen that would Coo-Coo every hour. My mother loved her Black Forest Coo-Coo clock. She said it reminded her of Bavaria. I would watch her as a child as she carefully wound the clock by pulling on the long chains that hung underneath the dark wood clock with carvings of birds, deer, and other animals engraved in it. She would repeat this act every day to keep the clock's time accurate. It was the same clock that I now have in my kitchen and the same pulling ritual that I now perform.

My mother was a terrific cook. She cooked German meals such as *wiener schnitzel* or breaded pork, *kartoffelsalat* or potato salad, and my favorite Black Forest chocolate cake. Most of the German food we ate, though, consisted of frankfurters, hamburgers, liverwurst, smearwurst, and pork chops from the local German butcher shop.

My father, Benjamin Franklin Jennette, was born in 1834 in Virginia. He was a brown skinned man of African and some say Arabic heritage who was equally proud. Benjamin migrated from Virginia. He was searching, like so many other colored folks, for employment opportunities and to escape Southern racism in the bustling urban industries of the North. So many blacks moved from down South to New Jersey that there was even an all-black community that was founded in South Jersey in 1901. It was comical that the town was called Whitesboro and many black folks from North Carolina migrated to and populated that town. Booker T. Washington was one of the towns' investors.

My father died on August 1, 1883, when I was only three-years-old. He was 50-years-old when he died. I don't remember much about him. I was told many wonderful stories about my father from my mother. My mother remarried Franklin Marshall, who was also a black man who migrated from Virginia. Frank was a blacksmith who had worked with my father. On September 21, 1885 Frank tried to run across the trolley tracks ahead of a trolley car and was struck. He had to have his right leg amputated below the knee.[15] Frank didn't work for a long time after the accident and we were forced to struggle through some very difficult times. Frank told us many stories of the hardships that black people suffered down South. He told us about segregation and the Jim Crow Laws and how blacks and whites used separate bathrooms and hotels. The South sounded like a scary place. I had no interest to visit Southern States and often in my youth I had horrible nightmares about the South.[16] I had one particular nightmare over and over. In it I boarded a train that was supposed to head north to Albany but instead by accident I boarded a train that headed to the Deep South. When the train finally stopped I would get off only to see a scary-looking tall white man with a cowboy hat on his head and a whip in one hand and shackles in the other hand. He looked down at me and said: *"I've been waiting for you boy. I got you now!"* I would run as fast as I could as the man chased me. The dream always ended the same way, with me waking up in a cold sweat.

My favorite foods from Frank's native Virginia included fried chicken, black eyed peas, corn bread, yams, sweet potato pie, and juicy watermelon. Frank would occasionally buy a foot or two of "Virginia Twist" for himself from the general store. "Virginia Twist" was chewing tobacco twisted up and sold by the foot or yard. My older brother Daniel would sneak a piece of Frank's twist when no one was looking. Boy oh boy if Frank would have caught Daniel he would've given him the beating of his life.

My siblings were Annie, born in 1874 from my mother's first husband, Phillip Bernhardt. Daniel, born in 1875, Marshall 1877, and Agnes 1882, from my father Benjamin. We added nine more siblings from my step-father Frank and my Mother's marriage. Mortimer born in 1884, Herman 1886, Edward 1888, Frank 1889, Pauline and Marshall, twins 1890, Matilda and Grace, twins 1892, and Marcella born in 1893. By 1893 there were thirteen of us children living in the same apartment. Annie was my only sibling that had a white father. I cannot remember it ever being an issue in our house growing up. The only problems Annie encountered were when she brought friends home. Some of her white friends accepted her mixed family, some did not. Annie's father Phillip died suddenly after she was born. Unfortunately five of my siblings, Pauline, Mortimer, Herman, Edward, and Marshall, would die from various illnesses as children.

The blacks who migrated from down South were not welcomed into

---

[15] *Jersey Journal* September 23, 1895.
[16] *Marriage beyond Black & White* by David & Barbara Douglas pg. 10.

factory work. Most of the jobs available for black males were as laborers, porters, chauffeurs, waiters, and servants, while the women were employed as laundresses, dressmakers and domestic servants. White women also struggled, as they could only work low-paying factory and servant jobs. Women were not allowed to vote at the time.

My father Benjamin had been a farrier by trade. He learned the trade in his native Virginia. The work was grueling. Unlike a blacksmith, forge, or smithy, a farrier dealt specifically with the shoeing of horses. He repaired wheels for carts by fitting new steel rims on the wheels. He also repaired many broken metal tools and objects for people in the community. Most of his customers owned horses and wagons and were employed by the local breweries. I started taking a great interest in horses because of all the stories everyone told me of how talented my father was working with horses.

My father used special coal to heat the metal which he had purchased from the Jagels and Bellis' Coal Company. His motto was: "every hoof is balanced, fit, and finished to perfection." My father was especially keen at noticing a foundering horse. That is one that is trying to relieve the pressure or strain of standing because of a loss of circulation to the legs and hooves. This ailment, which was commonly caused by overeating, could prove costly to the owner or deadly to the animal if not detected and corrected in time. Everyone in the area knew that my father was a specialist at spotting this ailment, and I was told he was extremely proud of this talent. I wanted to work with horses like my father did.

I loved my mother and stepfather Frank very much, but it was very difficult growing up in a mixed marriage in nineteenth century New Jersey. My mother's family migrated from Germany in the 1860s and they were well established, as were many German immigrants in the area. Frank always told my mom how sorry he was that her status in the community was diminished because of her marriage to him, a colored man. My mother would tell him to shut up and that he shouldn't dwell on what ignorant people thought. She told him everyone was just jealous of them. My mother had a grueling job in an embroidery factory. She was careful not to tell anyone at her job of her mixed marriage for fear of losing her job. Most of Frank's family still lived in Virginia, so we did not see much of them. There weren't many colored families living in the area. You could count them all on one hand.

My mother's parents' names were John G. Schultz and Ann Margaret Schultz. They lived nearby as did their children, my uncles Frank and Joe and their wives, both named Emma. Imagine that, they were both married to women with the same name.

Early in life I became well aware of racism. Marshall was the darkest colored of us children, with dark brown skin. Daniel and I had lighter brown skin, and Agnes was very light colored but not enough to pass for white. She had curly hair not "good hair" as they called it when it was very

23

straight and not curly.

Whenever my Aunt Emma and Uncle Frank came to visit we would stay inside the house, even if it was a hot summer day. I didn't realize until years later that they did not want to be seen in public with their brown nieces and nephews. My Grandma Anna was very nice and close to my mother but Grandpa John almost never came over to our apartment. On those rare occasions when he did, he always sat at the kitchen table having serious-looking conversations with my mom and Grandma Anna. When he did come over, it always seemed to be when Frank was at work.

When Frank was home from work on Sunday he would talk about his favorite topic, Virginia. Frank would sit on the couch and my brothers, my sisters, and I would sit on the floor and listen to his stories while he chewed his tobacco and spit in the spittoon. He would tell us about the beautiful hills, valleys, and streams in Virginia. I would close my eyes and think of these beautiful places.

Frank also taught us to be proud of whom we were and not to worry about what other people might say about him and mom being married. He told us that those people didn't understand our family. He would tell us all to come close and he would whisper a secret to us: *"Only we know,"* he would say: *"that people are all the same inside here,"* as he pointed to his heart. *"That's our secret,"* he would whisper.

Frank worked under my father as a farrier's apprentice. Frank said my father loved talking about the heroics of the Civil War and all the courageous soldiers who died so we could live free. Frank loved to share one of my father's favorite stories about General Phillip Kearney. My father worked under Kearney as a farrier during the Civil War. He would tell Frank exciting tales of how Kearney, who lost his left arm from grapefruit shot in the Mexican War, would ride into battle with a sword in one hand and the saddle reins in his mouth. He told Frank that Kearney would yell: *"I'm a one armed son of a gun, follow me!"* and *"Don't worry, men, they'll be firing at me!"* Kearney died on September 1, 1862, at the Battle of Chantilly at Fairfax County, Virginia, when he was shot in the spine. Frank would tell us if General Kearney could ride into battle with one arm we could overcome any obstacles in our lives.

Some Sundays in the summer, Frank would take us all to the beach down at Long Branch where many famous people vacationed. Several presidents vacationed there, and many famous theatrical personalities performed at Long Branch. I remember when Frank was sitting on the beach sifting sand through his dark brown toes. He motioned me to come close to him. He would speak to me in his deep Southern drawl. *"Joie,"* he said, *"do you see the waves that come crashing to the shore and disappear back out into the sea? Your life as a colored man is going to be like those waves. Every time you move forward in your life something is always going to try to pull you back out. You're gonna' have to keep fighting so you're not sucked out into the deep water. Whatever you do, Joie,"* he said as serious as he ever spoke to me, *"never give up moving your arms. You'll only drown out there, son. Remember, if you keep trying, eventually you'll get a friendly wave that will pull you in."*

When we were home in our kitchen and Frank was having a drink of his whiskey he would shout out to my mom, who was in the kitchen most of the time: *"Isn't it true, Sabina, what Frederick Douglass said about white folk and colored folk blending together and being happy. Just look at us."* Dad would point to the picture of Douglass that hung in our living room: *"Even Douglass is married to a white woman,"* he would shout.

"It's funny isn't it, Sabina, that white folks and colored folks aren't supposed to marry but the white men down South had no problem sneakin' around with colored girls. Isn't that true, Sabina?" Frank would proclaim more than ask. My Mom would tell Frank to shush up with that kind of talk around the children. Frank would always reply: *"They got to learn this stuff sooner or later."*

Frank would tell us that we had to work twice as hard as white people to succeed. He also told us that the color of our skin would affect us negatively every day of our lives. At the time we didn't understand what he meant. He told us that even if we were ninety-nine percent white we would still be considered colored to some white people.

One Sunday Frank told us the story about Sally Hemings and Thomas Jefferson. He said President Jefferson had a marriage just like his and mom's but Jefferson kept his a secret. He would tell my mom: *"The only reason you don't think like these white folk is because your family is from Bavaria and you aren't drunk with hatred like the rest of them."* Frank would tell us: *"You children marry whoever you want. If you're in love that's all that matters. Sometimes I feel like I get more evil stares from my own people than the whites."* He would say: *"I sometimes think colored ladies are more upset about me marrying a white girl than the whites are. Douglass isn't a coward and neither am I."* He continued: *"One day people won't be so ignorant. They'll see that love is color blind."*

My family was very poor, like most families in the area. Struggling to eat and keep warm in the winter. We would close the living room in our apartment in the winter to save on how much coal we used to heat the apartment. The coal stove was located in our small kitchen. When there wasn't enough money for coal we used wooden logs and branches. We would search for the logs in the woods over the train tracks behind the swamps. We used candles and kerosene lamps to light the apartment at night. We all took baths in the kitchen sink which had a section that was removable so adults could bath in it as well.

The main streets were lit by gas lamps. Each night the lamp-lighter would come by with his long lighting stick and turn on the gas and light the street lamps. Whenever the almanac predicted moonlight the town would keep the lights off to save gas. If it was cloudy or stormy the streets would be in complete darkness. My brothers and sisters and I would be really scared on those dark nights.

25

You never had to guess when the first of the month was in our neighborhood. Around the 29th or 30th of each month the streets would be filled with mattress carrying families moving from one apartment building to another. Carts would be loaded up with clothes and children as the monthly exodus from one flat to another took place. Our neighborhood didn't have many four-story tenement buildings like the towns up the hill, but still there were lots of people moving to and fro.

Color was never an issue in our home, but boy it sure was when we went out into the streets. People were always looking and whispering when we walked with our parents. My brothers and I would often get into fights with kids in the neighborhood. The main fighting theme was our parents' mixed marriage. My older brother Marshall was the real fighter. Any time neighborhood kids would bother us he would fight back with his fists. There was always some white kids who would call us "niggers," "darkies," and "coons" when all the while our Mother was whiter than most of them. It still gives my skin chills when I think of the looks my mother would get when she walked around town with us and Frank. Don't get me wrong, there were some very nice people and most of our neighbors were especially nice but the mean people always seem to stand out in my mind.

One day someone wrote "coon lover" on our porch in chalk. It was directed at my Mother. I ran in the apartment and filled a bowl with water and ran back out to wash the writing away before my Mother saw it. When I finished washing the words away I brought the bowl back into the house. My Mother caught me with the bowl and she was very angry that I took it outside. She told Frank and I caught a terrible beating but I never told anyone why I had taken the bowl outside. With every strike of the belt I hated my skin color more and more. I have to admit I hated being black growing up. Not because I didn't like my skin color, but because of all the problems I had to face because of it. I wasn't alone in that thought. My sister Agnes would cry and tell my mother: *"I hate my skin. I hate my ugly skin. I want skin like Annie's."* My mother would tell her not to say such things. She would tell her how beautiful her skin was and how lucky she was to have such beautiful brown skin. My mother would tell Agnes: *"All the white people sit in the sun to get beautiful skin like yours."*

Northeast of our flat about a half-mile up the hill was the "Drescher's Woods." It was a wonderful tree-filled swampy area, except for the mosquitoes in the summer. In the woods we would hunt for rabbit and birds. It was like going away and becoming Daniel Boone. I would play the Indian with Marshall, and Annie and Daniel would play the cowboys, and then we would switch. I was very sad when they cleared the woods in 1890. There were apple orchards up in Union Hill and grape vineyards over by the Palisades owned by the Loss family. Years prior the area had been named Lossburg. My Mother would send Marshall and I up to the orchards for a barrel of apples during the picking season in September and October or over to the Loss' farm for some grapes when they were in season.

One afternoon my brother Marshall and I were playing on the Palisades with some friends when we saw a group of boys climbing up the hill from Hoboken. I was 10-years-old at the time. When the boys got closer to us, one of them yelled: *"Hey, you guys and your darky friends better get off of our cliff."* I looked at my brother and his friends to see their response. The silence seemed to last forever until it was broken by Marshall, who yelled back: *"Why don't you go home and take a nap on your bed-bug filled mattresses!"* That was it, out came the bean shooters. Everyone loaded up their slings with rocks and pelted each other. Marshall screamed for me to take cover behind a tree. After about five minutes of fighting the Hoboken kids retreated back down the cliff. We were victorious!

In school that week the cops came in and checked all the desks and bags for bean shooters. Apparently too many windows were being broken and a woman was even hit in the eye by an errant rock. Thank goodness Marshall didn't bring his bean shooter to school that day.

One day we were walking home from school and we noticed a large crowd gathering in the street. Apparently someone had fallen into an open manhole. As I stood by I heard some adults talking that the man who fell into the hole was a boxer and he likely didn't see the open hole because he was probably punch drunk.[17]

When we were small Christmas was always the most special time. My sisters would want dolls and my brothers and I would want tin toys or lead soldiers. One Christmas I got a horse-drawn trolley toy. I used to make believe I was changing the shoes on the horse just like my father did. My sister Agnes always wanted a doll her color but they did not make any, or if they did, my parents could not find one. Frank got her a doll and he painted the skin light brown for her.

My brothers and I were the darkest colored kids in the area, with our brown skin and curly hair. The kids who knew we were from a mixed marriage would call us "zebra's," "marble cake," and "German chocolate."[18] Those comments hurt more than any sling shot hit could.

I was a stockily built kid with some baby fat just like my brothers. I was about five-foot nine-and-a-half-inches at full growth. My full name is Joseph Jeremiah Jennette but my family and friends all call me Joe or Joie. I spelled Joey with an ie instead of ey. My son would spell his name the same way.[19]

1892 was the year that Ellis Island opened its doors to the immigrants of the world who sought a new beginning. February 12 was officially named a national holiday honoring Abraham Lincoln. On June 7, Homer Plessy was

---

[17] Conversations with Joseph Louis Botti.
[18] *Interracial Intimacies* by Randall Kennedy pg. 129.
[19] Interview with JoAnn Flannery-Mostaccio Joe Jennette's great-niece.

27

arrested for sitting on a whites' only rail car in Louisiana, leading to the landmark case, *Plessy vs. Ferguson*, which upheld racial segregation.

I was 13-years-old in 1892, growing up in the shadows of New York City and the Hudson River. New Jersey was the home of the great Thomas A. Edison and his laboratory. His assistant William Dickson had just invented the motion picture machine.

When I was 14-years-old, Cracker Jack's and Jell-O were invented. The first Hershey bars rolled out the next year, in 1894. Every Sunday, Frank would buy us a special treat. The treat that would give me the most problems, especially when it came to making weight for fights in later years, was Coca-Cola. I was seven-years-old when Coke was introduced to the public in 1886, and I have been hooked ever since. Of course, on Sunday mornings we would all get dressed up and attend Mass at the New Durham Baptist Church. Reverend Giles and later Reverend Wardell would preach the sermons each week.

I was a very active youth, and my mother, because of her German background, got my siblings and I enrolled in the Turnverein Gymnastic Association Center in Union Hill on Lewis Street. The center was directly across the street from the Hudson Theater. The Turnverein was started in Berlin, Germany back in 1811 by Friedrich Ludwig John. John was known as the *Turnvater*, or father of gymnastics. I am sure that my mother went through a lot to get us into the program because we were the first colored children to attend that school. I learned many acrobatic exercises in the program that I used throughout my boxing career, including walking on my hands and back flips. Fifteen United States Olympic gymnasts would train at the Turner Hall in the years to come.

In the 1890s there were a lot of traveling salesmen. They would walk through the neighborhood yelling out their services or the wares they tried to sell. There was the knife sharpener and the tin man. The tin man would buy and sell metal objects. The umbrella man would sing as he walked around with his backpack singing: *"Toodle luma luma."* The fruit and vegetable man would sell all of the ripe fruit for that time of the year, yelling out fruits such as: *"Fresh watermelon!"*

We had the clothing salesman who would darn socks and clothes that were ripped. My mother would send us out with a bucket when the Javelle water man came around. Javelle water was a mixture of water with bleach powder and soda ash that the Javelle man usually mixed in his basement. All of the mothers in the neighborhood would use Javelle water to clean their apartments.

I can still remember how happy my mother was when my father brought home glass jars for the first time. Everyone used pottery because it was cheaper, but all the women in the neighborhood wanted glass jars instead. My mother was very proud of her glass jars.

Growing up we never seemed to notice how little we had. All the families

28

in the neighborhood were just as poor as the next, which is why I guess nobody noticed. We always had food to eat though. Food, including meat, was not expensive to buy back then. I guess food was cheap because if it was too expensive no one would have had enough money to buy it anyway. In the hot summer months my brothers and I would travel up the hill to Union Hill, to the Ice House. Outside the Ice House we would find fresh ice shavings on the ground after ice was scored and we would have a free treat on the hot summer days. We made sure that we scooped up the shavings of ice that did not touch the ground. If we were lucky we would have an orange or lemon to squeeze over the shavings to have a real special treat.

My family had a German neighbor named Franz. Occasionally when he was too tired to walk he would give me a coin and send me to the local pub with his tin bucket. Back then if you brought a bucket to the pub the bartender would fill it up for you. *"A bucket of suds for Franz,"* I would demand. When I brought the bucket back to Franz he would throw me an Indian Penny. If he was feeling really happy from the suds he would toss me a Liberty Nickel!

Jersey City was a stone's throw south of our apartment, and there were enough colored boys for my brothers and I to play with down there. We loved baseball and we played it any chance we could get. I also had a great love for basketball and handball. It was playing baseball in Jersey City in 1892 when I was 13-years-old that I realized I had a very special talent. It was mid-August and we were having a game behind a dye factory on Saturday morning. It was a mixed game, whites and colored, and I don't remember now who won the game or if we even finished it. My brother Marshall made a tag on Nate, who was the fastest Negro base runner in Jersey City Heights. An argument started because Nate thought he was safe.

Besides being a fast runner, Nate also had a reputation for being a fierce fighter. He was 16-years-old, tall and lanky, and close to six feet in height. Wanting to get back to the game, I stepped between the two of them and pleaded for them to stop arguing and get back to playing. While I was looking at my brother with my hands stretched out, holding both of them apart, I felt a crashing against my face, followed by numbness and a ringing feeling in my right ear. After a couple of seconds I realized that Nate had sucker punched me. The ringing in my head grew louder and a surge of energy built up in me like I never felt before. My brother tried to jump at Nate but Nate stepped back and screamed at him to let me fight my own battles. I was so angry I couldn't think straight. Tears were streaming down my face. The next thing I knew I was pummeling Nate into the ground.

When I was finally pulled off of him, there was blood coming from Nate's nose and mouth. Everyone, including myself, was shocked at what had just transpired. As a kid, most of my fights would end up with us wrestling around on the ground, but not this one. After I was pulled off of Nate, there was a strange silence, with the exception of Nate's sniffling and moaning on the ground. The silence was broken by one of the players yelling: *"Did you see that! Joe Jennette's some fighter!"* Another boy yelled: *"I'll bet he could probably beat the Boston Strong Boy."* Yet another proclaimed: *"He's another Joe Gans. No, Peter Jackson!"*

The Boston Strong Boy they were talking about was none other than the great John L. Sullivan, the world's heavyweight boxing champion. Even though I was nervous and out of breath from the fight, deep inside me I had to laugh. Me, beat the great John L.! At 13-years-old, even though it was a joke, a part of me wondered if I could one day be a good boxer if I really tried. Those thoughts and feelings were very real on that day. They would be suppressed for another twelve years, until they reemerged with a vengeance.

I'll tell you, if I knew ahead of time how that day would unfold, I would have never gone to play ball. Now that the fight was over, the kids were all looking at me differently. I was also feeling different. Not only did I take to task the Jersey City Heights tough guy, but that also meant I took his reputation as well. To be honest with you, it was a good feeling. Even though I did have some challenges in the next few years, and I mostly came out victorious, I was still living off of my reputation from that Saturday baseball brawl.

I was first exposed to boxing a year prior to the fight with Nate, in 1891, when Marshall and I had snuck down the hill to Hoboken to try to see the boxing match between Frank Slavin and Jake Kilrain. We couldn't sneak in the building but we heard the cheering from outside. After the fight ended we heard the people who were leaving talking about Slavin's spectacular knockout victory. Peter Jackson of Australia was the most talked about colored heavyweight fighter at the time. Word was he hit as hard as a mule kick.

Chapter 4

Introduction to the Art of Boxing

I was not very outgoing and I didn't have much interest in school as a child. I was, however, very interested in automobiles. By the time 1904 rolled around, I was 25-years-old and had been shoveling and delivering coal for several years for Jagels and Bellis' Coal Company. Being Benjamin's son helped me get the job because he was a regular customer of theirs with his farrier business. I started out breaking in horses for Jagels and eventually moved up to driving a truck when they stopped using horses. I lost the tip of my left middle finger in an accident when I first started working for the company.[20] Shoveling coal was no easy job. There are not many pains that can compare to the numbing feeling in your fingertips when you are shoveling coal on a frigid February day from the back of a wagon in freezing weather while your ears feel like they are going to crack off from the wind chill and your knees are shivering from the burning cold that seems to pass right through your body.

I learned to block out the weather because the pay was good and it helped to put food on the table. In the winter we would put the milk and eggs on the fire escape or in a window box which helped prevent the milk from freezing unless it was extremely cold outside. My mother would make her own butter by leaving milk out in a pan overnight. She would scrape the cream from the top of the pan and whip it up until it turned into butter. Sometimes this took hours. In the summer we had to buy ice for the icebox or the milk would spoil. When we wanted ice we would place a sign outside of our window with the amount of ice we wanted written on it. The ice was broken down into pounds, from 12 ½ to 25 pounds. The ice man would come down the street in his horse-drawn wagon every day in the summer months. He would cut the piece wanted off of a giant 300-pound block that was on the wagon. He would then take the cut piece of ice off of his truck with large ice tongs. He would pull the piece of ice up over his leather-covered shoulder and lug it up to whatever apartment requested it. He would place the ice in the top part of the wooden insulated ice box. The bottom part was where the food was kept. A trick we used to keep the ice from melting too fast in the hot summer days was to take sawdust from the local lumber yard and sprinkle the sawdust around the ice, which helped to slow down the melting process.

Some of the neighborhood kids would beg the iceman for shavings to have a treat, and some kids tried to scrape shavings off of the block of ice with a shoe horn when the iceman was making a delivery. If they got caught the ice man would chase them away or call for their parents. When I came

---

[20] Interview with JoAnn Flannery-Mostaccio Joe Jennette's great-niece.

home after work, my family and I would look through the Sears catalog and dream about all the nice things we would buy from the catalog if we had the money.

Another way my family got entertainment was when the song pluggers came by in their horse-drawn wagons. They had a piano on the back of the wagon and they would play all the popular songs of the day. Songs such as "In My Merry Oldsmobile," "Come Josephine in My Flying Machine," "Bill Bailey Won't You Please Come Home" and "Meet Me in St. Louis, Louis." There were also songs that echoed the racial prejudice of the times such as "All Coons Look Alike to Me" and "The Dark Town Strutter's Ball." The Pluggers would collect coins in a tin cup for their entertainment and they would also try to sell sheet music to whoever was lucky enough to have a piano in their parlor. Sometimes Frank would take the family to eat out at a place with a nickelodeon and we would hear all of the top songs and rags of the day. I loved music. I taught myself how to play piano by ear because we didn't have enough money for me to take lessons.[21]

The Borden's milk delivery wagons would make my stomach growl each time they passed. We could not afford much milk so we mostly drank tap water. When we did have enough money for milk we would dilute it with water to stretch it out. When we received a milk delivery my siblings and I all tried to be the first to run outside and bring in the bottle and open it. There was always some delicious rich cream at the top. Frank liked to use the cream in his coffee. We made sure Frank didn't see us taking the cream after the morning milk delivery and we always took just a finger licking amount so he had enough for his morning coffee. When I was a young boy the milk was purchased by bringing out a bucket and having the milkman use a ladle to dispense the milk to customers. On occasion, when the milk was spoiled, whole neighborhoods would get bellyaches. By 1904, however, bottled milk had taken over as the preferred method. The milkman would leave the bottles of milk on your porch in a metal box and take the empty bottles back for refills.

Vaudeville and burlesque theaters in the area were growing with popularity as the shows would have slapstick, strip tease, and all the top songs and dances from "Tin Pan Alley."

I didn't do much besides work. I would play baseball, basketball, or handball for fun when I could find the time. I was now built like a man. No more was I carrying the baby fat. It had turned into hardened muscles on my arms, back, and legs from all the shoveling of coal into homes. The only vice I had was smoking cigarettes.[22] I had picked up the habit from my co-workers at the coal company.

I had played around a little with boxing in a barn up in Union Hill behind

[21] Interview with JoAnn Flannery-Mostaccio Joe Jennette's great-niece.
[22] *Hudson Dispatch* August 19, 1912.

Cox's Corner, a general store, where sparring sessions, or "smokers," were held by the store's owner. Members of the club would square off against each other. In my first Cox's Corner match, my opponent, a large muscular German, whispered to me that we should take it easy because it was only an exhibition. I was surprised because when training in the barn with him I got the feeling that he didn't like me much. I trained hard for the match.[23] As we were entering the roped off area to box I heard him tell his friends in German: *"Legen sie etwas geld auf mir, ich werde diese coon knockout,"* or as translated in English: *"Put some money on me, I'm gonna' knock this coon out."* I sure am glad I had learned some German from my Mother because I was about to get set up. The bell was rung, and he waded in close to me. He had a determined look on his face as he grunted: *"Come on and fight."* I leapt at him with an overhand right that flattened him cold. His friends brought him back around with a bucket of cold water. As he was carried from the ring he shouted: *"You double crosser! I thought you were going to fight an exhibition?"* I shouted back in German: *"Was ist los sie verloren etwas geld?"* which translated meant: *"What's the matter you lost some money?"*

On February 29, 1904 the Olympia Athletic Club held wrestling and boxing exhibitions at the Turn Hall in Union Hill. The main event pitted wrestlers George Bothner of New York and Emil Selva of Paterson. Selva was offered four hundred dollars if he could throw Bothner twice in an hour. Selva failed to throw Bothhner once. I competed in one of the two boxing exhibitions, boxing three rounds against William Diehl.[24]

One night in August I went to Jersey City with some friends to see a boxing show. There were seven scheduled bouts, but four were cancelled and the crowd was booing and wanted more fights. The ring announcer asked if anyone in the crowd was man enough to get in the ring with Arthur Dixon, whose opponent did not show up. Dixon was a journeyman professional with a pan-caked nose, cauliflower ears and punched down eyelids which gave him a sad looking appearance. He was tall and looked every bit the part of a pugilist. My friends tried to get me to go in the ring but I would have no part of it. Eventually their pleas turned to taunts and finally to a straight out dare.

I turned to my friends and I told them I didn't want to wind up falling into any manholes. They looked at me like I was crazy and continued to dare me. I thought I could handle myself, so eventually I gave in. My friends raised their hands and screamed to the announcer that I was willing to challenge Dixon. I remember the tension in my body as I walked up the stairs into the ring. I wanted to turn around and walk out of the warehouse that was holding the fights, but to do so would bring a shame with which I could not bear to live. Instead I was resigned to being humiliated in the

---

[23] *Afro-American* January 25, 1947.
[24] *Evening Journal,* Jersey City March 1, 1904.

ring.

My hands were wrapped with medical gauze and sealed with insulation tape by an old boxing pug, which made them rock hard. After the gloves were laced on my hands I was waived to the center of the ring by the referee. While the instructions were being given, I could not take my eyes off of Dixon's nose. I was prepared to do anything to protect my nose from being smashed in like his. After the bell rang, Dixon came at me with the confidence of a bull. He circled me and out of sheer panic I swung first and missed wildly. Again I swung as he purposely left his face within striking distance and then pulled it away at the last second, but this time he countered with a straight right that made my face numb, as his cast-like punch crashed against my cheek bone.

I was hearing the same ringing in my head I had heard in the ballpark fight so many years ago. Just like then I became a different person. I attacked Dixon with everything I had and even though he had much more experience my sheer willpower kept me afoot for the six round no-decision bout. After I left the ring with my five-dollar purse the crowd was still cheering the show we put on. All my friends were slapping me on the back and congratulating my effort: *"Great job, Joe!"*

Even though I was well aware that I had little experience in boxing, the match left a burning feeling inside of me. I knew that I was sloppy and off balance for most of the fight. This boxing was nothing like the street fights I had in the past. Most of them wound up with wrestling on the ground. This type of fighting was much more difficult and tiring.

While I was still catching my breath and toweling the sweat off of my body an Irishman with a deep brogue accent named George Armstrong came over to introduce himself to me. Armstrong was the manager of a lightweight fighter named Johnny Dohan.[25] He told me he could help me get fights and make money. He was a tough-looking, fast-talking character who cut straight to the point. He said he liked my athleticism and determination and said with the right training I could be a successful boxer. Like I said, I had no desire to have my face punched in like Arthur Dixon but that five dollars was a lot easier and quicker to make in eighteen minutes of fighting than it was to shovel coal for a week. Boxing might give me the opportunity to raise the money I needed to enroll in veterinary school.[26] Armstrong invited me to the National Sporting Club in New York the next day and I told him I'd think about it. I was seriously thinking about taking up boxing so I decided to quit smoking after the Dixon bout.

I was very excited about getting the opportunity to learn boxing. I didn't sleep all night, thinking about how I would fight with proper training. I went to work the day after the Dixon fight a renewed man. Even though I

[25] *National Police Gazette* 1905.
[26] *Boxing* Annual 1914: 'That World's Title by Joe Jeannette pgs. 42-43.

might not make it in boxing, at least there was a hope that I could. For me it was an opportunity.

The day after the Dixon match, I was back at work shoveling coal, and believe me, it didn't take many shovels worth to get me thinking about going to that boxing gym. At three o'clock when work ended I paid a liberty-head nickel and took the trolley at the West Hoboken transfer station to the Weehawken ferry. The ferry took me across the river to Manhattan. I could see all of those tall buildings in Manhattan getting closer and closer. As I looked back I saw the smoke-stacks of the William Peter Brewery up in Union Hill growing fainter as the ferry approached Manhattan. The National Sporting Club gym was on the top floor of a garment warehouse. I stood outside and all I could hear was the humming noises of the garment machines still hard at work at four o'clock. I thought I might be at the wrong address. I opened the door and entered the hallway and I heard the grunting of the boxers and the wind whipping of leather jump ropes over the noise of the garment machines. I heard the slapping noises of leather hitting leather as the boxers were striking sawdust-filled leather punching bags. I could also hear the rhythmic beat of the light bag, or speed bag as they now call it, as it bounced off of its hardwood platform. The echoing of the gym noises were filtering down the five-story stairwell.

I was having second thoughts and was preparing to leave the hallway and head back to Jersey when a young boxer arrived with a wide smile and a hop to his step that let everyone know he had full confidence in himself and his athletic abilities. He introduced himself as Willie and he had a duffel bag slung over his shoulder. He had a deep lower-east-side "dead end kids" accent. He asked: *"You goin' up to train?"* I nodded yes and up we went. I was walking behind Willie and he turned around and shouted: *"You're walkin' like a 'toytle.' Hurry up."* *"Toytle? Whats a toytle?"* I replied. *"You know dat ting whit da shell dat swims."* *"Oh turtle."* Was this guy really speaking English? His name was Willie Lewis and we would become great friends over the years.

When I entered the gym, the first thing that hit me was the smell. There is no smell like that of an active boxing gym. The stale odor of old sweat pungently hangs in the air as a kind of memorial to all the training sacrifices made by the boxers who passed through its doors over the years. The leather of the boxing gloves and punching bags mixed in, as did the smell of the sawdust from the punching bag every time it was struck. The worst smell was the spit buckets that were sprinkled around the gym. The stale water and saliva mixture had a smell all its own. The top floor had the punching and striking bags and a makeshift boxing ring, and the roof was used for jumping rope, calisthenics, and additional sparring when the gym was too crowded, which was most of the time. There was an older man sweeping the floor and piling discarded gym clothes into a garbage can. Over the years I would see that scene replay itself over and over. It must have something to do with being hit in the head that makes boxers leave their gym clothes on the locker room floor. No matter how bad the economy is or how poor the boxers are, you will always find socks, shorts, and shirts left in gyms on a daily basis.

Armstrong, who was sitting in a corner, waived me over: *"I'm glad you decided to come by, Joe,"* he said. I was a little surprised that he remembered my name. Armstrong asked in a motherly type of way: *"Are you sore from last night Joe?"* Me sore, heck no. I am sorer from shoveling coal every day, I thought. I just answered: *"Nah, I'm okay."*

For the next several weeks we went through drill after drill after drill. First I was brought in front of a mirror, where George told me: *"Do you see that guy there, he is the only man who can stop you from being successful in this racket and the only one who can make you do the impossible. Take a good look at him."*

I stared at myself in the mirror for several seconds. George taught me proper stance and how to use my body when punching instead of just winging my arms. My wrists and knuckles were sore at first but they eventually healed. I was taught distance, range, and the proper bend in the knees for balance, power, and the ability to absorb and roll with a punch. He taught me how to turn my punches over to make them much stiffer when they landed.

George tied twine from one of my ankles to the other to help me with my balance. He only gave two feet of slack, so I lost balance a lot in the beginning, before I got the hang of it. I was given a half-inch thick piece of manila rope about eight feet long for jumping. I tripped over it many times before I learned the proper way to jump the rope. At first my calves were sore but the pain went away after a few weeks as my calf muscles grew.

After two hard weeks of training George finally put me in the ring to spar. He told me this was practice and not like competitive fighting and I was just to work on what he wanted me to. *"The most important thing you need to learn, Joe,"* he would say, *"is to listen to your coach. The noise of the crowd can be deafening but you have to recognize and listen to my voice and no others!"*

The first round, all jabs. The second round, only body punches. The third round, foot-work and feinting. This went on for several more weeks. The second day I sparred my nose was smashed by a hard right hand. I felt my nose bone crush into the skin that covered it. The bleeding wouldn't stop. You have to remember, we sparred with six-ounce gloves. After the sparring session George told me to go home and put some salt in a cup with a little warm water and add some lemon juice. He told me to snort the mixture up the nostril that bled. This would help seal the scab. Boy did that burn! It worked though. That nostril never bled like that again.

Finally, in November, George told me I was ready for my first fight. He also told me I was starting boxing at a very late age, 25, and if I was to make real money I would have to fight often and increasingly tougher opponents. *"I can't baby you, Joe,"* George would say.

After each day's workout George would have me dunk my head and hands in a bucket of beef brine or rub my eyebrow bones and forehead with beef brine and emery cloth to toughen my skin. The beef brine was obtained from a local butcher shop. This, he said, was necessary to prevent cuts. There are several things that you don't ask in a boxing gym, and I learned those things right away. When George told me I would be sparring for the first time, I asked him who I would be sparring against. George yelled loudly for everyone in the gym to hear: *"Who are you sparring with! Never ask that question again!"* He appeared to be talking more to the whole gym than to me. Like a politician on a stage he continued his speech: *"Do you see anyone in here that has three arms? I don't think so? If you want to box for me you get in the ring with whoever I say. It doesn't matter who you spar or how big he is. If you got the proper technique you can box with anyone. If you don't trust me then find another trainer."*

Right after his speech he took a swig from a decanter in his back pocket. I never asked that question again. To toughen up my jaw George had me chew on pine pitch every day after training was complete. Training in a boxing gym can be grueling work. In the hot summer months the gym was so blistering that the petroleum jelly that George put over my eyebrows dripped like hot oil down my face, and when I jumped rope the sweat that was mixed with my body salt would burn as it rolled from my forehead into my eyes. On the flip side, the gym was so cold in the wintertime I had to put three layers of clothes on to break a sweat, and when the petroleum was put on it felt like globs of ice.

Another thing you never did was question what George was telling you while you were sparring: *"I can see more standing outside this ring then you can inside of it."* He would say: *"You will never be a success unless you trust what I say one hundred percent. If you don't listen to me here where there is no pressure how are you supposed to listen to me when someone is trying to take your head off in a fight?"* George continued: *"If I tell you to walk in the middle of the ring, close your eyes and sing ragtime with your hands down you have to follow my instructions blindly. Then and only then will you be a successful boxer."*

Occasionally someone would walk into the gym who was a friend or relative of one of George's boxers. You could almost sense when one of these visitors was the kind who was going to open their mouth. George could sense it too and he zeroed in on these types of visitors. He wouldn't warn them about instructing one of his boxers, though, as a sign on the entrance to the gym gave that warning. He would wait for them to make the fatal mistake. When that certain boxer started sparring or striking the heavy bag and the friend or relative started giving "pointers" you could see George's face start to cringe. He would walk right up to the boxer and stop him from sparring or hitting the bag. The whole gym would stop and all noise would cease. George would turn to the friend or relative and say: *"You got a lot of nerve coming into this gym and giving my boxer instructions. Maybe tomorrow I'll go to your job or house and I'll give you instructions."* He would then turn to the boxer and say, matter of factly: *"Make up your mind kid, you can have him instruct you or me, but if it's me, that guy either leaves or shuts his mouth."* I can't remember anyone ever leaving when George gave that ultimatum.

Every once in a while an old-timer would walk into the gym and say he trained with John L. Sullivan, Paddy Ryan, or James J. Corbett. George would keep a close eye on those types. As soon as George saw them pull one of his boxers to the side he would run over and get right in the old-timer's face: *"Anything you want to say to my fighter you can say to me!"* He would yell. There was an unwritten rule in the gym that trainers abided by. They never talked to each other's boxers in private and they never gave instructions to each other's boxers.

George would take a swig of his whiskey every half hour or so. You knew George had a few belts of the ol' jug when his face turned beet red and he talked about the bare knuckled boxers of the old days and how they were so much tougher than the gloved boxers of today.

Chapter 5
My First Regulation Bout 1904

I returned to Cox's Corner for a "smoker" bout against Johnny Carroll in October 1904. Carroll was from Brooklyn, New York. In the second round I knocked Carroll out, through the ropes, right into his father's arms.[27]

On Thursday, November 10, George and I took the train down to Philadelphia to look for my first official professional boxing match. My brother Marshall came along with us. The fights were being held at the Manhattan Athletic Club on Friday. When we arrived at the club all of the boxers were huddled into a locker room while the managers haggled over who would fight who and for how much. After my first few fights, people would say many negative things to me about George and how he was overmatching me and collecting money on the side against me. I knew a lot of boxing managers would spread these rumors to try to steal boxers away from their managers. A fighter always has to be wary, not only about the guy he is getting into the ring with, but also about the matchmakers, promoters, and sometimes even his own manager. I trusted George and had full confidence in him. George would never let anyone approach his boxer, and he told me: *"If anyone asks you anything your answer is always the same. My manager is George Armstrong of New York City, any questions you have, go ask him."*

What I didn't like most about Armstrong was that he was drinking from his flask most of the time. His decision-making ability when drinking was compromised, and that was not good for my career, both business-wise and health-wise. I overheard other boxers in the locker room at the club talk about how the best managers to get hooked up with were Jack "Doc" Kearns and Dan McKetrick, the newspaper editor.

After about an hour of negotiating only four matches were made. George came back to me and told me that he wanted to get an easier fight but all the boxers looking for matches had experience. He told me that we were lucky to get one of the four matches. He said my opponent was Morris Harris, a local Negro boy. He was around the same height and weight as me, which George liked. He said Harris had nine fights, and if I wanted to, we could wait another day to find a match. I replied: *"Heck no. We traveled all the way down here and I need the money."*

There was one good thing. Harris had just lost his last fight and he hadn't boxed since March. The purse was ten dollars. Well, that's the cut of the purse that George gave me.

I was surprised at how nice and relaxed I was in the locker room as I lay down waiting for the show to start. The show's promoter, a small Jewish-looking older man with a toupee, came back into the dressing room and

---

27 'Boxing' Annual 1914 'That World's Title' by Joe Jeannette pgs. 42-43.

told all the competing boxers: *"Now let's put on a good show out there, boys."* *"What did he mean by that?"* I asked another boxer while we waited to be called to the gym to fight. The boxer replied: *"Don't you know this is the opponent's dressing room? We are all supposed to lose, but he don't want us to go down too fast, you know, give the fans something to cheer about."*

I needed to talk to George in a hurry about this opponent stuff, but George was busy talking to other managers outside by the ring apron. The scrap was scheduled for six rounds. George came back into the locker room and told me: *"It's time to get wrapped, kid."*

He wrapped my hands slowly with bandage while he spat water from a bottle onto the gauze. George said this was to pack the bandage like a cast. He coated the gauze with insulation tape, which made the fist rock hard. The only thing on my mind was, did my opponent have the same rock hard cast on his hands as well? A few years later, insulation tape would be banned from the sport because of its hardening qualities. I questioned George about the opponent statement and he said not to listen to other boxers, that they didn't know what they were talking about. *"Besides, even if this is the opponent dressing room,"* George said, *"there is always one upset a night and tonight you'll be it. If you want to get to the 'A side' dressing room, beating an 'A side' fighter is the only way."*

After George was done wrapping my hands he filled up a bottle with water and sat it next to me. He told me he was going out to the gym to check on the bout order. George told my brother Marsh, who was also going to work my corner, not to take his eyes off of the bottle of water. Marsh nodded his head. At about seven-thirty p.m. we were called out. The gym was filled with cigar smoke. The spectators were shouting bets and odds to each other. *"He's a strong looking Negro,"* someone yelled, *"gimme two on him."* Another commented: *"I'll take the coon in the brown shorts."* I tried to block out these comments. Anyway, the joke was on them because I was taking their money.

I was still feeling relaxed until I got to the ring stairs, that's when my legs started to feel weak. Unless you make that walk up the stairs and under the ropes you have no idea how much of the battle takes place in your mind during those precious moments. When I entered the ring, my feet sunk into the canvas. The ring floors of my "smoker matches" were not this soft and our practice ring had a wood floor. This worried me. I might get tired quicker in this ring. I tried to act tough waiting for Harris to enter the ring. I still wonder today how I looked to the crowd, and if they saw my nervousness. The referee walked over to me and asked me how to pronounce my name. I remember opening my mouth and telling him: *"Jennette, Joe Jennette."*

Finally, after what seemed like an eternity, Harris entered the ring. The referee motioned the smoke-filled room to quiet down. Then he yelled to no one in particular: *"Gentleman, may I have your attention. Tonight's first match will be in the heavyweight division. First, to my left, boxing out of New York City, New York, wearing brown trunks with a red, white, and blue sash, weighing in at 162 pounds, Joe Jennette!"* I actually lived in New Durham, but I was announced out of Armstrong's address. *"And his opponent, weighing 192 pounds, wearing red trunks, boxing right out of our great city of Philadelphia, Morris Harris! These two boys will be boxing six rounds or less."*

It was the less part that worried me. I was giving up thirty pounds to Harris. George told me Harris lost his last fight but other boxers in the dressing room had told me it was his only loss in nine fights! George conveniently left that information out. We were motioned to the center of the ring and touched gloves. Harris gave me a smirk as though this would be a pushover bout for him. Was he right? Did I really belong in this ring with him? Okay Joe, I said to myself. Get a hold of yourself. Harris was only five-foot ten-inches, so he did not have a height advantage on me.

We were motioned back to our corners. George quickly warned me to keep my tongue tucked behind my teeth when in close quarters, as there were no mouthpieces in those days. Seconds later, the cow bell was rung. The first three rounds, I was horrible. The more I tried to connect the more he made me look foolish. I would miss wildly and he would counter smoothly. After the third round, George whispered in my ear that Harris was getting tired. I could feel that his punches were coming less frequently and that they had less steam on them. He was also holding me more on the inside now. The final three rounds, I was landing much better because of Harris' slower pace. After the final bell the newspaper decision went to Harris. I had lost.

Funny thing is, a few years later I would beat Harris so badly that a spectator gave him a one hundred dollar bill.[28] Harris asked the fan why he was giving him the money, and the fan said it was because he felt bad, not for the beating Harris took, but for the way he courageously took the beating.

The next day, we were preparing to return home via train, and we stopped to get some coffee. George bought a newspaper and he showed me the sport section that mentioned my fight the night before. I had made the newspaper! That was one of the most exciting moments of my life. I took the paper from George and put it in my gym bag. When I arrived home I clipped out the article with my name on it and put it in a shoe box for safe keeping.

Four months later, George brought me back to Philadelphia for a return bout with Harris. On Thursday, March 2 we clashed again, this time at the Broadway A.C., with Harris again winning a newspaper decision. The *National Police Gazette* described the bout: *Joe Jeanette, of New York, made*

---

[28] *New York Times* October 1, 1910.

Morris Harris, the colored heavyweight, fight himself out in order to obtain a decision over him at the Broadway A.C., Philadelphia, on March 2. In fact, it looked as though Jeanette would be returned a winner during the early rounds, but he weakened after Harris drove home a number of right-hand swings to the stomach. Almost on the verge of collapse, Jeanette fought back like a demon, but he had shot his bolt and at the end was in need of bellows.[29] This time many people at ringside thought I had won. The consensus, though, was that the decision could have gone either way, and Harris was, after all, the hometown boy. Pennsylvania did not officially give decisions at the time unless there was a knockout. The fights were officially called "no-decisions." If the bouts went the distance the verdicts were decided by newspaper reporters for betting purposes. They were called "newspaper decisions."

Later on in my career I learned that the reporters were influenced by the records and hometown of the fighters. If a fight was close you could bet the guy with the better record or the "house fighter" would get the nod. Of course there was a lot of pressure put on the reporters by the promoters, managers, and big betters and there were even some reporters who placed bets on the side through third parties. That's the way it was in those days.

On Thursday, April 20 I returned to the Broadway A.C. against a Negro boxer called "Black" Bill. His real name was Claude Brooks and he was boxing out of Memphis, Tennessee, although he lived in Merchantville, New Jersey. Bill was a right-handed boxer, around six-foot in height, and he weighed around 170 pounds. He was a veteran of close to thirty fights. Bill had fought for the colored heavyweight championship twice, losing both times to the "Galveston Giant" Jack Johnson. Bill was taller than Harris and I paid the price for not gauging his range accurately. I jabbed well in the first round. Bill was much more selective with his punches than Harris. Bill's punches did not feel as heavy as Harris' either. In the second round I threw a jab that landed and I guess I did not bring my jab back fast enough. The next thing I knew the referee was standing over me counting. I was the victim of a counter overhand right. At first I just stared at the grains in the canvas and the blackened round blood spots, which were neatly sprinkled around the canvas from previous warriors who spilled their blood. Bill had set me up. He was purposely throwing light punches to make me relax my defense. When he saw a solid opening he let me have it. I would use that same trick on some of my opponents in future bouts.

I could hear the referee counting, but he sounded far away. My head was ringing. Suddenly I snapped out of it. I realized I had been knocked down. I pulled myself upright just before the referee had reached the count of ten but he waived the fight over anyway.[30] George came running up the stairs and through the ropes. First he complained about the stoppage and then he

---

[29] *National Police Gazette* March 18, 1905.
[30] *Philadelphia Inquirer* April 21, 1905.

asked me if I was okay. I felt dizzy and his voice sounded like a whisper as it made its way through my punch-clogged ears. Instinctively I answered: *"I'm okay."* I felt that I had beaten the count and I argued with the referee to let me continue. The referee patted me on the back and said: *"Another day son, another day."*

The lesson I learned was no matter how light a boxer's punches feel, a shot on the sweet spot with four-ounce gloves can send you straight to "queer street" in a hurry. The day after the fight the *Philadelphia Inquirer's* headline read: *Joe Jeanette Quit.*[31] I stared at the headline for what felt like hours. I swore to myself that I would never again let the papers write that I was a quitter. I would get back up before the count of ten and continue regardless of how hurt I was.

The year 1905 was an important year because it was the first year a black athlete, Bob Marshall, of the University of Minnesota, was selected for the All-American football team. This was a big accomplishment for black Americans and it also brought hope that soon we would be able to participate in professional sports such as baseball and basketball. It also brought me the hope that soon a black man would get the opportunity to box for the heavyweight championship of the world.

---

[31] *Philadelphia Inquirer* April 21, 1905.

Chapter 6
Meeting the Galveston Giant in the Ring

On May 9, 1905, we returned to Philadelphia. There was a lot of buzz at the Knickerbocker Athletic Club. The colored heavyweight champion was scheduled to fight on the card. I couldn't wait to get a look at Jack Johnson in action. Many boxing insiders thought he could beat James Jeffries, the world's heavyweight champion. There were also rumors that Jeffries would announce his retirement soon. Two of the top contenders being mentioned to replace him were Marvin Hart and Jack Root. Hart had recently defeated Johnson over twenty rounds. Upon arrival, I weighed in on the scale and proceeded to the locker room area to rest. When George came back to the locker room he explained to me that he couldn't get me a fight but he did get me an exhibition match. I asked him how much I would be getting paid. He told me I would get sixty dollars for the match.[32] That was strange to me. Why would they pay me sixty dollars for an exhibition match? We walked down Market Street and I questioned George as to why I was getting paid so much for the exhibition. I also asked George who it was that I would be fighting. He shrugged off both questions. *"It's only an exhibition,"* he said. *"It's not important who you're boxing. You're just gonna' move around and make it look good. You know, put on a show for the fans."* I didn't see any reason to press him further. After all, I was getting paid and George didn't seem concerned with the match.

Philadelphia was a large city, but not as big as New York City. I had heard people call it a dull city, but they sure loved their sports. The baseball A's were playing in Washington that day. They were tied for third place in the American League. I hadn't been playing much baseball lately, as I was spending more and more time in the boxing gym after work trying to hone my skills. I would have liked to see the A's play while I was in Philly.

I overheard some passersby saying that the contender Jack Johnson was fighting on the show tonight. I couldn't wait to see him in action myself. I was always hungry to learn and figured I could pick up a lot from Johnson. I asked George what he thought of Johnson. He said he thought Johnson was overrated. I didn't care. I was excited to get a chance to see one of the top heavyweights in action. George was very quiet during our walk and I knew he wasn't himself. When I questioned him again on whom I would be boxing the exhibition against he finally blurted out: *"Jack Johnson."* *"Jack Johnson!"* I said as I stopped in my tracks. *"The colored heavyweight champion, Jack Johnson!"*

George tried to calm me down. He told me it would be like sparring in the gym. He said that Johnson would be fighting another boxer named Walter

---

[32] *Newark-Star Ledger* March 11, 1956.

44

Johnson after my bout and he would be conserving his energy for that second bout. I was still suspicious but I figured George knew better than I did.

"I told you we have to move you quick, Joe. You're not starting out at a young age. This is good experience and it is only an exhibition. Just like sparring." "Move me quick!" I shot back astounded. Johnson was a veteran of over thirty fights and one of the most talked about boxers in the country. *"Isn't that a little too quick?"* I said. George didn't reply. He just reached into his coat and took out his flask of whiskey and took a swig. We arrived at the club at six o'clock. This would be my first Tuesday night match, but the gym was packed with many more people than the Friday fights. You could feel the excitement in the air as the crowd anticipated the Galveston Giant's arrival.

It was rather quiet in the dressing room as I was changing into my trunks. The other boxers were whispering: *"That's one of the opponents that's going in with Johnson."* There was that "opponent" word again. It just sounded so dirty when it was used in the boxing dressing room. Just then a large crowd arrived. There were newspaper reporters, well dressed with their brimmed hats with press cards sticking out of the top. Photographers were popping flashbulbs. As the group passed me, I got my first look at him. He looked about six-feet one inches tall and he had a slim athletic build. He had a shiny bald head and he flashed a wide, bright, golden smile from his gold capped teeth. He was accompanied by a beautiful colored woman named Etta Reynolds.[33] I was told he was from Texas, and when he spoke he sounded more like an orator or a preacher than a boxer. He walked with a fancy cane and never stopped talking. I was star struck.

Johnson obviously enjoyed the attention, and he boasted to the reporters that he would whip the white Heavyweight Champ Jeffries. He further stated that Jeffries was afraid to fight him. Johnson never mentioned me or the other fellow that he was boxing that night. Johnson was saying how Jeffries was old and no match for him. He said he was the greatest fighter in the world and he would prove it tonight. Prove it tonight! What did that comment mean? He knows this is only an exhibition doesn't he? I pressed George about Johnson's comments and he repeated that there was no need to worry, as he took his flask out and took a drink. He said Johnson was just playing to the reporters.

The noise faded a little and the reporters were ushered out of the dressing room as Johnson went through his preparation for the matches. He was on the other side of the locker room behind a sheet that was strung up over a rope just for him. He even got his own dressing area! I tried to sneak a peek at him warming up but I couldn't get close to him, as he had friends blocking off his warm-up area.

---

[33] *'Jack Johnson is a Dandy'* by Jack Johnson, pg. 51.

Walter Johnson, the other boxer Johnson was going to fight, arrived. He was much smaller looking than Johnson. He did not have the athletic prowess of Johnson either. He sat eerily quiet not ten feet from where I was sitting. I watched him get dressed with absolutely no emotion. He looked my way several times with scarred and drooping eye lids but he never spoke a word to me. His scars had wide depressions that looked to be the result of cuts that were not treated properly. We both laid down on the locker room benches. I tucked a towel under my head and tried to think about anything else but getting in the ring with Johnson. At eight o'clock I started stretching out and shadow boxing to work up a sweat. I had learned the hard way that going into the ring cold was a dangerous proposition.

Around eight-thirty I got the call to make my way into the ring. I heard some clapping and whistling from the crowd, mixed in with boos and some comments such as: *"You'll get yours tonight, kid."*

Jack entered the gym and the crowd arose and erupted with applause. He walked to the ring like he was on a Sunday stroll through the park. He slipped under the ropes and waved to his supporters. He had a confident look that I had never before observed on the face of a fighter preparing to do battle. He looked like he just exited a swimming hole. He had sweat running down all over his body. I sat on my stool and looked down as my gloves were being laced on. They still had fresh blood that was coagulating on them from the previous bout. George nervously wiped the blood off of the gloves and told me to stay focused.

After my gloves were laced up, I sat and waited. The referee quieted the crowd down and made his introductions: *"To my left, wearing brown trunks with a red, white, and blue sash, weighing 167 pounds, hailing from New York City, New York, Joe Jennette.*[34] *And to my right, coming to us all the way from Galveston, Texas, wearing light blue trunks with a yellow sash, weighing in at 185 and 3/4 pounds, the current colored heavyweight champion of the world, let's hear it for the Galveston Giant, Jack Johnson!"* The crowd let out a great roar.

George had me announced as being from New York because he was trying to build a fan base for me and anyway that is where he trained me. He told me after I had established a name for myself I could use my real hometown. After Johnson was announced, we were brought to the middle of the ring, where we touched gloves. The referee reminded us that it was only an exhibition match. Johnson looked at me and with his proper sophisticated accent said: *"Don't worry kid, let's just give the crowd a show."*

Johnson had worked up a good sweat and he did not look at all like he was ready for some easy sparring like George said he would be doing. The bell rang and Jack came running over to me, but he did not swing. I threw a right hand instinctively out of survival and he just leaned back, smiled, and

[34] *'Boxing'* Annual 1914 'That World's Title' by Joe Jeannette pgs. 42-43.

swatted it away with an open right glove. Later in the round I charged him and he landed a straight left jab that sent a shock wave from my neck down my spine all the way to my tail bone. I tried to counter to the body but he tied me up. After that things really started heating up. I learned more tricks in that first round than I did in six months of sparring.

Over the next two rounds, "Lil" Artha' kept trying to back me up, but I refused to give ground. A couple of times he even tried talking me into letting up. George was shouting instructions on how to land and slip blows. Johnson was smiling and talking back to George: *"Why don't you change seats with Joe, George,"* he said. *"Maybe you could show him how it's done."*

Johnson took the time to know all the names of the men who worked my corner. I took a knee in the second and third rounds after hard rights to the jaw. Both times I came back with several hard hook-cross-hook combinations. The blows got both Johnson's and the crowd's attention. Johnson's face changed from a smile to anger. This was a real fight! Johnson was still talking to George: *"You want to be my manager, Georgie?"* and *"How you getting home tonight, Georgie? Can we share a ride?"*

Harry Preston, a British sportsman, would later comment about Johnson talking to his opponents during a fight: *"A very cunning fellow was Johnson in the ring... He set out to try to goad his opponent into attacking him by talking at him in the ring. This was less of a matter of temperament than a deliberate bit of craftiness. A wonderful defensive fighter, who preferred to hit a man coming at him rather than force an attack, he kept up a flow of provocative talk in order to infuriate his opponent, and lure him into an unwise attack."*[35]

Johnson was a great counter puncher and he used his taunts to get me to step in with my punches. At the beginning of the third round I landed a hard punch to Jack's stomach. Johnson suddenly turned tail and galloped around the ring with me in pursuit.[36] He didn't stop running until the end of the bout.

After the final bell rang, I was still standing! Even though it was only an exhibition, there were times when Jack tried to push me around and drop me to the boards, but I had held my own. I would never walk into the ring feeling any doubt in my abilities again. I knew I belonged and I knew with the right conditioning and experience I could beat Jack Johnson. George slapped me on the back and said: *"See Joe, I told you he wouldn't try to knock you out. Just a friendly exhibition."* *"Friendly exhibition!"* I shot back stunned. *"Are you kidding. He was trying to kill me in there!"*

I exited the ring and sat in the back of the club toweling myself off. I watched as Walter Johnson made his way into the ring. He glanced over at where I was sitting. He slipped under the ropes and bounced around the ring. Jack was leaning over the ropes talking to people outside the ring. He

[35] *'Memories'* by Harry Preston pgs. 96-97.
[36] *Auburn Citizen* April 17, 1909.

didn't even notice that Walter had entered the ring. The ring announcer let out a yell: *"Ladies and gentlemen. Your attention please. To my left, fighting from the city of Philadelphia, weighing 173 and 1/4 pounds, Walter Johnson. And to my right, once again, from Galveston, Texas, Jack Johnson!"*

After the cow bell rang Jack went right at Walter. Walter took a terrible beating in the first round. What happened to the exhibition? In the second round Walter was dropped with a right to the jaw. In the third round Jack landed a hard jab to the forehead of Walter followed by a picture perfect right hand that landed square on Walter's jaw.[37] Walter was straightened up and he was out cold as he fell back as stiff as a board. As the crowd stood cheering, Johnson turned to walk to his corner. All at once he stopped, turned, and looked straight at me with a menacing look for several moments. I heard a bystander whisper that Walter's seconds should have tossed up the sponge instead of letting him take those extra punches when he was out on his feet. After Walter crashed to the boards I turned to George and said: *"Just an exhibition? Nothing to worry about?"* Armstrong shrugged his shoulders and grinned meekly.

A newspaper report of the fight stated: *Big Jack Johnson caught a tarter in Joe Jeannette at Philadelphia several nights ago. The colored heavyweight champion was contracted to stop Walter Johnson and Jeannette in three rounds each. Joe... was practically unknown, besides being heavily handicapped in both weight and height, the spectators expected to see Jack "clean" him in a hurry. Instead he tore into the big black champion and made it decidedly interesting for him in each of the three sessions.*[38]

Another report on the fight stated: *The double stunt tried by Jack Johnson, colored heavyweight champion of the world, in meeting two men for three rounds each in the wind-up at the Knickerbocker Athletic Club last night proved to be more of a surprise than the champion was looking for. Joe Jeanette, of New York, went on first, and although greatly handicapped in weight and height and eclipsed in experience, he gave Johnson as hard a three-round reception that the latter has run across while in this city.*

Jeanette not only held his own, but actually forced the milling in two of the rounds. He repeatedly got home to Johnson's body and face with a good left jab and landed a few right hand wallops which caused the crowd to yell its approval. Jeanette was not any too gallus, however, by his success and he invariably cleverly covered up whenever the big fellow came rushing in after being stung by some of Joe's punches. Johnson seemed unable to get to Jeanette with any of his blows effectively, although the New Yorker took the count more than once to gather his wits about him when the milling got a bit warm. Johnson did not seem to try very hard in the first round, but after Jeanette had made himself solid with the crowd Johnson sailed in for the second round like a hurricane.

For a time things went badly for Joe, but before the round was over he was giving just as good as he received. The third he easily held his own, despite Johnson's desperate efforts to land the "ender" punch. The crowd went wild when the bell ended the bout with Jeanette

---

[37] *Boston Globe* May 10, 1905.
[38] *Chicago Daily Tribune* May 14, 1905.

fighting Johnson savagely. Walter Johnson then essayed to go the same distance, but a clip on the jaw just as the men had shaken hands in the third round settled that bout.[39]

From this moment I knew that boxing would be my career. I gave up any thoughts of being a veterinarian. Johnson met me in the dressing room after the fight and told me: *"You're a tough kid, Joe. Keep it up and you will have a fine career. Work on your balance and your defense. You're a little off."* He followed with this advice: *"Show me a fighter's stance and I will estimate his abilities. In my fights, I spend three out of four rounds padding backwards. Defense always wins in the end, if it's good enough."*[40] Johnson continued: *"Remember Pete Jackson, Joe? He died as much from a broken heart as he did from tuberculosis. The white man didn't give him the shot at the title that he deserved. I am not gonna' wind up like Old Pete. I'm gonna' get my shot!"*

[39] *Philadelphia Inquirer* May 10, 1905.
[40] *Champions of the Ring* by Gerald Suster pg. 53.

Cox's Corner in West Hoboken where
Jennette fought "Smokers" in 1904.

Bert Williams & George Walker.

Joe Jennette's first automobile. Jennette is in front passenger seat, circa 1908.

Joe Jennette's brother Marshall driving a Jagel's & Bellis coal wagon, circa 1906.

Sabina Marshall's delicatessen & ice cream parlor in Homestead, New Durham, North Bergen, N.J. L to R: Joe Jennette, sister Grace, mother Sabina Marshall, sister Agnes, & brother Marshall, circa 1907.

Pacific Street on the "Barbary Coast" where Jennette performed exhibitions in 1907. The So Different Café is left of The Bear.

Joe Jennette & the Olympia Athletic Club basketball team, circa 1908.

Joe Jennette Paris, France, circa 1909.

Charlie Mitchell, Bob Fitzsimmons, Jem Mace, Joe Jennette, & Willie Lewis
at fundraising exhibition for Mace in London, England, May 26, 1909.

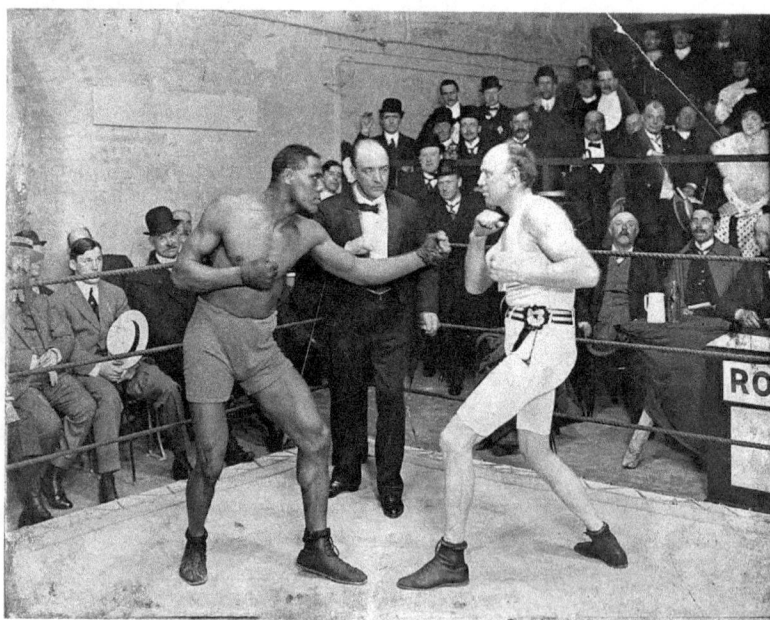

Exhibition bout between Jennette & Fitzsimmons May 26, 1909.

Jim Pratt, Willie Lewis, Dan McKetrick, & Joe Jennette, Paris, France, circa 1909.

Joe Jennette & son arriving in Paris at St. Lazare Station January 7, 1909.

Jennette teaching son boxing in the courtyard at Neuilly, France, 1909.

Willie Lewis postcard pose, circa 1909.

Willie Lewis, Paris, circa 1913.

Willie Lewis practicing with Joe Jennette, Paris, circa 1909.

The Fearsome Foursome

Joe Jennette "The Hoboken Iron Man"

Jack Johnson "The Galveston Giant"

Sam Langford "The Boston Tar Baby"

Sam McVea "The California Rail Splitter"

Joe Jennette Baseball Photo Shoot For La Vie au Grand Air Paris, France

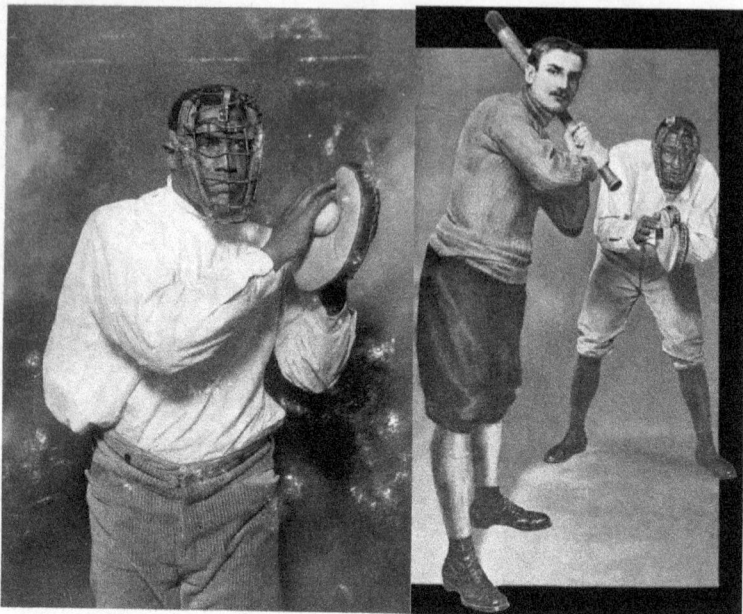

Joe Jennette poses wearing catcher's mask, December 4, 1909.

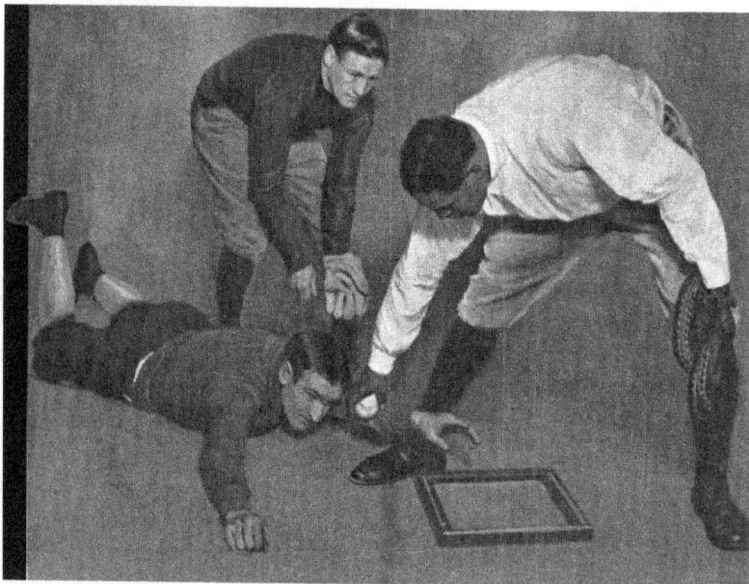

Charlie Hitte wearing glove while Joe Jennette applies tag to John Kelly, December 4, 1909.

Joe Jennette sparring with Marc Gaucher in courtyard, Neuilly, France, 1909.

Joe Jennette on horseback at Jim Pratt's estate Neuilly, France, 1909.

Olympia Athletic Club photo, circa 1909, Union Hill N.J. Joe Jennette, only black member, seated in middle. Boxer Al Benedict to right of Jennette with elbow on Jennette's leg. Gregory Speciale's Great-Great-Grandfather Jean Baptiste Lehe sitting in window sill in upper right corner.

Joe Jennette promotional postcard photos, Paris, France, circa 1909.

Joe Jennette fighting pose, circa 1909.

Joe Jennette in automobile, Joe Junior in toy car, at 503 Central Ave,
West Hoboken N.J., circa 1909.

Joe Jennette in automobile, West Hoboken N.J., circa 1909.

Joe Jennette in automobile, West Hoboken N.J., circa 1909.

Joe Jennette postcard, circa 1909.

Joe Jennette working on his automobile, circa 1909.

Joe Jennette poses, circa 1909.

L to R standing: Caspar & Joseph Atzingen. Joe Jennette's mother Sabina Schultz-Marshall.
Sitting L to R: Robert, and Anton Atzingen.

Adelaide Atzingen-Jennette.

Chapter 7
My Swiss Princess

Two months later, I returned to the Broadway A.C. for another match with "Black" Bill. I knew "Black" had been knocked out by Jack Johnson five weeks earlier, and this gave me new confidence. There was a flyer with the names of the contestants and I noticed that my name was again spelled Jeanette instead of Jennette. I complained about this to George and he said not to worry, he would correct it later. After six grueling rounds against Bill the final bell rang. I used my jab effectively and made sure that I did not get caught by Bill's heavy overhand right. We both landed hard uppercuts in the sessions but I felt confident I had the edge. After the bout we both waited as the newspaper reporters at ringside huddled over who won. After several tense minutes they gave their verdict. One of the reporters shouted out: *"After six rounds of boxing the decision goes to Joe Jennette."*

Dan raised my hand up and a chill went through my body. A lot of people had told me how talented I was at boxing, but until you win a fight the doubts in your mind continue to magnify. Still I was just cutting my teeth as a pro. The money was good, but did I really want to keep doing this? I saw what the "opponents" looked like. They looked like they were supposed to lose. All beat up looking and out of shape. I was not ignorant to the fact that I was dressing in the same area of the locker room as they were and that I was also an opponent. I was hearing all the locker room chatter again that Jack Kearns and Dan McKetrick managed all the top boxers, and that George Armstrong was a nobody. That he delivered the dead bodies to the shows to lose. They called him one of the "meat wagon" managers. I told myself I would give this fight game six more months to see where it would take me. I was not resigned to being an opponent, and I definitely was not coming to lose any fights.

I returned to the Broadway A.C. on July 6 and faced George Cole. Cole was one of the top fighters in the country. He was a veteran of over 130 fights. Cole had just beaten tough Jack Blackburn a month prior. George was a New Jersey native. He fought out of Philadelphia but he lived in Bordentown, N.J. Cole was only five-foot seven-inches tall and weighed 154 pounds at fight time. He was a fast, scrappy boxer who was a ten-year veteran of the ring. The six round bout was filled with action. The newspaper decision was awarded to Cole. The *National Police Gazette* described the action: *It was a hard fast battle and Jeanette made a great showing with his more experienced opponent. He started right in as soon as the bell rang and, using his left effectively, he sent it often to Cole's face and body, the latter, countering with a right to the face that brought blood from Joe's nose. Again Joe used his left in the second sending it to the face and body and cleverly blocking a vicious left from Cole. Joe then jabbed and Cole tried for the jaw but missed. In the third Cole sent a left to the head and Joe repaid this with a right to the body. Cole put his left to the face and Joe jabbed. Before the bell rang Cole sent two hard lefts to the head. The fourth round was a hummer and some hard and fast exchanges were witnessed. Cole was now bleeding. Cole tried hard to send his right to the jaw in the last two rounds, but Joe always had his jab in reserve. Cole sent some hard shots to the body and both fought in grand style. It was a great contest and at the finish Cole had a shade on the New Yorker.*[41]

I boxed Cole again on August 28 at the National A.C. in Philadelphia. The bout was ruled a no-decision. The *Philadelphia Item* thought I won the fight while the *Philadelphia Inquirer* gave the edge to Cole. George gave me a lot of trouble when he got underneath my punches. I would learn that I was much more comfortable fighting taller opponents. This problem with smaller fighters would again resurface when I met Sam Langford in later bouts. I liked using a crouching style which worked well with taller boxers like Johnson. The crouching style, though, made me easier to be reached by the smaller boxers I fought.

On October 7 I returned to the ring in North Bergen, N.J. against debuting Pat O'Rourke of New York. It would be one of only a few times I would box in my native Hudson County. Working my corner for the fight was my brother Marshall and Jack Johnson.[42] Johnson was impressed with my exhibitions against him in May and he asked if he could second me. Marshall and I were excited to have Jack in my corner but we were also a little leery that he might be trying to pick up on my fight strategy. I knocked out O'Rourke in the fifth round of a scheduled six round affair. There were over one hundred sports at the scrap which took place at the "Old Gut," Guttenberg race track. O'Rourke came out the aggressor and had me hurt in the second round. In the third round I knocked O'Rourke down four times. O'Rourke survived the fourth round on guts alone. In the fifth I caught Pat with a hard right hand that sent him toppling over. Referee John McDonald, a New York newspaperman, didn't even bother to count. O'Rourke's seconds put up no argument, as their charge was out cold. I weighed 168 pounds for the bout, and O'Rourke weighed 197. The gate for the show was one hundred and fifty dollars. I received twenty-five dollars for my effort.

Four days later, on October 11, I met "Black" Bill again, this time in Wilmington, Delaware. It was my first scheduled ten rounder. Martin "Fiddler" Neary helped prepare me for the jump in rounds. I was 1-1 against Bill but I was nervous about having my first ten round fight. I had gone six rounds six times. Until you actually go ten rounds in a real fight the doubts are there. I never sparred more than eight rounds in the gym up until that point. It didn't matter, because the fight never reached the tenth. The *National Police Gazette* described the bout: *One of the hardest fights ever seen*

---

[41] *National Police Gazette* July 22, 1905.
[42] *Hudson Dispatch* October 9, 1905.

at the Wilmington Casino was the windup between Joe Jeanette and Black Bill, of
Merchantville, N.J. After a terrific battle Black Bill was knocked out in the seventh of
what was to have been a ten-round combat. In the second Bill got a blow on the jaw
which knocked him down and seemed to take the steam out of him. He rallied and
showed strong in the third. The men fought well until the seventh, when another blow put
Bill through the ropes. He came up again, and was floored three times in succession, the
last blow putting him out.[43] It was during this bout that I discovered that my
grueling training habits paid off more the longer the bouts went.

Next I boxed Jim Jeffords on October 26 at the Broadway A.C. in Philly.
Jeffords' had over fifty fights going into the contest. He was a six-year
veteran who was very tall at six-foot four-inches. Jeffords had beaten the
great Peter Jackson, stopping him in the fourth round. In the dressing room
before the match, a reporter asked me how I felt about boxing Jeffords
being that he had killed a boxer named George Feeley in the ring two years
prior. I tried to act like I knew about the ring death, but I didn't. It was the
first time I heard of it. I tried to act like it was no big deal to me, but it was.
I was careful early on in the bout, until I felt Jeffords blows and realized
that he couldn't hurt me. The *National Police Gazette* described the action:
'Jeanette Bested Jeffords.' Jeffords had the advantage in height and reach, but the stocky
colored man bore in and made Jeffords wince with his lefts. Joe stepped in at the start and
shot lefts to Jeffords' face. In the second he reached the nose with such success that it
started to bleed. Jeffords did better in the third, putting a terrific right hand uppercut to
Joe's face. The fourth was furious, Jeffords swinging hard rights. Jeffords took much
punishment in the fifth, and in the sixth was plainly tired. He repeatedly hung on to Joe
in the clinches.[44] I defeated Jeffords via a six round newspaper decision.

On October 28 I returned to the ring against George Cole at the National
A.C. in Philly. The fight almost didn't go off, because I outweighed Cole by
almost 40 pounds. I weighed in at 185 pounds to Georges 146. I easily beat
Cole in six rounds. On November 2, I drew with "Black" Bill in
Wilmington, Delaware, over six rounds. My career was going well and my
confidence in my abilities was growing exponentially. I helped my mother
open a neighborhood store with some of my boxing earnings.

One night Marshall and I went to a dance party at a hall in Jersey City.
When we got to the entrance we were told it was a "paper bag party." Not
knowing what that meant we just smiled and tried to enter but we were
stopped and told that we had to roll up a sleeve and put an arm up against
the paper bag that was taped to the door frame. At first we thought it was
some kind of joke, but it wasn't. I rolled up my sleeve and put it next to the
bag. We asked what the bag was for and were told that if a person was the
same color or lighter than the bag they would be allowed to enter the party.
If a person's skin color was darker than the bag they would be denied

---

[43] *National Police Gazette* October 28, 1905.
[44] *National Police Gazette* November 11, 1905.

entrance. The bouncer at the door motioned me to enter. When Marshall put his arm up the bouncer stated: *"I'm sorry pal, I can't let you in."* My brother laughed at him and said: *"You have to be kidding me."* The bouncer replied: *"Listen, we don't want any trouble but that's the rules."* I stepped back outside and grabbed Marshall who I could see was getting angry. On the trolley ride home we both stared out the windows and didn't speak a word. I was later told that "paper bag parties" had originated in New Orleans.

One Saturday night Marshall asked me if I wanted to go to the Liberty Dance Hall, at Shippen and Spring Streets, in West Hoboken. My sisters Annie and Agnes were also going. I loved ballroom dancing almost as much as boxing and basketball. It was mostly a white dance hall but we felt comfortable because everyone knew us from the neighborhood. Never in my wildest dreams did I think that fate would be at that dance hall waiting for me. I was dancing with Agnes, who was not too skilled with her footwork. While spinning her, our feet got tangled and I fell to the floor. I heard a giggle from a woman standing on the side. Her face was turned away but she was the only one wearing a burgundy dress. I got up and brushed myself off.

After the song ended I noticed the woman with the burgundy dress walking towards the exit. I followed her. At the exit I tapped her on her shoulder and asked: *"Do you think I am going to let you laugh at me and leave without dancing with me?"* She turned around to reply to me, and I immediately felt like I was struck by lightning. She was the most beautiful woman I had ever laid eyes on. She had brown hair and hazel eyes. My heart was filled with excitement. All at once I caught myself and my excitement turned to terror. This woman was white and I am black. Although my family accepted interracial relationships almost everyone else did not. I was afraid to speak. I was one of only seven colored people in the hall. I must have been crazy to think she would talk to me.

In boxing gyms and at the fight halls, whites and blacks mingled as though there was no racism in the world. But outside of the boxing world, racism wasn't just a word; it was a hard, cold reality. As real as an uppercut to a raised jaw. I could hear my sister Agnes screaming those words so many years ago: *"I hate my skin, I hate my skin!"* Once again I was so frustrated with this color barrier. I didn't have a clue of how to deal with it.

While I was standing there frozen she spoke: *"Hello my name is Adelaide Atzingen but my friends call me Addie. I'm sorry but I cannot dance with you."* My heart sank. I turned to walk away and she grabbed my shoulder. As I turned back she was smiling brightly. She said: *"You didn't let me finish. I was going to say I cannot dance with you unless I know your name. I never dance with strangers."* We both laughed: *"I am sorry ma'am my name is Joseph Jennette but everybody calls me Joe."* We started dancing. Addie asked me what I did for a living and I told her I drove a coal truck and boxed professionally. *"Isn't boxing dangerous? Why would you want to do that?"* She asked. I told her I started boxing as a dare

70

and kept at it for the money and I made sure I protected myself as best I could. We didn't speak for several moments after that, as we just stared into each other's eyes. We danced for hours that night. Addie told me she was supposed to meet a girlfriend at the dance hall, but when her friend never showed up, she decided to leave. She said she was waiting for the song to end when I fell in front of her. It wound up that her friend had an outbreak of measles that day!

We talked about everything from sports to politics and religion, not noticing at first the stares that would accompany us throughout our lifetime; the stares that only interracial couples know. We seemed to connect on every subject we discussed. After the last song ended I asked Addie if she wanted to go for a walk. We talked for hours as we walked above the Palisades Cliffs overlooking Hoboken and the Hudson River. I knew that night that I wanted Addie to be my wife.

If not for her support and love I would have never accomplished half of what I did in this world. How a love like ours could be looked upon as being threatening is something I will never understand. Unfortunately, to some people it was and still is. Adelaide was of Swiss heritage. She was born in Hoboken, New Jersey, and was just as fair skinned as my mother. Even though I was the product of a mixed marriage, there were rarely mixed marriages at the time. In most states, mixed marriages were not only unwelcome, they were illegal.

We had our first date in mid-November. We walked along the Palisades where Aaron Burr long ago dueled against Alexander Hamilton, and we sat and had a picnic lunch. We watched the ships sail in and out of the Hudson River, and the trolleys going to and from the ferry down below the cliffs. After lunch, we took a walk past Lovers Leap in Weehawken. The location had a spectacular drop from the hill-top. Addie's father, Louis Von Atzingen, had died when she was only seven-years-old. Her father was struck by a train while driving a milk delivery truck in Haverstraw, N.Y. We were both unfortunate that both of our fathers died when we were children.

When I was at work or training in the gym I found myself thinking of Addie. I would sing "Sweet Adeline" to myself, changing Adeline to Adelaide: *Sweet Adelaide, My Adelaide, At night, dear heart, for you I pine. In all my dreams, your fare face beams, You're the flower of my heart, sweet Adelaide.*[45]

With every date I grew fonder of her. Eventually I knew that we would have to discuss our future and the prospects of a mixed marriage. I loved her so much that I wanted to protect her, even if that meant saving her from me and my skin color. I knew if we married it would be a very difficult life for her, more difficult than she could ever imagine. She would not only be marrying a black man, but she would probably be divorcing

---

[45] "You're the Flower of my Heart, Sweet Adeline" 1903

herself from most of her family and friends in the process. She would be marrying into the racism that I was born into. Life with a colored man might be too much for her to handle. I would never want Addie to experience the vicious stares and comments that I had to experience in my young lifetime.

I finally told Addie I wanted her to meet my family. When we arrived at my mom's house, I hadn't told Addie that my mother was white. When Addie and my mother met, my mother was not as accepting as I thought she would be. I don't think race was an issue, my mother could see how in love we were, I think she wanted to make sure this girl was right for her son. She spent the better time of our visit studying Addie. Addie of course was fully aware of this and she was visibly uncomfortable. My stepfather, my brothers, and my sisters were all cordial. I could not read any disapproval from the way they acted. My sister's Annie and Agnes were very excited to meet my girlfriend.

Two weeks later, Addie brought me home to meet her family. I was very nervous. Surprisingly, Addie's family was very respectful, although somehow I got the feeling that they didn't think we were as serious as we were. Addie's mother's name was Josephine, and she had two other daughters named Alois, 16-years-old, and Mary, 14-years-old. Addie also had five uncles on her father's side named Caspar, Melchoir, Joseph, Anton, and Robert. The first time Addie's mother saw my car she was scared half to death. She had never seen a car so big before.[46]

I know how difficult it was dealing with racism in my mother and step-father's marriage. I struggled over telling Addie how I felt deep inside. When I finally got up the nerve to explain how I felt, Addie shocked me with her reply. Adelaide told me her love for me was stronger than any hate the world could ever show towards her. She told me she wanted to marry me and said the only protection she needed would be provided by our love for each other. We embraced each other as tight as we could.

At first we worried what people might think and say, but after a while we realized if they were really our friends they would understand, and if they weren't, it didn't matter what they thought. We told my family, and they all seemed happy for us, as they knew how in love I was with Addie. When Addie and I told her family, however, the response was somewhat different. Addie's mother had constantly tried to get her to break off her relationship with me. She tried making her feel guilty by telling her that Addie's sisters were being teased because their sister was dating a black man. She berated Addie for not trying to find someone of her own Swiss heritage. Addie's uncles told her they loved her, but they were worried that she wouldn't be prepared for the hard life she would have to live. Addie turned to her

---

[46] Interview with JoAnn Flannery-Mostaccio Joe Jennette's great-niece.

72

mother and asked for her blessing. Her mother pleaded with her to reconsider. Her mother stated that I was a fine young man but she didn't want her daughter to suffer through the hardships of an interracial marriage. When Addie insisted that she was to be married, her mother screamed at her: *"What will the neighbors think!"* Addie replied: *"Ma, I don't care what the neighbors think. They aren't marrying Joe, I am!"* With tears in her eyes, her mother said: *"If you don't care about yourself what about the children?"*[47] Addie replied: *"What children, Ma?"* *"Do you want to be responsible for the hardship that those poor mongrel children will face? I gave you everything growing up. What did I do to deserve you hurting me like this? When I told your aunts that you were dating a black man, all they asked was, 'How dark is he?' I will never approve of this marriage. Never!"*[48]

Addie burst out of the house crying hysterically. I caught up with her and we held each other closely. *"I can't believe my mother,"* she cried. *"Mongrels! Is that what she thinks my children will be!"* I told Addie that her mother loved her and was just trying to protect her and that she was worried about our future. She would come around, I said. Addie still had tears in her eyes when she softly replied: *"When I thought of all the qualities I wanted in a man to marry I never considered that for my family, skin color was one of them."*

We planned to marry in January 1906, and we went to city hall to get our marriage license. The clerk gave us a cold stare and told us to wait in the lobby.[49] We watched her as she walked back to talk with another clerk, and they both looked over at us. I felt like we were criminals. The silence was deafening. When the clerk returned, I was preparing to speak, when Addie shouted loud enough for everyone in the office to hear: *"Is there a problem with our application!"* *"Oh, no,"* the clerk replied. *"I was just checking to make sure it is legal."* *"Make sure it is legal!"* Addie screamed. *"I'm sorry, ma'am."* The clerk said: *"I was just making sure this is legal in New Jersey. You are the first couple that... well, here is your license."* Addie ripped the license out of the clerk's hand, grabbed my arm, and stormed out of the building. We both came to the conclusion that through our example, over time, we would have to teach people that interracial marriage was not a crime. We would be ambassadors of interracial love. When I asked one of my female cousins on my father's side why I got angry looks from some black women when I was with Addie, she explained her opinion: *"For many black women the thought of black men, especially successful black men, dating or marrying white women is like being passed over for the prom by the boy of their dreams, causing them pain, rage, and an overwhelming sense of betrayal and personal rejection. It is considered the ultimate insult or racial disloyalty. Others look at it as white men are marrying white women. If black men start*

[47] *Mixed Messages* by Fred & Anita Prinzing pg. 111.
[48] *Marriage beyond Black & White* by David & Barbara Douglas pg. 54.
[49] *Marriage beyond Black & White* by David & Barbara Douglas pg. 47.

marrying white women, who will be left for us to marry?'[50]

---

[50] *Interracial Intimacies* by Randall Kennedy pgs. 152, 120, 116.

Chapter 8
Decision Match with "Lil" Artha'

I had reeled off four straight wins with one no-decision when I returned to Philly on November 25. Once again I was matched with "Lil" Artha,' but this would be a decision match. The bout was held at the National A.C. Johnson had only one loss in his last 25 contests with that loss coming to current world's heavyweight champion Marvin Hart. Hart, nicknamed "The Kentucky Plumber," won the title vacated by James J. Jeffries on July 3 in Nevada defeating Jack Root by knock out. Jeffries refereed that bout.

Johnson would be defending his colored heavyweight championship against me. Once again, my name was spelled wrong on the flyer. This time they spelled my name with two n's, Jeannette. Johnson arrived at the weigh-in with a crowd, but this time he was with a different colored woman. She was just as beautiful as the woman from our last fight, Jack called her Sadie but her name was Clara Kerr. At the scale, Jack weighed 185 pounds. I tipped the scales at 162 pounds. I went back to my hotel room and rested. I played cards with George to pass the time. At night we returned to the club for the fight. Johnson passed me in the locker room and whispered so only I could hear him: *"Hey, Joe, you're a nice fellow, black eyes and a scarred face wouldn't look too good."* I ignored his comment.

Finally it was fight time and we entered the ring. After the introductions, the announcer slipped outside the ropes, and we waited for the bell. Johnson had a look of concentrated anger I did not see in our two previous encounters. My heart was once again beating rapidly, but my breathing and thought processes were much more relaxed. This, I would later realize, only comes with the experience of several ring battles.

When the bell rang, Johnson attacked immediately. There would be no feeling-out process in this match. Earlier, Jack had fielded questions about the competitive exhibitions we had, and he did not seem to appreciate the fact that reporters were questioning him about my abilities. His aggressive tactics appeared to be his attempt to try to silence the doubters. The first round was loaded with heavy punches. I would land a hard uppercut and Artha' would follow with a stiff counter hook. In close, we both landed hard body shots followed by uppercuts and hooks. The pace was frightening. I could feel my body punches going deep into Johnson's midsection. I could hear him wince as I buried the punches into his ribcage. I landed a solid uppercut that snapped Jack's head back, the crowd roared with approval. Johnson was visibly shaken.

In the second round we continued where we left off. I found an opening to land an uppercut right on the tip of Artha's jaw. The blow sent Jack's jaw twisting upward, while his knees quivered and buckled underneath him. He somehow unleashed a counter right on wobbly legs and the thumb portion

75

of his glove pushed deep into my eye socket. I suddenly saw five Jack Johnsons circling around in my thumbed eye. I kept blinking over and over in panic until my eyesight recovered.

I smelled an opportunity as Artha' was clearly wounded. I unloaded everything in my arsenal. Lefts, rights, uppercuts, this was no time for conserving energy. This was the opportunity I was waiting for. This was my chance to dethrone the great Jack Johnson. This was my opportunity to be a world famous fighter, to start earning serious paydays, and to leave forever in my past the opponents' section of the dressing room.

I could feel my foe breaking and wilting with every punch that broke through his guard. I was only a blow or two away from ring immortality. No, sports immortality! I looked deep into Artha's glazed-over eyes and I could see that he knew what I already knew. The end was near for him. He was not the hunter anymore, but the hunted. Only in boxing can that change occur in a moment's notice. The title, the money, the fame, it will all be mine. I must keep throwing and throwing. Suddenly, I saw Johnson's face change from bewildered punch drunkenness to a wide-eyed survival look. He rushed at me and landed a hard right to my stomach. My body went stiff and I could see Jack cocking his right shoulder back. As he leaned forward with a right to the jaw I bobbed underneath and weaved a hard right uppercut to his stomach followed by a hook to his jaw. Jack's legs buckled again, and for a moment he appeared to be sitting back, getting ready to fall. Then he recovered. He wouldn't go down! He just kept coming! What an athlete. The more I hurt him the more he dug in.

Jack was raining punches down on me and I was slipping them all and countering cleanly to his jaw. This was my night! Jack pushed me back to a corner and threw several body punches. Two in a row went below the belt with the second punch nearly scraping the canvas as it ripped up from the floor directly between my legs and into my groin, crippling me over. I watched as Jack looked the punch straight into my groin.[51] It was no accident. As I was falling from the illegal blow, Johnson hit me twice on the back of the head. A loud raging roar broke out from the crowd, followed by boos.

The blows sent me straight down. I was unable to move for close to ten minutes. I lay in a fetal position in a corner of the ring. Policemen had to circle the ring to prevent a riot. After several minutes, I was awarded the win on a disqualification. Although I won on a disqualification, I knew and the crowd knew what Jack had done. It was no accident that he landed the punches where he did. He'd rather lose by a foul from his own punch than be counted out from my punches. He'd rather take himself out of the fight than fall to a boxer with twelve months experience. No matter, the title of

---

[51] *Boston Globe* November 26, 1905.

colored heavyweight champion was now mine. Now I would make the big payday and get a world's championship match. He denied me the satisfaction of knocking him out, but he could not deny me the title. Two doctors were brought into the dressing room to attend to me.

What happened next was more devastating than the ending of the fight itself. Although Artha' was the loser, he still proclaimed himself colored heavyweight champion because he was disqualified and not beaten. The reporters would not fall for this. The promoter would not fall for this. The public would not fall for this. But they did! He erased my victory and my title and they let him do it. He told them how a champion should not lose his title on a mistaken punch. I collected my purse and was taken to a nearby hospital for treatment.

I seriously contemplated quitting boxing at that moment. George kept trying to cheer me up, but I blocked him out. I realized at that moment what a dirty game I was involved in. I now held a win over Jack Johnson, but I was disgusted. This was not a sport. This was a racket. What did I win? A win over Jack Johnson, with no title. A win over Jack Johnson, with no glory. A win over Jack Johnson, with no big purse in the future. I was denied the title that I rightfully deserved, and no one cared. No one except George, who was protesting at the top of his lungs, yet no one paid him any mind. He followed his protests with a swig from his flask. Everyone was in awe of Jack Johnson, and that hadn't changed one bit with this fight.

The local constable was not in awe of Johnson, though. In the dressing room there was a loud commotion. Johnson was arrested by the police on the constable's order and taken to the Second District Station House on a complaint of assault and battery. Someone had taken action against this injustice. After I recovered I was brought to the station house and asked to file a complaint, but I refused. I wanted to exact my revenge in the ring, not a courtroom.

The *Boston Globe* described the bout: *Joe Jeannette of New York went down in the second round of the wind-up with Jack Johnson, the Negro heavyweight champion, at the National A.C. tonight, from a foul blow, and 10 minutes later he was carried from the ring suffering intense pain. The blow was delivered about the middle of the second round and when both men were fighting fast. Johnson rushed Jeannette into a corner and one of his many swings went foul, the blow landed several inches below the belt. Jeannette's seconds worked over him five minutes, and then carried him to his dressing room. Jeannette to the surprise of everyone, had all the better of the first round. He was fully six inches shorter than his opponent, and 25 pounds lighter.*

Commencing the second round, Johnson sent a hard right to Jeannette's body and swung another right for the jaw, but Jeannette was out of harm's way and came back with that bad left to Johnson's jaw. This appeared to anger the big champion, and he went after Jeannette. Many of the blows, which had steam enough behind them to drive Jeannette through the ropes, missed, and as Jeannette straightened up after each ducking he nearly always managed to tap Johnson's jaw. Johnson fought Joe around the ring, and finally getting him in a corner, rained rights and lefts on his body, one of which blows went low and Jeannette fell to the mat. Johnson, not knowing he had hurt Jeannette, struck him at least twice while the latter was falling.[52]

The *Hudson Dispatch* reported the following: *In the middle of the second round of a fast, interesting contest, at the National Athletic Club last night, Jack Johnson, the colored heavyweight champion laid low Joe Jeannette with a terrific left hand uppercut which landed very low on the Gotham boy. As Jeannette sank to the canvas with a startling groan, the crowd threatened to the title holder bodily harm, and it was due to the fact that a squad of armed policemen entered the ring, in time to prevent some lovers of the Queensbury rules from starting into the ring.*

Jeannette was carried unconscious from the ring to his dressing room, where Doctors Ferris and O'Connor, failing to revive him, sent him to the Pennsylvania Hospital. Johnson was placed under arrest and locked up in a nearby station house where he was held until Jeannette entirely recovered from the blow. Jeannette was taken to the station house, but he refused to make any charges against the champion.

Johnson and Jeannette were the principals in the star boxing show at the National Club's weekly boxing show. The former had every natural advantage, towering over the Jersey man, outclassing him in reach and outweighing him many pounds. There was considerable money bet that Jeannette would not last four rounds, Johnson himself having put up $200.

When the bell summoned the men into action, Johnson appeared the cleverer of the two, having it all over Jeannette. The latter soon got down to business and a long left jab was continually reaching the champion's jaw. A hard right to the body shook Jack up considerably.

Jeannette kept these tactics in the second round, and Johnson maddened at the thought, threw all reason and rules to the wind, and started to go in and "rough house" it.

Near the end of the second round, he rushed in, swinging both arms wildly, Jeannette backed into the ropes, and as he did so, Johnson released a terrific left uppercut from his knees, hitting the local fighter very low. Jeannette then slowly sank to the floor.[53]

On December 2 at the National A.C. Artha' once again defended his colored title against me. It was tough for both of us to find opponents, so we fought each other again. This was another brutal contest. Before the bout, I was told that Johnson was very angry about his arrest in our last bout.[54] The *National Police Gazette* described the action: *Johnson started after his rival at the tap of the gong, and Jeannette knowing the power of the man facing him, protected himself well. The fourth round was the best of the night, for the New Yorker. He came out of his crouch and met Johnson. Then the milling waxed warm, and the crowd began to yell. Jeannette did not retreat, but stood and let fly as best he could, and Johnson smiled in glee to think that he would soon find a vacancy and bang it on Joe's jaw. This was Jeannette's round, and the gallery yelled in delight at the promise of some*

---

[52] *Boston Globe* November 26, 1905 pg. 13.
[53] *Hudson Dispatch* - Golden Jubilee 1924 pg. 30.
[54] *National Police Gazette* December 23, 1905.

rare swatting yet to come. Jeannette encouraged by his showing in the round previous, began to go after Johnson in the fifth round, and just when the New Yorker came strong he bumped into a stiff short right to the jaw, which put him on the floor for the count of nine. In the last round Jeannette went to the floor twice and took the full limit on each occasion. He was not trying to evade the short taps to the jaw, and the mill ended with Johnson actively engaged in a desperate endeavor to end the go and Jeannette there to stay.[55] I was a little overanxious in the bout which caused me to get caught by a few of Jack's right hands. In my opinion: *"Jack was powerful and a wonderful defensive boxer, but he didn't believe in overworking or taking chances.[56] If you didn't hurt him, he didn't hurt you."[57]*

After the end of the six round affair the result was another no-decision because there wasn't a knockout. Once again the colored heavyweight title eluded me. I was making better money now, and I was making a name for myself. All I could do was go back to the gym and train harder. In many of my bouts with Johnson, the newspapers were unanimous in naming me as winner of the no-decision bouts, of which I shall be pleased to show anybody who may doubt this statement.[58]

Whatever I lacked in experience I made up with sheer determination. Funny thing, "Lil" Artha' got real friendly with me in the dressing room before this third meeting. I wondered if it was a ploy to soften me up or he really wanted to be friends. Either way, we brawled hard again. Johnson was a master at parrying blows and feinting, but with each punch he'd feint and parry, I was learning. Johnson's sparring partner "Gunboat" Smith said of Jack: *"Johnson was a fellow that used to stand flat-footed and wait for you to come in and when you came in, he'd rip the head off you with uppercuts, cut you all to pieces. That's the way he fought."[59]*

I could feel the difference when fans looked at me now. They looked at me like I was a somebody, like I belonged. The great Jack Johnson even knew me by name now. In the dressing room before the third match with Johnson the other fighters were whispering again. Only this time they whispered that I was the chap who gave Johnson such a tough time a week prior. I pretended not to hear them, but it sure felt good to be recognized. Once again, the morning after the bout I ran to a corner coffee shop and purchased the New York papers and the *National Police Gazette*. The papers wrote that I was Jack Johnson's equal! My friends and stable-mates back in Hudson County and New York were as excited as I was. Of course, this was after I showed off the Johnson articles to them. I cut out every article and put them in my shoe box when I got back home. I went from being a

[55] *National Police Gazette* December 16, 1905.
[56] *'The Ring'* magazine September 1958, Joe Jeannette quote pg. 47.
[57] *Champions of the Ring* by Gerald Suster pg. 57.
[58] *'Boxing'* Annual 1914: 'That World's Title' by Joe Jeannette pgs. 42-43.
[59] *Champions of the Ring* by Gerald Suster pg. 54.

nobody coal-shoveler to a boxing celebrity virtually overnight.

Every once in a while I would take the articles out and look them over and read about how much I was improving. This motivated me to work harder. Johnson called the December 2 fight with me: *"a disputed six rounder."*[60]

The *National Police Gazette* wrote another article about our December 2 match: *Somebody ought to tell Jack Johnson that being fancy and "gallos" don't get a "coon" anything in the fighting game. That battle he put up the other night with Joe Jeannette rather suggests that the white lights and blandishments of swell colored society have been too much for the Texas "smoke" and unless he "cuts out" something his days as a person of importance in the fighting world is over. With every natural advantage at his command- height, reach, and weight- he failed to put Jeannette away, and the latter must still be considered a novice, having only figured in the game for a little over a year. There can be no doubt but that Johnson tried his best to win, and as quickly as possible, at that. Besides being angry at Jeannette for his arrest a week previously on the latter's claim of being seriously injured by a foul blow, he wagered considerable money that he would knock the New Yorker out before the final bell. He also had his friends bet liberally. But Johnson failed miserably in his efforts to make good.*

From the time the initial bell called the pair to battle Johnson was ever after his man. Jeannette, who was in none to good condition seemed to be somewhat bewildered at the viciousness of his darker opponent's attack and got several hard lefts which staggered him in the opening number, but he fought back gamely. In the second, third, and fourth rounds, Jeannette used a straight left which rattled the gold-filled tombstones which were displayed when Johnson smiled. Jack didn't like these tactics and throwing science to the smoke, which filled the arena, rushed in, in true Joe Walcott fashion to end it all. But Jeannette either clinched or stopped the big fellow's rushes with his left. In the fourth round Jeannette kept away and the round was a most delightfully lop-sided and uninteresting affair.

Johnson was desperate in the fifth, and as Jeannette tired Johnson battered him handily, sending him to the canvas for the full count. In the sixth, Jack was like a maddened bull and showed his man no quarter. Jeannette was tired but showed good generalship and smothered up. Twice Johnson sent him down for the count. Both men were tired at the end. Johnson bested his man, but that is not anything for him to brag about.[61]

On December 21 I returned to the ring against Walter Johnson in New York. Walter had been KO'd by Johnson right after I fought Jack back on May 9. Johnson was a ten-year ring veteran with twenty-three bouts under his belt. The three round bout was ruled a no-decision. I was very disturbed over the report that I faked the fight.[62] When I went in with Walter the club officials told me it must be a friendly exhibition, and that's what Walter and I made it. I had hurt Walter in the second round with a hard right and

---

[60] *La Vie Au Grand Air* March 4, 1911 "Mes Combats" by Jack Johnson.
[61] *National Police Gazette* December 23,1905.
[62] *Boston Daily Globe* December 25, 1905.

Walter went reeling to the ropes.[63] I pulled back because I was honoring the arrangement we had made before the contest. The *St. Louis Post-Dispatch* stated: *Jeanette could have stopped his man with a punch, but he chose the other course, and the spectators hissed him when he left the ring.*[64] The *New York Morning Telegraph* wrote: *The semi-windup of the session was a corking good go between big Joe Jeannette and Walter Johnson of Providence, two Negro boxers. Jeannette proved the better of the pair and had Johnson very much worried at the finish, though he could not put him away.*[65]

It was around this time that I was dreaming of even bigger goals than just nice paydays or the light heavyweight title. Imagine if one day I could get a chance to fight for the world's heavyweight championship. I didn't understand why skin color would prevent this. What were people afraid of? Many of my friends and stable-mates were white, and so was my manager, not to mention my own mother! Maybe, just maybe, if I kept improving I might be the first black world's heavyweight champion. Wouldn't that be something! Just think, if that came true it might even open the door for us to play in other sports such as professional baseball or basketball. We had already been allowed to box for world titles in lower weight classes. George "Little Chocolate" Dixon became the first black world's champion in 1890 at Bantamweight, and Joe Walcott won the world welterweight championship in 1892, while Joe Gans, the "Old Master," won the lightweight title in 1902. Though they were great accomplishments, none of them could equal the recognition and honor of being the first colored heavyweight king. That would be a major leap forward for our race.

I had to keep training harder and harder. It just might be destiny for me to win the world's heavyweight title and use it as a tool to bring blacks and whites closer together and end that ridiculous fear they had of each other. After all, we are all Americans, aren't we? We are all human beings. My heart would race the more I thought about it. Imagine all the better job opportunities that we would get. Imagine better pay and integrated schools. I would take my title down South and help bring togetherness to the states that my stepfather told me were so unwilling to give us the same opportunities that white people had.

I remember as a small child I would talk to an old blind man that sat on a porch not far from where I lived. His name was Mr. Benson and he was a white man. We would sit and talk about music and sports and anything else that came up. He would give me advice on every subject we talked about. Eight months into our friendship we were sitting talking on his porch when a young woman walked up to us. She gave me a searing look that I can still see as clearly today as I did back then. She said: *"Excuse me, young man. Let's*

---

63 *New York Sun* December 21, 1905.
64 *St. Louis Post-Dispatch* December 22, 1905.
65 *New York Morning Telegraph* December 22, 1905.

go in the house, dad." I never saw Mr. Benson sitting on the porch again. Obviously his daughter didn't want her father sitting and talking with a colored boy. Would it ever be possible that someday people could be as blind to color as Mr. Benson was? He didn't see me for my color. He saw me for the person I was inside. At the time, I remember hating the world and my parents for bringing me into it.

I wished so much that I would become a champion. If I became champ I would show the world that there was nothing to fear about whites and blacks living, working, and marrying together. After all, my parents had found the ability to thrive in an interracial relationship. I had found, through my parents, the answer to end segregation forever. I would be the spokesperson to bring us all together at last. If my mother and father could find love without being blinded by color, then surely the rest of the world could be taught this also.

Chapter 9
The Boston Tar Baby

On Christmas Day 1905 I traveled to Lawrence, Massachusetts for a bout. Although Adelaide and my mother were upset that I was on the road at Christmas time, we needed the money. I would enter the ring that night against the boxer I would grow to admire more than any other. A boxer with more determination and courage than ten men combined. A boxer with horseshoes in his hands. What he lacked in size and weight he made up with speed and power.

His name was Sam Langford. He was only five-foot six inches tall but he had a seventy-two-inch reach, and it was like he swallowed a tornado before every match and unleashed its fury through his fists.

They called him the "Boston Tar Baby" for his dark complexion. Some called him "Old Ho Ho" for his hardy laughter. He hailed from Boston but he was born and raised in Nova Scotia. Langford had a soft voice with a Canadian accent, not a Southern drawl.[66] He was rumored to eat six pounds of pork a day. The papers called him the "Caveman" that all boxers fear. Once again I was on the road in the opponent's dressing room when I fought him the first time. Langford was so confident in his punching power, he would point to the location where he would drop his opponents. Even the crowd would get in on the fun and yell: *"Drop him over here, Sam."*

Langford had been boxing professionally since 1902 and had participated in over fifty fights. Sam had knocked out my stable-mate Willie Lewis the year prior. Willie told me that Sam could punch like a pole ax. I entered the affair with due caution. Sam had also mixed it up with the dangerous Jack Blackburn several times. Blackburn would go on years later to train heavyweight champion Joe Louis. Willie and Blackburn were smaller fighters than I. I hoped my size and weight would give me an advantage against the "Tar Baby."

Sam fought welterweight champion Joe Walcott a year prior, and though it was called a draw, the consensus circulating amongst local boxing sages was that Sam got the better of Walcott. I had fourteen professional fights going into the match.

Sam attacked me from the opening bell like a buzz saw. He constantly pressed forward fearlessly with his small, solid frame. I landed precision shots at will. I was now becoming sharp at directing my punches and I landed many shots that would have crumbled lesser foes. I was catching many of Sam's hard punches on my shoulders.[67] I started to target Sam's left eye as it was swelling up. In the eighth round I cut Sam's swollen left

---

[66] Untitled Article from Joe Jennette's scrapbook. Courtesy Ben Hawes collection.
[67] *Sam Langford: Boxing's Uncrowned Champion* by Clay Moyle pg. 48.

eye with a right cross. Sam's head movement had slowed down substantially.

During one of the heated exchanges I positioned a right hand on the left side of his temple and Sam was transformed into a drunken sailor. He retreated on unsteady legs. He was wobbling all over the ring. I was careful not to headhunt because I knew he would be protecting the spot I had just connected with. I unleashed a left to the liver and his hands dropped down by his side. After the bell rang ending the eighth round, Sam refused to come out for the ninth. The referee went over to Sam and asked him: *"Sam, aint you gonna fight no more?"* Sam replied: *"Why sure I'm gonna fight some more."* Then he peered over and saw me standing waiting for the bell to ring and he looked back up at the referee and his cornermen and said: *"but not tonight, men, not tonight."*[68]

Sam's corner threw in the sponge. Sam was unable to see out of his left eye. I was awarded the victory by technical knockout in the eighth round. It was after this bout with Langford that newspaper reporters gave me the title "Hoboken Iron Man."[69] Though I still lived in North Bergen, I trained in West Hoboken when I didn't have a fight scheduled or if I didn't have time to travel to New York City. The reporters frequently confused Hoboken with West Hoboken. The *Boston Journal* described the bout: *In the first round both boys started in to feel each other out and after a few hard exchanges Langford looked as if he was up against it and seemed to lose all his courage. In the second round Jeannette shot out of his corner with fire in his eye and stung Langford with three successive rights and lefts to the jaw and one going to the left eye which closed that optic, worrying Langford very much.*

In the fourth round Langford shot up a wicked left uppercut, which made Jeannette wince and he started to hang on, but the men were quickly broken by the referee. In the seventh Jeannette tore in some terrific body punches that weakened Langford and following up with terrific rights and lefts had him hanging on when the round ended. When Langford went to his corner he was covered with blood and had both eyes closed and a big cut down the left side of his cheek. Blood was flowing in large streams and he was too weak to go on with the next round and his seconds threw up the sponge.[70]

I entered 1906 with sixteen professional fights. My right arm was giving me problems. In sparring I was experimenting on adjusting the angles I was throwing it from to alleviate the deadness that would come after I threw a hard punch. I noticed shorter straight rights and uppercuts did not affect my arm strength but I could not throw hard overhands or long straight rights anymore without risking severe pain and deadness in my arm. I started turning my body to the right in fights. I learned to whip my left jab from that position while drawing my opponents in for uppercuts and right

---

[68] *Millbrook Round Table* February 11, 1949.
[69] *Plainsboro Dealer* December 21, 1945.
[70] *Boston Journal* December 26, 1905.

hands.

On January 5 my manager issued a press release: *Joe Jeannette, through his manager, George Armstrong, has issued a challenge to Jack O'Brien. Jeannette weighs about 165 pounds, and agrees to make that weight. His easy victory over Sam Langford at Lawrence opened the eyes of some of the fight followers. But they evidently forgot that he won from Jack Johnson, and had all the better of a go with the "Pink Pajama Man" until Jack remembered how Sandy Ferguson lost; and fouled Jeannette. Armstrong ridicules the claims that Jeannette had twenty pounds on Langford. He declares "Laughing Ho Ho Sam" is a middleweight, and that he would have hard work to weigh in under 155 pounds. Jeannette has a fine record and has defeated Jim Jeffords and other heavy men. Armstrong realizes that O'Brien has drawn the color line, although why at this late day he cannot understand, for he has met George Cole, Young Peter Jackson and others in the ring.*[71]

On Saturday, January 13, Addie and I were married. A local newspaper called the *Evening Journal* described the wedding and my upcoming Johnson bout in New York City: *Tonight the star bout at the week's boxing entertainment of the Sharkey Athletic Club will be a three round slugging bee between the colored heavyweight pugilists Joe Jeanette of North Bergen and Jack Johnson. They will meet for the fourth time. Twice the North Bergen fighter won and the other bout ended in a draw. The fight tonight will be sort of a honeymoon celebration for Joe Jeanette. He became a Benedict Saturday night by marrying Ms. Adelaide Atzingen, 19 years of age, who resides in Union Hill. The ceremony was performed by Joe Kennel of New Durham, a Justice of the Peace.*

The bride is a comely white woman. She received a wedding gift from the groom, a diamond ring. The witnesses to the ceremony were Mrs. Joseph Kennel, wife of the Justice and Mr. and Mrs. George Quilter. Jeanette will fight harder than ever now that his incentive for victory has become a double one and is confident of putting it over Jack Johnson this evening.[72]

Joe Kennel was a close family friend, which is why we asked him to perform the marriage. We didn't have a chance for much of a honeymoon because I was in training for a bout on January 16 against Jack Johnson.

We both wanted a Church wedding but money was tight and we realized the commotion it would cause. Anyway, Addie saw no point in one. If her mother wasn't going to attend, that would keep many of Addie's other family members from going as well. The city hall wedding on Saturday, January 13 lacked the Church atmosphere, but we didn't care. We promised each other we would have a beautiful church wedding when we could afford it. I wore a fine tuxedo and Addie wore a beautiful wedding dress that she bought at Holthausen's department store on Bergenline Avenue in Union Hill. What we both wanted most was to be together. We went shopping at a local bakery for a wedding cake. We didn't have much money

---

[71] *Washington D.C. Evening Star* January 5, 1906.
[72] *Evening Journal* Jersey City January 16, 1906.

so we bought a cake that we could afford. Addie wanted to have the marriage figures on top of the cake. There were no mixed couple figures in the bakery. I told Addie to buy the white ones. It wasn't a big deal to me. Addie gave me that look that meant she was going to get her way. I told her to buy the white figures and my sister would color the grooms face brown. She smiled. Addie's sisters Alois and Mary came to the wedding.

After we exchanged vows at city hall we headed home for a small reception. We planned on staying with my family in New Durham until we saved up enough money for a place of our own. After dinner and cake with some family members we took the trolley to the Weehawken ferry, which brought us over to Manhattan where we saw the musical "Little Johnny Jones" at the New York Theater. The musical was written by George M. Cohen and was about a horse jockey who was in love with a copper heiress. It had some lively songs such as "Give My Regards to Broadway" and "Yankee Doodle Boy."

After the show we were walking back to the ferry when a group of teens walked passed us. As soon as they passed, one of the males yelled: *"Look at that nigger lover."* Addie turned to the crowd without raising her voice and replied: *"Nigger lover. Is that what you call me? You couldn't be more wrong. I am his wife not his lover. Just got married today."* Addie held me with one arm while she flashed her diamond ring with her free hand. *"I doubt if you will ever be able to buy a girl a ring like this."* Addie could sense I was going to break loose and jump at the boy who made the remark. She held my arm tighter and whispered in my ear: *"Let it go, Joe. They are just jealous. You are my man now, they can yell, curse, and throw things at us but nothing is going to change the fact that you are my man. You're stuck with me."*

We both looked at each other and broke out laughing. We held each other tightly as the group gave us a strange look and walked away. Addie didn't realize that by marrying me she had lost her rights as a white American citizen and had become the undesirable wife of a black man.[73]

When we went to church the first week after our marriage, no one spoke to us. It was as though we were invisible to everyone. They all ignored us. We must have been very naive to believe that in a church people would be different than out on the street, but they weren't. Several parishioners walked out when they saw us sitting together. An elderly white man even came up to us and said: *"You two should really read Deuteronomy 22:9."*[74] When we got home we looked up the passage in the Bible and it stated: *"Do not plant two kinds of seed in your vineyard; if you do, not only the crops you plant but also the fruit of the vineyard will be defiled."*

Addie scoured through the Bible all week to find the right quote. The next Sunday when we arrived back at church she walked straight up to the man

---

[73] *Marriage beyond Black & White* by David & Barbara Douglas pg. 81.
[74] *Mixed Messages* by Fred & Anita Prinzing pg. 93.

and said: *"Good Morning Sir. Thank you so much for your advice last week. I have a Bible quote for you too. You might want to read Acts 17:26, which states, 'God made from one man every nation of mankind.'*[75] *I'll repeat that: 'from one man.' So you see, you and my husband are related by blood. You're actually brothers!"* Addie turned away, grabbed my arm and led me to our pew while the man stood there frozen. Addie, who was a Catholic, converted me from Baptist to her faith soon after. We started attending St. Michael's church in West Hoboken.

Adelaide's family, as well as my own, were very understanding, with the exception of her mother. Although they feared for us they all supported us. They knew we were deeply in love. I now knew I had to support the two of us, so I decided to make fighting my full time job. Adelaide told me how worried she was about my boxing. She supported me fully but she told me if I quit boxing we would be able to survive. The problem was there was not many ways for me to make a decent living. I told Adelaide that I promised I would only box long enough to give her a comfortable life and a nice home.

We were not the only ones who suffered from our interracial marriage. Addie's sister Mary began getting into fights with other students in high school. Mary, who was only fifteen at the time, was teased so much at school that she had to drop out.[76] The students called Mary all kinds of terrible names.

I told George that I wanted to fight as often as possible. My dream was to buy a nice home for Adelaide and to make enough money to start a business. I did not want to end up like all those broken down old boxers in the "opponents" dressing room who had absolutely nothing but the clothes on their backs and the shoes on their feet. I had to give Addie a better life.

Addie and I had an important decision to make when it came to choosing where to live. Most of my family had migrated south to Jersey City where the black community had a growing section by the Bayonne border. They felt more comfortable there because the North Bergen-Union Hill section, where we were raised as children, was predominately German, Austrian, Swiss, Armenian, and Irish. Addie and I decided that when we saved enough money we would look for an apartment in either Union Hill or West Hoboken instead of Jersey City or North Bergen. We were unsure where we would have a more difficult time in our mixed relationship. No matter where we lived we would probably be treated as outcasts, so it really didn't matter much to us. To our dismay, many black people looked at us with the same disdain as white people did.[77] Some expressed that they thought I was giving in to white dominance.[78] The stares would follow us

---

[75] *Mixed Messages* by Fred & Anita Prinzing pg. 95.
[76] Interview with Charles Hartleib, Ada Atzingen's nephew & JoAnn Flannery-Mostaccio.
[77] *Marriage beyond Black & White* by David & Barbara Douglas pg. 44.
[78] *Interracial Intimacies* by Randall Kennedy pg. 34.

everywhere we went, at dinner, movies, or just taking a walk in the neighborhood. There were also considerate people, both black and white, who would smile at us and treat us as a normal couple.[79] We learned to ignore people who stared at us. We saw no need in making someone else's problem with interracial relationships our problem.[80]

Mixed marriages in the U.S. dated all the way back to John Rolfe and Pocahontas in 1614. Addie and I discussed the "one drop rule" that Booker T. Washington had spoken out about.[81] He said that if a person had ninety-nine percent white blood and one percent black blood, that person was considered black. The white blood counts for nothing. Not only was a black and white marriage taboo but other European mixed marriages were also discouraged at this time. Irish, Italian, Polish, and English persons were considered part of separate "races." The practice of not mixing races was common. The only difference was that the English, Irish, Italian, and Polish could hide their heritage if they wished. I could not hide my skin color. The only mixing of races that was illegal in some states involved colored people.

Some blacks who were very light colored used to perform what we called "passing."[82] They acted as though they were white. Some of the people who "passed" were rumored to have told their own relatives to ignore them if they saw them in public. I would never divorce myself from my heritage. I was as proud of my African blood as I was of my German blood. Trying to forgive blacks who "passed" was not easy. Some felt that those who "passed" cursed the memory of their African ancestors.[83] Still others complained that passers were "living a lie."[84]

We were fortunate not to have anti-miscegenation laws in New Jersey. Some states had these laws on the books and people would actually be sent to jail if they were involved in a mixed marriage. We did not know it at the time but our struggles with this issue would last a lifetime.

The January 16 bout with Johnson was once again for the colored heavyweight title that we fought for previously. Jim Buckley was the promoter for the Sharkey A.C. Since boxing exhibition matches were only permitted between club members in New York, Buckley had to announce the participants as members of the club before the match. This was a dilemma for Buckley. The Sharkey A.C. was a whites-only sports club. When we entered the ring all the club members waited anxiously to see how we would be announced. If they announced Jack as a club member you could bet he would be back the next night lounging around the club.

[79] *Marriage beyond Black & White* by David & Barbara Douglas pg. 24.
[80] *Interracial Intimacies* by Randall Kennedy pg. 151.
[81] *Interracial Intimacies* by Randall Kennedy pg. 223.
[82] *Marriage beyond Black & White* by David & Barbara Douglas pg. 55.
[83] *Interracial Intimacies* by Randall Kennedy pg. 330.
[84] *Interracial Intimacies* by Randall Kennedy pg. 325.

Buckley quieted the crowd down. Then he proceeded to announce Jack as the club's janitor and me as the club's fireman! That was very smart thinking on Buckley's behalf.[85]

The affair was only three rounds and Artha' did not take any chances. He used his reach and countered from the outside. Whenever I got too close he would tie me up. I landed some solid body shots but I was too cautious to try the overhand right. The newspaper decision was awarded to Johnson, who boxed well and used his height to his advantage. Johnson's game plan was to avoid contact as much as possible. The fans disliked the lack of action but Jack didn't seem to care. Newspaper decisions were extremely controversial. Not only because the reporters were biased one way or the other but also because they were pressured heavily by the promoters, managers, and most importantly, the bookies and the gamblers. You could feel the tense looks on the hustlers, betters, and the bookies as they huddled around the writers, while awaiting their decision. Some reporters were intimidated so much they would not render their verdict until the paper was printed the next day.

On January 18, the *Evening Journal* wrote another article about my wedding: *Joe Jeanette a gentleman of color, who won fame in the pugilistic world, went out the other evening and put an opponent to sleep. Jeanette then found enough time to go forth and make love to a pretty girl. She is white, but when it comes to love-making, the color line is lost. Jeanette, with his pugilistic laurels, seemed to Ms. Ada Atzingen, Fulton Street, Union Hill, to be a real hero, and she promptly agreed to annex him and his fame. The colored fighter had to surrender and he is now happy in the role of husband. The young woman's friends registered a protest against her marriage, but that did not bother her in the least. Love was color blind, and she felt that the path of duty for her led to the office of a Union Hill Justice of the Peace, and the said Justice made Jeanette and Ms. Atzingen one. The fighter is well known in North Hudson. He has lived in North Bergen for many years. The couple will reside in North Bergen after returning from a honeymoon trip.*[86]

On March 14, I dropped a fifteen round decision to Johnson in Baltimore, Maryland. The contest was much like the previous ones. Johnson was constantly trying to build up points while I bored in behind the jab looking to land uppercuts and hook-cross combos. Jack received the close decision. Once again, many ringside observers felt I was the aggressor who had landed the harder, cleaner blows. I had forced the exchanges, while Jack was content to counter from the outside and avoid any infighting.

A few years later, Johnson commented on the amount of times we faced each other in 1905 and 1906 and on how tough the Baltimore fight was: *"In 1906 I met Joe Jeanette four times. Joe and I met so often that it became a game for us and we took much pleasure in the bouts. In our second meeting, which was a six rounder,*

---

[85] *Amsterdam Evening Recorder* March 18, 1925 pg. 7.
[86] *Evening Journal* Jersey City January 18, 1906.

it was a very serious match because we had much knowledge of each other by now, I was beaten on a foul in the second round. Later in the season, we met again in Baltimore, and I won a fifteen round decision. I reckon that was one of the best fights of Jeannette's life.'[87]

The best thing about the bouts with Johnson, besides the experience and exposure I was gaining, was the purses. I was pulling in close to five hundred dollars after George took his cut.

On April 5 I fought a rematch with Sam Langford in Chelsea, Massachusetts. In the locker room after the weigh-in the other boxers talked of my fight ledger: *"You're fighting Langford again!" "Doesn't your manager care about you?"* and *"Didn't you just fight Johnson a couple of times?"*

When I talked to George he told me he was doing the best he could and that no one wanted to box me. Langford and Johnson were my only options. He told me every boxing insider knew that my bouts with Johnson were close, and no one wanted to risk putting their charge in against me. He told me that Langford and Johnson suffered from the same dilemma.

The Langford bout was close again as described by the *Boston Herald*: *For the first three rounds the fighting was pretty nearly even, though it might be accredited to Langford on a pinch. The New Jersey man set the pace, getting to Langford hard and often. At the same time Langford hammered in some terrific body punches, and when in clinches banged Jeannette pretty hard on the kidneys. In this way he appeared to hammer Jeannette down rather gradually until the fifth round, when he got to the visitor rather hard, and at one time Jeannette went to the mat partly from the effects of a punch and partly through slipping. However, Jeannette was up quickly enough and at it. In the next round Langford tried to finish the bout, and, though he fought hard and fast, Jeannette fought him back. Again in the seventh round Langford whipped a clean left hook to Jeannette's jaw and the latter took the count.*

Then it was terrific fighting for the rest of the contest. Jeannette at times appeared to grow stronger as the contest progressed and after being pretty well punched in the eighth round he sent Langford to his corner at the end of the ninth round a bit weak. From the ninth to the end of the fifteenth round the pair tried hard to stop each other and though Langford had Jeannette a bit to the bad at times, he was not able to put over the knockout punch. The pair finished the battle tired from the fast pace and tremendous punching that they had been through.[88]

Of course the crowd was supporting their home-town favorite. I had won over the support of many crowds during my road fights with my aggressive determination, but I always longed for the chance to box before my own cheering partisan crowd. A fighter always wants to box in front of his own fans. I lost a close decision to Langford.

There weren't many bout offers after the Langford match. On April 18, the City of San Francisco suffered a terrible earthquake. The quake, along

---

[87] *La Vie Au Grand Air* March 4, 1911, "Mes Combats" by Jack Johnson.
[88] *Boston Herald* April 6, 1906.

with the fire that sprung from it, destroyed most of the city's waterfront area. Three hundred and seventy-five people died in the tragedy. The quake lasted over forty-seven seconds. Even though the Japanese government headed the list of contributors to assist with the recovery from the quake, in October, the San Francisco Board of Education tried to segregate the school system by removing all Japanese, Chinese, and Korean children. The segregation was sparked by an influx of immigrant laborers from these countries. The segregation attempt would later be rescinded.

My manager had received offers for me to go out to the West Coast and box exhibition matches in Vaudeville houses there. I would receive about fifty dollars a week for the performances. I decided to accept the offer because I wasn't getting any calls for fights. Addie stayed home, as she was four months pregnant with our first child.

I arrived in Oakland with George Armstrong in May and we took the ferry over to San Francisco on a dark night.[89] From the water it was amazing as the electric lights on Pacific Street lit up the bay. A passenger on the ferry saw my amazement as I looked up at the lights. I turned to him and asked: *"Is that Pacific Street?"* The man replied: *"To visitors it's called Pacific Street but to us locals it's called Terrific Street!"*

I performed nightly at Chutes Theater, which was a Vaudeville house. I would perform exhibitions against different boxers, but mostly a local black boxer named Sam McVea.[90] The talented song and dance team of Bert Williams and George Walker performed there. They were hilarious slapstick performers. Williams performed a song that I would think of often in my life called "Nobody." The lyrics, written by Alex Rogers, were hauntingly sad but at the same time comical. The lyrics went as follows:

When life seems full of clouds and rain,
And I am filled with naught and pain,
Who soothes my thumping, bumping brain?
(Pause) Nobody...
When winter comes with snow and sleet,
And me with hunger and cold feet,
Who says, "Here's two bits, go and eat"?
(pause) Nobody...
I ain't never done nothing to nobody,
I ain't never got nothin' from Nobody, no time!
And, until I get somethin' from somebody sometime,
I don't intend to do nothin' for Nobody, no time!
When summer comes, all cool and clear,
And my friends see me drawing near,
who says "Ah, come in and have some beer?"

---

[89] *National Police Gazette* December 30, 1905.
[90] *New York Amsterdam* News June 16, 1945 'Brown Bombers of Yesteryear' by Casey Jones.

(pause) Nobody...
When I was in that railroad wreck,
and thought I'd cash in my last check,
who took the engine off my neck?
(pause) Nobody...
I ain't never done nothing to nobody,
I ain't never got nothin' from Nobody, no time!
And, until I get somethin' from somebody sometime,
I don't intend to do nothin' for Nobody, no time![91]

When Williams and Walker finished a performance the crowds would roar with approval. Walker would yell back: *"No applause just throw money!"*

Williams was a tall, light skinned, colored man who held himself up with poise and dignity. When he went onstage he portrayed an inept colored man. He wore disheveled suits and broken shoes. He put on a wig with kinky hair and rubbed burnt cork on his face to make his skin a charred black color. I often wondered how frustrating it was for Bert to portray black people in this fashion but I never had the heart to ask him. I spent a lot of time with Bert in San Francisco. Bert would say: *"People sometimes ask me if I would not give anything to be white... most emphatically, 'No.' How do I know what I might be if I were a white man. I might be a sandhog, burrowing away and losing my health for $8 dollars a day. I might be a streetcar conductor at $12 or $15 a week. There is many a white man less fortunate and less well-equipped than I am. I have never been able to discover that there was anything disgraceful in being a colored man. But I have often found it inconvenient... in America."[92]*

When I asked Bert if, like me, it bothered him that he was discriminated against by the very same people that came to watch him perform, he replied: *"It wouldn't be so bad... if I didn't hear the applause still ringing in my ears."[93]*

Once I was sitting with McVea as we watched Bert and George perform at a local theater. After the performance they were leaving the stage and a white stagehand asked the theater manager Maurice Barrymore what he thought of Bert. Barrymore said he thought Bert was: *"terrific."* The stage hand nodded: *"Yeah he's a good nigger. Knows his place all right."* Bert over heard the comment and as he was walking away he stated: *"I know my place alright. Going there now. Dressing Room One!"*

Sam and I couldn't stop laughing. Bert showed as much guts as any colored pugilist. Once when we were in a bar with Bert he ordered gin and the white bartender, who did not appear happy we were in the bar, said: *"Gin is fifty dollars a glass."* You could hear a pin drop as Bert stared at the bartender. McVea and I waited to see what Bert's reply would be. After

---

[91] "Nobody" Published 1905, written by Bert Williams and Alex Rogers.
[92] Lost Sounds: Blacks & the Birth of the Recording Industry 1890-1919 by Tim Brooks pg. 174.
[93] "Broadway: The American Musical" 2004 from American Decades CD-ROM 1998.

several tense moments Bert flashed his famous wide grinned smile and reached into his pocket and plopped a five hundred dollar bill on the bar as he proclaimed: *"Sounds great, give me ten shots!"*[94] The bartender's face turned beet red. Bert knew how to handle those tense situations better than anyone. Inside though I knew he was feeling the same frustrations that Sam and I felt. W.C. Fields called Bert: *"The funniest man I ever saw and the saddest man I ever knew."*[95]

Bert would become the first black man to lead the Ziegfeld Follies and the first major black recording artist. Booker T. Washington would later say of Bert Williams: *"He has done more for our race than I have. He has smiled his way into people's hearts; I have been obliged to fight my way."*[96]

At the famous "Barbary Coast," which is what the area was called, I met Sam King and Lewis Purcell.[97] They were former Pullman porters and they ran several "Black and Tans" on Pacific Street. "Black and Tans" were the name for clubs where blacks and whites were allowed to mingle together. Most of the patrons were white and most of the performers were black. Jazz, or "Fillin' and Fakin' " as the locals called it, blossomed in this area with great musicians such as pianist and saxophonist Sid LaProtti, Benjamin Franklin "Reb" Spikes, and Clarence Williams Sr. perfecting their trades here. King and Purcell owned several clubs such as the So Different Cafe and The Ivy. Drunkenness and prostitution was abundant on the "Barbary Coast." It was common for police to shut down all the clubs in the area at night only to have them open up again the next day. Other famous performers who plied their trades on Pacific Street were Sissiretta Matilda Jones, Ada Overton Walker, and Ferdinand "Jelly Roll" Morton, who came to San Francisco from the South like most blacks, to avoid the Jim Crow laws.

One of the most interesting characters I met on Pacific Street was barbershop owner Richard B. Spikes. He would talk for hours about his ideas, while cutting hair. Spikes would go on to invent many things such as the railroad semaphore, the beer keg tap, the automatic car wash, and the automobile directional signal.

Even though I was boxing in exhibitions I had to be careful with Sam McVea. He was a very big and strong fighter with a tremendous left hook. He was not, however, a soft spoken man. Sam was very arrogant and cocky. We got to know each other well while we boxed three round exhibition bouts for small crowds of a hundred and fifty or less paying customers. Most of the crowds were white and we were often the subject of cruel and

94 "BlackFace" by Ken Padgett.
95 "Broadway: The American Musical" 2004 from American Decades CD-ROM 1998.
96 "Jass.com Bert Williams & George Walker" by Thomas L. Morgan.
97 *New York Amsterdam* News June 16, 1945 'Brown Bombers of Yesteryear' by Casey Jones.

vulgar remarks by some of the patrons. King and Purcell were big fans of boxing and they treated Sam and I like kings at their clubs.

Before and after the exhibitions McVea and I would sit and talk about boxing and other topics. Sam and I frequently talked of our frustrations in dealing with racism in boxing. Colored boxers did not receive the opportunities that white boxers did. We got paid much less and had to take tougher fights. We talked about our bouts with Jack Johnson. McVea fought Jack three times, losing all three, with one by knockout in the twentieth and last round. Sam was an inexperienced 18-year-old when he first fought Artha'. McVea lost several teeth in that match and his face looked: *As though a goat had chewed it.*[98]

Sam told me in his last bout with Johnson some of the racist white fans threw lit cigars at Johnson's back while he was sitting on his stool between rounds.[99] After the fight ended, Johnson, his back blistered from cigar burns, grabbed a bucket full of water, blood, and spit and threw it at his antagonizers.[100] As he threw the liquid mixture at their faces he yelled: *"Allow me to serve the refreshments!"*[101] Jack ran from the ring and quickly left the building. We both agreed that Jack had a lot of guts for doing that. McVea and I had more in common than just boxing. We were both married to white women.

Right before I left California, McVea and I got into a heated exchange. At first Sam would just tease that he would knock me out if we ever fought for real. After a while he started saying the jokes around other people. I told him to stop because people didn't know he was kidding. Sam turned to me loudly so everyone could hear him: *"I ain't kidding, Jennette. I'll knock you out any day of the week."* I was fuming with anger. I composed myself and before walking away I shot back: *"Maybe one day you'll get your chance to try it, Sam. Maybe one day."*

In late August, George and I returned to New Jersey. On September 6, 1906, I took on "Black" Bill at the Broadway Athletic Club in Philly. I had the best of the first three rounds with my left jab. During the fourth round I caught Bill rushing in with a left hand flush on his jaw. I followed it up with a right hand punch under the heart.[102] Bill crumbled to the floor, where he was counted out.[103]

After knocking out "Black" Bill I boxed a return six round bout with Jack Johnson. The bout was on September 20 and it was also in Philadelphia. Johnson again won a newspaper decision in a heated six round session. The

---

[98] *Champions of the Ring* by Gerald Suster pg. 56.
[99] *The Heavyweight Championship* by Stanley Weston pg. 74.
[100] *Champions of the Ring* by Gerald Suster pg. 56.
[101] *Champions of the Ring* by Gerald Suster pg. 56.
[102] *National Police Gazette* September 22, 1906.
[103] *Philadelphia Inquirer* September 7, 1906.

National Police Gazette described the action: *Johnson had every advantage over Joe being twenty pounds heavier and considerably taller. The men mixed it up for the first two rounds. The first was in Johnson's favor, his left frequently reaching Joe's face, and his right catching Jeanette on the body as Joe rushed in. Early in the second round Jeanette cut Johnson over his eye with a long left swing. Johnson rushed hard but was wild and Jeanette three times reached his eye before the bell rang. Joe continued to hold his own though Johnson brought all his skill into play. Jeanette's good work surprised the crowd, and judging by the way he fought Johnson he would make it warm for any of the big fellows.*[104]

On September 22, 1906, in Atlanta, Georgia, an anti-Negro riot left twenty blacks and two whites dead, and dozens injured. Over ten thousand whites stormed the streets to protest several minor incidents that involved black men and white women. One of the incidents alleged that a black man was seen peering in a white woman's window. Another incident allegedly involved a black man hiding in the bushes by a white woman's home.

Black people were pulled from cars, beaten, and in some cases even shot in the street. The riot was sparked by white supremacy tensions. Black men in the South were charged with rape for just touching a white woman. Winking or smiling at a white woman could get a black man lynched. Addie and I were fearful that the tensions in Atlanta could creep their way up North. We prayed that they would not.

On October 17, 1906, I was training for another match with Johnson when I received a message to hurry home as Addie was ready to give birth. Addie and I celebrated the birth of our first child on that day. We named our son Joseph Daniel but I often called him Junior even though we had different middle names. He was born in my parents' home at 349 Paterson Plank Road in North Bergen. Addie was lying in bed after giving birth and she started crying. I asked her what was wrong and she told me she had always dreamed that her family would be here to share in this moment with her. She was most upset that her mother wasn't there. Addie later told me she felt more separated from her family that day than at any other time in her life.

The birth of Joie would bring us a major surprise. About a week after Junior's birth there was a knock on the front door. Addie was napping because she was up all night with the baby. I went to answer the door and was almost knocked over with surprise. It was Addie's mother! She had baby blankets and a toy in her hand. Behind her was Addie's uncles and her sister Mary. Mary winked and smiled at me. I invited them in and showed them our child. Addie's mother cried out: *"Oh what a beautiful baby. May I?"*

I nodded and she picked up her grandson and held him close. She turned to me and started explaining how sorry she was for the way she acted. She

[104] *National Police Gazette* October 6, 1906.

told me she was concerned for her daughter, not because of me, but because of the way people would treat Addie. She told me she knew I was a good man and a good husband. I told her I understood.

We sat down in the living room as Addie's mother tended to Joie. After about forty-five minutes Addie woke up and came into the room. She was still groggy. When she laid eyes on her mother holding Joie, she was speechless. Her mother stood up and said: *"What a beautiful Grandson I have. Will you ever forgive me?"* Addie had tears in her eyes as she and her mother embraced for several minutes. Within an hour they were fussing over Joie as if they had never fought at all. Addie's mother realized that our child, her grandson, was her own flesh and blood. Things improved after that, but one thing I noticed, there was never a picture of Addie and I or our children hung in her mother's home. Although her mother proudly displayed pictures of her other grandchildren throughout her home the pictures we gave her were always kept in a dresser drawer.[105] It was comforting that Addies sister Mary hung pictures of us in her home.

Not long after Junior's birth we moved to our own apartment at 480 Spring Street in West Hoboken. We lived at that address for a few months after which we moved to 503 Central Avenue in West Hoboken. It was a nice three-family home. The house was close to the West Hoboken Transfer Station area. The area was so named because the location, on Paterson Plank Road, was where commuters transferred from one trolley to another en route to their destination. Many Naval personnel traveled from ships, which were docked in Hoboken, through the station on the trolley cars.

Sometimes the seamen were forced to wait for prolonged periods for the next trolley to arrive. Of course the soldiers needed something to occupy their time and the locals found this dilemma as an opportunity to make some income. Before you knew it, bars and burlesque theaters were popping up everywhere at the station. Friday and Saturday nights were particularly noisy as the intoxicated travelers, as well as locals, would be fighting and arguing in the streets as the bars let out at three in the morning. For a stretch of three blocks there must have been close to fifty bars. Every Saturday night looked like New Year's Eve, as policemen on horseback would push the crowds out of the area. I knew I did not want to raise a family in this area, and the only way for me to raise the money to move to a better location would be to keep fighting with my injured right shoulder.

On November 26 I boxed a ten round draw with Jack Johnson in Portland, Maine. Jack commented on the fight: *"We gave a spectacularly beautiful encounter for the pious people of Portland (Maine), the ten rounder ended in a draw."*[106]

---

[105] *Mixed Messages* by Fred & Anita Prinzing pg. 35.
[106] *La Vie Au Grand Air* March 4, 1911 "Mes Combats" by Jack Johnson.

Right before we were to enter the ring, Johnson gave an ultimatum. If the bout went the distance it must be declared a draw or he would not fight.[107] Obviously Johnson was not too confident in his chances of victory. Johnson's manager Alex McLean admitted that I had long been a stumbling block for Johnson.[108] I had no option but to accept the terms or the bout would have been cancelled. The bout went the distance and was called a draw. Johnson was very smart in his demand as he would have lost had a decision been rendered. The *National Police Gazette* described the action: *In the presence of two thousand spectators big Jack Johnson and Joe Jeannette, of New York, fought a fast ten round draw at Portland, Me., on Nov. 26. Johnson, though having twenty pounds advantage in weight, besides a much longer reach, could do nothing with Jeannette who recently had a shade over the big fellow in a six-round argument at Philadelphia. Jeannette did practically all of the leading up to the sixth round, and most of it from that time on, Johnson fighting inside and on the defensive, while Jeannette played with a reaching left-hand jab. Upon entering the ring Johnson expressed his desire to meet any heavyweight in the world, Jim Jeffries preferred.*[109] I met Jack in the dressing room after the match and he offered me some advice when boxing white fighters: *"For every point I'm given I'll have earned two, because I'm a Negro."*[110]

One day, Addie was shopping at a local store with baby Joie in her arms. A woman approached and asked her to see the baby. The woman stated: *"My what a lovely baby but isn't he dark?"* Addie replied: *"Yes, isn't he dark and handsome?"*[111] Addie always knew how to say the right thing at the right moment.

Christmas of 1906 held great memories. I was making good money and I showered Addie and Joie with many gifts. On Christmas Day we were relaxing after opening up all the presents. Addie asked me who the last gift was for that was left under the tree. I hadn't noticed the wrapped box behind the back of the tree. I knew all of the gifts I bought were opened already. I picked up the box and read the card which stated: *"To my loving husband Joe. Thank you for a wonderful life, Love Addie."* I turned to Addie and hugged her. After our embrace she yelled: *"Well aren't you going to open it?"*

I tore open the box. Inside was a beautiful green leather-covered oversized book. I opened the book and saw that it was a scrapbook. Even more startling was that Addie had taken all of the newspaper clippings and photos I had collected from my career and neatly placed them in the scrapbook without my knowledge. Next to my children's birth and my marriage to Addie, it was the greatest gift I had ever received.

---

107 *'Boxing'* Annual 1914 'That World's Title' by Joe Jeannette pgs. 42-43.
108 Untitled Article from Joe Jennette's scrapbook. Courtesy Ben Hawes collection.
109 *National Police Gazette* December 15, 1906.
110 *Unforgivable Blackness* by Geoffrey C. Ward pg. 120.
111 *Marriage beyond Black & White* by David & Barbara Douglas pg. 62.

Chapter 10
1907-1908

When I entered 1907 I had boxed professionally in twenty-two contests. I turned professional without any amateur bouts. My only experience was the few "smoker" bouts I had. Looking back now I considered my first three years as a pro as my learning stage. All the experience I had lacked when I first started boxing I now held from the tough competition I faced. I now held what one might consider a master's degree in pugilism.

In 1907 there was a great run on the banks. Several large companies such as Westinghouse Electric and Knickerbockers Trust failed, which set off the Panic of 1907. It was a very scary time. I had saved a considerable portion of my fight purses in banks to buy a house. Neighbors were taking their money out of the banks and keeping it at home under their mattresses. This of course led to more daytime home burglaries. Industries in our area were struggling to survive. Local breweries did not, though, as they flourished in the bad economy. Many people tried to drink their problems away. The embroidery industry also continued to do well. When walking past the embroidery factories one could hear the machinery working well into the night as the factories had three shifts.

On January 11, 1907, I faced Sam Langford again in Lawrence, Massachusetts. The bout was ruled a twelve round draw. The *Boston Herald* described the bout: *Langford had the best of the first three rounds, but after that Jeanette strengthened and kept Langford running away from his vicious lunges for the head and body. Jeanette closed Langford's eye in the fourth round. Jeanette gave most of his attention to the body in the ninth and tenth, and Sam weakened under the right uppercuts to the heart and stomach which Jeanette sent in. Langford, at the end of the bout, was very weak, but the decision of the referee was received with approval.*[112] The referee wanted Sam and I to box one more round to decide the winner but Sam refused.[113]

Jim Jeffords was next in Portland, Maine on February 11. I knocked out Jeffords in the seventh round of a scheduled fifteen round bout. Jeffords, a white heavyweight, was a veteran of thirty-six bouts. The *Jersey Journal* described the bout: *In the seventh round of what was originally scheduled as a fifteen round battle. The white opponent of the North Hudson fighter was badly punished and during the encounter was knocked down eight times, being floored three times in the sixth round. Jeffords showed he was no match for the Hudson County boxer and took one of the hardest beatings ever handed to any fighter in the ring in Portland.*[114]

On March 3, 1907 at 12:13 a.m. a Pennsylvania Railroad's storage house of

---

[112] *Boston Herald* January 12, 1907.
[113] *La Vie au Grand Air* January 16, 1909.
[114] *Jersey Journal* February 13, 1907.

dynamite exploded in Homestead, New Durham. The dynamite was being used for the Pennsylvania tunnel project. The explosion was felt for a radius of fifteen miles. My mother was cut by flying glass from the explosion. At least five men were killed from the accident.[115]

On March 8 I faced the very capable "Young" Peter Jackson. Jackson had been boxing professionally since 1895 and had participated in over one hundred boxing matches. The bout was held at the Spring Garden Athletic Club in Philadelphia, Pennsylvania. "Young" Peter's birth name was Sim Thompkins. He was from Baltimore, Maryland. Although he was only five-foot six-inches tall, Peter was a tough customer. The affair was a six round newspaper decision in my favor. Jackson refused to stand and trade with me as the *Boston Journal* described: *Joe Jeannette of New York proved to be entirely too much for Young Peter Jackson of Baltimore at the Spring Garden A.C., Philadelphia, tonight. Joe had Jackson on the run during the entire six rounds, the once famous Baltimorean giving a most wretched exhibition. Jackson did nothing but back away from the New Yorker and at no stage of the game did he stand up and fight. Time and again he went to the floor without being struck and the crowd vigorously hissed him for his dirty and cowardly tactics. Jeannette did his best to draw him on but Jackson was there to stay and stay he did. He was almost mobbed as he left the ring.*[116]

On April 15, 1907, I faced Sam McVea for the first time in a non-exhibition bout. Sam had come to New York from California to take a steamer to Europe to box there. We were matched against each other a few days before he sailed off. I thought about the time we spent together in San Francisco. Sam was heading off to Europe because he heard that blacks were treated more as equals to whites there. That would mean more opportunities to make decent purses. Sam still held a grudge against me. When I tried to shake his hand at the weigh-in he told me: *"Now I am getting my chance!"*

I didn't know it then but our paths would cross again in epic proportions in the future. The fight took place at Lyric Hall in New York City under the banner of the National Sporting Club of America. There were rumors that the show would be cancelled by the police, but a large crowd turned out anyway. We were the main event. McVea, who had sixteen pro bouts, was fighting out of Los Angeles. I was fighting under Armstrong out of New York City. I weighed 185 pounds while McVea weighed in at 208 pounds.[117] Seeing that McVea had me outweighed by 23 pounds, George and I decided that I should box him.

The *New York Times* described the bout: *It was an interesting encounter, punctuated with many telling blows and a good show of science... Jeannette was speedier on his feet, and resorted to long range work. McVey on the other hand, scored at close*

---

[115] *New York Tribune* March 3, 1907.
[116] *Boston Journal* March 9, 1907.
[117] *New York Times* April 16, 1907.

quarters, depending on a right swing and a right drive for the wind. McVey looked like a winner in the second round. After mixing it McVey countered with the right. Then Jeannette tried to shift, and as he did so McVey hit him and brought him to his knees. At the end of the bout McVey's face was puffed and bruised and his right eye was cut. He was also bleeding from the mouth.[118]

The *Trenton Evening Times* wrote: *The bout was one of the fastest held between two big men here since the repeal of the Horton law. The California heavyweight outweighed his opponent by about twenty pounds, but Jeannette's superior cleverness kept him out of the way of McVey's heavy punches. In every round but the ninth, Jeannette did the better work. In the ninth the men were boxing fast, and Joe was landing some stiff jabs, when Sam suddenly let loose a short left hook that caught the New Yorker flush on the jaw. Jeannette wobbled and sank to the floor like a kite without a "tail." The bell rang as he arose to his feet. In the tenth and last round Jeannette staggered McVey with a volley of jabs and hooks. At the end the Californian was bleeding from the mouth and nose, and his left eye was cut and closed.*[119] I was awarded the newspaper decision.

Sam's nickname was the "California Rail Splitter" but it would soon change to the "Colored Globe Trotter" because of all the time he would spend boxing around the world. In June of 1907 Sam sailed to London to fight Ben Taylor. He didn't return to box in the United States again until December of 1914. He would box in Australia, France, Belgium, and the United Kingdom.

After having fought six times in 1906, I wound up only having five fights in 1907. I won four bouts, two by knockout, and I boxed one draw with Langford. George told me word was spreading on how tough I was and it was getting more and more difficult to find fights. The final bout for me in 1907 was against Morris Harris on June 11. I knocked Harris out in the fourth round at the Consolidated A.C. in New York City.

On July 13, 1907, I issued a statement to the press calling on heavyweight champion Tommy Burns to fight me.[120]

On July 16, I was called to give former heavyweight champion Robert Fitzsimmons sparring at Dunellen N.J.[121] Fitzsimmons had a fight set with Jack Johnson for the next day. Several boxing insiders thought it was a bad idea for Fitz to spar the day before the fight, because he could risk being injured. Fitz stated he needed to get in some rounds. During the sparring session I threw a solid body blow and Fitz tucked his right elbow in to block it. Upon impact Fitz immediately fell to the floor screaming in pain. It appeared as though the blow had torn a ligament in Fitz' arm.[122] Fitz had a local doctor look at the arm, which was swollen and had a large blood clot

---

118 *New York Times* April 16, 1907.
119 *Trenton Evening Times* April 16, 1907.
120 *Indianapolis Freeman* July 13, 1907.
121 *Los Angeles Times* July 18, 1907.
122 *Jersey Journal* July 18, 1907.

forming on it.[123] Fitz refused to cancel the fight, which was held in Philadelphia. When Fitz entered the ring and took his robe off the referee Tommy Keenan took one look at his arm and declared he would not referee the contest because Fitz's arm was clearly damaged. Fitz, who was sitting on his stool, jumped up to his feet and declared that a doctor had examined the arm the day before and determined that the arm was not broken. To this day I don't know if Fitz needed the money that bad, or as he claimed, he did not want to disappoint the paying customers. The crowd cheered: *"Go on, Go on."*

Several appeals were made to the referees at ringside to ref the match, but all refused. The promoter McCarney declared if no one was willing to referee the contest he would referee it himself, and he did. The first round started slowly as both Fitz and Johnson were cautious. Johnson landed a left hook and grinned as Fitz responded with his own left but neither blow did any damage. The first round ended. In the second round Johnson deliberately put his arm under Fitz's injured arm and threw him to the canvas. The crowd hissed at this dirty tactic. Fitz was visibly in pain but he refused to protest the foul. Fitz rose to his feet and put his hands up. Johnson stepped in and landed a right to Fitz's jaw. Fitz fell to his knees and was counted out. The crowd, who had wanted the fight to go on, filed out of the building in disgust.

In November of 1907 I changed managers. Armstrong was a nice person, but as a manager he wasn't getting me enough fights, and I didn't feel he had the connections or wherewithal to get me to a title shot.

I was introduced to Billy Elmer while fighting Morris Harris at the Consolidated Athletic Club. Elmer ran the club and showed a desire to manage me. He ran bi-monthly shows out of his club which was located at 114 West 65th street in New York City. I decided to leave George Armstrong and let Elmer manage my career. I never signed a contract with Armstrong and I didn't with Elmer either.

Elmer had a different approach to boxing than most people I had previously met in the game. I'll let Billy explain his methods himself in an interview he gave to the *Elmira Gazette* in 1905 as he spoke about being bumped into by someone who gave him a surly look and instead of fighting, Elmer apologized and deflated the situation: *A friend who was with Elmer remarked: "Why the fault was with that fellow. Why didn't you resent it. You could make him look like a two-spot." "That's the reason I didn't," replied the boxing teacher. "Because I can, I won't." This sounded like strange philosophy and they asked Elmer for details. "The greatest advantage in knowing how to box and being able to take care of yourself in an emergency," said Elmer, "is that it teaches you to keep your temper and renders you far less quarrelsome than if you thought the other fellow was your*

---

[123] *Los Angeles Times* July 18, 1907.

physical superior. You are conscious of the fact that you can resent an insult, and for that very reason feel that you are not imposed upon.

"I teach boxing, but none of my pupils have any idea of ever boxing in public. They are businessmen who take the lessons for the benefit they derive from the exercise. Idleness puts fat on them, and fat is the source of many ills. It prevents them from enjoying life. They are short winded. They can't eat what they like. They have to be continually dosing themselves with pills. There is no exercise that keeps men of this kind in such good physical condition as light boxing. There is no slugging in my shop. The pupil always feels that he is never in danger of being handled roughly by the instructor. This is the only way to teach the beginner.

"Returning to your first query, when a man has acquired a knowledge of boxing he feels confident of himself. There are a hundred and one dangers that men are exposed to in the streets every day. The training that the boxer receives, the quick eye, the nimble feet, the ready arm, saves him from many a bump that he might otherwise receive. He avoids a trolley car or an auto instinctively. And he passes up a slight because he is too sure of himself to feel his self-love injured. He has been made good natured by the healthy expansion of his lungs and he doesn't mind having his corns trod upon because he hasn't any corns."[124]

On December 16, 1907, Billy Elmer and I were arrested at the Consolidated A.C. on warrants related to committing crimes in regards to prizefighting.[125] Judge Wahle placed Elmer under one thousand dollar bond, for one year, ordering him not to violate the law in regards to sparring exhibitions. The charges against me were dropped. Boxing exhibitions were only allowed to be held between members of the club.

1908 would prove to be a much busier year for me, as I would take part in ten bouts under Elmer. Elmer, unlike Armstrong, was a former fighter who had competed in the welterweight division. He had boxed out of San Francisco and had eight professional fights between 1897 and 1900.

On New Year's Eve 1908 I took Addie to Times Square. The city was holding a special ceremony where they dropped a ball in the square to signify the coming New Year. We didn't know it at the time but this would be the first of what would become an annual event in the square.

On January 12, I played basketball with the Olympia's of Union Hill.[126] We faced the South Hudson championship team at Westside Hall in Bayonne. I played center for the team. Basketball helped to keep my footwork sharp.

I had my first bout of 1908 on January 13 at the Consolidated A.C. in New York City. Elmer thought it would be a good publicity stunt if I fought two boxers on the same night like Jack Johnson had done. My first opponent was Joe Phillips. I let Phillips control the action, as he was much

---

[124] *Elmira Gazette* November 28, 1905.
[125] *Boston Herald* December 17, 1907.
[126] *Jersey Journal* January 11, 1908.

less experienced than me. In the third round the crowd got restless so I countered Phillips' lazy jab with a hard overhand right which sent Phillips down in a heap for the ten-count. After a short intermission, Griff Jones was brought into the ring and I finished him off with a hard right to the body followed by a hook to the jaw in the third round. On January 27 I returned to the Consolidated A.C. and knocked out Jim Jeffords in the second round.

After the effects of the Atlanta riots died down, talks started circulating again of a black fighter being given a shot at the world's heavyweight title. A lot of the rumors had to do with the fact that the best boxers at the time in the States were believed to be colored, and more important than race for the U.S. sports fans was bringing the title back to the United States. Tommy Burns, a Canadian, currently held the title.

1908 was the year that Louisiana addressed what some called the South's "yellow peril."[127] They enacted a law making concubinage between a person of the Caucasian race and a person of the Negro race a felony. A few years later they enforced the law and arrested a German-born white man. The indictment against him charged that he had lived with a Negro woman and fathered three children by her. Soon after the indictment the man died. When the mother of his children, who was the beneficiary on his life insurance policy, attempted to collect on it she was denied the insurance even after filing suit.

Jack Johnson was following Tommy Burns everywhere, from England to Australia, taunting him for a shot at the title. Burns was really an overblown middleweight when he won the vacant title from Marvin Hart on February 23, 1906. I must give Johnson credit. He would not be denied. He hounded Burns until he finally got his shot. Johnson bought ringside seats to all of Burns' fights and he would taunt the champion. Unfortunately, I did not have the resources or finances to follow Burns around as Johnson did. I had a family to support and I needed to fight to support them.

Johnson had apparently learned a lesson from Peter Jackson, the great colored boxer from the 1880s. Jackson never called out an opponent and this lack of self-promotion, along with John L. Sullivan drawing the "color line," led to Jackson never getting a title shot.

1908 was also the first year that amateur boxing formally became an Olympic sport. That made all of us who boxed for a living very proud. Boxing was now considered a real sport and not just a violent business.

On February 17, I took on George Cole of Trenton at Billy Elmer's Consolidated A.C. The *Boston Globe* described the contest: *Jeanette was the aggressor from the beginning, and it soon was evident that he was the master. In the first round both fought cautiously and neither did any damage to the other. In the second*

---

[127] *Interracial Intimacies* by Randall Kennedy pg. 218.

session Jeanette went after his antagonist and made him wince from lefts and rights to the body. Jeanette landed a left to the jaw that staggered Cole, and the latter was tired when the bell rang. In the third round the local fighter popped his opponent twice with lefts and rights to the jaw, and again the bell saved the Trenton man from a knockout. Cole looked tired when he responded for the fourth round, and after a few seconds of feinting, Jeanette hooked his left to Cole's jaw. He repeated the blow twice and Cole sank to the floor. Before he could rise one of his seconds threw a sponge onto the ring. Cole was carried to his corner.[128]

On March 2 the press described Johnson's ducking me: *Jack Johnson is 'salving' us every day- spreading it on a foot thick. Johnson tells us he is trembling with eagerness to fight anybody in the wide wide world. And all the time this Jack is dodging and sidestepping one Joe Jeannette with extreme agility. Why is he sidestepping Mr. Jeannette? Simple enough, Jeannette is very likely to lick him if they fight. Jeannette has one decision over Johnson, and the other four bouts they have fought have been draws. Jeannette is a tough, dangerous coon, and Mista Johnson is drawing the color line harder than Tommy Burns ever drew it.[129]*

On March 4, 1908, I traveled up to Boston to take on Sam Langford again. The bout was scheduled for twelve rounds at the Armory AA. The *Boston Journal* described the bout: *The Armory A.A. never held such a crowd. Every seat in the vast amphitheater was occupied and the meeting was a grand success. It was estimated that 2,200 lovers of the manly art saw the contests scheduled. Joe Jeannette has the most wonderful left hand displayed around these parts since the days of Young Griffo. The big New Yorker jabbed and jolted Langford at will with this member during the entire contest and it was only superb blocking by the Cambridge boy that saved his face from being badly marked...*

The first round was a hummer, Sam going right to the copper-colored boy: flooring him for a count of four seconds before the fight was a minute old. The left hook made Joe cautious, but he gained confidence in the second period and evened up matters with that wonderful left which he poked into Langford's face with telling effect. In the third the two wrestled and clinched all over the ring. Sam missed several dangerous right swings and worked on the kidneys. Jeannette kept at work and the round was his by a good margin. In the fourth Jeannette rested somewhat after starting in well, and Sam went to work with rights to the head and left and right kidney punches.

The fighters opened the fifth by standing toe to toe and swapping punches. At one period during this round Sam looked to be weakening, but his continual leading in the early part gave him the advantage. In the sixth round Langford led by a mile and Joe looked bad. In the seventh Joe started finely, but Sam rallied and beat the big fellow back with four wicked right hand punches without a return. Jeannette came on strongly the last part. In the eighth the New Yorker had a big margin and opened the left optic of the Cambridge scrapper, who was weak as he walked to his corner.

The ninth was an even round, both men showing the strain of the hard fight. In the

[128] *Boston Globe* February 18, 1908.
[129] *Auburn Citizen* March 2, 1908.

tenth Langford maintained lead enough to offset the rush of Jeannette in the middle of the round and Sam also finished up strongly enough to gain the eye of the referee. In the eleventh and twelfth it was all Jeannette and the crowd rooted hard for the underdog up to this point. Langford was a beaten man in the eleventh and had to stall to finish. He did not fare much better in the closing round, as Jeannette had the bothersome left going like a piston rod.[130] I don't know what kept Sam up. In the eleventh and twelfth stanzas Sam's knees and gloves touched the canvas several times as much from exhaustion as from my punches.[131] The bout was ruled a draw. The crowd cheered the effort we both gave forth.

On March 9, I returned to the Consolidated A.C. to take on Sam Campbell. I knocked Campbell down six times in the contest. The referee tried to stop the fight in the fourth round but Campbell's seconds insisted on the fight continuing. One minute into the sixth and final round, the referee stopped the fight because it was plain to see that Campbell was not going to last the round. In one of the rounds I broke a small bone in my right hand when I struck Campbell on his forehead.[132] I took a month and a half off, on advice from a physician, to rest the hand. After the fight, my manager Elmer stated to the *National Police Gazette* reporter covering the fight that I was an equal to Jack Johnson. He also told the reporter that he would issue a challenge to heavyweight champion Tommy Burns as soon as Burns returned from Europe. In mid-April I started hitting the bag with the hand and it felt okay. I started preparations for my upcoming battles against Jim Barry and Sam Langford.

On April 14, the *Boston Journal* reported that Jack Johnson and Tommy Burns had agreed to fight. A colored boxer was finally going to get a crack at the heavyweight title!

On May 8, I fought Jim Barry, a veteran of twenty-one fights, at the Consolidated A.C., in a no-decision bout. The twenty-one year old Barry was a five-foot ten-inch heavyweight from California.

Elmer was keeping me busy but my purses were much less than I was getting when I was with Armstrong. Elmer was constantly complaining about ticket sales at the Consolidated. I felt Elmer had conflicting interests in promoting his club and managing me. I told Billy that I didn't want to fight for him anymore. To my amazement Elmer tried to claim that I owed him money even though he cut my purses on nearly all of his shows. I would make sure that my next manager was not also a promoter.

Jimmy De Forest offered to train me and get me fights. Jimmy helped me gain more speed on my jab. Jimmy spent many hours carefully showing me the proper way to throw the left jab. He showed me how to lean forward on my left toe, turn my left shoulder, and flick the left out with a snap.

---

130 *Boston Journal* March 4, 1908.
131 *Baltimore Sun* March 5, 1908.
132 *Syracuse Herald* March 20, 1908.

Jimmy explained: *"Joe the jab is the key to opening all the doors in boxing. If used properly it is like an annoying fly in your opponents face. It is a weapon and a distraction all in one."* De Forest also helped Jack Johnson perfect his jab.

On September 1, I faced off against Sam Langford in New York City. The bout was ruled a draw by the *New York Times* and a win for Sam in the *NY Sun* and *NY Evening World*. Sam knocked me down three times in the bout. I hit the floor twice in the first round and once in the fifth. I dug down deep and rallied hard in the bout and felt I had earned the draw. I injured my right elbow during the contest so De Forest had me double up on my jab. In the dressing room after the contest I was approached by Emil Fuchs and Billy Elmer.[133] Fuchs stated he was Elmer's attorney and demanded half of my purse. I told Fuchs and Elmer to "pound salt" because Elmer actually owed me money. Things were getting heated when De Forest broke it up and pulled me away.

In Springfield, Illinois, Abraham Lincoln's hometown, on August 14, there were massive riots by whites against blacks.[134] At the end of the riots seven people were dead and forty homes were destroyed. The riots were fueled by a white man named Clergy Ballard who had his throat slashed in July. While he was dying Ballard stated that a black man named Joe James had broken into his home and attacked him and attempted to rape his daughter. Whites in the town beat James unconscious. When the authorities stepped in to protect James the townspeople turned their anger on other black families and white people who were protecting them. The August 14 riots were also fueled by a white woman named Mabel Hallam who stated she had been raped by a black man. The state militia was called in to restore peace.

On August 15 the mob approached the shop of black shoemaker William Donnegan because he was married to a white woman named Sarah Rudolph. The 79-year-old Donnegan had fitted boots for Abraham Lincoln. The rioters set fire to Donnegan's shop. They dragged him outside and beat him with bricks. His throat was then slashed. Still breathing, he was dragged across the street into a courtyard not far from a statue of Lincoln, where he was hoisted up a tree with a clothesline, and hung by his neck. His 49-year-old wife and infant daughter escaped the mob with the help of a neighbor. The next day, the tree was demolished by townspeople seeking souvenirs of the murder.[135] The incident, and the fact that an interracial couple was targeted, shook Addie and I to the core. Could our neighbors do such a thing to us?

It did not appear likely that a black man would be given a chance at the heavyweight title now. Fear was spreading amongst us black fighters that we would be given even less opportunities to earn a living from boxing than

---

[133] *Evening World* September 2, 1908.
[134] *Beyond The Ring* by Jeffrey T. Sammons pg. 41.
[135] "Blanche Hawkins Interview" University of Illinois at Springfield.

we were currently getting. Rumors were spreading that Northern black boxers would be forced into Battle Royal matches to make a living. Blacks down South engaged in Battle Royals to make money. Battle Royal matches consisted of six black boxers in the ring, sometimes wearing blindfolds, attacking each other for the amusement of the white crowd. When a boxer does not see or is unprepared for a blow to the head the knockouts that result can be very violent and deadly. The last fighter standing was the only one who received the money, or sometimes the last two boxers standing would fight four rounds for the purse. Usually the purse was only a couple of dollars. White boxers never had to humiliate themselves by fighting in Battle Royals.

Despite arrests and indictments of the riot leaders in Illinois, there was only one conviction in the Springfield Riots, it was for a theft of a militiaman's sword. Mabel Hallam would later admit that it was a white man who had raped her. After the rioting, two thousand blacks left the city.

On September 15, De Forest took me up to Boston to fight Sandy Ferguson at the Armory. I won a twelve round decision against Ferguson although my right arm was still in great pain. Sandy was a big heavyweight, standing six-foot three-inches in height, and weighing close to 220 pounds. He was durable and capable and ducked no one, black or white, in his career. The *Boston Globe* reported: *Though he (Ferguson) stood head and shoulders over his opponent and had a much longer reach, he was awfully afraid of the colored boxer. He did more foul work and hugging than boxing and in the whole 12 rounds did not land a half dozen punches... Jeannette, who was in grand shape, forced the boxing from the start. He was quick and at times had Sandy bewildered by his sudden attack. Jeannette did the greater part of his work with his left and he repeatedly jabbed and hooked Sandy in the face. The colored boxer got in some good wallops with the right on the kidneys and face.*

In the middle of the tenth round Sandy surprised the spectators by making a lead with the right, and it proved a bad move for him, as Jeannette avoided the blow and countered Sandy on the jaw with a right, putting Sandy to the mat. About every time that Jeannette jabbed him Sandy would go into a clinch and hang on for all he was worth. Sandy acted so badly that the members were well pleased when referee Donnelly declared Jeannette the winner.[136]

After the Ferguson bout I decided to leave De Forest. He was a very intelligent trainer but he had too large of a boxing stable. I needed someone who could focus on my career. Fred Schubert, a basketball coach for the Liberty team, offered to help me find fights. I rounded out 1908 with a six round decision win over Morris Harris on December 7 at the West End A.C. in Philadelphia, Pa. I wore an elastic support on my right elbow to help with the discomfort. The *Cincinnati Enquirer* wrote that the elastic

---

[136] *Boston Globe* September 16, 1908.

support: *Seemed to interfere with his action of that member somewhat.*[137]

I now had competed in thirty-seven professional fights. Having the opportunity to compete with boxers at a lesser level than Johnson and Langford helped to boost my record and more importantly my confidence. I learned a great deal from all of the different styles I faced. This helped me become a more complete boxer.

When a boxer enters a contest without experience, everything appears to be happening so much more rapidly than it really is. Instead of having the time to think of what move to make, a boxer with no experience is forced to react to his opponent, thereby giving his opponent the edge in setting the tempo and exchanges. Experience in the ring brings relaxation, which in turn helps to slow down the mind, which slows down what you see happening in front of you.

Experience makes it much easier to control the action in a bout. Controlling a fight is what boxing insiders call "ring generalship." I learned how important "ring generalship" was in the Johnson matches. Although I had equal athletic ability and a strong desire to win I had not yet discovered those other intangibles that help a boxer succeed.

I was excited about my prospects in the sport with the current winning streak I was on. I was now perfecting "ring generalship" along with all the other facets of my game. The injury to my right elbow forced me to come up with a new style that offset the handicap of my injured arm. I was perfecting how to turn my left shoulder inward toward my right side, which protected my right elbow and gave me better defensive coverage while also drawing in my opponent for my right cross.

---

[137] *Cincinnati Enquirer* December 8, 1908.

Chapter 11
A Barrier Broken and Hope for a Title

On December 21, 1908, the headline in the papers screamed off of the pages when I read it. "Burns and Johnson to fight for the World's Championship."[138] The bout would be held in Sydney, Australia. Almost as thrilling was the purse of thirty-five thousand dollars, of which Burns was guaranteed thirty thousand. Johnson would take home fifteen hundred dollars for the fight. The match was really going to happen!

Up until this point I had never taken home more than a few hundred dollars in a bout. I believed that if Johnson could win the title, we would most certainly meet again, and I would finally be in line for a major payday. The Burns-Johnson bout was scheduled for December 26. All of the colored boxers that I knew, myself included, were thrilled that we were going to get a chance at fighting for the world's heavyweight championship.

Former heavyweight champs James J. Jeffries and John L. Sullivan both voiced concerns over a black man being given a shot at the title. It was common knowledge in boxing circles that the champ Burns was not regarded as the best heavyweight of the day. Burns was enticed into the Johnson bout by the large purse offered by Snowy Baker via former pie salesman and current promoter Hugh Macintosh. Although many fight fans and bettors disapproved, the promoter Macintosh would also referee the bout. The title fight was a sellout.

I will never forget receiving the news of the fight on Friday around eight o'clock in the evening on the 25th of December 1908. Because it was Christmas night, Addie had originally protested, but she finally gave in to my brother Marshall and I going over to Manhattan to hear the results of the fight. We took the trolley to the ferry and sailed over to Manhattan. The *New York World* newspaper would be announcing the results of the big fight outside of its building located at Park Row and Frankfort Street. The skyscraper held the distinction of being the tallest building in New York City and the world from 1890 to 1894. In 1894 it lost that honor to the Manhattan Life Insurance building. The *World* building was three hundred and nine feet tall and twenty stories high. The *World* had a ticker tape machine inside. A reporter was standing outside the building on a platform with a megaphone in his hand preparing to announce the results, as they came in, to the large crowd that had gathered. When it was discovered who I was, Marshall and I were ushered inside of the building to hear the results of the fight with the *World's* editors and reporters. It was a cold December night so we were glad we were let inside.

As fate would have it, one of the editors I was introduced to was the

---

[138] *Augusta Chronicle* December 21, 1908.

Scottish fight manager Dan McKetrick. McKetrick was a huge boxing fan and he managed several boxers including my stable-mate Willie Lewis. I had observed McKetrick around the gym talking to Willie but we were never formally introduced. He told me he had been at several of my fights and he explained that if I had the right manager I could be champion of the world. Dan said he would use the press to force the heavyweight champion to fight me. McKetrick told me he was going to France with Willie Lewis and if I was interested in making some money he would take me with him. Dan gave me his business card and asked me to look him up. I looked at his business card and replied: *"Count me in. Let's go to France!"*

I decided at that moment that Dan McKetrick would be my new manager. Dan, in partnership with Harry Pollock, would eventually take over the National Sporting Club where I trained and rename it the Forty-Fourth Street Sporting Club.[139]

We listened intently as the reporter prepared to read off the results, round by round. The fight was taking place at Rushcutter's Bay in Sydney. We were told there were between twenty to thirty thousand people watching the fight live in Sydney. Several seconds into the bout Johnson landed a nasty uppercut that sent Burns to the canvas for a six count. Several seconds later Burns was floored again by a straight right to the chin. I looked outside a window at the largely white crowd on Park Row. The crowd was eerily silent. For the next eight rounds Johnson pitched a shutout. The only positive thing that was being said about Burns was how courageous he was in absorbing such an enormous amount of punishment. During the fourteenth round the ticker tape went silent. We thought that the machine had broken but the ticker tape operator said the machine was fine, as he tested it. We were all wondering why the results from Sydney had suddenly stopped.

I looked at Marshall, and he at me, and we both were thinking the same thing. Johnson was well on his way to an easy victory. Something must have happened. Was there a riot? Had Johnson been shot, as several anonymous people had threatened to do? There were many threats made that he would be killed if he fought Burns. Did the police stop the fight? We waited for what seemed like hours as the silent minutes went by. After about ten minutes the machine started ticking again. The clerk shouted out: *"The fight has been stopped!"* His eyes scanned the tape as it continued to punch out information. The crowd was growing anxious as it awaited the verdict. Did Johnson finish Burns off? Did Burns come back and land a knockout punch? The clerk motioned with his hands for the reporter with the megaphone to quiet the restless crowd down. A serious look came over the clerk's face. The clerk continued: *"The Sydney police department has stopped the*

---

[139] *New York Press* December 15, 1912.

fight during the fourteenth round. John Arthur Johnson, a Texas Negro, the son of an American slave, tonight is the NEW heavyweight champion of the world!"

The mostly German-Irish crowd became eerily quiet once again. The silence was broken though by the winning gamblers wanting to cash in on their bets. Before the bout there was mixed feelings about bringing the title back to the United States versus a Negro winning the title. Dan McKetrick approached Marshall and I and said it would be better for us if we stayed inside the building until the crowd dispersed. We waited for over thirty minutes until we were able to leave. We were careful not to show our emotions on the street. There were those who were happy that the title was coming back to the U.S. but most showed no emotions.

Johnson was just too big and strong for the smaller Burns, and the contest was ended in the fourteenth round when police stepped into the ring and ordered the mismatch stopped. Burns had been dropped hard by a Johnson blow just prior to the stoppage. Johnson was clearly toying with Burns. It is not farfetched that Jack purposely carried Burns so as not to set off a riot by blowing the white boxer away, but more likely Johnson carried Burns to sell more moving picture reels. A longer bout helped when it came time to sell the reels of the match. Johnson was well aware of this fact.

As soon as we arrived back to New Jersey Marshall and I embraced each other. We were overcome with joy. We had finally broken the racial barrier in the heavyweight division. We could not contain ourselves. Johnson had defeated Burns and the world had its first black heavyweight champion. I would definitely get a chance at the title now. The world was changing for the better. For many blacks, Johnson was a long-sought liberator, the deliverer and up-lifter of our persecuted race. To others, his reign as champion was the most satisfying event since the end of slavery.[140] In all the little towns, in the houses and cotton fields of Texas, Louisiana, Georgia, Tennessee, Alabama, and Mississippi, colored folks were praying, weeping, and dancing. Jack Johnson was the black Jesus, the deliverer, after so long a wait in hopelessness.[141]

The famous writer Jack London stated of the Burns-Johnson fight: *"The fight, there was no fight. No Armenian massacre could compare with the hopeless slaughter that took place in the Sydney stadium today. But one thing now remains.[142] Jim Jeffries must now emerge from his alfalfa farm and remove that golden smile from Jack Johnson's face. Jeff, it's up to you. The white man must be rescued."[143]*

The term "great white hope" was coined. It was a term that would haunt me and become an insurmountable obstacle to my title aspirations. Up in

---

[140] *Beyond The Ring* by Jeffrey T. Sammons pg. 46.
[141] *The Big Black Fire* by Robert H. DeCoy pg. 76.
[142] *Champions of the Ring* by Gerald Suster pg. 60.
[143] *The Heavyweight Championship* by Stanley Weston pgs. 76-77.

Harlem the streets were filled with celebrations. Although the bout took place on the afternoon of the 26th, Australia is sixteen hours ahead of New York time, so we actually received the news on the 25th in New York.

Marshall and I were overwhelmed with joy. The joy was for the first black heavyweight champion as well as for the knowledge that I was one of the top two or three challengers for that throne. Now that we were given the opportunity to fight for the heavyweight title my turn for a title shot would not be far off. If I became heavyweight champion Marshall would be able to quit his job as a coal driver and help train me full time. When I arrived home, Addie had already heard the news. She had tears in her eyes as she hugged me tightly. Her voice trembled as she spoke: *"See, Joe, I told you times have changed. The days of discrimination in this world are finally coming to an end."* Her statement would be short lived.

The next day I signed a contract with Dan to fight for Victor Breyer of Paris. I was to engage in six bouts in Europe for ten thousand dollars. Dan and I spent several hours charting our plan to a title shot. We figured Johnson would rest and tour the country cashing in on exhibitions, before the public would force him to defend his title against an able opponent. I couldn't count more than two or three heavyweights that were as worthy of a title shot as I was. I hadn't lost a bout in two years and I was the last boxer to hand Johnson a loss. Johnson had lost only two bouts in the last seven years, the disqualification loss to me and a disputed decision loss to Marvin Hart.

Willie Lewis signed a similar contract for ten bouts. We were to head to Paris on January 5, 1909. Willie had taught me much in our time training together. He taught me how to defend against the many fouls in boxing. Willie knew all of the dirty tricks. He knew the "shoestring trick," when you point your glove at your opponent's feet and tell him his shoe is untied and then hit him. He taught me the thumb to the eye punch, and the elbow to the jaw. He taught me how to step in with your front leg and bring it behind your opponent's leg and punch him while pulling your leg back causing him to lose balance and fall. If you were positioned right the referee would not see this move. He taught me two "fingering" punches. One was punching your opponent with an open glove to the throat. The other was punching your opponent to the eyes and mouth with an open glove. Others were the head butt, the punch below the belt, pulling your opponents head down, and laying your glove on his shoulder while pushing your thumb into his throat. I never used any of these illegal punches, but thanks to Willie I was aware of how to defend against them.

Willie was also very good at getting into his opponent's head. One such incident took place on December 26, 1907, at Long Acre A.C. in New York when Willie took on Pat O'Keefe. I will let the famous fight referee Eugene Corri describe what happened: *"An amusing example of bluff among boxers, practiced especially by American boxers, is told of Willie Lewis... Going into Pat*

112

O'Keefe's dressing room immediately before the contest, he started chaffing him about his appearance, and, pointing at the big fellow's stomach, he said: 'You're a ver' good fella, but you can't go into the ring with a stomach like that; if I hit you there I might kill you, and I don't feel like going on with the contest until you've trained that down a bit.' His opponent protested that he was all right, and that he was not bulging with fat, but with muscles. Lewis, however, persisted until the fellow got his stomach on the brain, so that when they squared up in the ring he immediately guarded it with his left forearm, leaving himself exposed to Lewis, who promptly hit him a terrific punch on the point. 'Outed' by bluff!'[144] Willie knocked out O'Keefe in the first round. Boxing is truly ninety percent mental.

[144] *Thirty Years a Boxing Referee* by Eugene Corri pg. 220.

Chapter 12
A Tour of Europe 1909

The Springfield riots of 1908 led to the formation of the civil rights organization called the National Association for the Advancement of Colored People, founded in New York and led by W.E.B. De Bois on February 12, 1909.

In 1909, Abraham Lincoln's image replaced the Indian portrait on the penny. This was very important for black America. The great emancipator was being honored on the penny. It made me think back to when my stepfather used to sing the song: "Give us just another Lincoln." Lincoln was the first president to have his image on a coin. President Theodore Roosevelt commissioned Victor David Brenner to design the coin which was released on the one hundred year anniversary of Lincon's birth. Roosevelt was the first president to invite a black American to the White House when he entertained Booker T. Washington in 1901.

Dan McKetrick, although only 27-years-old, was now my new manager. McKetrick had many connections in the boxing world from his newspaper position. He was a small Scotsman who stood only five feet in height. Dan told me he was going to work out a deal for a possible fight with Jack Johnson by summer. We were hopeful that our European tour would drum up support for a Johnson rematch. Dan figured if we received enough international support it would force Johnson to fight us more quickly.

We left New York City for Paris, France, in mid-January. As we steamed out of New York Harbor I could see the William Peter Brewery up in Union Hill, with its smoke stacks working overtime, as it towered over the other buildings in the area. The trip included Dan, his wife Anna, Addie, Joe Jr., Willie Lewis, and his wife Tillie.

Each of us felt the sickness that comes with a long journey on the seas. Several times we were all sick at the same time. The never-ending rolling waves grabbed hold of our stomachs, and its effects lasted for days. The nauseous feeling lingered in my throat. We looked ghost white when the seas overcame us. At this time of the year the winds were very strong and cold on the Atlantic. To help deal with the sickness we spent a lot of time on deck breathing in the salty ocean air. We would watch large icebergs that looked like small islands drift past us as we steamed east.

Upon arrival in France on January 7 we took a train to the Saint-Lazare station. When the train stopped I walked my two-year-old son Joie to the stairs to walk off of the train. I was completely caught off guard by the attention our arrival had stirred up. There were well over one hundred people at the train station to greet us. Besides the fans there were many reporters and photographers. They were snapping pictures of us as we stepped off of the train. I could tell immediately that boxing was a bigger hit in France than it was back in the states. A local magazine called *La Vie au Grand Air,* or *The Great Outdoors* in English, covered our arrival. They also covered the arrival on January 11 of the famous flying machine discoverer Orville Wright and his sister Katherine. Victor Breyer, the boxing promoter, was also a newspaper reporter for *Grand Air.* He wrote that when Orville and his sister arrived on the same platform in Saint-Lazare as we did there were only fourteen people there to greet them.[145] He was amazed at both how many people turned out for our arrival and of how few turned out for Orville's arrival.

Jacques Mortane of the *Grand Air* covered our arrival as well. He wrote an article that was printed on January 16. In the article Mortane thanked the Company for the Propagation of Boxing in France and the Wonderland Arena for helping to bring me over to France. He stated: *Thanks to them, we will see Sam McVea have to work. He will have to fight. It will not be enough for him to enter the boxing ring to destroy, with two or three light blows, the adversary which will oppose him.*[146]

Mortane wrote that although I was not as colossal in size as Sam I was still physically imposing. He stated that Sam would be in for a real fight for the first time since he arrived in France, as Sam had blown away his previous opponents. Sam had won all nine of his matches since leaving the States in April of 1907, with all nine wins coming by way of knockout. Sam's longest match was against Ben Taylor. That fight went eleven rounds. In all nine bouts Sam averaged only four rounds a fight.

Mortane wrote that he believed Sam had gotten rusty in Paris. He believed I was too much for Sam to handle. Jacques thought that Sam had matured as a fighter age wise, but he had lost his hunger and drive. Jacques stated that the referee, who decided my decision loss to Langford just before I sailed to France, was "hooted" by both the spectators and the press. He mentioned my January 11, 1907, match with Langford. In that match, the referee declared the fight even after twelve rounds and wanted Langford and I to fight one more deciding round. Langford refused, stating he could not see out of his swollen eyes. Jacques also mentioned that I had defeated McVea on April 15, 1907 in New York, via newspaper decision.

The weather in Paris was just as harsh as it was when we left the U.S. We didn't mind, though, we were excited and went about sightseeing immediately. Addie and I visited the Eiffel Tower, which was the tallest structure in the world at the time. There were those in Paris that actually wanted the tower torn down because the twenty-year lease was up on its land. Paris was magical.[147] We strolled along the boulevards and wandered down narrow ancient streets. We admired the extravagant architecture. We

---

[145] *La Vie au Grand Air* January 16, 1909.
[146] *La Vie au Grand Air* January 16, 1909.
[147] *Paris Noir* by Tyler Stovall pg. xii.

toured the monuments at Notre-Dame and the Arc de Triomphe. We visited the museums, bookstores, shops, and art galleries. The food in Paris was delicious. We ate some of the finest cheese I ever tasted at a new cheese shop called Androuet.

After we toured Paris for a few hours we returned to our hotel room. Addie and I immediately noticed the difference between Paris and America. In Paris, when we walked down the street together there were no whispers or second looks. For the first time we did not feel alienated. We did not feel like criminals. We even stayed in a hotel that white people stayed in! Back up in the room I slipped into my work boots and went out for a jog in the crisp, cool, January Paris air. Running in boots was a trick we used to feel light on our feet when we fought.

When I returned, Addie and I went for a walk to the Louvre to view the art work. Afterwards we walked along the Champs-Elysees and visited Montmartre and the Latin Quarter. The French treated us with affection and respect.[148] In Paris it appeared that a color-blind society could be possible after all. Addie and I were slapped back to reality when we were looking through a local magazine called *Le Petit Journal.* There was a full page artist's depiction of a lynching in Kentucky. The drawing was of a black man on horseback, facing the rear of the horse, his hands tied behind his back, with a noose prepared to be hung around his neck. The end of the rope was tied to a tree branch. There was a mob of white men around him cheering the lynching on. One had a pitchfork. Another was playing a banjo. No matter how far we traveled, there were always stark reminders of home.

My stable-mate Willie Lewis had traveled to Paris the year prior and he left a very good impression on the Parisians. Willie won all six of his fights in France in 1908 with five coming by way of knockout. One of Willie's biggest wins was his fourth round stoppage of England's Curley Watson. Watson had over one hundred fights, winning most of them, at the time of their meeting. Curley was considered one of England's top fighters. Unfortunately for Curley he would be killed in the ring on March 5, 1910, by a boxer named Frank Inglis, who had only three professional bouts. Curley had lost eight straight bouts in six months with five losses by stoppage leading up to that fatal knockout. His tragedy taught me a great lesson. Never underestimate your opponent no matter what their experience level might be. It also taught me that when my skills erode and I am not competitive anymore I'd better retire or I could risk my health or even my life. The biggest win by Willie in 1908, as far as the French were concerned, was his fifth round knockout over Walter Stanton in a scheduled twenty round affair. Although Stanton had only five professional

---

[148] *Paris Noir* by Tyler Stovall pg. xiii.

bouts going into the match he was extremely popular in France. This win propelled Willie into star status in the country. Dan promised that I would be just as popular if I beat my old foe from California, the rail splitter, Sam McVea, who had become very popular in France.

We only stayed in the hotel in Paris for a few days, as we moved onto the property of millionaire English sportsman Jim Pratt. Pratt had a villa in Neuilly where we would be training. Pratt, who owned many horses, also let me take morning rides on his colts.

I picked up a copy of the local sports magazine *La Vie au Grand Air* when I arrived. On the second page was a photograph of Sam McVea knocking out Jiu-Jitsu champion Tano Matsuda in the first round. Matsuda was knocked out with the very first punch that McVea landed. Matsuda was one of the first martial artists who fought a boxer in a mixed fighting match.

On our France trip Willie Lewis was the first to fight. On January 16 Willie knocked out Bill Curzon of London at the beginning of the fourth round with a right cross to the jaw. Willie was twelve pounds lighter than Curzon going into the match. Mortane described the bout: *Willie Lewis was in splendid form and he has not lost any of the beautiful qualities that made us admire him last year. During the second round, in particular, he had fun just dodging punches, seeking not to carry the least bit of an attack. And it was a marvelous spectacle to see this man, his opponent's arms swinging, let blows arrive within a millimeter of him and to be satisfied to move back slightly or to the right or the left, letting the punches strike the air.*[149]

The papers celebrated the return to Paris of Willie Lewis. He had made a huge name for himself on his previous visit to France. The fans were applauding Willie's quick combinations and his slick defensive moves, especially the way he rolled with the punches.

My first bout in Paris was against Englishman Ben Taylor. In boxing you learn rather quickly that an opponent's record can be quite deceiving. This is especially so if the fellow's competition was stiff. Such was the case with Ben Taylor. He had fought all quality competition, even though he lost his last five bouts in a row. Ben's opponents included Jack Johnson, Sam McVea, Iron Hague, and Jack Scales. He had been stopped by Johnson in eight rounds. Dan told me that if I could stop Taylor faster than Jack and McVea did, Sam stopped Ben in three and eleven rounds; it would help stir up support for the McVea bout and a possible title shot with Johnson. I started training for Taylor with local boxers Marc Gaucher, Bob Scanlon, Marcel Moreau and Adolphie Cocu.

On January 23 I entered the ring in Paris with thirty-seven fights and twelve knockouts. Taylor was twenty-nine years of age and he had forty-one pro bouts. I was as focused as could be. We fought at the Wonderland in

[149] *La Vie au Grand Air* January 23, 1909.

front of a packed house. I gave up twenty-four pounds to Taylor in the match. I easily dispatched of Taylor in three rounds. Strangely enough, Taylor, who was born on New Year's Day in 1880, would die on New Year's Day in 1915 at only thirty-five years of age. In the *Grand Air*, Jacques Mortane stated that my upcoming bout with Sam McVea would: *"constitute the great event of the year."*

Mortane gave a prediction on who he thought would win the upcoming bout between McVea and I: *Jeannette gives the impression of being much faster than McVea, and I must acknowledge, much more skillful. We will see whether I am wrong, at the time of their meeting on February 20. While waiting, I believe that the victory, in spite of the variation of weight, must belong to Joe Jeannette, he is more scientific and more quick. I ask for forgiveness from you to go against your preference, which undoubtedly is Sam McVea, but you will excuse me to speak to you in all frankness. Jeannette cut down Ben Taylor several times during the second round and knocked him out at the beginning of the third. In 1908, Sam McVea needed eleven rounds to obtain this result, Jack Johnson, eight.*[150]

Mortane also talked of how furious the fans were at McVea's last fight. The January 23 blowout, against 0-1 novice Bill Rickard, lasted only six-seconds. Mortane wrote of how such mismatches could harm the sport: *The other evening, I must acknowledge that all the spectators... were furious and proclaimed they would not be taken by a mismatch again.*[151]

Sportswriter George Prade promised his readers he would never again mention in his column mismatches such as this one. Mortane thanked McKetrick for bringing championship quality fighters to France and not souring the sport by bringing fighters like Bill Rickard.

In Chicago, my old friends Bert Williams and George Walker were ecstatic about Jack Johnson winning the world title. They were so confident in his abilities they pledged a five thousand dollar bet that Johnson would defeat any white boxer put before him.[152]

On February 1 Willie Lewis met Charlie Hickman in Paris. Hickman had won only one of his nine professional fights. Dan was worried that Willie was not in the best of shape as he was staying out late with wealthy French and American sporting men. Before the Hickman bout Willie walked into Hickman's dressing room with Jim Pratt. Willie walked up to Hickman and said: *"How are you feeling, Mr. Hickman?"* Willie slapped Hickman on the back. Hickman said he was feeling fine, not knowing he was talking to his opponent. *"Fine, Fine, I'm glad to hear it. Now, young man, you must put up a good fight. Try to last as long as you can. You mustn't disappoint the crowd."* As Willie turned to walk out of the room he whispered into Dan McKetrick's ear loud enough for Hickman to hear: *"Dan, Dan, why did you match me with this*

[150] *La Vie au Grand Air* January 30, 1909.
[151] *La Vie au Grand Air* January 30, 1909.
[152] *Indianapolis Freeman* January 23, 1909.

poor fellow? Why I'm afraid I'll kill him!"

Later, when the fight started, Willie dropped Hickman with a one-two combination in the first round. As Willie walked back to our corner he was taking his gloves off with his teeth. Dan yelled up at him to stop, that Hickman wasn't hurt, the fight wasn't over, and Hickman was going to get up. Willie replied: *"Get up nothing! I scared the life out of him in the dressing room!"* Hickman stood down and was counted out at two minutes and forty seconds of the first round. Mortane wrote: *If we do not have longer fights involving Willie Lewis and Joe Jeannette, whose fault is it? Is it theirs? Are they the reason? No, not a hundred times no: but fault lies rather with the English boxers, who do not have the comparable talent as that of the American champions...[153]*

I followed up the Taylor win with a second round knockout of his fellow countryman Charley Croxon on February 6 in Paris.

My bout with Sam McVea was becoming highly anticipated. Mortane wrote: *Sam McVea is, for the large majority of Parisians, the man unbeatable, the invincible one. And this opinion was born in the spirit from people following his victories over Frank Craig, Jack Scales, Harry Shearing, Ben Taylor, Jewey Smith, Herbert Synnott, and, if I dare to point out this bad memory, on Bill Rickard... Otherwise interesting and instructive are his three meetings with Jack Johnson, in America. They make of him a marvelous boxer, having all the qualities which one can claim of a champion, but those of Joe Jeannette on paper, and, I believe, next Saturday in the boxing ring, are thoroughly much higher.*

A man who can praise himself to have made the matches that he provided with Jack Johnson and Sam Langford, two champions over which he has triumphed (on a foul, it is true, with Johnson) is a true boxer, and if we are sportsmen before being sentimental, we should all make him the favorite of this great meeting.[154]

Fourteen days after the Croxon bout I met Sam McVea for the second time in my career. The fight was billed as being for the colored heavyweight championship of the world as Johnson now held the world's heavyweight title. McVea was the betting favorite among the boxing locals. He was called the "Idol of Paris" because of how endearing he was to the French.

A local magazine called *Le Plein Air*, or *The Outdoor Life* in English, predicted that I would be victorious. The article claimed that I had had the better record against Jack Johnson and had been in with tougher competition. Therefore they believed that I would be the victor. The build-up to the bout by the local promoter, Victor Breyer, was amazing. The talk was all over Paris about the battle to take place at the Cirque de Paris.

It was an extremely important match for both McVea and I. We both knew that a world championship match with Johnson and a career payday most certainly awaited the winner of the bout.

I trained vigorously for the fight. The following was my training regimen:

---

[153] *La Vie au Grand Air* February 6, 1909.
[154] *La Vie au Grand Air* February 6, 1909.

7am- I wake up.
8am- Running, foot chases, high jumps and long jumps.
11am- Lunch in the company of my wife and child.
2pm- Punching the ball for a quarter hour, shadow boxing for ten minutes, sparring (aiming at the arms and neck) for ten minutes, practicing for a quarter hour with two-ounce gloves, hard sparring for twenty or thirty minutes with three sparring partners, taking turns, using four-ounce gloves.
4pm- Soak and massage.
5pm- Take a walk.
630pm- Dinner
10pm- Go to sleep.
Such is the schedule that I invariably keep when I am preparing to fight. I have not had to modify my training in a long time. I will finish with this advice: avoid all temptations, avoid all excesses. And this is, without any doubt, the most difficult part of training.[155]

I ran every morning while Jim Pratt followed behind me in his car with Mr. Fred Egan and Mr. G. Mayer, with Dan McKetrick behind them on horseback. Dan loved riding horses and Pratt loved raising them.

The morning of the affair, after weigh-ins, I had my usual pre-fight breakfast which consisted of three poached eggs, dry toast, and orange juice. For lunch I had a salad with asparagus, cauliflower, and spinach, along with a cup of tea. My dinner, which I always ate three hours before leaving for the arena, was a rare steak along with a raw salad and a banana. I chewed the steak and swallowed the juice before spitting out the meat. As usual I avoided all milks, creams, and butters as they sit in your stomach and do not dissolve quickly. As with all my bouts, Dan had Willie Lewis or some other trusted person go out to order my food or buy the needed groceries. We were very cautious of attempted poisoning of my food or water. The buildup to the match had reached peak proportions as described by Mortane: *The great day finally has arrived! It is indeed today, in the Cirque de Paris, that the question of superiority between Joe Jeannette and Sam McVea will be solved in a final way. Never, in France, was a match preceded with more verbal sparring matches and epistolary. Everyone, even those who know nothing about boxing, especially those, have given their opinion, on which one would be the winner and why.*

In the Vie au Grand Air, faithful to our policy, we have preserved our whole independence. After having published the list of the principal performances of each adversary, we have explained why our preference went with Joe Jeannette rather than with Sam McVea.

We must acknowledge, however, that Sam will be a hot favorite. Why? Because he has demolished with an extreme ease all of the men of third order who opposed him. However, these victories were enough: the French public believes he is absolutely invincible. And, as I said it in the last edition, we remembered the same fact, at the time of the Lewis-

---

[155] *La Boxe* 1910, Counsels of Joe Jeannette, pg. 198.

Stanton match. *Willie Lewis, a man of great class, was not in Paris for two months, everyone knew little about him and no one wanted to study his record. This record would have shown that Stanton could not survive in front of him. Stanton, certainly, was a boxer of value, but of second order in America. He did not have any major victories.*

Only, he had beaten Dick Bailey, Peter Brown, Costello, Tiger Smith, Pat Daly, and that was enough for the French sportsmen. They concluded from it at once that he would also overcome Lewis. This one was easy, in the fifth round of their match, Lewis proved to us the exactitude of the forecast of the Vie au Grand Air and all those which had taken the care to study the performances of the two involved athletes.

I believe that we will see, this evening, a replication of the Lewis-Stanton match. Obviously, Sam McVea is a good boxer, a very good boxer, but, on paper, is he better than Joe Jeannette? Besides the three defeats which were inflicted on him by Jack Johnson, his record is not brilliant. These failures were very honorable, since Sam went 20 rounds each time, was beaten twice by points and the third time by knock-out. While Joe Jeannette has met Jack Johnson six times. The result of these engagements is as follows: 3 without decision, 1 victory by a foul, 1 null match, 1 defeat.

As well, since their last match, Jack Johnson has always refused to meet him again. He is doing with Joe what Burns did with him. The career of Joe Jeannette is summarized as follows: 34 combats, including 6 victories by knock-out, 8 by points, 14 matches without decision, 4 null, 2 defeats.

Few men can show a record more shining. Joe Jeannette is one of the best current heavyweights. And, on paper, he cannot be overcome. In a few hours, we will know if our forecast is right. In any case, whatever the result, we wish that the best man triumphs![156]

The *Grand Air* also wrote: *It seems to us interesting to ask Marc Gaucher his opinion on the combat. The champion of France, in all categories, is in better position than anyone to make an opinion since he has been involved for a long time with both men. "I believe in the victory of Joe Jeannette," he answered us. "I saw the two adversaries fight and I have worked with both of them. I had always believed that Sam was invincible. Since I saw Jeannette at work, I have to change opinion. One cannot have an idea of the endurance, science and speed of this man. He is more quick, more scientific, and as hard a striker as Sam. Consequently, he should triumph, in spite of the large variation of weight which separates him from McVea."*

We admire the Californian because we are not yet accustomed to true boxing. But we are convinced that we have seen of him enough to know him. Moreover, it is malignant, and I guarantee you that if he felt it necessary to beat Johnson, Sam Langford, Phil. Jack O' Brien and others, he would return to America or he would find engagements more lucrative than those which he can garner from time to time in Paris. I am astonished that he has agreed to meet Joe Jeannette, since, with his victories, he has moved back in front of Tommy Burns whom Joe Jeannette would beat, as I believe it.

This opinion is interesting to note. Boxers Bob Scanlon, Herbert Synnott, Dick Green, and Piet, are all convinced that Sam McVea will triumph. We will see if their reasons

---

156 *La Vie au Grand Air* February 20, 1909.

are correct, I continue to defend the prediction that I have never stopped supporting: Joe Jeannette will win, for he is far superior to Sam McVea. And it will be interesting to see the winner of the match with Jack Johnson.

Jack Johnson, Joe Jeannette, Sam Langford, and Sam McVea make up a beautiful quartet of Negroes that want to fight for the title of champion of the world. They proved to us that... the black ones are worth more than the white ones. It is true that we will soon see arrive a fifth heavyweight, who will be Phil. Jack O'Brien who will be among us in a month.[157]

The Cirque de Paris was a wonderful place to hold fights. When I entered the arena it was filled to capacity. The way the balcony was set, it almost felt as though the fans were hanging right over the ring. I sensed that Sam knew, as I did, the enormous importance of the bout to both of our careers. This was evident in the caution we both displayed as the bout opened up. Sam had a terrific left hook and he could punch with both hands.

The large crowd on hand to witness the twenty round affair was extremely vocal. Although the Paris crowd was not as vicious as the U.S. crowd was, you would still hear the occasional shouting of: *"Kill that coon!"* along with shouts of: *"darky, nigger,"* and *"shine"* as well as other demeaning words. It was never easy swallowing those comments but I thought back to George Walker's credo of: *"No applause, just throw the money."* Knowing that I was taking their money to feed my family helped me to deal with the remarks.

I established the jab from the opening round and felt I was in control of the contest. Two times in the bout Sam got inside of my reach and landed "trip hammer" like blows that sent me to the canvas. From the second round forward my right arm muscles tightened up and the arm was in terrible pain. After the bout, my hand was raised by the referee. The locals who supported Sam started booing. The referee then put my hand down and raised Sam's.[158] I turned to Dan with a quizzical look. Dan protested but to no avail. Most in the crowd on hand booed the decision. They started throwing all sorts of items into the ring such as papers, programs, lorgnettes, opera glasses, walking sticks, hats, women's mesh bags, hatpins, and Lord knows what else.[159] Many bettors were furious over the change of the result by the referee. Besides the decision controversy, some thought Sam and I had an arrangement not to hurt each other. Can you imagine that! I was knocked down two times and some thought the fight was a fix. What more did they want, one of us dead?

Mortane wrote of the fight: *Sam McVea has triumphed by points over Joe Jeannette. There must be a rematch. In any case, your colleague admits he was wrong in his prediction. There were two knockdowns and the two antagonists took turns with the advantage until the last round, many viewers thought the fight was a draw. But no*

---

[157] *La Vie au Grand Air* February 20, 1909.
[158] *La Vie au Grand Air* December 25, 1909 pg. 482.
[159] *The 100 Greatest Boxers of All Time* by Bert Randolph Sugar pg. 174.

matter, they are not extenuating circumstances, because I was convinced that Joe Jeannette would knock his opponent out...

During the fight we were able to observe that one was much more scientific than the other, we were enthused by his feints, dodges, and agility, while Sam, who we considered the king of the fighters who fought in Paris, seemed clumsy and lacked precision. Twice, however, he managed to reach Joe on the right spot and send him to the ground. These knock downs certainly influenced the opinion of the referee. We can give the following statement of the meeting: A thinner man, a scientist, was beaten by a boxer who clapped like an anvil. His attacks were substantially equal to that of the victor, but he was knocked to the ground twice and seemed in trouble in the seventeenth round. I think this is the reason behind the referee, Mr. Watson's, decision...

I heard it said that Negroes do not want to hurt each other. This phrase... is just stupid when you saw how hard the opponents were trying to hit. I know the feelings one has towards the other and I know how much importance they attached to the victory. These were two men, two champions, who each had a great reputation to uphold and for who a defeat would be a significant loss. They wanted to show their best to the world and those who think otherwise do not know anything...

Two first class pugilists struggled to make beautiful attacks, while also artfully dodging. That is why all the shots did not reach their destination. We have finally seen a real fight, two men so close in skill to each other that right up until the end, it was unknown who would be the winner. I would be happy to see more meetings of this kind.[160]

Several reporters also thought the fight was a set-up. Some of them wrote that Sam and I had prearranged the bout. Why would I do that! I had a potential bout with Johnson for a big payday on the line. Although Dan and Willie told me not to pay attention to the crowd or the reporters, I was hurt. The last thing I wanted was for these rumors to affect my title chances. McVea received three thousand dollars and I took home two thousand for the fight. *Le Monde Illustre* magazine reported: *They say the wolves do not eat themselves; Negroes either. We saw that last Saturday at the Cirque de Paris, where the famous match between Sam McVea and Joe Jeannette was held. This meeting was slightly disappointing. Admittedly it was a good storm, but nothing more. At no time, was it exciting, we realized the opponents did not want pity: they were content to fight scientifically, but would have been apologetic had they hurt each other. At no time did one or the other fighter appear to have this fire in their attack, the fury that their impressive muscles could support.*

And yet these two champions are really wonderful athletes, amazing boxers. Their styles are quite different. Jeannette is more lively, more feline, Sam more powerful, more varied. Jeannette is better at the dodges and the feints and Sam at the attack and the parry.

The first seventeen rounds, three minutes each, were conducted without the benefit of a mark on either antagonist. Joe Jeannette was perhaps a bit more lavish moving forward with impetuosity, but Sam landed the more terrible direct hits, and swung at Jeannette

---

[160] *La Vie au Grand Air* February 27, 1909.

with a smile on his lips.

In the eighteenth round Jeannette had a slight malfunction which was quite short, Sam McVea slightly overpowered, and the last three rounds were even. Jeannette protested when the Arbitrator, Mr. Watson, proclaimed Sam, who looked almost as fresh as the start, the victor.

Is it necessary to add how substantial the crowd was? We could not find an empty seat in the vast confines of the Cirque: the biggest figures in the world of sports, literature, and arts were all present, and the revenue reached a record 85,000 francs, of which the winner received 20,000 ($3,000) francs and Joe Jeannette 15,000 ($2,000) francs.[161]

We immediately set out to sign a contract for a return bout. One might wonder why McVea would sign to box me again after the victory. Dan was one of the shrewdest managers in boxing. He convinced McVea's manager that if Sam and I did not box again and erase the negative publicity of our performances, neither one of us would get a chance at the world title. He said that if it was widely believed that we were just going through the motions to make a payday it would negatively affect both of our careers. Some were saying that two black fighters would never go all out against each other, and they used our bout as an example. The return bout was set for April 17 in Paris and it would once again be for the colored heavyweight title.

After the McVea fight, Willie and Dan noticed I was feeling down. They talked Addie into letting them take me out for a "boy's night" on the town. It took them more time talking me into going out than convincing Addie to let me out. Our first stop was the famous Moulin Rouge with the big red windmill on the roof. Inside the club the music was loud and the girls were very risqué. On stage, courtesans would perform the can-can dance while exposing their breasts and lifting their skirts. Willie introduced me to "Coco" Chanel, who sang at the club, and "La Goulue," The Queen of Montmartre, who was a famous can-can dancer. "La Goulue" did not perform at the club anymore but she stopped by on occasion for a night out. We watched Jane Avril, another famous can-can dancer perform. After about an hour and a half I told Willie I was bored and wanted to head home. Willie could tell I wasn't enjoying myself and agreed that we should leave. Willie told Dan and I that he knew of a place where it was guaranteed that we would have a good time. We went to a private villa where everyone knew Willie by first name. Willie told me that we were going to see a famous performer who rivaled Harry Houdini. The performer was Joseph Pujol or *Le Petomane* as he was called. The name *Le Petomane* in English meant fartomaniac. His profession was *flatulist* or *farteur*. At the entrance I tried to turn around and leave but Willie grabbed me with tears in his eyes from laughing, and through a crackling voice said: *"Please Joe, you gotta see this,*

---

[161] *Le Monde Illustre* February 27, 1909 by E.H.

please!" I took a seat next to Dan and someone stood and announced: *"Now I give you the great Le Petomane."*

Pujol began his performance by placing a candle on a table. He walked several yards away, turned, and gave the audience a serious stare. The room was silent. He then quickly turned around dropped his pants and proceeded to blow out the candle from several yards away with a fart! The crowd was hysterical with laughter. I have to admit I laughed myself. Pujol then ordered us to be silent. He then placed a bottle on a wooden crate. He was handed a pan of water which he put on the floor. Pujol then pulled down his pants and sat on the pan. He then got up and proceeded to shoot water out of his rectum, knocking over the bottle with water he had inhaled. The crowd went berserk again. Pujol ordered quiet once more. *"Now,"* he said, *"for the grand finale!"*

Pujol pulled down his pants and inserted a rubber tube called an ocarina into his anus and proceeded to play "O Sole Mio" from his anus. Once again the audience went wild. I have to admit Willie did get my mind off of the McVea fight. When I returned home to Addie I told her we went to Moulin Rouge but I never mentioned *Le Petomane* to her. She probably wouldn't have believed me anyway.

On March 13 Willie was scheduled to box a ten rounder against Steve Smith of England. Smith had a poor record of only one win in four bouts to Willie's fifty-six bouts. These types of bouts can be dangerous because it can be difficult to work up that needed motivational anxiety which makes your punches and defensive movements crisp and fast. Willie was usually good at avoiding this pitfall but the day of this fight he made a huge error in judgment.

Willie and I were very popular in Paris. Whenever we walked the streets people would approach us with words of encouragement. Willie took a prefight walk to relax and he ran into some boxing fans who recognized him and asked him to join them. They stopped in a cafe and someone ordered a round of drinks. Willie did not usually drink when in training and especially not the day of the fight, but after several attempts to bypass the offer he agreed to have one. The drink was absinthe, or the "green fairy" as the locals called it. The drink was made of herbs and it had a natural green color and a high concentration of alcohol in it. Willie did not know that the innocent-looking pale green drink had a terrific kick.[162]

One drink quickly turned into twelve. As fight time approached, Willie miraculously found his way into the arena. I was busy being swarmed with reporters about the McVea rematch and I did not notice Willie's obvious intoxicated state. Dan didn't notice it either as he was busy drumming up the McVea rematch. When Dan started wrapping Willie's hands he smelled

---

[162] *Bill Stern's Favorite Boxing Stories* pg. 16.

the alcohol and noticed Willie was drunk. After screaming at Willie, Dan said he was calling off the fight. Willie pleaded with Dan that he was fine. He talked Dan into letting him fight because Smith was easy to beat, and more importantly, Willie needed the money. When Willie made his way into the ring we thought everything would work out okay. After the fighters touched gloves, Willie came back to our corner and asked what round it was. Right there we should have known we were in trouble. The bell rang for the first round. Willie walked right up to the referee and shook his hand. The referee looked puzzled. Willie then cocked his right hand and knocked the ref out cold. The crowd was hysterical with surprise and laughter. *"That's one way to change refs!"* Someone yelled.

As the unconscious referee was carried from the ring and a replacement was being looked for, Dan looked at me with his mouth wide open. I could do nothing but shrug. We called Willie back to the corner and told him he was in no shape to fight and we were going to stop the fight. Willie turned away from us and started pumping his hands in the air, working up the sporting crowd.

We tried to talk to Willie in the corner but he told us not to worry. He said that he was fine. He said he made the mistake of hitting the referee because of the poor lighting in the arena. The lighting looked fine to me. Once again Dan threatened to stop the fight but Willie would have none of it. Finally, a new referee, Emile Maitrot, was located and the bell was clanged again. For the next ten rounds Willie alternated between attacking his opponent and chasing the poor referee around the ring. The ref was screaming: *"No, monsieur! I am not the man you are fighting! There is the man you want to hit! I am the referee! Oh, mon dieu, this crazy American is trying to kill me!"*[163] To which Willie replied: *"Come on, Frenchy! Let's give the people a show! Put up your fists and fight!"*[164]

The crowd roared with laughter round after round. The fans were enjoying the show so much, when they saw Willie dancing around the ring, they started singing the song: *"Waltz me around again, Willie. Around, around, around!"* When the final bell clanged the referee looked more relieved than Willie's opponent. To top it off, Willie was awarded the decision! Smith was content to cover up, block, and just survive the fight. When he did lead, Smith's punches had no sting on them. Willie, who dropped Smith several times, hurt his right hand early in the contest. The reporters had no idea that Willie was intoxicated during the fight but Dan begged them not to print that Willie had attacked two referees. He told them Willie had taken a lot of punches in sparring and wasn't quite himself.

Reporter Mortane wrote: *People who did not attend the ten round combat have no idea of the savage energy spent by Lewis, trying with all his force to finish and knock out*

[163] *Bill Stern's Favorite Boxing Stories* pgs. 16-18.
[164] *Bill Stern's Favorite Boxing Stories* pgs. 16-18.

Steve Smith. He could not reach that point, but the result was even more beautiful than if he did score a knock out.[165]

After the match we led Willie back to his hotel room, where he slept like a baby. The next morning, besides his hangover, Willie had no recollection of the previous night's fisticuffs. Needless to say, Willie never touched absinthe again. I began preparation for my April 17 return bout with McVea.

On March 10, Jack Johnson returned to the ring in Vancouver, British Columbia. His title would not be on the line. He boxed a six round exhibition bout against Victor McLaglen, dropping McLaglen in the first round, then carrying him the rest of the way.[166] McLaglen would go on to have a successful acting career, earning an Academy Award in the movie *The Informer.* Johnson looked heavy and out of shape in the match, but he did earn five thousand dollars for his efforts. I was watching Jack's every move now. I hounded Dan on a daily basis to make a match with Johnson. I was not the same fighter who had faced him early in my career and I wanted a chance to show the boxing world what I could do.

"Young" Otto arrived from New York and joined us at Neuilly. His real name was Arthur Susskind. He was called the "King of the Knock Out" because he had twenty-seven first round knockouts and forty-four total knockouts in fifty-eight fights. In 1905 Otto had a string of fifteen first round knockouts, from May until October. Otto debuted in Paris by knocking out George Proctor in the third round of their scheduled ten round bout on March 21 at the Wonderland.

In France, Dan purchased a white horse called Snowy. The horse had won first place in a horse show in Wales. Dan was planning on entering Snowy in horse shows in Paris.

Addie was pregnant with our second child. The papers were talking up a storm about which white fighter could beat Johnson. They even mentioned Stanley Ketchel as a potential threat to Jack. Stanley Ketchel! He was a great middleweight fighter, but he was just that, a middleweight. I was the one who deserved the title shot, not Ketchel.

The articles were finally signed for a McVea rematch. Originally, we were going to box forty rounds, but to help promote the event, it was agreed the fight would be a finish match. Finish matches were now outlawed in most countries. Dan was hoping a finish fight would garner much needed press and ticket sales. Dan also hoped it would minimize reporters writing about our last match being a fix. It was very difficult to prepare for a finish fight. I wanted to box enough rounds in training camp to have the stamina needed to win the fight, but I did not want to over-train and leave my fight in the gym.

---

[165] *La Vie au Grand Air* March 20, 1909.
[166] *Champions of the Ring* by Gerald Suster pg. 60.

127

I never sparred more than ten rounds a day in training. I ran eight to ten miles a day and performed an hour of calisthenics. I trained on the pulley bars and the light and heavy bags. Willie and I worked on defensive and offensive moves, over and over. Dan tied my feet twenty inches apart to help me with my balance. I walked around the gym on my hands to help with my upper body strength and to help me withstand blows to the chin. To build up my stomach muscles I leaned back off of a chair, face up, and I let sparring partners take turns punching my abdomen.

Jack Johnson

Sam McVea

Joe Jennette & Sam McVea promotional photo, Paris, France, circa 1909.

Jennette knocking out Ben Taylor KO-3 Paris, France, January 23, 1909.

Depiction of a Kentucky lynching in French magazine *Le Petit Journal*, circa 1909.

McVea (L) and Jennette clinching during February 20, 1909, 20-round bout.

Joe Jennette down for 9-count in 21st round of 49-round finish fight, April 17, 1909.

Jennette on floor taking count in 19th round of 49-round bout, April 17, 1909.

Official program from April 17, 1909 "finish fight."

133

Artist depiction of Joe Jennette fighting Sam McVea
from April 17, 1909 "finish fight" program.

Sam McVea (L) and Jennette square off during 30-round bout December 11, 1909.

Jennette throws his son in air as Mrs. McKetrick looks on, Paris, circa 1909.

Joe Jennette & Marc Gaucher practicing "catch as catch can" wrestling, Paris, France, circa 1909.

Billy Elmer in his fighting pose, circa 1890s.

Jennette poses in parents' yard, circa 1909.

Joe Jennette clowning with friends in Paris. Notice how Jennette is holding photo of his two children. From L to R; Jacques Mortane, Joe Jennette, John Kelly, Henri Piet, Charlie Hitte, and Marc Gaucher, circa 1909.

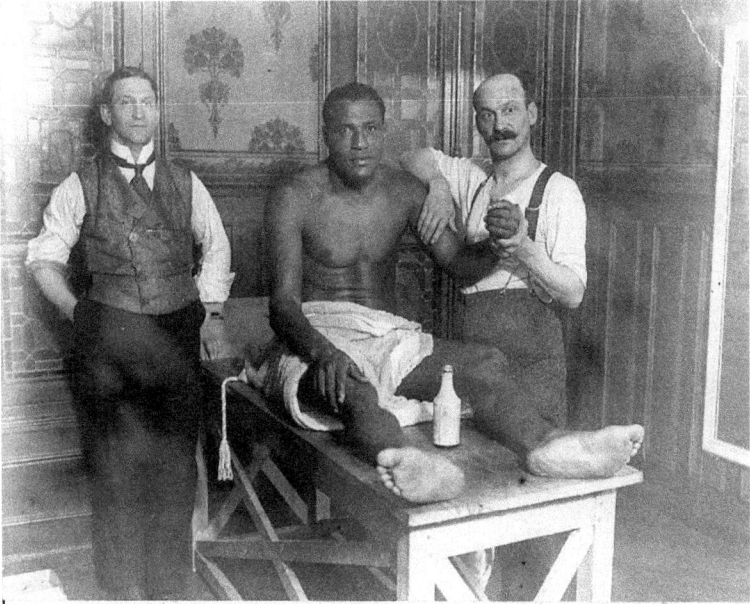

Joe Jennette receives a rub down. Trainer Gus Wilson on left, circa 1909.

Joe Jennette, Dan McKetrick, & Jim Pratt, Paris, France, circa 1909.

Joe Jennette poses in his mother's yard in the Homestead, New Durham section of North Bergen, N.J., circa 1909.

Family members wishing Joe Jennette good luck & success on his Paris voyage, circa 1909.

Joe Jennette in his automobile, circa 1909.

Joe Jennette attempts to get his son Joie to look at the camera.
Paris, France, circa 1909.

Toweling off after training for Sam McVea fight April 1909.

Chapter 13
The Match without Mercy

I needed to avenge the loss to McVea in order to generate interest in a Johnson rematch. A Johnson fight would give us the opportunity to make enough money to buy our own home. My family depended on me making this fight a victorious one. The purse for the McVea return bout was 30,000 francs, or six thousand dollars U.S., that would be split between McVea and I, three thousand dollars each. After Dan took his cut and I paid Willie for helping to work the corner, I would end up with about two thousand dollars. The purse would go a long way towards getting us the home we wanted.

I started appearing on several cigarette sports cards. It was exciting to see my name and likeness on the tobacco cards. Once again my name was misspelled. By this time I gave up complaining to Dan about the misspellings. Some of the cigarette cards I appeared on were Ogden's, Copes, Will's, Cohen & Weenen, Scissors, and Mecca. I quit smoking cigarettes when I began boxing but I made sure any friends that did smoke saved my card for my kids. That is if they were lucky enough to get my card in their pack or mail order.

Upon arrival in Paris I immediately set out for my revenge on McVea. I knew that I was in great shape, but this would be my first finish fight, so I was still very nervous. I had heard many stories of finish fights of the past and how boxers had died or suffered serious injuries in those battles. Some of the rumors that circulated suggested that boxer deaths were caused by the fighter over-eating too close before a bout and not digesting his food properly. Others thought deaths were caused from the boxer not controlling his stress level and being over-excited before the bout.

I heard the story of how Andy Bowen was killed in a finish fight over ten years earlier. His death was blamed on an indigestion ailment, not on the fact that when he went down he hit the back of his head on an unpadded ring floor. I was told how he was unconscious in his dressing room after being knocked out and although he was unconscious, through pure reflexes, he was still blocking and throwing punches as he lay dying on the rubbing table. He was swinging as though he was still boxing in the ring.

I could immediately see the impact Sam McVea had on Paris from his recent decision victory over me. There were giant billboards with McVea's black caricature on it. He was smiling next to a battered and beaten white fighter. The advertisement was for Sen-Sen chewing gum. On the ad a quote attributed to McVea stated: *Me always winner, always smiling, never knocked out, because me always chewing.*[167]

---

[167] *L'Auto* March 28, 1909 "After the Match-Sen Sen Chewing Gum."

McVea's meteoric rise in France was described by a newspaper reporter: *As he won fight after fight he became more and more idolized. Crowds followed his carriage in the streets. Noblemen invited him to their estates and were proud to dine with him in the cafes along the boulevard. Much feminine adulation too, had McVey. Jeannette (is) the opposite of McVey. He is well educated, quiet, gentlemanly and unassuming. He (is) as handsome as McVey is ugly. He has fine features, almost Arabic in type. He only weighs some 175 pounds against McVey's 205.*[168]

This bout would be France's second boxing contest of forty-five rounds or more. The first was a forty-five round draw between Henri Piet and Adolphie Cocu.

Boxers can tell when their reflexes are peeked for a fight. They call it "being in the pink." Adelaide would tell me I would flinchingly parry and throw punches in my sleep. I guess when your nerves are peaked for battle it is a natural muscular occurrence. I have personally witnessed boxers knocked out in the ring, lying on their backs, still throwing punches as though they were doing battle. Unaware that they already lay victim to the ending that all boxers fear the most, but never seem to want to talk about. No matter how many ring deaths occur each year, talk of them is mostly avoided as taboo in boxing gyms.

When word spread that Paris would be hosting a "finish fight," many English and American sportsmen started buying tickets. Finish fights were becoming extinct, and this helped to sell tickets.

I trained for the McVea fight at Jim Pratt's Neuilly estate again.[169] Pratt was a good friend of Willie Lewis'. Pratt was very wealthy and had estates all over the continent. Dan had appointed Willie my chief trainer and he brought in Frank Moran and Jim Stewart to be my sparring partners. Pratt built a beautiful gymnasium for training. There wasn't enough room in the building for the ring so it was set up outside in the open air. A young, skinny Georges Carpentier hung around during training, always asking questions. Carpentier was only 15-years-old but he already had eleven professional fights. He turned professional at age 14.[170] Dan and I both thought he was much too young to be fighting professionally. He couldn't have weighed much more than 100 pounds at the time. Willie and I gave Georges many pointers during our breaks in training. I gave Georges a lot of conditioning tips and Willie taught him the American boxing technique. Willie taught Georges the importance of the jab and combination punching. Willie called it the one-two or *un due* in French. In between my serious training I would lace on the gloves and spar with the young Carpentier.

During one of my training sessions Carpentier walked in as I was walking around the gymnasium on my hands. When I finished, Carpentier

[168] Untitled Article from Joe Jeannette's scrapbook April 18th 1909. Courtesy Ben Hawes.
[169] *Evening Telegram* January 7, 1923 pg. 9 Willie Lewis Interview.
[170] *Shake Hands & Come Out Fighting* by L.A.G. Strong pg. 109.

approached me and asked: *"For what do you do such a thing?"* I responded: *"Well, my boy, I'll tell you. By turning yourself upside down you so employ and test your brain centers so that when you are hit on the jaw your head is less likely to go spinning round. No man alive can keep his feet if he is hit properly and heavily on the point: but if you will follow this particular exercise which means that I shoot my feet in the air and walk round on my hands, you become less susceptible to that kind of drunkenness which is induced by a clip on the jaw."*[171] Carpentier thanked me for my advice. I was always the type to break from the stereotypical training methods if I felt an exercise could help me in battle. If Willie and I would have known then that we would both fight Carpentier in the future, maybe we wouldn't have taught him so much.

McVea was training at the White Hart Hotel. There was a training facility set up in the barns behind the hotel for him. On the morning of the 17th I went through my regular prefight routine. The weigh-in went as usual. McVea had weighed in at 201 pounds to my 184 pounds.[172] Although I already knew the importance of the bout, Willie and Dan kept reminding me of it over and over again. After lunch I went for a walk with Willie to loosen up my legs and take in some fresh air.

I picked up a copy of *La Vie au Grand Air*. Jacques Mortane discussed the bout and why it was not necessary: *It is this evening, at the Cirque de Paris, that the revenge of Sam match will be disputed. Like all large matches, the combat of this evening made much ink. Most of this ink could have been saved without regret... It is well known that this meeting is not essential. Why? The reasons I will give are too puerile to have fun to discuss them.*

An unquestionable fact, an indubitable fact for all true sportsmen, for all those who like the sport and who do not mix their convictions with mercantile thoughts, it is that this match is not essential any more. This revenge is obligatory, and it would have been remiss of the sporting tradition not to organize it...

The two men are equals of each other, which is why it was interesting to require that they had to combat to the finish. Twenty-five rounds were not enough, in that time they could not make an appreciable advantage. Only a match without mercy could give us an exact idea of the superiority of one of the two men. Who will triumph? After the first bout, rationally, it would be necessary to answer Sam McVea. But the science of Joe Jeannette is such, his dodgings are so brilliant, that I persist to believe that it is extremely possible that he will take a bright revenge. Moreover, it is of importance, in the first match, a muscle injury to his (Jeannette's) arm, in the second round, handicapped him and prevented him from doing what he wanted. But I will state that I am less sure of myself than I was two months ago.[173]

The magazine also displayed several photographs of Sam and I. I was playing with my son Joe Junior while Sam was relaxing, playing piano and

---

[171] *Weekly Irish Times* March 14, 1931 pg. 3.
[172] Measurements from Official Program Sam MacVea vs. Joe Jeannette April 17, 1909.
[173] *La Vie au Grand Air* April 17, 1909 by Jacques Mortane pg. 251.

guitar with his Caucasian wife.

At nine o'clock we arrived at the arena and I pulled two chairs together. I laid towels out on the chairs and pulled my feet up to relax. Willie was in charge of watching the water bottles so no one could "slip the peter" to me. Dan was out in the arena wheeling and dealing. Willie had just won a decision seven days prior over Englishman Jewey Smith. He had been fighting steadily in Paris since January, winning all seven of his bouts. Willie now had sixty pro fights and was eyeing the British welterweight championship held by "Young" Joseph.

There were five preliminary bouts and they were all four round affairs.[174] Georges Carpentier and his trainer-manager Francois DesCamps tried to get in to watch the fight for free. They thought because Georges had fought for the promoter he would give them passes. The promoter kicked them out onto the street.[175] They wound up listening to the cheers of the crowd from outside the arena.

Dan came back into the dressing room at about ten forty-five and I started going through my pre-fight stretching routine. First I stretched out my legs and arms. Then I loosened up my neck muscles and jaw bone. Dan wrapped my hands, spitting water between each layer of gauze to pack the wraps in like a cast. The gauze was hard as a rock because Dan had saturated the bandages in a solution of gun cotton and whiskey.[176] Dan then compacted the gauze with insulation tape. Dan went through his check-list of supplies. One large sponge for the face and one smaller sponge for the mouth area. Both sponges were in a large bowl. Two towels and one bottle of alcohol.[177] The alcohol was for cuts and muscle tightness. Usually we had one or two bottles of water, but today, due to the possibility of many rounds, Dan had ten bottles of water. Dan left the room and came back in wheeling a tank on a hand truck. I asked him what the tank was for. He told me that because we were fighting a finish fight the French Boxing Commission was allowing both fighters to use oxygen. I had never observed anyone use oxygen in a boxing match before.

McVea made his way into the arena around eleven-fifteen. As I waited at the doorway of the dressing room Sam starting bouncing down the aisle. Nearly the entire audience stood and looked on. Someone in the crowd starting singing the French National Anthem, "La Marseillaise." Before long, all the French fans joined in: "Allons enfonts de la Patrie, Le jour de gloire est arrive!, Contre nous de la tyrannie, L'etendard sanglant est leve!" Or in English: "Ye sons of France, awake to Glory, Hark, Hark! What myriads bid you arise! Your children, wives and white-haired grandsires, Behold their tears and hear their cries!"

---

174 Official Boxing Program, MacVea versus Jeannette, April 17, 1909.
175 *Anaconda Standard* March 21, 1920; *Atlanta Constitution* May 21, 1920.
176 *The Big Black Fire* by Robert H. DeCoy, pg. 44.
177 *'La Boxe'* 1910 "Les Devoirs D'un Second" by Dan McKetrick pgs. 222-3.

McVea really was the "Idol of Paris." They had adopted him for their own. When Sam entered the ring he took a seat on his corner stool. As I entered the arena of the Cirque de Paris the aroma was overwhelming. The aisles that led to the ring were adorned with all types of beautiful flowers.[178] I took a deep breath and was consumed by the smell of the gourdons, irises, roses, and of course the lilies, or *fluer-de-lis* as the French would call them, that decorated the aisles in large urns. My Addie loved Iris butter, which is made from the rhizomes of the Iris plant. If the sporting crowd on hand knew that I was thinking about flowers as I walked to do battle they would have thought I was insane. You could hear a pin drop as I made my way down the aisle. Willie, who already had a few drinks, started shouting out his own tune: *"I'm a Yankee Doodle Dandy, A Yankee Doodle do or die."* Before Willie hit the second line all of the American and English fans started singing along: *"A real live nephew of my Uncle Sam's, born on the Fourth of July. I've got a Yankee Doodle sweetheart, she's my Yankee Doodle joy. Yankee Doodle came to London, just to ride the ponies, I am a Yankee Doodle Boy!"*

The atmosphere was electric. The French fans were backing Sam and the English and American fans were backing me. Willie had sung in a church choir as a child and he still knew how to carry a note. The Parisians were all dressed in formal attire. The men wore suits and bow ties and the women wore long dresses with large bonnets on their heads. In the United States, women rarely attended fights. When they did they usually had to dress as men to hide their gender. I bounced down the aisle behind the singing Dan and Willie while drinking in the atmosphere. Dan best described the Parisians' buzz for boxing: *"This city has the fight bug in its bonnet and the craze is even greater than ever... One of the good points is that not only a male portion of the family are fans but also the female, for just as one takes his wife or sweetheart to the theater so does he take in the bouts, and in many instances the men take their mothers. What a sight it is. No rowdyism, no shouting and no caustic remarks. On the contrary the spectators wait until the round is over to show their appreciation of the boxers' efforts and then they wave their handkerchiefs and clap their hands or shout Bravo! And what good sportsmen they are. The loser, if he puts up a game fight, is as well received at the end as the victor...*

"As a sight, it reminds me of the opera. It is bad form to attend in anything but evening clothes, and the ladies are all in décolleté. Only those that are in the cheap seats, or what we term 'gallery gods,' are not attired in their 'happy' suits. Only two clubs are going, and only one is considered the 'place' by the fans. That is the one operated by the people who have the best boxers under contract. The other is a small place, and caters to the mob, while the rival organization is patronized by the smart set. The bouts are held on Saturdays. When the event is a big one it is held at the Cirque de Paris, while the small shows are held at the Wonderland. The Cirque is the finest boxing hall in the world. It

178 *Evening Telegram* January 7, 1923, pg. 9; Willie Lewis Interview.

seats 6,500, with standing room for several thousands more. It is a sort of cyclorama, and the ring, which is in the center, is surrounded by four rows of seats. These are for the 'swells,' and they cost about 100 francs each, and more if the bout is a big one such as... Jeannette-McVea... Around these seats comes a row of boxes. Each box holds seven persons, and they are sold as one. The price is 300 francs. Then for the remainder of the house, which is circular, the prices range according to location. All the seats are of a turquoise blue, with plush backs of a lighter color, and with brass trimmings. It is certainly a pretty place, and every American that attends remarks at first sight. Wouldn't this make a hit in the States?"[179]

The crowd was visibly smaller than the one present at our last contest, with a lot of empty seats in the balcony or gallery area. Most of the floor seats were taken up by American and English fight fans. The lack of a sell-out was probably due to the rumors that our first fight was a setup and that two colored fighters would never fight full out for a white crowd. Many fans who attended the first match voiced their displeasure with the referee changing the verdict. Either way there was a considerable amount of empty seats in the balcony for this contest. There were approximately 2,500 fans present at the opening bell.

I finally made my way up the ring stairs and slipped under the ropes. Stepping onto the canvas I looked up, the arena was built so that people in the upper seats appeared to hang over the ring. I was glad that I was not claustrophobic or I might have run right out of the arena. I gazed at the chandeliers that adorned the arena's domed ceiling overhead.

One of McVea's seconds checked my wraps as Dan went and checked Sam's wraps. As we awaited the official announcement of the participants, Dan told me the referee was new, or green, as the sportsmen called it. His name was Emile Maitrot. He was a famous French strong man with little boxing refereeing experience. He was the substitute referee that Willie chased around the ring when he fought drunk. Maitrot was presiding over the French Propagation of English boxing in France. Sam and I were both told by Maitrot to be extra careful boxing on the inside, as far as fouls were concerned. We were given our gloves which were of the standard four-ounce size, and one of McVea's cornermen looked them over. The gloves were brand new and made by a local sporting goods manufacturer called Tunmer.[180] Tunmer supplied all the gloves for matches at the Cirque de Paris as well as the Wonderland.

Willie skinned the gloves as he put them on me. Skinning is when you use the laces to pull back the leather front of the glove as much as possible, which packs the glove's horse-hairs against the knuckles tightly. Early in my career I didn't want much gauze on my hands because I wanted my opponents to feel my power. After a couple of hand injuries I now knew

---

[179] *Washington Post* January 23, 1910, pg. 4, by Dan McKetrick.
[180] Official Boxing Program, MacVea Versus Jeannette, April 17, 1909.

better and welcomed a healthy amount of gauze on my hands. McVea was in the opposite corner and I'm sure his seconds were skinning his gloves as well.

After the announcements, and both the American and French National Anthems, the dignitaries left the ring. It was just me and Sam along with our seconds, staring across at each other. The referee called us to the center of the ring and Willie led me out to where the instructions were given. Willie was looking around and he said: *"This has got opening night at the Metropolitan lashed to the mats."*[181] He glanced around some more then added: *"There's a good forty thousand dollars in the house, Joe, and you've just got to win."*[182] We were reminded that this bout was a fight to the finish. We touched gloves and returned to our corners. Willie slipped under the ropes and whispered to me to pay close attention to McVea's lethal left hook. He also advised me: *"Feint him, Joe! Cuff him now and then about the face and threaten him, but don't land a solid punch to the head until I tell you. Keep pounding away at heart and wind. That's the way to wear him down. It will be time enough to try the jaw after you have softened him up."*[183]

Willie was worried I might break my hand on Sam's hard head. It was well documented that many boxers had broken fingers and wrists on Sam's skull.[184] Willie thought it was a better game plan to soften up McVea with body blows and save the head shots for the later rounds. A finish fight was new to all of us. Whether to start aggressively or cautiously was anybody's guess. Willie turned to McKetrick, Stewart, and Moran and screamed: *"Not a drop of water on Joe. Not one of you! It'll only stiffen him up. I'll give him water on the head if he ever gets far enough gone to demand it, but don't let a drop go on his body."*[185] The referee pointed to the time keeper, Jim Pratt, who rang the bell for round one. I could hear the French women in the crowd yell out: *"En Garde! En Garde!"*[186]

I started out strong in the first two rounds, landing many crisp jabs followed by solid straight rights, but I concentrated mostly on the body like Willie told me.[187] The action was slow, though, as we were both trying to pace ourselves for a long battle. There was a lot of feinting and clinching in the first few rounds. Sam got the better of the third and fourth by counter-punching and side-stepping. After the fourth round the crowd started yelling all sorts of insults at us because we weren't fighting at the pace they expected. I peeked over to see Sam's reaction and he was yelling back at some of the agitators.

---

181 *Evening Telegram* January 7, 1923 pg. 9 Willie Lewis Interview.
182 *Evening Telegram* January 7, 1923 pg. 9 Willie Lewis Interview.
183 *Evening Telegram* January 7, 1923 pg. 9 Willie Lewis Interview.
184 *Ring Noir* pg. 32.
185 *Evening Telegram* January 7, 1923 pg. 9 Willie Lewis Interview.
186 *St. Louis Post* May 10, 1908 "Those Lovely Prizefighters."
187 *Paris Herald* April 18, 1909.

Sam came out furiously for the fifth, no doubt spurred on by all the between-round insults. In the fifth McVea nailed me with a left to the body followed by a hard right hand under the heart. I made the mistake of looking the punch in and right behind the right was a left hook to the jaw that I never saw. I toppled over like a wet sack to the canvas. The next thing I knew I was staring at the referee's shoes. It is amazing how much detail in Maitrot's shoes I observed during those few seconds. I arose at the count of eight, more stunned than seriously hurt. Hats were sent flying in the air at ringside by McVea's supporters who thought that the fight was about to end. McVea's bettors were yelling to my supporters to ready their money for dispersal. I held on to Sam as much as possible for the rest of the round, trying to clear my head, although the referee tried in vain to keep us separated. In the corner after the round, Dan said: *"Take it easy, Joe. Let it wear off. Keep away."*[188] According to Dan I did not speak a word in the corner for the next thirty rounds.[189] Dan would later say it was because I was: *"Out as cold as a dead sardine or haddock."*[190] Dan poured some water on my head but Willie cautioned him: *"I told you not a drop of water on his body!"*[191]

In the sixth round, Sam came out like a gang buster with an angry, scowling look on his face. He swung wildly at me until I forced a clinch. In the seventh round Sam seemed to have punched himself out a bit and he was warned several times for holding my right arm. At one point in the round he grabbed my right arm with his left arm and continuously punched my face with his right. The crowd yelled all sorts of threats at McVea for his fouling tactics. The referee had to pry Sam off of me and give him a stern warning for his illegal methods.

In the eighth round I chased McVea all over the ring trying to trap him so I could land head shots. He followed back with counter hooks underneath to my mid-section. At the end of the eighth I landed a big right on McVea's jaw that really got his attention, but the bell rang before I could follow up and inflict any further damage.

I got the better of Sam in the ninth. I was beating him to the punch and I drew a trickle of blood from his nose. I started noticing he was swelling around his left eye, and I continuously tried to target that eye.

Sam came out hard for the tenth round but I landed a solid right on his swollen left eye again. Sam staggered. He didn't see the punch. I charged in and ripped a straight right to Sam's stomach and Sam doubled over in pain and fell into a clinch with me when I tried to follow up on the blow.

In the eleventh round, time had to be called as my corner worked on my right glove, which was splitting open at the seam. They used tape to hold

[188] *Utica Daily Press* October 29, 1938.
[189] *Cleveland Plain Dealer* February 9, 1942 pg. 12.
[190] *Cleveland Plain Dealer* February 9, 1942 pg. 12.
[191] *Evening Telegram* January 7, 1923 pg. 9 Willie Lewis Interview.

the glove together. In the twelfth and thirteenth rounds Sam seemed to get a second wind and was getting the better of the exchanges. Sam abandoned his wild rushing tactics and started to settle in. He was landing crisp hooks with greater accuracy and frequency.

In the fourteenth, Sam was landing crisp short hooks and crosses on the inside. During one exchange I feigned a left with my shoulder and Sam leaned into a hard right hand. The blow brought a roar from the crowd as his legs buckled. Somehow Sam recovered and lasted out the round.

Time was stopped again in the fifteenth round because my taped glove broke open again. A new glove was brought to the ring. Dan complained that if I had to put on a new glove so did Sam. He argued that Sam's right glove was already broken in. The complaint fell on deaf ears. Later in the fight, one of Sam's gloves would also tear open and have to be replaced.

In the sixteenth round, Sam dropped his head to slip under my jab. I quickly crouched and uncorked an uppercut. Sam slipped to his right and countered with a hard right cross to my jaw that dropped me. The referee picked up the count. I couldn't get the blood flowing back into my legs. The referee was up to the count of eight when the bell rang. Willie and Jim Stewart jumped into the ring and dragged me back to the corner and propped me up onto the stool.

At the end of the eighteenth round I heard a sigh from the crowd. At the time we did not know why. Later we were told that one of Sam's seconds, Bob Scanlon, lanced Sam's left eye with a razor because Sam was complaining that he could not see out of it. Scanlon not only lanced the eye but he proceeded to suck the blood out of the cut and spit it into the water bucket. Many fans in the crowd were forced to look away. Scanlon would continue this act, after every round, for the rest of the fight. After the eighteenth I was administered oxygen for the first time in the bout.[192] After a couple of inhales I felt fresh again.

By the nineteenth round, Sam was bleeding and swelling around both eyes. My confidence was building. We were both slowing up considerably but I was still beating Sam to the punch with regularity. I was utilizing my jab more. We fell into a clinch. The referee ordered us to break, and as we did, McVea snuck in a murderous left hook to my jaw. I saw a bright, white light camera flash in my eyes, but there was no camera in the ring. Sam's fist was the source of the white flash. I dropped as though struck by lightning.[193] I fell sideways and my face landed, jaw first, onto the canvas. Immediately the bees started humming inside of my head. The roar of the crowd in my ears was both magnified and muffled all at once. As I lay stretched out on the rings canvas the fans celebrated at what they perceived was the end of the contest. A newsman from England named Norman Hurst later reflected on

---

[192] *Evening Telegram* January 7, 1923, pg. 9, Willie Lewis Interview.
[193] *Thrilling Fights "The Battle of the Black Giants"* by Norman Hurst pgs. 75-80.

the punch. He said I: *"looked as dead as if shot. There was not a tremor in the bronze-colored form that sprawled inert on the white canvas."*[194]

Sam himself had no interest in watching me rolling around on the floor trying to muster up enough energy to rise to my feet. He was too busy raising his hands to the crowd in victory as the fans stood and cheered their "Paris Idol." Sam believed, as did the crowd, that I was finished for the evening. Sam began dancing around the ring to the crowd's cheers, a victory dance. Both Sam and the crowd were wrong.

Through the muffled roar of the crowd I could hear one voice shrieking in terror. My eyes zeroed in on the familiar voice and I saw Dan through my hazy vision. He was standing up holding his hands cupped around his mouth to make his voice travel farther: *"No! No! Joe!"* he yelled. He already knew what Sam and the crowd did not know. He knew that I was going to get back up and continue. He knew me better than anyone in that arena. My memory flashed back to the headline several years prior: "Jeannette Quit." I would never let reporters type those words about me again. I started hearing Bert Williams singing in my head: *When life seems full of clouds and rain, and I am filled with naught and pain, who soothes my thumping, bumping brain? Nobody...*

My legs were numb and trembling as I willed blood and strength to flow back into them. *I ain't never got nothin' from Nobody, no time!* If I was going to do this I was going to have to do it alone, right here, right now.

I felt the cool wet sensation of raindrops. I remember lying on my back, as a child in Drescher's Woods as the rain snuck through the tree leaves and trickled onto my face. Suddenly I was snapped back to reality. The water raining down on me was from Dan and Willie's sponges. They were taking advantage of the green referee Maitrot. They were soaking the sponges in water, running around the sides of the ring, and squeezing the sponges as they threw their arms out in my direction. As the water rained down on my prostrated form I could see Sam, out of the corner of my water-logged eyes, smiling to the crowd as they were crowning him victor. He was bathing in the crowd's electrified applause. He was dancing the Irish Jig in the middle of the ring. I had had the same vision in a dream several days before. I closed my eyes and I could feel myself falling deeper and deeper. Sinking into the cushioned canvas floor until it consumed me and swallowed me whole. I could hear a familiar voice calling me. It was my mother Mina. She was saying: *"You'll be late for school, Joe. I told you, you need to get to bed earlier."* I turned over in my bed, covering my ears with my pillow, but I kept hearing her: *"Let's go, Joe. You'll be late. Get up, Joe. Get up!"* Suddenly my mother's voice changed to a manly voice. It was Dan's frantic voice screaming as he banged his hands on the ring apron: *"Get up, Joe! Get up!"*

---

[194] *Thrilling Fights "The Battle of the Black Giants"* by Norman Hurst pgs. 75-80.

I was not going to let this dream become a reality. I shook my head and slowly motioned my limbs to move. I staggered to my feet as the crowd, suddenly quiet, stared on with unbelieving eyes. Sam jumped between me and my corner as he tried to prevent the water they threw from reaching me. Sam realized I had regained my senses and that I was not yet finished. He turned his frustrations towards the referee as he angrily complained about my corner's water sponging. His complaint was disregarded. He was still complaining as I stumbled upright. I began stamping up and down trying to get the needle-tingling feeling out of my feet and legs. Sam, seeing that the referee was ignoring his pleas, slowly and methodically walked up to me as a hunter would his mortally wounded game. He sized me up as I tried to balance myself upright. He wound up with all his might and delivered a crushing right to the left side of my temple. Down I went again, as Hurst described: *"with a crash that seemed to shake the very building."*[195] Again I arose.

Some fans pleaded and cried for the referee to stop the fight before I was killed, while others cheered, their craving for more violence unfulfilled. As I pulled myself erect, a stunned McVea stopped and looked down in bewilderment at his right gloved hand as if there were something wrong with it, as though it was loaded with rabbit fur. Never before had a man risen after being struck with such solid blows from Sam. Only the bell saved me from further punishment. When I stumbled back to the corner, Dan squeezed a sponge of water over my head while Willie complained: *"Let me get the towel around his neck first! I don't want him stiffening up!"* Dan shot back: *"He's out as a haddock and if he doesn't wake up he won't have to worry about being stiff cause Sam will stiffen him out for good!"*[196] Willie thought about what Dan said and dumped an entire bucket of water over my head.[197] Dan shouted to Willie: *"I thought you said no water on his body? That it would stiffen him up!"* Willie replied: *"Forget about that. Joe will be knocked out stiff if we don't wake him up and quick!"*

Ringside officials jumped up into our corner and tried to remove Willie because he threw the entire bucket of water on me, drenching the ring canvas in the process. Dan yelled at them that there was nothing in the rule books forbidding such revival techniques. I sensed that my corner might be losing control. I tried to keep myself calm. Dan put one of the oxygen tubes up against my mouth and he told me to slowly breathe in as the oxygen filled my lungs. *"Take slow breaths,"* he said. Sam's corner was also using oxygen. The oxygen helped to relax me.

After the nineteenth round, Dan implored me from the corner to clinch with Sam until my head cleared. Willie, Dan, and Jim Stewart were doing an

195 *Thrilling Fights "The Battle of the Black Giants"* by Norman Hurst pgs. 75-80.
196 *Utica Daily Press* October 29th 1938.
197 *The 100 Greatest Boxers of All Time* by Bert Randolph Sugar pgs. 174-75.

excellent job in my corner, while Sam's corner appeared to hamper his recovery efforts. I had three cornermen tending to my needs while Sam had five seconds falling over each other, and they appeared to do more harm than good. Sam's seconds were Bob Scanlon, Henri Piet, Grognet, who ran a boxing school in Paris, Jem Styles, and Sam's manager, Emil Guiller. Sam also had a healer in his corner who was smoking a black pipe.[198] The healer used vials of some type of energy booster that he injected into Sam with a syringe. He also rubbed embrocate on Sam's body.

Just before the bell rang to start the twentieth round, Willie whispered in my ear: *"Now, Joe, now... go to the head."*[199] At the start of the twentieth round I waited for Sam to punch and then I fell into a clinch with him. The referee kept stepping in to separate us. My legs were still tingling and I kept holding on as much as possible. Sam knew I was hurt and he was desperately trying to finish me.

As I attempted to fall into a clinch I made the fatal mistake of leaving my shoulders square and my chin exposed. Sam bent low and ripped a terrific uppercut. I just turned my jaw to the side in time to take away the solid impact of the blow. Still the punch had enough effect to drain me further. I kept telling myself; Joe, keep your eyes on him. Don't look down or blink.

In the gym, when I first started training with George Armstrong he told me two things that I never forgot. One, the only person who can defeat you is here, and he pointed to a mirror where I observed my reflection. Two, never take your eyes off of your opponent. He showed me this by telling me he was going to smack me in the face and then he did. He then told me to close my eyes and that he was going to smack me again. Not being prepared for the second hit made it hurt much more.

McVea rushed in with a sweeping left hook that sent me crashing down. He stood over me looking confused as I started to pull myself up again. Ringside fans were on their feet pushing towards the ring as the Paris police tried to push them back. Some were screaming for me to get up, while others pleaded for me to stay down. Once again I pulled myself up.

At the end of the twentieth round, Willie doused my head with water as Dan screamed for more water to keep me alert. It was the same pleas after every round: *"More water, Willie. Get me more water!"* I later found out that fans were complaining during the rounds because their view was being blocked. Willie had enlisted the help of several friends and they had started a bucket brigade from the corner all the way back to the shower room.[200] The manager of the Cirque complained to Dan that the fans were moaning that their view of the fight was being obstructed by the water brigade. Dan shot back: *"My fighter either gets water or the fight is over!"*

---

[198] *Ring Noir* pg. 34.
[199] *The 100 Greatest Boxers of All Time* by Bert Randolph Sugar pg. 175.
[200] *Lexington Herald* November 14, 1915 Interview with Dan McKetrick.

The manager and Dan continued screaming at each other. Willie Lewis recognized a fireman friend of mine in the audience. He asked him if he could run us a fire hose from a hydrant outside to our ring corner. The fireman said he could. Willie told Dan and the manager of his idea. All parties agreed to the fire hose. The fireman ran the hose to ringside, charged the line, and we were back in business. Both corners used the hose to fill up bottles and buckets between rounds.[201]

The twenty-first frame was more of the same. Again I was trying my best to clinch when fighting on the inside, to regain some strength. Every time Sam threw a hook or cross I slipped underneath. In the early rounds I would bob and weave back up with my own hook or cross but fatigue now prevented this. When Sam was throwing his hooks and crosses he was also timing me for an uppercut when I ducked underneath. In this round, Sam caught me clean with an uppercut and down I went. This uppercut was the hardest punch I was hit with during the bout, and I was hit with many. At this point I started thinking about why I should continue. I knew clearly now that it was very possible that I could lose my life in the ring tonight. Was this what Andy Bowen was feeling moments before he collapsed in the ring?

Each blow that landed on me was having more lingering effects. I started thinking about Adelaide and Joe Jr. and the baby we were expecting. I thought about living around the corner from the train yards as a child and being woken up by the rolling freight cars or the screaming herds of cattle they transported. I thought about the trapped goat in that freight car so long ago. I was not going to give up. I had the ability to fight my family out of poverty. I had to continue, but I didn't want to lose my life in the ring. Who would care for my family if I died? I had to fight to keep these thoughts from consuming me. I had to push such thoughts out of my head. A win tonight would put me that much closer to a Johnson bout and financial freedom. I had to utilize all of my strength to push my body and mind onward. I would not let my family down.

In the twenty-second round I found a second wind. I scored often. My head appeared to clear out the cobwebs. I was winning the frame handily when I was caught by a counter right and down I went again. I banged my glove on the ring canvas in disgust as the referee picked up his count. Why was my body letting me down? I trained so hard for this fight. This time it was more fatigue than the actual strength of the punch that knocked me down. I could hear an American fan at ringside yell: *"I'll give a million to one on McVea!"* I took the full nine-count and pulled myself up again. Why did my legs keep betraying me? Don't let me down, legs, I pleaded to myself.

In panic, Sam's corner started putting oxygen into Sam's eye after the

---

[201] *Lexington Herald* November 14, 1915 Interview with Dan McKetrick.

twenty-second round, to bring the swelling down. During the twenty-third through twenty-eighth rounds the action was back and forth, we were both surviving on adrenaline, supported by the crowd's electric roaring desire for more blood and more bone-shattering blows.

In the twenty-eighth round I hit the canvas again from one of McVea's sledge-hammer-like blows. The buzzing noise of the bees returned. I could also hear the sound of ocean waves crashing inside of my head. When I looked up at the referee, one of my eyes was focused on him while the other was staring up at the ceiling dome. I blinked several times but my one eye was still looking up. Did the referee see this? When I pulled myself up I closed my eyes hard for a second and when I opened them again my vision straightened out.

I went down several more times in the following rounds but I had already decided that if need be, I was committed to taking my final breath in this arena tonight. Dan had noticed how McVea's corner was dousing him with ice-cold water after every round.[202] Dan knew that all that cold water would stiffen up Sam's muscles. After the thirtieth round Dan grabbed my face, looked straight into my eyes, and frantically asked me if I could hold on. I replied: *"I'll hold out, Dan."*[203]

I was hurt badly again in the thirty-second round. The bees started humming inside of my head, mixed in with sounds of tin garbage can tops clashing together. The pain in my head was so great I thought at any moment my head would explode. My head felt like it had a balloon inside of it that was expanding against the walls of my skull.

At the end of the round, Dan pushed Willie aside. He cradled my head in his hands again, and looking straight into my eyes, he told me he was stopping the fight. He had tears in his eyes and his voice was trembling. I looked back into his eyes and told him if he tried I would fire him. He asked me how I felt and I answered as all boxers are conditioned to answer: *"I feel good."* Why do managers even ask that question? From the first day a boxer enters a gym he is conditioned to repeat the same three words: *I feel good.* The boxer learns very quickly that saying anything else might cause his seconds to stop the fight. If a boxer has bled every ounce of blood in his body he would still whisper those same three words. If Andy Bowen could have spoken as he lay flinching, dying in the dressing room, he would have spoken those same three words: *I feel good.*

I fought much better in the thirty-third round. It was one of my best rounds in a long while. I started noticing that Sam's punches did not have the sting that they had in earlier rounds. When I went back to my corner after the round Willie told me he thought I looked better than at any stage of the fight and that he felt I would certainly win. I answered him: *"Sure I'm*

[202] *Brooklyn NY Daily Eagle* February 2, 1933.
[203] *Brooklyn NY Daily Eagle* February 2, 1933.

going to win, Willie. Sam is losing his punch. He can't hurt me anymore."[204]

The thirty-fourth round was another devastating round for me. McVea had gotten another wind and I was trying my best to avoid his powerful swings. I got cornered and dropped for another nine-count. Sam tried hard but he couldn't put me down again in the round.

Around this time, word had spread outside the arena about the battle that was taking place inside. A crowd was gathering at the entrance. The amount of knockdowns was unheard of. Some fans inside were so tired that they left the arena, while others fell asleep during the rounds only to be awoken by the clanging of the gong as each round ended and began.[205]

From the thirty-fifth to the thirty-eighth rounds we both lost a lot of strength as well as blood. I utilized my jab well in these rounds. I was continuously targeting Sam's left eye. Sam had started the bout smiling, but that expression faded after the tenth stanza. His smile had returned after I landed a hard body shot after missing wildly to his head twice. I wondered why he was smiling. Was it because he was still standing? That we both were still standing? Some of the women in the crowd became hysterical from the carnage they were witnessing. Several of them left the arena. I remember hearing one of them shrieking as she was led out of the hall: *"Dear God somebody stop this before one of those poor boys are murdered!"*

In the thirty-ninth round I rocked McVea with a hard right hand. I followed with a crashing left hook that dropped Sam like a log.[206] Sam was dead game and was up at the count of five.

At the end of the fortieth round I sank onto the stool and asked Dan: *"What's going on here?"* Dan replied: *"You're taking the mother and father of an awful licking Joe. Do you want to go on?"* I answered: *"Yes, I feel good now. What's the round?"* Dan answered: *"It's the fortieth round."* I shot back: *"My God man. Where have I been?"*[207]

By the forty-first round, we were both drained and leaning on each other. We fell into a clinch and were both working to free up a hand to deliver liver and kidney shots as well as shots to the washboard area of the midsection. Both of Sam's eyes were swollen nearly shut. I targeted the eyes as much as possible. I wondered what was keeping Sam fighting. Was he fighting for his family? Was it purely for money? Was it pride? I landed three solid uppercuts in succession, ripping Sam's head upward with each landing blow. What was keeping Sam up? With about a minute left in the forty-first round I could feel Sam's energy draining rapidly. He was giving ground easier now. I drove him back to the ropes and landed three more hard uppercuts. I could feel my knuckle bones smash into his skull with

[204] *Evening Telegram* January 7, 1923, pg. 9; Willie Lewis Interview.

[205] *Ring Noir* pg. 34.

[206] *Evening Telegram* January 7, 1923 pg. 9 Willie Lewis Interview.

[207] *Utica Daily Press* October 29, 1938.

each blow. What was keeping him up?

At the end of the forty-first round we both staggered back to our corners. Sam clearly looked the more spent. We were both being administered oxygen in our corners. Out of pity the referee let our seconds do whatever it took to keep us going. During the last couple of knockdowns, Dan had actually thrown buckets of water over the top rope onto me. Again, the referee made no complaints. Maitrot had transformed himself from the third man in the ring to just another fan hypnotized by the event he was witnessing unfold, powerless to influence the savagery. He was pulling for both of us. He would not be the one to stop this battle. He couldn't. The crowd would break into a riot. He wouldn't be able to make it out of the arena alive if he stopped the fight.

Sam was stiffening and slowing up. When he came out for the forty-second round he moved like a mechanical doll. His leg movements were jerky and forced.[208] He was completely drenched with water by his seconds, the worst possible thing to do in a long fight. My face was virtually unmarked, but both of Sam's eyes were shut, his nose was broken in two places, and his lips were swollen to four times their normal size.

The referee and the spectators were all a part of this historic event: The fans, by their cheering for us to continue, infused our veins with adrenaline. The ref, by purposely overlooking whatever measures our corners used to keep us upright. The canvas floor in both of our corners looked as though a painter had spilled several gallons of red paint on it from all the blood we poured.

In the forty-fourth round I dropped Sam with a hard right. Sam got back up and wrestled me into a clinch. I tried to free my arms because I knew Sam was seriously hurt. Sam whispered in my ear: *"I'm all through."* I shot back: *"No, sir, you ain't. This is a finish fight and I'm gonna finish it. Keep-a-comin'."*[209] Sam continued on.

The forty-sixth and forty-seventh rounds were won by me. We had both slowed down significantly, but Sam appeared as though his will was waning. It appeared as though he could not see out of his left eye at all now. He did not or could not slip any rights that I threw. Each right I threw landed solidly behind my sweat soaked, gauze wrapped, horse-hair padded, four-ounce glove. I felt the stinging of the blows up my arm as my knuckles slammed into McVea's skull, over and over. I could feel my knuckles bury deep into Sam's swollen skin and smash up against his eye-socket bone. When my blows landed, blood squirted out from Sam's lanced eye. The thick meat under Sam's skin was exposed from his cut. What kept him up? Sam's punches had no power at all, yet his tremendous will kept his arms throwing. Were the fight fans finally convinced that two colored fighters

---

[208] *Evening Telegram* January 7, 1923 pg. 9 Willie Lewis Interview.
[209] *Utica Daily Press* October 29, 1938.

would go all out against each other?

In the forty-eighth round, I beat McVea from pillar to post. I connected with punches from all angles. I felt his energy sapping like sand through an hour glass. What was keeping him up? Dan explained what happened next: *"About halfway into the forty-eighth round, Jeanette got a left drive into the stomach of McVey, and like a flash, crossed his right over to the point of McVey's chin. Down went the powerful McVey and he was unable to do more than keep his arms up around his head for the remaining minute and a half of the round."*[210]

As the bell sounded ending the forty-eighth round Sam reached for and used the top rope to guide him back to his corner. His cornermen jumped into the ring to help assist him back to his stool.[211]

I had earlier feared and then accepted that I might die in this ring tonight. Now I contemplated that I might actually kill another man in the ring. It was close to two-thirty in the morning and the crowd sounded like a dog after several hours of barking. Their voices were as strained as my overworked lungs. Sam and I were both sucking on oxygen in our corners like it was the last air on earth. Dan was screaming through his crackled voice that Sam was ready to go at any moment now. He had made that exact same prediction at least a dozen times during the fight. I paid him no mind.

I leaned to the side to peer at McVea while Dan was attending to my muscles with alcohol. I could see Sam's chest heaving heavily as he sucked in as much air as his lungs would allow. I wondered if the air he was taking in burned as much as mine did as it made its way down my throat into my lungs. Sam won't quit. He can't quit. He is the "Idol of Paris." Sam has been the victor on many glorious nights in Paris. He is the hero of the French. His cheek bones and eyes were swollen and hammered into one congested mass. The referee yelled: *"Seconds out!"* to start the forty-ninth round.

I pulled myself off of my stool with the help of Willie and Dan and through glazed eyes I saw Sam being helped up by his seconds. He appeared to be miles away from me as I squinted at him through my swollen eyes. Sam looked like a drunken sailor as he stumbled out to meet me before the bell rang. Why was he in such a rush to start the round when the bell hadn't even rung yet!

As we neared each other in the center of the ring, the entire arena fell silent. The ringing of the bell echoed eerily throughout the building. I drew back my right arm to deliver the executioner's blow. The spectators held their collective breaths, as though watching a matador deliver the final sword to its staggering, battle weakened foe. As Sam drew closer his heavy breathing almost sounded as though he was trying to speak. I focused in on

[210] *Capitol Plains Dealer* October 18, 1936 Interview with Dan McKetrick.
[211] *Evening Telegram* January 7, 1923 pg. 9 Willie Lewis Interview.

his jaw. Throughout the battle I had looked at his face as merely a target. Now I looked at it as a human face; a defeated face. His eyes were swollen shut, his eye lids were both punctured, his nose was crushed, his mouth was bloodied and missing several teeth. His body was shaking as though he was experiencing cold chills. He was trying to speak. I could not understand him at first because my water-logged swollen ears felt as though I had soaked-cotton jammed into them. My eardrums were thumping loudly from all of the hooks and crosses Sam slammed into them. Dan later described the moment: *"The huge Californian had sensed by now that the object before him was nothing short of an iron man and in nowise anything human."*[212]

Sam reached out his gloves, apparently feeling for me through the air. Again he whispered to me. This time I could hear his words: *"You're not human, you win Joe, my eyes are closed, and I can't see you anymore: it's your fight."*[213] He continued: *"I can't see you, Joe, I can't see you, Joe, and I couldn't raise my arm to hit you if I could. I've gone as far as I can. You win."*[214]

When Sam finished speaking he reached out and shook my hand. He then collapsed face first onto the blood-smeared canvas.[215] His corner threw in the sponge signaling they were retiring their charge. They did not know Sam had already ended the affair. His corner pushed the stool back into the ring. After hundreds of punches thrown, the fight was ended by a strained whisper. Sam's cornermen rushed in and picked up their fighter, carrying him back to his stool.

The remaining crowd erupted in a tremendous roar. They rose as one. I'm sure they were cheering both of our efforts. Every ounce of vocal power that remained in their lungs was cast out over the ring in crescendo. I swallowed as I tried to force my heart to convert to a normal rhythm. As I was trying to digest what had just transpired I was slammed from behind. Willie and several other people had entered the ring and were jumping ecstatically over my back. I was pushed against the ropes where Dan jumped up on the apron by our corner and almost pulled me over the top rope in excitement. Dan was screaming at me: *"Corking good fight, Joe!"*

I tried to tell them to take it easy but my voice was too weak. Willie, finally realizing my weakened state, yelled for everyone to give me breathing room. I was led back to my corner, where I sat on the stool. I bent my head down and worked hard trying to breathe in as much air as I could. I felt a cool feeling on my head and back as a bucket of water was thrown over me. *"Is Sam okay? Is he okay?"* I whispered my query through airless crackling lungs.

As I raised my eyes up through the smoke-filled room I looked across the ring, and there sat Sam. He was sitting all alone in his corner as his seconds

---

[212] *Capitol Plains Dealer* October 18, 1936 Interview with Dan McKetrick.
[213] *Evening Telegram* January 7, 1923 pg. 9 Willie Lewis Interview.
[214] *Evening Telegram* January 7, 1923 pg. 9 Willie Lewis Interview.
[215] *Capitol Plains Dealer* October 18, 1936 Interview with Dan McKetrick.

were shaking hands with my cornermen. I wanted to go console him but my legs were without feeling. I glanced out into the crowd. Mixed in with the smiles and clapping hands I saw many of Sam's fans crying as they gazed at his limp form. His swollen-shut eyes looked like slits as he turned his head sideways to listen to the celebration in my corner.

I was bombarded by reporters wanting to know how I felt and what Sam had whispered to me. I tried not to be rude but I ended the interviews as quickly as possible. I just wanted to get back to the cottage.[216] Addie did not go to the fight because she was pregnant and watching Joie. Reporters approached Sam and he gave the following statement: *"I had no luck. I had to fight most of the time with only one eye. I failed to follow up an advantage in the nineteenth round and for the last few rounds my left eye was helpless. I had arrived at the end of my strength. I did not dope as Jeannette did. Nevertheless I was beaten. I am nevertheless glad that I did not manage to knock Joe out as he is the finest fellow I have ever met in the ring."*

I finally found the strength to pull myself up and stumble over to where Sam was sitting on his stool. He didn't see me standing over him. He was screaming at his seconds as they were removing his gloves: *"Don't lose these gloves. I want these gloves! Don't let anyone take them, Bob!"* Bob Scanlon, one of Sam's cornermen, promised to secure the sweat and blood-soaked leather mittens for Sam. I reached down and whispered in Sam's ear: *"Great fight, Sam."* Sam returned: *"You're not human, Joe. I wish I had that nineteenth round back. You're not human."* *"Great fight, Sam,"* I said again as I stumbled back to my corner.

After the official decision was read, Willie dropped me off at my cottage. Addie was wide awake, waiting for me. Dan had already visited her and told her I had won.[217] I was so sore I could not sleep. It was around four in the morning and my hands were still shaking from all of the trauma they were forced to endure. I was feeling an excited paranoia mixed with nausea from all of the head shots I had received. This was a feeling that I felt on occasion after bouts in which many hard shots were landed on my head. The bout lasted three-and-a-quarter-hours.

Around six o'clock I still couldn't sleep, so I put on my running boots and togs and went to the hotel where Dan and Willie were staying. I asked the concierge at the front desk for the mail and to lead me to Willie's room. The concierge took me to the room and knocked on the door. After several hard knocks, Dan demanded that Willie see who was knocking at such an hour. The concierge stated: *"Monsieur Jeannette is here with the mail and says he must see you."* Willie opened the door wearing his robe. He looked at me and turned back to McKetrick and said: *"Dan, it's either Joe Jeannette or his ghost!"*[218]

---

[216] *Evening Telegram* January 7, 1923, pg. 9; Willie Lewis Interview.
[217] *Newark-Star Ledger* March 11, 1956.
[218] *Evening Telegram* January 7, 1923, pg. 9; Willie Lewis Interview.

I told Willie I felt a little sore and I wanted to join him on his morning jog. I knew that Willie had a fight coming up in a week and that he would be doing his roadwork. He looked at me as though I was insane. *"Are you crazy! I got plenty of road work going up and down the stairs with the spit bucket last night!"* *"What's the matter, Willie?"* I replied. *"Aren't you going to do your road work? You know your fight with (Honey) Mellody is only five days off."*[219] I talked him into running. I wanted to breathe in the fresh morning air that comes along with a good run as this helped to alleviate the paranoid feeling that came from all the head shots.

Willie told me he had run almost five miles with all the running up and down the stairs after every round. He laughed at me and said I was crazy. Once again I reminded him that he had a fight coming up next week. He dutifully pulled on his running boots and we went for a jog. I did not want to run alone as I was still feeling nauseous from all the shots and I wanted someone with me just in case I passed out. A boxer would never speak these feelings, though, as they could bring on bad luck in the form of the thoughts coming true.

We headed off on our run and made our way through the quiet morning streets of Paris. As we worked our way back to the hotel we passed the Cirque de Paris. As I jogged past the main entrance I saw a canvas poster advertising my battle with McVea. I told Willie to go ahead and I stopped and stared at the promotional poster. Overnight my face had swollen and my left eye was nearly shut. I looked around to make sure that no one was looking. I ripped down the poster from the gate to which it was tied. I folded it up and tucked it inside my waist band. I took another look at the exterior of the hall. Flashbacks from the fight started rewinding in my head. I closed my eyes and could see the referee standing over me counting.

After I opened my eyes I saw several people approach a custodian at the door of the arena. I could hear them tell the custodian that they attended the fight the night before but left before it ended. They asked if the fight was still going on! I started laughing to myself. After several moments of reflection I turned and jogged back towards the hotel. After the run I returned to my room and slept. After I awoke I picked up the *Paris Herald*, which had a nice write-up on the fight. I borrowed scissors from the front desk clerk to cut out the article. I noticed I could not keep my hands steady. They were shaking uncontrollably, no doubt from all of the trauma they endured punching Sam's hard head the night before. I asked Addie to cut out the article and she did so. I placed the article and the poster from the fight safely in my suitcase. I would place them in my scrapbook when I returned home.

Dan told me how the states were abuzz with talk of our three-and-a-

---

[219] *Evening Telegram* January 7, 1923 pg. 9 Willie Lewis Interview.

quarter-hour marathon bout. He assured me the publicity of the bout would force Jack Johnson to meet me. My bout with McVea was being called the greatest fight in France since John L. Sullivan and Charlie Mitchell fought a 39 round draw in Chantilly in 1888. Later the same day, I accepted a request to fire the starter pistol to begin a bicycle race between Victor Dupre and Thorwald Eelegaard at the Buffalo Velodrome. The race took place late in the afternoon.

The *Universal Sports Illustre* magazine wrote the following about the battle: *The rematch of these two great fighters was not only the best we've seen in France, but perhaps the toughest and wildest in the history of boxing worldwide. The Burns-Johnson fight in Sydney, was faster, but certainly no more cruel, and lasted much shorter. "I do not think so," writes George Dupuy, "from what we learned from the news, that Burns was found at the end in worse shape than McVea, the Negro was tough skinned, leaving after half past two, one eye completely closed, his eye lids punctured, his nose crushed, his mouth toothless and bloody, a crushed left wrist, a dislocated right shoulder and his body shaking with fever, while Jeannette's figure did not have a scratch, not on his face or chest. McVea, gifted with incredible strength, is certainly one of the best men presently who can endure punishment at least as easily and stoically as Sharkey did in his prime. So what can we say of the value of Jeannette? My impression is that Johnson would not have come after McVea as fast as Jeannette did, that Jeffries would succumb to McVea in a few rounds, and finally that Johnson would probably beat Jeffries, for one and the other, the greatest difficulty would be in crushing Jeannette, because of his beautiful craftsmanship and his disconcerting vitality. Joseph Jeannette is a fine boxer in every sense of the word. Older, wiser, and finer than McVea, more courteous and accurate too. I do not think Jeannette, if McVea was on the ground, would rush forward to prevent aids from throwing water on the face of their man... This is precisely what made McVea, among other things, show a lack of self-control during the battle.'*[220]

Later that evening, Dan told me that the local sportsmen wanted to honor me for my great effort the night before. I tried to decline but Dan reminded me that any publicity would help bring about a Johnson match. When we entered the hotel ballroom I was stunned more than any punch I received the day prior. All of the 135 guests were dressed in tuxedos and the room was prepared as though a royal wedding was taking place. I was thoroughly embarrassed that I was only wearing slacks and a blazer. We took our seats and the sportsmen and reporters proceeded to honor me as though I was the world's heavyweight champion. I received two medals in leather cases. The first was a beautiful gold medal with an enameled boxing figure on the front and an inscription on the back that read: *Presented to Joe Jeannette by the S.P.B.A. Paris championship of Europe. Joe Jeannette beat Sam McVey, 3h. 15m. 49 rounds. April 17, 1909.*[221] The second, smaller bronze medallion, made me laugh immensely. It was a smaller version of the gold coin. On the back it

[220] *Le Sports Universal Illustre* April 1909.
[221] *Hudson Dispatch "Jeannette Prizefighter"* by Virginia Smith August 19, 1912.

stated: *Presented to Joe Jeannette Jr., to record his father's great fight in Paris, April 17, 1909.*[222] The front of the medallion had the same pugilistic figure and underneath the figure it read: *May he grow up as straight and as game.*[223]

The most surprising gift I received that evening, however, was an oil painting of myself by Count Hubert de La Rochefoucauld. The 47-year-old count was an accomplished artist as well as an art collector. He said he was inspired to create the painting from my courageous performance the night before. The painting was of me throwing a punch and was extremely detailed, showing every muscle in my body. The count spoke with great passion about the fight game, as well as his love for art. One of his favorite artists was Vincent Van Gogh. He owned several of Van Gogh's paintings. I decided that the artwork should stay in France. I donated it to be placed in a local art museum.

F. H. Lucas described the awards banquet: *"As was to be expected, and following a principal that the society of propagation of English boxing have instituted, a banquet was given to Joe Jeannette in honor of his recent victory over McVea. About a hundred people were present, and the evening was voted a great success. The eminent author, Tristan Bernard, gave us another of those crisp, humorous speeches for which he is famous. Both Mr. Breyer and Mr. Vienne having done their share of spouting, Cuny obliged with an excruciating bit of oratory. Presentations of medals to various officials followed, and the chief guest, Joe Jeannette, was the recipient of a beautiful oil painting of himself executed by the Comte de la Rochefoucauld. Jim Pratt, having, as usual, managed to put away enough food for a whole regiment, festivities terminated with song and music."*[224]

I believe I suffered a concussion from McVea, for the next several days the ground looked as though it was sinking and rising up in front of me. I must have looked very funny when people observed me trying to walk. I worried I might wind up like some of those boxers that walk on their heels. There is a saying that boxers start their careers on their toes and they end them on their heels. I didn't want to wind up like that. The hearing in my right ear was coming and going from all of Sam's left hooks. It took several days until my hearing fully returned.

My friend Jim Pratt, who was the time-keeper of the fight, remembered the ending of the match: *"It was about two o'clock in the morning. Historically, most spectators were gone to bed, considering that this fight would never end. Some returned the next morning before going to work to see if Sam McVea and Jeannette were still fighting in the ring at the Cirque de Paris. Others had fallen asleep and our hammer on the gong awoke them with a startle at the beginning of each round. We saw men raise oxygen tubes, maneuver pressure taps. A healer handled syringes and vials, another smoked a black pipe in his mouth insensitive to Sam McVea. Bob Scanlon sucked Sam*

---

[222] *Hudson Dispatch "Jeannette Prizefighter"* by Virginia Smith August 19, 1912.
[223] *Hudson Dispatch "Jeannette Prizefighter"* by Virginia Smith August 19, 1912.
[224] *Mirror of Life and Sport* April 24, 1909.

McVea's eyelids in the hope of reopening his colt's swollen eyes... Among us the master Tristan Bernard sometimes dozed quietly in his beard.'[225]

When asked his thoughts on the bout by *La Vie au Grand Air*, Sam McVea explained: *"I sure did give him an awful pasting with everything I had. Jeannette just wasn't human. Every time he hit the floor I thought I could pull off my gloves an' call it a night. At the beginning of the forty-ninth we were both badly banged up, and it was a tossup which of us was in worse shape. My legs were gone and I was dizzy. 'Come on boy,' Joe said. 'I'm gonna knock the daylights out of you.' 'No Joe,' I said. 'I'm through for the evening. You spend the rest of it figuring out how many times I knocked you down.'"*[226]

The article continued: *"I did not have a chance,"* Sam McVea told us. *"I hoped well to be victorious in the nineteenth round, then again in the twentieth round, but the seconds of Joe Jeannette threw water on him and thus allowed him to get up again. I would have triumphed. But it is not important, I was obliged not to give up and this does not declare me deposed. To incline myself in front of such a man as Joe Jeannette in the forty-ninth round during a combat so terribly carried out, gives proof of the value of recovery. And I believe that I have merited more in the spirit of the sportsman while being overcome, then I had done knocking out all of my adversaries up until now with two or three blows of my fist."*[227]

La Vie au Grand Air interviewed both of our managers: *What the managers say, The manager of Joe Jeannette, Mr. Dan McKetrick declares: "Many howled when Willie Lewis and I threw water on the figure of Joe Jeannette while he was on the ground. It was claimed that we did not have the right. They are absolutely false... show me the text of the page in which a similar act is prohibited. In the rules of the Marquis de Queensbury, in the rules of the National Sporting Club, no article prohibits this case. And I defy anyone to prove the opposite to me."*

"Acknowledge that you have not yet seen a boxer like this one in Paris," states Willie Lewis. *"And Joe Jeannette had thirty more rounds in his legs at the time of the finish... The more the match lasted, the more fresh our fighter was. He was not a boxer, he was a rammer who has more endurance and energy than any man. Some experts who do not know anything, claimed that Jeannette had triumphed, thanks to the care of his seconds. Nothing is any more inaccurate. We are all looked after in the same way in America. Joe won because he was the best, and he has proven it well, from the beginning to the end."*

Mr. Guillier, manager of Sam, sees even more reasons with the defeat, than his fighter himself. *"There was help for Joe Jeannette. He was given oxygen after he was on the ground. The ten seconds lasted half an hour. I conclude that Sam McVea was victorious in the tenth round and that Joe Jeannette was finished."* Obviously, any opinion can be correct. But I believe that Mr. Guillier exaggerates a little: for his fighter, his eyes are a little too biased. Let us take a look at his objections. Admitting that Joe Jeannette was given oxygen, but Sam McVea wasn't looked after, also, didn't he have oxygen given to

---

[225] *La Vie au Grand Air* April 24, 1909.
[226] *La Vie au Grand Air* April 24, 1909.
[227] *La Vie au Grand Air* April 24, 1909.

him? Is he saying that those which made use of it with regard to the winner were more expert, but is this acknowledgment the fault of Joe? Moreover, Bob Scanlon sucked the eyes of Sam McVea. Jeannette did not complain any. I believe, moreover that, Sam could not find this very pleasant. Moreover, Mr. Guillier made the black Californian absorb a potion of an unpleasing aspect. Lastly, I do not dare to doubt that he omitted to employing embrocate on the body of Sam McVea.

Eh well! Don't all these proceedings belong to the field of doping? If one wants to blame his adversary of proceeding not strictly and incorrectly, it is necessary oneself to be above any reproach. With regard to the sprinkling of Joe when he was on the ground, Dan McKetrick answered this objection. I join him and I defy anyone to show a rule prohibiting this means. Only, the referee could prohibit it... Mr. Guillier was wrong when he claimed that the ten seconds exceeded normal time. He thus questions the good faith of people who are above any suspicion and affirms an inaccuracy. It looks like Joe has much better character. At the time of his defeat, he did not seek excuses. He had an injured arm, he did not proclaim he was defeated because of this... Why does Mr. Guillier seek excuses for the admirable Sam McVea? Does he wish to decrease the glorious battle he took part in?

The final question, Dan McKetrick speaking in the name of Joe Jeannette, can answer: "You claim that Joe was finished in the tenth round? Please explain to all the spectators of the match who know who was the best man up until that moment, who had been the best since the beginning, who had until the very end given up only the tenth, twentieth and Twenty-first rounds? Three rounds of inferiority in forty-nine, is so little. You affirm that Sam could have killed Joe, then why didn't he do it? Then, why was he a three step distance away from his adversary, as the photographs of the Vie au Grand Air attest to? I do not think that what you say holds any breath! You complain unceasingly. You affirm the superiority of your fighter? Maybe, but what you did not point out, are the illegal blows which are prohibited that Sam McVea threw during several rounds causing the arm of his adversary (Jeannette) to be immobilized and him (McVea) being able to strike him (Jeannette) without fear. When Joe had to change his glove, the recovery was not more than two minutes, when Sam imitated his example, the rest reached four minutes."

Here is what Dan McKetrick could have answered. But he kept silent, not being offensive to Guiller's fighter. He could have in this case, preferably spoke of all the true sportsmen present who supported his victory. It is probable that he will never overcome this, Mr. Guillier will never give in to Joe having wanted this more. This is an assessment matter.[228]

McVea admitted that I had knocked him down about sixteen times.[229] Altogether, according to several reports, there were fifty-two knockdowns in the fight. A reporter for the *National Police Gazette* wrote: *Of the Victor, no words of mine could speak in too high eulogy. Not so much for his victory, but for the extraordinary and positively superhuman courage he displayed to the end. And that,*

---

[228] *La Vie au Grand Air* April 24, 1909.
[229] *New York Amsterdam News* October 3, 1936.

164

mark you, won him the day. Exactly how many times he was floored and apparently finished I've almost forgotten, and yet this extraordinary mass of human fighting material would always rise and plug on and on, until I began to wonder whether the man was really human.[230]

McVea, Langford, and I were so intimidating at that time that the English boxing newspaper, *Mirror of Life and Boxing World*, stated: *It is well known that Jeannette, Langford, and McVea, if unrestrained, could start out any evening after dinner and devastate almost the entire white hope association without having to hurry to catch the last train home.*[231]

La Vie au Grand Air interviewed me after the fight: *Without a doubt, the combat of April 17th was the most beautiful, up until now, in all of Europe. All of the sportsmen present will never forget the marvelous spectacle that was the science and endurance of Joe Jeannette and the power and force of Sam McVea. Joe Jeannette has proven how correct we were to have unshakable confidence in him and he has justified the opinion of Jack Johnson. The champion of the world has, indeed, affirmed that he regarded Joe Jeannette to be James Jeffries' superior. And I believe one cannot give any more beautiful a compliment to a boxer.*

Joe Jeannette's opinion

"*I have to affirm, I, Joe Jeannette, have never fought as hard a combat as I have against Sam McVea... The matches of forty-nine rounds are rare, and even rarer those where the combatants show similar eagerness. I have triumphed and I regard this victory as the most beautiful success of my career... I had the greatest confidence in the ending of my match. Initially I had followed a very serious methodical training regimen, which put me in danger of overtraining. I remembered a useful lesson from our previous meeting. I had only one fear, that was to be the victim of an accident, like an injury to an arm muscle. In truth, in the twenty-fifth round, I hurt my right hand, but I overcame the pain and did not show my weakness to my adversary. But this wasn't the only incident which really worried me; the other incident coming from the fact, of course, that in the twentieth round, I was almost put out of combat.*

"*Sam McVea hit me a terrible blow directly on my nose. The blow came so quickly, was so brutal, that I did not realize I was on the ground. I fell back, my arms crossed, and most surprised when I rose, was poor Sam, who I have been told, had danced the jig, at seeing my prone body. In the twenty-first round, I found the ground again, by a violent left hook to the jaw. I feared I would not be fresh enough to continue the fight, but, thanks to the energetic care of my marvelous seconds, Dan McKetrick, Willie Lewis, and those that helped them, I became myself again after the rest.*

"*Until the thirtieth round I had but one objective: to damage Sam McVea. And I took from some of the applause from the spectators, that I carried out my desires. Besides that indicator, despite all of my efforts, I could not arrive to knock out this colossus, so I changed my tactics. I simply changed my tactic to force Sam to give up, by my repeated blows to the sides and to the stomach. And be certain that the fact that he gave up in the*

---

[230] *National Police Gazette April 1909.*
[231] *The 100 Greatest Boxers of All Time* by Bert Randolph Sugar pg. 174.

forty-ninth round, was only thanks to the violent number of these blows which one could say could break one in two.

"I was very happy with my victory, I highly state that I have never met a man as resistant as Sam. He is better than Johnson as a puncher, that fact is indubitable. He is less of a scientist, but his endurance and his power would enable him to claim victory in a match until the finish with the current heavyweight champion of the world. And as for my part, I would strongly support and bet on the chances of Sam McVea." It is obvious that one cannot pay enough beautiful homage to the courageous Californian.[232]

Le Monde Illustre magazine commented on the fight: A boxing match that will go down in the annals of sport was disputed last Saturday between the two Negroes Joe Jeannette and Sam McVea. One remembers, no doubt, that the two famous American boxers had met recently, and after the twenty round match, the referee declared Sam McVea the victor and this decision was challenged by Joe Jeannette's supporters. The organizers of this match did not dare, after this meeting to again have two blacks compete in a decisive match for fear of being accused of bias, which would have been completely unjustified if you know the leaders of boxing action in France...

The match last Saturday, which ended in the defeat of Sam McVea, was, however, for almost the entire duration of the fight, to the advantage of McVea, who weighed heavier than his rival, demonstrated the same speed as him, but infinitely less spring to overcome punishment. It is unfortunate that the rules of English boxing had been broken in the nineteenth round, which might well have changed the outcome of the meeting. At that point Sam hit with such a terrible left hook that Jeannette collapsed. If he would have stayed on the ground for ten seconds he would have been defeated. Sam waited for Jeannette to rise. He succeeded but was soon extended two additional times.

It was then that his handlers threw water on him, which enabled him to move, thanks to their reaction, and find himself standing before the fatal time. At that time, had I been the referee, with some regret I would have immediately declared the victory to McVea. Anyway, the meeting continued and, in the 26th round, Jeannette collapsed again. The bell announcing the end of the round allowing him to regain his senses during the minute rest and this wonderful man once again faced his formidable opponent. However, he fell again in the 28th round but he found enough resources to get up by the ninth second. The battle continued and, after facing his opponent for three and a quarter hours, Sam shook hands with Joe and abandoned the fight after 49 rounds.

Certainly Jeannette has won the greatest victory of his life, but Sam McVea, who was proclaimed the winner the last time, was not deprived: it is therefore said that both men are great in the eyes of the English boxing fans, because they were able to partake in the most memorable fight that has ever occurred[233]

Sam McVea, who stated that I was the toughest fellow he ever met, was bedridden for two weeks after the bout.[234] Years later, Dan McKetrick commented on the match: "The thing about Jeannette and McVey, they didn't like

---

[232] La Vie Au Grand Air May 1, 1909 pg. 282.
[233] Le Monde Illustre April 24, 1909.
[234] New York Amsterdam October 3, 1936, Black Dynamite "Fighting Furies" Fleischer pg. 182.

each other much. And they had nothing to lose. So I matched 'em for a finish fight, and they put on the greatest exhibition of strength and stamina and plain hatred that was ever displayed to a paying audience."[235]

End of finish fight April 18, 1909 at 2:30 a.m. McVea sits on his stool in background while Jennette is being mobbed along the ropes on the left.

Joe Jennette after finish fight.

Sam McVea after finish fight.

Count Hubert de La Rochefoucauld painting of Joe Jennette
presented to Jennette on April 18, 1909.

Joe Jennette poses in Paris, France, circa 1909.

Joe & Adelaide Jennette, circa 1909.

Joe Jennette firing pistol to start the bicycle race between Victor Dupre & Thorwald Eelegard at the Buffalo Velodrome on April 18, 1909.

Jack Johnson & Sam McVea playing pool
Paris, France, circa 1908.

Sam & Mrs. McVea playing piano
Paris, France, circa 1909.

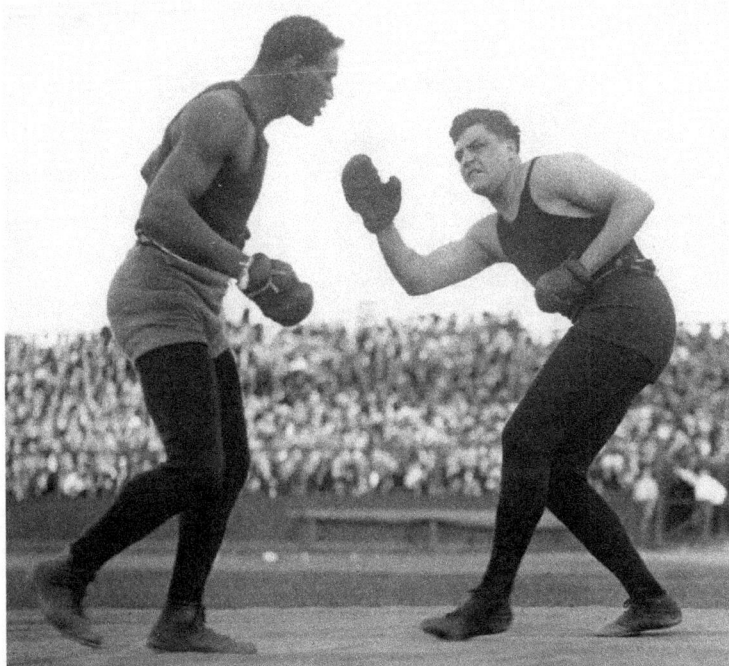

Joe Jennette & Jim Stewart re-enacting Johnson-Jeffries fight, Hilltop ballpark, July 4, 1910.

L to R : Adelaide Hartlieb, Mary Hartlieb, Agnes Jennette, Adelaide Jennette, Joe Jennette, Joe Jennette Jr. & Oswald Hartlieb, circa 1914.

Joe Jennette sparring on roof with Jim Stewart, circa 1913.

Tom Kennedy & Jennette after sparring, circa 1912.

Joe Jennette poses alone & with children Agnes & Joe Jr., circa 1913-14 Paris, France.

Sam Langford

Agnes, Adelaide, Joe, & Joe Jr., circa 1913, Paris, France.

Chapter 14
Battle of the Century

After the McVea fight, Dan got to work on pressuring Johnson to give me a title shot. Dan was interviewed by a reporter who wrote the following: *The extraordinary contest that was brought off by our friends, Mr. Breyer and Mr. Vienne, and their colleagues in Paris last week, between Sam McVea and Joe Jeannette, has been talked of less in England than it otherwise would have been had the championship contest taken place at the N.S.C. on Monday. The presence in London of Mr. Dan McKetrick, Joe Jeannette's manager, gave us an opportunity of learning something of the personality of the coloured man who has been able to lower the colours of the Parisians idol.*

'Dan' is the admirer of his protégé as well as being his manager. He tells us that Joe is 'a splendid boy,' quiet, well-behaved, and fond of the seclusion of his own home, and deeply attached to his wife and child. "He is the gamest boxer in the whole world," declared his manager, "and I have so great confidence in him that I am prepared to back him against Johnson if the champion will meet my man in a finish fight in Paris, or any other place that will offer any kind of a purse. It is not a question of a purse with us, but a question of the championship. We will agree to fight Johnson, winner to take all. In Jeannette's opinion, McVea is a better man than Johnson. He is bigger, stronger, and carries a much harder punch. When Johnson boxed McVea the latter was only 19 years of age, and at that time was an easy victim for Johnson, which shows that McVea has improved wonderfully in the last few years. Johnson can probably get more money fighting Jeannette in Paris than by meeting any other man in America- barring Jeffries. It will be time enough to talk about fighting Jeffries when Mr. Johnson has cleaned off the other heavyweights now in the limelight."

"I cannot understand- can you?"- said Dan, "why the English people do not make an effort to see in this country my champion, who has beaten McVea, and whom Jack Johnson himself declares to be a better man than Jim Jeffries." Here is what Johnson says of Joe Jeannette: "I think that Jeannette is a tougher man than Jeffries, and it is harder to make an impression on him. I do not say this because Jeannette is a man of my own colour; it is my candid opinion. I have fought him, and I know. I studied the other man, and I think that I am expert enough to pass a proper opinion on the relative merits of the men." "You see," continued the manager of Jeannette, "I have some reason for saying that my man has some right to a contest with the best boxers in the world. We leave in May for the States, but if any enterprising promoter is prepared to stage a contest we are prepared to return."[236]

Another article was written by Jim Corbett, the former heavyweight champion, who gave his opinion on a matchup of Johnson and me: *If Johnson boxed under the rules of the State Athletic Commission, Jeannette would outpoint him, for Jack would be compelled to break clean and couldn't hold. Johnson isn't a hard hitter. He confines his punishing to the breakaways and is strictly a defensive*

---

[236] Untitled article from Joe Jennette's scrapbook. Courtesy Ben Hawes collection.

fighter. He isn't a clever boxer when it comes to feinting and footwork. Jeannette is. I think, he is the best long-distance fighter in the ring, and could whip Johnson in a finish contest.[237]

I was now the idol of France after my forty-nine round bout with Sam McVea. Until Saturday night McVea was considered invincible by Parisian boxing fans. I was now looked upon as the greatest heavyweight in the world by the French. I took Addie to the opera and when we entered the theater the opera audience, bejeweled in ivory, rose to their feet and chanted: *"Vive l'american! Vive Jeannette!"* A proposed match between Jack Johnson and I was the talk of the boulevards. I felt as invincible as the Parisians thought I was.

On May 8, Willie knocked out Honey Mellody in four rounds at the Cirque de Paris. Mellody was one of the top welterweights in the world. He was the former welterweight champion, having beaten Joe Walcott for the title in 1906, but he lost it to Mike "Twin" Sullivan in 1907. Mellody was down five times in the fourth and final round. Willie commented on Mellody after the fight to *Vie au Grand Air.* *"My Compliments, Melody, you strike very hard."* Mellody, who had stopped Lewis both times in their previous meetings in 1906 and 1907 via third and fourth round knockouts replied: *"You made great progress since our last matches."*[238] As always Willie started the bout by making the sign of the cross and he ended it by kissing his wife.[239]

On Sunday, May 16, I was honored to be asked again to fire the starter pistol for the bicycle race at the Buffalo Velodrome race track. The race included sprinter Major Taylor, who had agreed for the first time to race on a Sunday. Taylor, a black American, failed to win the race, but he performed admirably.

I traveled east with Addie to the town of Nancy, France. Nancy was holding an exhibition on Arts and Industry. Terrain Blandan housed the seven main exhibition palaces. The central pavilion was the Palais des Fetes which showcased horticultural exhibits. There were beautiful art and sculpture exhibits as well as displays devoted to electricity, food, civil engineering and transportation. Addie was now seven months pregnant with our second child.

On May 19, 1909 in Philadelphia, Jack Johnson defended his title against "Philadelphia" Jack O'Brien. O'Brien was a tough comer who gave Jack problems. The bout was surprisingly close; many ringsiders thought that O'Brien had the edge. The contract was for a no-decision bout, pursuant to Philadelphia law, which meant that the light punching O'Brien could only win if he knocked Johnson out. Johnson did not look impressive in his bout

---

[237] Untitled article from Joe Jennette's scrapbook. Courtesy Ben Hawes collection.
[238] *La Vie au Grand Air* May 15, 1909.
[239] *La Vie au Grand Air* May 9, 1909.

with O'Brien. It appeared as though the title had softened Jack up. Many reporters called the bout a draw and some even thought that O'Brien had the edge.

On May 22, I faced Sandy Ferguson in Paris. Sandy had a forty-four pound weight advantage over me. Ferguson had defeated my friend Jim Barry by disqualification in the tenth round of their April 6 bout in Boston. Sandy, who was managed by Alex McLean, fought Jack Johnson four times in his career. I defeated Ferguson over twenty rounds on points. I won two more bouts in France; we then traveled to London, England.

On May 26, I participated in a fundraising exhibition for ex-champ Jem Mace at The Arena in London. Bob Fitzsimmons and I boxed a few rounds, and Charlie Mitchell, England's former champion, acted as the referee. The *Syracuse Daily Journal* stated that the exhibition: *was a sight unique enough to attract a monster crowd.*[240]

On May 27, I was scheduled to box three men on the same night. I won the first two bouts against Harry Sherring and Trooper Cooke. Both wins were by knockout. The third boxer entered the ring and was being given instructions by the referee. Apparently he had a change of heart; while the referee was speaking to him he turned and walked out of the ring.[241] After I exited the ring I was approached by a ringside fan from England. His name was Aleister Crowley. He told me he admired my fighting style and physique.[242] Crowley was a writer, mystic, mountaineer, and occultist. Crowley would later form a character for one of his short stories, *The Ordeal of Ida Pendragon*, after me.[243] In the story he wrote: *He is like a black leopard... Is anything as beautiful as that lithe black body?* The character in the story was a black boxer named Joe Marie, who defeated a white boxer and flirted with a white girl. I guess Crowley made up the last name Marie because my last name Jennette was also a girl's first name.

Also that same night at the Arena in London, Willie faced the five-foot ten-inch tall Andrew Jeptha. Jeptha was originally from South Africa but was now fighting out of London. Willie had made a statement a few days prior to the bout that he could trim an English fighter after each meal. I'll let Dan describe what took place during the fight: *"The crowd started to hiss and jeer him. Willie became angered as he sat in his corner waiting for the second round to start. He told me he was going to tell the spectators what he thought of them. I argued with him that he was a stranger in a strange land and could not afford to be an antagonist. 'Well I'll show them that they can't hoot at me,' he said as he walked out for a renewal of fistics. During the round he was made the butt of jibes and abuse and I thought he would jump out of the ring on a tour of assassination. He did not take a rest*

---

[240] *Syracuse NY Daily Journal* June 22, 1909.
[241] *Jersey Journal* August 25, 1949.
[242] *Champions of the Ring* by Gerald Suster pg. 56.
[243] *Champions of the Ring* by Gerald Suster pg. 56.

after the round but leaned far over one rope and made good on his threat. 'Do you know what I think of you creatures,' said he in a tone of voice that had poison in it. 'You wear dress suits but you are not gentlemen. The worst toughs on the Bowery are gentlemen compared with you. You are nothing. I can lick the whole pack of you one by one. There never was an Englishman that was game. I'll prove that to you in this round. I'll make this English boob I'm fighting quit cold.' With vengeance in his eyes he went out when the bell tolled and knocked Jeptha down. Standing over him and in a voice that all could hear, Lewis hissed: 'Get up you English quitter; get up and try to be a man.' But Jeptha took the count although he could have arisen. Then, turning to the audience, Willie relieved himself: 'There. There you are. Didn't I tell you every Englishman was a quitter? Now let's hear one of you hiss at me.' "[244]

Willie had twelve fights in Europe from January to May, winning all twelve with nine fights ending by knockout. He fought ten of his bouts in France and one each in England and Belgium. Willie had become a boxing superstar in France.

While we were in London, Dan introduced me to a very wealthy hotelier who was also a big boxing fan. His name was Sir Harry Preston and he treated us very hospitably. He was a great historian of the gloved as well as the bare-knuckled age. Preston also ran a profitable betting business on the side. Willie Lewis hit it off immediately with Preston and spent many nights out on the town with him. Preston loved to talk of all the great fights he witnessed and even of his own glory days as a young amateur boxer. Today most boxers think that there was more blood and savagery when the fights were fought with bare knuckles. This could not be further from the truth. As Preston explained: *"The old knuckle-fights were not really as brutal as the modern generation have been led to believe. The endurance of a modern boxer fighting twenty rounds is astounding. Wonderful as they were, I doubt if the old-timers could have survived it. A blow with a gloved hand, scientifically delivered is harder than a blow from a naked fist, even when that fist has been carefully pickled. Heads, and chins, and cheekbones, and shoulders, and ribs are very tough things to drive your naked fist against; and many a bare fisted fighter of old had his knuckles driven in by contact with an opponent's bone. This led to a man being careful about his blows. He seldom struck full force, since he did not want to break his hands. You did not get the lightning and complete knock-outs that you get so often in the modern prize ring. A good many of the old-timers tried to wear their opponents down by glancing and ripping blows, in order to save their knuckles from a direct impact."*[245]

Preston stated of Willie Lewis: *"Here I may say that it was Willie Lewis who, more than any other man, taught the French boys to forget 'Savate,' and how to use their fists in the Anglo-Saxon manner."*[246] Preston spoke of Willie's prefight visits to his opponents' dressing rooms: *"He was an astonishing fellow- the first boxer, I*

---

[244] *Plain Dealer* January 5, 1913 Interview with Dan McKetrick.
[245] *Memories* by Harry Preston pgs. 90-91.
[246] *Memories* by Harry Preston pg. 114.

believe, to wear a dress suit. He would don this evening dress suit and pay a visit to his opponent in the latter's dressing room. The boxer, thinking this was a 'toff' come to see him, would stand up, or pull his forelock; anyway, he would be very respectful. 'Are you so and so?' Lewis would say disdainfully, 'I'll let you off easy tonight. Knock-out in the second round, d'you see? Not the first.' 'Who are you?' The astonished opponent would ask. 'Me? I'm Willie Lewis.' This put the Great Fear into quite a lot of men."[247]

Before my return to the United States, *La Vie au Grand Air*'s Jacques Mortane wrote the following in the May 29 issue: *'The Last of Joe Jeannette'*

For his last combat, Joe Jeannette has proven his marvelous science once more and his courage has passed every test. It is not without a certain sadness that we have attended the last combat of Joe Jeannette in Paris. It is painful for us to note that this marvelous athlete is going to leave us. He gave us so much enthusiasm and we would have liked to keep him among us. But he has engagements in America calling him. And he is forced to say to us, Au Revoir, but he will return at the end of the year.

It is not exaggeration in saying that he is the best heavyweight applauded up to now in France, most scientific, more enduring, and most courageous. None can be compared to him with this triple point of view, even Sam McVea. It is sad to see him leaving at the time when men who are lower than him are arriving. His friends will hasten to ensure that if Joe had been matched against them, they would have been crushed...

For his last combat, Joe Jeannette was opposed to an excellent American heavyweight, Sandy Ferguson, weighing 103 kilos (226.6 pounds) and frame in proportion. The two last matches of Ferguson ended in a victory over Jim Barry and a null match with Sam Langford...

During his meeting with Jim Barry, he was declared victorious following repeated fouls from his adversary. As he was guilty of many fouls against Joe Jeannette, we can conclude from it that the combat of these two men was rather a demonstration of prohibited blows of American boxing. As well, the flagrant fouls of last Saturday... did not prevent the yellow Negro from carrying out the dance from the beginning to the end and from answering the prohibited blows with science and uprightness.

Sandy Ferguson allowed himself to insult Joe during the match, starting with "dirty Negro." The other swearwords cannot be repeated in these columns. Jeannette did not answer, being contented to make boxing and not palaver. Ferguson must have regretted it besides, because he accepted a correction to which he was far from expecting, being given a broken nose, opened cheek, poached eyes and swollen body. One more thing...

Joe Jeannette, while involving himself with Herbert Synnott, days before the match, injured his right hand which was swollen in worrying proportions. He could not make use of this fist. In addition to this was a handicap of more than 23 kilos (50.6 pounds), he was thus a magnificent boxer with only one hand, the left. But it does not matter to a virtuoso of this scale. First round to the last, he carried out the combat as he wanted it. He could not, however, drop this colossal tower which was opposite of him. "Too big!" Joe Jeannette said to me.

---

[247] *Memories* by Harry Preston pgs. 114-115.

But it is necessary to acknowledge that by his attacks which resembled those of a tiger precipitating on its prey, by his dodging, the Negro could attract the admiration of all the spectators. Sandy Ferguson, on the contrary, employed only his weight. He did not strike a shoulder or a deltoid, of the body. His blows were without much effect and speed. Joe Jeannette perfectly avoided the influence of the weight of the mass which was opposite him. He jumped, precipitated and struck.

Sandy Ferguson tried to employ all the prohibited blows, of which he attempted to make up by these means, the handicap of science which separated him from Joe Jeannette. At the same time as Jeannette, Willie Lewis will leave us. Their departure will plunge boxing into stagnation. We will undoubtedly applaud these brilliant champions next year. None will be able to make us forget the splendid masteries, ardor, the science and the energy of this famous fighter which is Willie Lewis.

No matter what occurs, this charming boy will always be entitled to the recognition of the French public. Isn't it he who has initiated us with the mysteries of the American method of which he has all the smoothness, all the rogueries? It is he who gave us our education. We will not forget him.[248]

After returning to the States I lost a decision to Sandy Ferguson on June 22 in Boston. The decision was unpopular and hissed by the crowd. The *Indiana Freeman* reported: *It was one of the hottest exhibitions of heavyweights ever seen in the ring. Jeannette did the better work from start to finish, landing cleanly with his left to head, and he cut Sandy over the eye early in the bout. The colored fighter had a wholesome respect for the big white man's right wallop, and was under it every time Sandy swung, avoiding some damage, but he could not escape Ferguson's left hooks, and one caught him in the third round, flooring him. The big Ethiopian, however, was up again without taking any part of the count.*

After getting his bearings Jeannette tore into Ferguson, who was always ready to clinch. Going the last half of the distance Ferguson took more chance of catching Jeannette as he rushed in, and planted some heavy welts with his left on the body and head. The announcement of the decision was received with jeers, as the biggest part of the house was with Jeannette, in spite of his color.[249]

I started pestering Dan again about a date for my title shot. He told me to be patient, that he would have a date soon. On June 30, Johnson defeated Tony Ross in Pittsburgh, via a six round newspaper decision.

On July 21, Adelaide gave birth to our second child, our daughter, Agnes Marie. Agnes was born in our apartment at 503 Central Avenue in West Hoboken. She was the most beautiful thing I had ever seen. When Agnes was old enough to talk, my sister Agnes would playfully say: *"I am Agnes number one, you are Agnes number two."*[250] Addie and I had learned a lot about raising a child from Joe Junior. One of the things we had learned to watch as parents of mixed children is what type of children's books to buy. Many

---

[248] *La Vie au Grand Air* May 29 1909.
[249] *Indiana Freeman* July 3, 1909.
[250] Interview with JoAnn Flannery-Mostaccio Joe Jennette's great-niece.

books displayed colored people in a bad light. We were very careful to avoid buying these types of books. Once, by mistake, we bought a children's book titled *The Adventure of Two Dutch Dolls* by Florence Kate Upton. The book was innocently enough about two Dutch dolls that roamed around in a toy store. The part of the book that enraged us was the evil Golliwogg doll in the story. The Golliwogg caricature was a male dressed in bright red trousers, a blue swallow tailed coat, a high collared white shirt, and a red bow tie. The Golliwogg had a coal black face; large red lips, wide white eyes, and messy nappy hair that made him look like a black minstrel character. The Golliwogg was often drawn with paws instead of hands and feet which made him look like he was part animal. He was made out to be very ugly and the two Dutch dolls would play a game by throwing rubber balls at him, knocking him over. The character was portrayed as evil, mean-spirited, incompetent, and a thief. When I read the story to Agnes I had to change the story line. I showed the book to Addie and she looked through it without saying a word. When she closed the book she opened the garbage dumbwaiter and threw the book down the chute. We never spoke of that book again.

Addie wanted to have another child. She discussed the issue with our priest at St. Michael's Passionist Church and he advised her not to have any more children.[251] When I asked Addie why the priest recommended that we have no additional children she said that he didn't give her a reason.

On August 13 at the Fairmont A.C. in the Bronx, Willie Lewis boxed Sailor Burke. Burke's real name was Charles Presser. Willie was knocked down in the first round, but he turned the tables on Burke, knocking him down in the second round. In the third, both boxers loaded up and threw bombs at the same moment. They both connected and were down for the count. Dan and I screamed for Willie to get up. He did but Burke beat the count also. Willie wound up stopping Burke in the sixth round. George Bannon, the famous New York timekeeper, said of all the fights he observed in his fifty years the Lewis-Burke fight that night was the greatest fight he ever saw.

I went into training for a rematch with Sandy Ferguson in early August at the Olympia Athletic Club in Union Hill. A sports reporter stopped by and wrote the following article: *I dropped into the training quarters of Joe Jeanette yesterday. Jeanette is training to fight Sandy Ferguson next week at the Fairmont. His training camp is in Union Hill, New Jersey. After seeing Jeanette in action it isn't hard to understand how he once made Sam Langford quit, or how he stopped Sam McVey in forty-nine rounds in Paris last spring. The only wonder is how McVey lasted so long against a man so absolutely tireless and endlessly active.*

Jeanette began by playing basketball for a quarter of an hour at top speed. He never

---

[251] Interview with JoAnn Flannery-Mostaccio Joe Jennette's great-niece.

stopped but was always after the ball as hard as he could go. Right after the basketball game came the boxing, several hard, fast grueling rounds, with Jim Stewart. Stewart, by the way, has entirely altered his style of milling since his poor fights with McCoy and Jack 'Twin' Sullivan. I venture to say that if he met either of these gentlemen today they wouldn't last over five or six rounds with him. Instead of standing off and boxing, as he used to, he tears in and roughs it every minute of the time, smashing away hard at close quarters. As Stewart weighs stripped 220 pounds or more, and is as strong as a horse, it's no joke to stand him off. He has a lot of speed and can hit.

Each three minute round was a slasher. Jeanette slugged hard and put many a hook on Stewart's chin that might have been the curtain signal for a man with a weaker jaw. Stewart mussed Joe up in return and seemed to enjoy the rough work as much as Jeanette did himself.

After the boxing Jeanette went through a long 'stunt' of acrobatic feats, and was as fresh at the finish as at the start. Jeanette plays basketball all the time with the Olympia Club of Union Hill. He thinks basketball the best all-around training exercise in the world. Jeanette weighs 191 pounds now, which will enable him to make it very hot for the Sandy Man from Boston.[252]

On August 27 at the Fairmont I stopped Ferguson in eight rounds. I pummeled Sandy's body in the bout, and he was taking a terrible beating when his corner tossed up the sponge. I didn't think the victory would cause the uproar that it did. With Johnson defeating Burns and myself annihilating the white Ferguson, paranoia started spreading that black boxers were going to dominate heavyweight boxing.[253] Johnson's success, as well as my own, seemed to spell doom for some in regards to white superiority in heavyweight boxing. If you add Sam Langford and Sam McVea into the mix it didn't look too promising for white heavyweights.

On September 18, I took on Al Kubiak in Philadelphia. The press reported on the fight: *After the first round in which the Michigan man showed much aggressiveness, it was all Jeannette. Kubiak took a great amount of punishment but gamely stuck to his task. The New York man, however, was too clever for him and gradually wore him down by hard jabs and body punches. In the first round both men set out at a hot pace. They exchanged hard blows to the body and face and near the end of the round Kubiak caught Jeannette on the jaw with a stiff left which staggered him.*

Jeannette came back strong in the second round and using his left hand with great effect, soon had Kubiak on the defensive. In the third round Jeannette dropped the white man with a right jolt to the jaw, but he was on his feet in an instant and clinched to save himself from the hot drives of the Negro. In the remaining rounds Jeannette appeared to be Kubiak's master at all times.[254]

We traveled back to France on October 2 aboard the steamship

---

[252] *Auburn Citizen* Aug. 23, 1909.
[253] *Beyond The Ring* by Jeffrey T. Sammons pg. 37.
[254] *Omaha World Herald* September 19, 1909.

Philadelphia of the American Line.[255] Ada stood behind with Joie and the baby. Delegates of the National Athletic Club of Brooklyn saw us off at the Brooklyn dock. We sailed to Southampton and then made our way to France. Jim Stewart accompanied us on the return trip. I was now 30 years old and the forty-nine round affair with McVea had taken its toll on me. I needed the bout with Johnson before my speed and reflexes eroded.

On October 16, Johnson defended his title against Stanley Ketchel in Colma, California. Ketchel, the middleweight champion, was no slouch, but Johnson outweighed him by over 30 pounds. It was now becoming more apparent to me that the public was more interested in seeing a white man attempt to beat Johnson than seeing Johnson beaten. At the Johnson-Ketchel weigh-in, Ketchel wore boots to look taller and he had an overcoat on with several layers of clothing underneath so he didn't look too small standing next to Johnson. Johnson knocked out Ketchel in the twelfth round of a scheduled twenty round bout. Johnson had now defended his title four times, and I was no nearer to a bout with him.

Also on October 16, the Pittsburgh Pirates defeated the Detroit Tigers 8-0 to win the World Series. I was a big baseball fan and I was extremely excited for Honus Wagner, who was a very good friend of mine. Honus, or Hans as we called him, and I played with each other on the Pittsburgh Southsiders.[256] I played shortstop. I also played on the Olympia's of New Jersey team.[257] Both teams were barnstorming semi-pro teams and Hans played with us to keep sharp in the offseason. I played semi-pro ball because colored players were not allowed to play in the Major Leagues. We called Hans the "Flying Dutchman" because he was so fast on his feet.

Willie Lewis started things off in Paris on the 23rd of October by beating Englishman Jeffry Thorne via a ten round decision at the Wonderland. Willie was upset that he didn't win by knockout. He looked a little sluggish, which was probably from the recent voyage overseas.

I met Kubiak in a return match on the 30th at the Cirque de Paris. The bout was scheduled for twenty rounds but I knocked out Al in the tenth round. *La Vie au Grand Air* described the bout: *Last Saturday the match that pitted Joe Jeannette and Kubiak was one of the most exciting that we have attended. Not that there was any doubt at all as to the outcome of the battle, Kubiak not fully recovered from the fatigue of travel, is currently in short form but the Polish fighter showed incredible courage in the ten rounds and he is really admirable. As for Jeannette he is always a wonderful boxer. He may even be growing stronger. He dealt terrible punishment to the courageous Kubiak, who in the tenth round fell in a heap from a violent hook to the solar plexus that put him to sleep for 30 seconds. Finally he resumed his senses and spit up the equivalent of two or three glasses of bloody fluid under the*

[255] *Brooklyn NY Daily Eagle* October 2 1909.
[256] *Chicago Defender* February 6, 1932.
[257] Untitled Article from Joe Jennette's scrapbook. Courtesy Ben Hawes collection.

anxious eyes of the brave Joe Jeannette who kept asking 'Is it serious, is it serious?'[258]

On Friday, November 5, at the Wonderland, my protégé Jim Stewart boxed Jewey Smith. In the fifth round Smith was knocked to the ground for an eight count. In the sixth round Jim dropped Smith for good with a hook to the stomach.[259] On November 13, I decisioned Australian heavyweight Sid Russell in a fifteen round bout.

On Sunday, November 14, *La Vie au Grand Air* held a special Gala at the Femina Theater. I attended the sports Gala along with Sam McVea, Willie Lewis, Al Kubiak, Jim Stewart, and Charlie Hitte. We performed demonstrations and exhibitions. Sports and literary celebrities as well as many sports fans attended the event. The master of ceremonies for the event was Mr. Victor Breyer, the president of the Society for the Propagation of Boxing in France. Willie Lewis discussed American boxing and the importance of shadow boxing. I exhibited the American method of boxing with a Frenchmen named Puai. I showed all of the punches, parries, dodges, and fouls that are used. Then we finished up with an exhibition match. Al Kubiak and Jim Stewart followed with an exhibition. Sam McVea then gave a punching bag demonstration as did I. The show wrapped up with a motion picture of all the past and present famous boxers of the world along with a showing of the Sam Langford-Jen Hague match. It was a very fun evening for everyone and a chance for us boxers to hang out together outside of the competition atmosphere.

On Saturday, November 20 Jim Stewart, whom the papers called the "Young Joe Jeannette," took on Sid Russell. The fifteen round bout was ruled a draw by referee Emile Maitrot, but most in the crowd thought that Stewart had the edge.[260]

On November 29, Dan wrote to a London newspaper expressing his feelings about Sam Langford and his manager Joe Woodman: *"Woodman was offered a good inducement to match Langford with Jeannette for a match in Paris. What did the great and only Langford answer? This: 'Get me John Willie or someone else.' That hardly shows that he is ready to meet the world, does it? Now Mr. Victor Breyer is prepared to offer Langford a match with Jeannette, and what is more, at terms that are far and away beyond the amount of money he receives for boxing in America, and more than he received for boxing and quitting cold to Jeannette.*

"I might add that Langford was defeated by Jeannette in eight rounds, and what is more, it was an inglorious defeat for Langford. The great one refused to leave his corner for the ninth round, stating that he had had enough. They boxed again in New York and Langford dropped Jeannette cold several times in the first rounds, but Jeannette kept boxing as hard as he could, and the great Langford was bucking and side-stepping before the end of the sixth session and Joe earned a draw. Then they went to Boston for a twelve

[258] *La Vie au Grand Air* November 6, 1909.
[259] *La Vie au Grand Air* November 13, 1909 pg. 357.
[260] *La Vie au Grand Air* November 27, 1909 pg. 377.

round contest, or, to be more exact, the match in Boston preceded the one in New York. At any rate it was a twelve round contest and was declared a draw and all the papers of the country including the Associated Press, declared it a 'Boston decision' which makes a verdict for the home man. It is what happens in nine contests out of ten in that section. The unbiased newspaper men and those who sign their articles said it was 'robbery'. Many declared that the referee was induced by the betting and that Jeannette was a winner by a mile.

"We were offered another contest in Boston just before we came across and I agreed to take the date provided the club would increase the distance to fifteen rounds and have some well known New England sportsman, not connected with the club, as referee. This they agreed to do, and when it was put up to Langford he refused to go over twelve rounds. Now Langford can prove his class by accepting a contest with Jeannette and there is no reason for him to sidestep, for he can obtain more money than he would receive at home."[261]

I arrived at the office of *La Vie Au Grand Air* to partake in a photo shoot. John Kelly, who managed Charlie Hitte and Al Kubiak, wrote a story about American baseball for the French magazine. John knew that I was an avid player and fan, so he asked me to assist in the project. I dressed up as a baseball player. One of the shots had me in a catcher's mask and glove. The photograph wound up being on the cover of the December 4 issue. We used an empty picture frame as home plate for the photos. It was a fun day. The article spoke of the high salaries that some of the baseball players were paid.

On Saturday, December 11 I took on Sam McVea again.[262] There were a lot of back and forth negotiations before the match regarding how many rounds we should fight. Sam wanted twenty rounds and I wanted another finish fight. Tristan Bernard, the famous writer, publicly stated that the fight should be thirty-five rounds to be fair to both sides. Bernard was the person who introduced the use of a bell to signify the last lap of a race. *L'auto* newspaper, as well as Jacques Mortane, both pushed for another finish fight. All parties eventually agreed to thirty rounds. *La Vie au Grand Air*'s Mortane had this to say of the upcoming bout: *Under these circumstances (30 rounds) who will be the boxer who triumphs? Is it Sam? Is it Joe? Sam McVea has for him power, a strength that makes the man feared by all. His punches are very hard though slower than Joe's, not difficult to dodge. I think he can overcome his opponent with a lucky shot... Joe Jeannette, however, is the scientific boxer in every sense of the word. His skill, his location of his punches, double hits, triple, his energy, his heart, his coolness, his sudden attacks, his remarkable dodges that place him among the leading boxers of our time. Only two men can now compete with him: Jack Johnson and Sam Langford...*

If Jack Johnson is able to triumph over Jim Jeffries, only one man should oppose him for

---

[261] *Denver Post* December 6, 1909.
[262] *La Vie au Grand Air* December 11, 1909 pgs. 412-13.

187

the title of world's champion: the winner of a Joe Jeannette Sam Langford match. That should tell you that tonight's match will be hotly contested because, if Sam McVea triumphs, he will become the third in line. Odds are with Jeannette. In the first meeting Jeannette sprained his arm in the second round. Besides the weight handicap, he had to endure the pain that prevented him from doing what he wanted... The second match fought to the finish gave rise to an incredible battle. Viewers who saw Joe Jeannette knocked down in the eighteenth round, arms outstretched, then get up, fight back, and eventually sicken and force his opponent to withdraw, will never forget this wonderful show of energy and indomitable courage. We must not forget if Sam can put over one of his terrible blows he may very well clinch the win.

In sum, despite my preferences, the outcome is uncertain. As for those who claim the encounter may not be sincere, we can only classify them under two labels: those who are ignorant and those who are in bad faith...[263]

Later that evening Sam and I clashed for the fourth time. I had won two of our first three fights and the loss was very controversial. The fourth match was described by Mortane: *The Joe Jeannette-Sam McVea match has ended in a draw... A match to the finish would have had a different outcome... The fight attracted a large crowd at the Cirque de Paris. Never before was a larger and more worldly supporting crowd observed in the vast lobby. It was impossible to find a seat near the center of the ring. The receipts passed one hundred thousand francs. Did the evening legitimize the take? I contend impartially yes, and for several reasons, the two Negros gave us a wonderful boxing exhibition full of science and strength, they proved to us that they are very similar to each other, but Joe Jeannette was beyond dispute, the best of both.*

Sam McVea himself is of the same opinion. The French public does not yet have a very advanced education in boxing. They think that as long as it is a fight, men must be horribly mutilated when the final gong sounds. But these scenes of massacre did not occur between the pugilists who are so different: one of the two hammered his opponent with such power that he bled profusely.

And besides, that is precisely what happened the other day. But you had to be at ringside to notice and observe the long streaks of purple blood on the face of Sam which is why some have written that the Californian did not bleed. And I assure you that from the twelfth round, when Joe began to hurt him, Sam McVea shed torrents of blood from the mouth and nose. For men so well trained for endurance, they struck with unusual force.

Joe Jeannette was prudent. Also note that Joe Jeannette has been knocked down by Sam McVea in all of their fights so far. In a fight to the finish whatever, but in a limit match, one must be cautious. The man who crowds the floor may well see the decision go against him. It was therefore necessary to prevent Sam from hitting him decisively. So Joe had one objective: to avoid as much as possible the attacks of his opponent and hit back as hard as he could. I think he couldn't have done better.

We observed the wonderful scientific dodges at the appropriate moments. And each time he returned, affecting especially the flank, which he knows to be the sore spot of Sam

---

[263] *La Vie au Grand Air* December 11, 1909 pgs. 412-13.

McVea. Sam's tactic was to swing very hard to try and knock out Jeannette. He did his best; he swung terrible blows that Joe was fortunate to avoid.

So far, it has been fashionable in the big fights to use referees from across the channel. What a mistake! At the first meeting between Joe Jeannette and Sam McVea we dealt with a man who first gave victory to Jeannette and then to Sam. This time Mr. Hulls, however, delegated by the Sporting Life, displeased many sportsmen by declaring a draw, When Joe had, in my opinion, a clear advantage. Suffice it therefore that the future is our national referee Emile Maitrot, who is certainly the best referee we have seen so far in France. It is very interesting to hear the opinions of the participants in this fight. What Joe Jeannette said,

"I am furious at the decision. I was definitely the winner of the match and I do not know what aberration made the referee declare: Draw! I was certainly better prepared and quite serious for this fight. Sam McVea was also at his best. I wanted to win and did everything to achieve that. All viewers thought I won except the referee which is weird. But I drew a lesson from this encounter: I will never succeed in knocking Sam McVea out, it is too hard. But I will always fight to the finish. Only my opponent, who knows as well as I do, doesn't want to."

Sam McVea's opinion,

"I cannot overcome this man if the rounds are more than twenty. I no longer agree to meet him under any other conditions. I was surprised with the progress he has made since last year. I confess that he was better than me the other night and I did not expect the decision of the referee."

Jeannette's seconds talked,

"Joe Jeannette is not liked in England," says Dan McKetrick. "Last year when he boxed your neighbors, he feared that his purse would be below that promised because of the receipts collected, he demanded to be paid before entering the ring. So he made the English change their process which they have usually maintained. I can only attribute that the referee's decision was biased, otherwise I'd be forced to admit that he ignored the basic rules of boxing."

"Sam McVea lost without a shadow of a doubt," said Lewis. "He could not contain himself from Joe's energy and courage. Since the fifteenth round he was a beaten man... Jeannette had one of the nicest, most scientific fights of his career..."

"I thought the victory belonged to my teacher," said Jim Stewart. "He dominated with such ease. He had the head and flank of McVea in such a state; I was convinced he would be declared the winner."

The opinion of an arbitrator,

Emile Maitrot, the French referee that made England envy us and who it would be prudent to use in the big fights, also believed Joe Jeannette was the victor. "I was hoping," he said, "we would take a good lesson of arbitration and I noticed the slightest gestures of Mr. Hulls. But I soon noticed that he was not an excellent teacher. The poor man, he looked unconcerned and he appeared so bored! He mediated and wrote down his meditations on his notepad. I thought the notes were related to the fight and I thought he would postpone his decision by reviewing them: Not at all! They were perhaps related to combat and his failing journal may have decreed his amazing draw that no one expected.

189

I saw clearly a Jeannette victory; it is to him I gave my decision."
John Kelly says,

Our colleague from Philadelphia, John Kelly, manager of Charlie Hitte and Kubiak too believes that Jeannette has triumphed: "The fight may have been monotonous," he told us, "but that is not surprising. Two men who are so evenly close and have so much interest in triumphing are obliged to be careful and not let a blow end their hopes. In addition, two heavyweights cannot provide a show with the speed of lightweights, especially when they are fighting until half past one. Sam McVea, a man who is strong, cannot do more than twenty-five rounds, while Joe seemed fresh as the battle stretched on. If the match had been thirty-five rounds, Sam would have been done."
The opinion of Kubiak and Hitte,

The two Americans also support a Jeannette victory, but they recognize that the fight was not exciting: They thought that the battle could have been fought harder. "The two men could have done better and issue a more severe battle. McVea's shots were very hard, but Jeannette blocked them wonderfully... And, Sam had a face full of blood, one eye swollen; we believe it would have been the kidney punches that would have forced him to abandon the fight in two or three more rounds."
Louis Doerrs' opinion,

"The fight was boring and slow, very slow," declared the professor Louis Doerr... "The fighters watched each other too much, and I think that if Joe Jeannette had been less afraid to get hit hard, he could have forced Sam McVea to retire before the thirtieth round. Moreover it was only a matter of time, and if the match had lasted a few more rounds, Sam would have been forced to bow again to the science and endurance of his opponent." As you can see, the opinions are almost unanimous, but the French public still needs more sports lessons.[264]

On December 12, we were entertained at the Femina Theater with a physical culture exhibition.[265] The lecturers were George Rozet, who spoke of past and present physical culture and its relations to sports. Emile Maitrot, the referee, followed with his secrets on physical culture. Mr. Gasquet, the Jiu-Jitsu professor, showed off his Apollo-like body. Finally, Jacques Mortane, the writer, displayed his world-record-breaking feat of card tearing. Gasquet and Maitrot showed how one can have a chest like a blacksmith, legs like a runner, and thighs like a mountain climber through various exercises.

We sailed home on the Teutonic several days later. To get my mind off of boxing I took Addie to New York to hear pianist Scott Joplin perform. He had moved to the city in 1909. Joplin composed the famous tunes "The Entertainer" and "The Maple Leaf Rag."

On Tuesday, January 4, 1910, I went to my brother Marshall's house to give him a gold watch I picked up for him in Paris.[266] Marshall and his wife

---

[264] *La Vie au Grand Air* December 25, pg. 482.
[265] *La Vie Au Grand Air* December 1909.
[266] *Jersey Journal* January 5, 1910.

Katherine were in the midst of a marital dispute. Katherine became enraged because I gave Marshall the watch and didn't bring her anything. She started attacking me. It was raining so I had my umbrella in my hand. I used it to fend her off. Marshall grabbed Katherine and tried to calm her down. Katherine broke free and stormed out of the house. Marshall apologized to me and I left for home. Unbeknownst to me Marshall's wife went to the police station and signed a complaint against Marshall and me for assault. We were both arrested. When I was brought to the police station Captain Marcy looked at me laughing. He told me that he had asked several officers to go lock me up after Katherine signed the complaint, but they all refused for fear of their safety. Finally Sergeant Kennell, a personal friend, heard that there was a warrant for my arrest. He said: *"Give that warrant to me, and you bet Jennette is going to come here."*[267]

Captain Marcy asked me when I was going to fight Jack Johnson again. I told him my manager was doing everything he could to make the match happen. While we were being processed Marsh turned to me laughing: *"With all the trouble Johnson is stirring up, you wind up in jail!"* *"Very funny,"* I replied. We were eventually released on five hundred dollars bail each. Addie was so angry with Katherine she stopped speaking to her. The charges were eventually dropped. I took a rest from boxing in the beginning of 1910 to spend time with my wife and children.

In late January 1910, Paris and its surrounding cities started experiencing severe flooding following months of torrential rainfall. The Seine River overflowed and flooded Paris. Water came up through the sewers, tunnels, and drains. Thousands of Parisians were forced to flee their homes and search for higher grounds until the flood passed. Paris was in a state of emergency. Dan McKetrick and his wife Anna were in France at the time staying with Jim Pratt at his home in Neuilly. Dan and Anna helped to keep thousands of Parisians alive during the flood by using their automobile to drive broth and meat from the countryside to the misplaced Parisians who had taken up residence in hovels on hills.[268] They made hundreds of gallons of broth which they brought to the victims. The French government did not overlook the assistance of the McKetrick's. They decorated Dan with the *Palmes Academique*, a ribbon which until that time had only been given to one other American, Mrs. William K. Vanderbilt. Anna McKetrick earned the title "Little American Ministering Angel," from the French citizenry for her assistance.

As unhappy as I was at not getting the opportunity to fight for the title I was truly happy for Willie Lewis when he got his shot. Or should I say, his shots! On February 19, 1910, Willie boxed Harry Lewis for the world welterweight title in Paris, France. Willie was floored twice and the twenty-

---

[267] *Jersey Journal* January 5, 1910.
[268] *Auburn Citizen* September 26, 1913.

five round bout was declared a draw. I felt very sad for Willie. He was devastated by the lost opportunity. Willie had fought the red-headed Harry three times prior, losing all three contests.

On March 19, Willie took on Billy Papke at the Cirque de Paris for top honors for the middleweight crown held by Stanley Ketchel. *Le Sport Universal Illustre* described the bout: *The words are too slow and too heavy, which are required to translate into clear sentences the overwhelming impression that we received at the Cirque de Paris Saturday night. Sustained lightning. I will long remember, the shocking vision, but this shocking is not the same as the match between Willie Lewis and Billy Papke. Papke is a "hurricane fighter," said Harry Lewis a few days before the meeting to a reporter who asked him his opinion on the newcomer in France.*

Having seen the work of Papke I understand the opinion of Harry. That battle will be decided soon... Willie Lewis is without a doubt a great athlete, of harmonious proportions, solid, well muscled. The smart and popular challenger appeared in good shape. Much better than during his match with Harry Lewis, when reaching the legal limit, he had to descend below his normal weight...

Papke is a living statue, the image of elegant force... He inspires confidence. If the physique does not lie, Papke I feel, must win. He walked in front of his rival... hands were half open in the glove... He looked like a cat getting ready to play with a little mouse. And the mouse was the man who has had trouble with champions, who has not tasted defeat in France. Papke let his opponent come to him; there was a nonchalance sureness in himself. 'Shoot First' apparently thought Willie. Willie took the offensive. Papke began to come alive. Willie was exhausting. Now Papke heats up and loads up. There was a rapid exchange of blows, Willie was pushed towards the ropes, and he suddenly collapsed. The room fell into a silent stupor. Will he rise? The judge counted the seconds. At the count of seven Willie was standing. It was an uppercut followed by a swing to the jaw, which threw him down. But he bounced back and finished the round bravely.

For the second time the bell rang. This time the two men rushed upon each other with fury, raining blows on each other. Willie was leading the dance. He took the advantage. He reached his opponent's jaw who obviously had a moment of weakness, a little fleet; he used the 'clincher.' In a burst of energy Willie spent himself thoroughly, and the crowd, already believing the victory was his, stamped, and shouted enthusiasms. All the spectators were standing. It was an unforgettable moment of frenzy. But Papke did not fall and the gong rang. Was he saved? Perhaps it would be too rash to suggest this.

A third time the men were facing each other. Such was the effort, that the spectators were tiring. This type of fighting could not continue much longer. Willie was still attacking and Papke took the offensive. He rushed his assaults. Yes, indeed, the man is a whirlwind. Here again he cornered Willie. The scuffle became hellish. Willie was struck three times on the button of the jaw so hard that he fell and didn't move. Papke, smiling, contemplated his opponent's demise, while the judge counted the seconds. At ten Lewis did not move. He was defeated. It was over, as his keepers took him away, his friends comforted him as he cried. The hero of so many victories just suffered the fate he inflicted on Stanton. It is the destiny of all great athletes, the tragic seconds. Willie Lewis is not

192

diminished in the eyes of the connoisseurs. He succumbed to a bigger man who outweighed him. But for the crowd who idolized his successes he has left this battle with some of that halo intact.[269]

On April 23, Willie and Harry went at it again and the results were the same. A draw over twenty-five rounds. Willie would later say: *"What Harry doesn't know about boxing isn't worth learning."*

Harry was of Jewish heritage. I got along well with Harry. He was a friendly fellow and a very good fighter. I used to kid Harry that he wasn't a good practicing Jewish boy because he didn't keep the Sabbath with his Friday and Saturday night fights. Harry replied that he practiced his faith the same way that the Hasidic Jews did. He explained that the Orthodox Jews boxed off an area with fish wire which was strung on poles in an area several blocks wide around the synagogue. Within the fish wired area the Hasidim were exempt from the Sabbath rule. Harry told me if the Hasidic Jews were exempt inside of their rope, he was exempt inside his ring ropes!

On May 24, I returned to the ring after a much needed five-month layoff. I knocked out Andy Morris in the third round in Boston.

On May 27, Dan threw poor Willie in with Stanley Ketchel, the top middleweight in the world. On the ride to the fight, which was being held at the National Sports Club in the Bronx, Dan stopped at a local church, St. Anthony's Roman Catholic Church, and took a quarter and lit a Votive Prayer Candle.[270] He prayed that Willie would knock Ketchel out. Fight manager "Dumb" Dan Morgan went along for the ride with McKetrick to help work Willie's corner.

Early in the fight, Willie nailed Ketchel on the nose, and a stream of dark red blood started to flow from Stanley's nose. The crowd went wild and Willie smelled an opportunity and jumped on Stanley as the three thousand plus fans in attendance roared with approval. Even McKetrick was stunned. It looked like the prayer candle idea was working. Every punch that Willie landed was like a stroke of a paint brush as the dark red blood was stamped all over Stanley's face by every one of the blows landed by Willie's blood-soaked gloves. In the corner after the first round, Morgan told McKetrick: *"I'm outta here."* McKetrick replied: *"What for we got Ketchel in big trouble."* Morgan replied: *"Oh no, Willie just got Stanley's attention and now 'The Slasher's' gonna kill that poor boy, you'll be responsible for picking that poor boy up when Stanley's through with him."*[271]

Morgan also reminded McKetrick that Ketchel was not nicknamed "The Slasher" for being a feather-fisted pug. Morgan proceeded to take a seat in the fourth row for the remainder of the fight. Sure enough, in the following round, Ketchel doubled Willie up with a one-two punch to the mid-section

[269] *Le Sport Universal Illustre* 1910 pg. 206 by P. Hamel.
[270] *Dumb Dan* by Dan Morgan with John McCallum pgs. 153-4.
[271] *Dumb Dan* by Dan Morgan with John McCallum pgs. 153-4.

and when Willie straightened up "The Slasher" struck him with, as Morgan described: *"one of the most terrible right hands to the face,"* that Morgan had ever seen. The blow drove two of Willie's teeth right through his upper lip. Somehow Willie was still standing but shortly after that big punch, Ketchel dispatched of the helpless but courageous Lewis. Morgan asked McKetrick after the slaughter: *"Did you ever think in your wildest dreams that young kid had a chance with a killer like Ketchel?"* *"Yes I did,"* McKetrick replied. *"I counted on the surprise element and sometimes forces are at work you don't know about. I gambled and I lost. It's not my fault the saints didn't stand up!"* After they carried Willie back to his dressing room he finally came around. When Willie opened his eyes, Morgan turned to McKetrick and said: *"Where the hell do you get your nerve? For a quarter you wanted the middleweight championship of the world!"*[272] All I can say is I'm glad I trained hard in my career and didn't rely on Dan's religious connections!

On June 3, I decisioned Brooklyn native Jim Smith at the National Sporting Club in New York over ten rounds. On June 25, the White-Slave Traffic Act was passed into law. It was commonly called the Mann Act after Congressman James Mann, who introduced the law.[273] I had no idea how much impact this act would have on my boxing career. There was a great deal of panic concerning this new law. There were rumors circulating that white girls were being abducted from Europe and forced to work in brothels in Chicago. The act specifically prohibited the transportation of women or girls for the purpose of prostitution or debauchery.

Unbelievably, Jack Johnson would become the first person charged with a violation of the Mann Act. It was obvious that white America was angry over his defeating its white champion and challengers. It was also upset over the way Jack flaunted his lifestyle, in particular his affection for white women. According to the charges Johnson had apparently crossed state lines with a white prostitute named Lucille Cameron. He wound up marrying Lucille to avoid prosecution. The authorities found another white prostitute that Johnson crossed state lines with. Her name was Belle Schreiber. Schreiber would eventually testify against Johnson and help to convict him. Would Johnson be stripped of the title? Would he give the title up? Would another black man ever be given a shot at the title?

Johnson was in the newspapers everyday with his out-of-the-ring antics. His drinking and carrying on with white women was constantly making headlines. Johnson started the year traveling in a vaudeville show. He was fired and returned to New York, where he was arrested for beating a man.

The papers were now saying that former champion Jim Jeffries was training to come out of retirement to fight Johnson. I hoped it was not true because I wanted my shot, but my worst fears were soon realized when they

---

[272] *Dumb Dan* by Dan Morgan with John McCallum pgs. 153-4.
[273] *Beyond The Ring* by Jeffrey T. Sammons pg. 43.

announced the bout in Hoboken N.J., less than a stone's throw from my house. I was now beginning to come to the realization that a bout with Johnson for the title would likely never take place. He was purposely ducking me. He was even telling reporters that he was going to be the only black heavyweight champion ever.

On June 26 a local reporter asked me who I thought would win a potential Johnson-Jeffries match, as I had fought Johnson more times than anyone else. I knew that Johnson hadn't been training properly lately and Jeffries was a very strong fighter. I told the reporter: *"Why, Jeffries can lose half his strength, have his endurance cut in two, carry a ton of extra weight and still whip Johnson. He has the head and heart to do it."*[274] I made the comment more with my heart then with my head. I was very upset with Johnson not giving me a shot at the title first. It was now becoming more difficult to prepare for matches. I felt I deserved a shot at the title but I still needed money for my family so I fought on.

On July 1, I took on Morris Harris at the National A.C. in New York City. The press reported on the bout: *Joe Jeannette easily defeated Morris Harris of Philadelphia in their ten round bout last night at the National Sporting Club. Harris received a bad beating throughout. Jeannette jabbed, hooked and landed right and left swings at will. He floored Harris twice... In the ninth round Jeannette jabbed hard lefts to the face and crossed some stiff rights to Harris' jaw. During the session one of his punches knocked out two of Harris' teeth. Jeannette went in for a knockout in the tenth. He dropped Harris twice with terrific right hand swings to the jaw. Harris took the count both times. He was groggy, but came back gamely. Harris was hanging on when the bell came to his rescue at the end of the tenth round.*[275]

On July 4, 1910, in Reno, Nevada, Johnson fought former heavyweight champion James J. Jeffries in a scheduled forty-five round bout. Leading up to the fight there were a lot of racial tensions. Jeffries was 35-years-old and hadn't fought in six years but he was the best hope to take the championship back for white America. Jeff's ring name was the "Boilermaker." He retired as undefeated champion with a 19-0 record with 16 knockouts. Johnson was 32-years-old but was in his fighting prime. Sam Langford and Johnson hated each other and Langford publicly backed and bet on Jeffries to win the fight. "Tex" Rickard promoted the bout and also refereed the contest, when both camps couldn't agree on who should be the third man in the ring.

Jeffries' strength-and-conditioning trainer was Martin "Farmer" Burns. Burns was a famous wrestler with a huge neck. It was told that Burns was once hung by his neck and he whistled "Yankee Doodle Boy" while hanging. Rumor has it he survived because of his twenty-inch neck. I enjoyed Burns' "catch-as-catch can" or freestyle wrestling. I practiced the

---

[274] *Wilkes-Barre Times-Leader* June 27, 1910.
[275] *Pawtucket Times* July 2, 1910.

style in France with Mark Gaucher.

Jeffries supporters had a song they were singing called the: "Jim-ada-Jeff Song": *Commence right away to get into condish, An' you punch-a da bag-a day and night, An'-a' din pretty soon, when you meet-a da coon, You knock-a-him clear-a out-a sight. Chorus: Who's dat man wid-a hand like da bunch-a banan! It's da Jim-a-de Jeff, oh! da Jim-a da-Jeff, Who gives-a da Jack Jonce one-a little-a tap? Who makes-a him take a one big-a long nap? Who wipe-a da Africa off-a da map? It's da Jim-ada-Jeff.'*[276]

The Johnson-Jeffries bout began with a rendition of "All Coons Look Alike to Me." Jeffries was quoted several times in papers using the songs title when referencing colored people. This only angered Johnson further. The song was actually penned by a black performer named Ernest Hogan. Hogan, for the rest of his life, stated he regretted ever writing the song. Word spread that there were going to be race wars over the verdict. The *Chicago Defender* stated that Johnson would be fighting: *race hatred, prejudice, and Negro persecution.*[277] Reverend Reverdy Ranson, a black Chicago leader, stated: *"What Jack Johnson seeks to do to Jeffries in the roped arena will be more the ambition of Negroes in every domain of human endeavor."*

Jack toyed with Jim. While Johnson was hitting Jeffries during the fight, he mockingly said: *"Package being delivered, Mr. Jeff."*[278] The white crowd seethed with anger. Johnson knocked Jeffries out in the fifteenth round. There were fist fights and shootouts between whites and blacks throughout the country. In Chicago, thousands of blacks poured into the streets beating buckets and dishpans, whooping and hollering, running and laughing, crying tears of joy.[279] Old-timers declared that they hadn't seen the likes since back when the Emancipation Proclamation was signed. Colored people had made up a street song that they were singing: *The Yankees hold the play, The white man pulls the trigger; But it makes no difference what the white man say, The world champion's still a nigger.*[280]

Riots broke out around the country as news of the results spread. The *Baltimore Sun* reported sixteen deaths, hundreds severely injured, and city jails filled with Negroes and whites.[281]

The *Indianapolis Freeman* described Chicago: *"Jack, Jack, J-A-J; Jack, Jack, J-A-J!" Time and again with a rhythm that was catching and inspiring, with enthusiasms born only of the intensity and excitement of the victor, Chicago Negroes celebrated the victory of John Arthur Johnson Monday evening when the iconic dispatch, "Johnson wins," was flashed over the wires and immediately placed on every bulletin board in*

---

[276] *Beyond The Ring* by Jeffrey T. Sammons pg. 38.
[277] *Beyond The Ring* by Jeffrey T. Sammons pgs. 38-39.
[278] *Beyond The Ring* by Jeffrey T. Sammons pg. 39.
[279] *The Big Black Fire* by Robert H. DeCoy pg. 124.
[280] *Beyond The Ring* by Jeffrey T. Sammons pg. 40.
[281] *Baltimore Sun* July 6, 1910.

Chicago.

"Jack, Jack, J-A-J; Jack, Jack, J-A-J." The refrain was sung by maddened, enthusiastic thousands, who swarming out of the saloons and resorts on State Street, crowded that busy thoroughfare from Twenty-fifth to Thirty-fifth streets. Fully ten thousand people joined in the celebration and State Street was blocked.

The refrain indicated above was caught up by the surging crowd, and keeping time, stamping feet, up and down the pavement, men and women sang and shouted; "Jack, Jack, J-A-J," occasionally varying the refrain with a joyous, "Oh, you Jack Johnson."[282]

Johnson's mother adoringly spoke of her child: *"Oh, ain't it fine- Ain't it fine for Texas," shouted the champion's mother. "All the South and all the North never turned out a hero like him... It's a very funny thing about Jack," she continued... "when he was little he was a regular cry baby. Every time he got in trouble he would cry and say how hard the boys hit him. Then his sister Janey would run out and beat up the boy who had beaten Jack. One day Jack came in blubbering, and I lectured him a plenty. 'Jack,' says I, 'Ain't you ashamed of yourself, letting a little girl like Janey go out to fight for you? If it happens again I am going to wallop you myself.' Ever since that Jack has been a fighter."[283]*

A colored man named Henry Crowder described his feelings and how the aftermath of the Jeffries loss was received in our nation's capital: *"A friend and I had just read the bulletins in a large Washington newspaper that Jack Johnson (Negro) had beaten Jim Jeffries (white) for the heavyweight championship of the world. Great, of course, was our elation. Hats in hand and yelling like madmen we started home down Pennsylvania Ave. towards 6th St. We lived in that section at the time. Passing 13th St. we noticed a terrific commotion in the doorway of a very noted Negro bar-room. I saw two or three men fall from blows delivered by one man in the doorway. The door was shut and with his back to the wall he was fighting a crowd of howling white men. The police charged in and we continued our way home still throwing up our hats and howling with delight.*

We later learned that the man fighting the crowd in the doorway was a giant Negro armed with brass knuckles, and that several white people had received cracked skulls before the police subdued him. I think he got a considerable term in the penitentiary. That night the white people gathered in thousands and took possession of Pennsylvania Ave., and no Negro dared show his face on that street. One Negro was chased down our street by a mob of whites. The Negroes quickly ascended to the tops of buildings and hurled brickbats onto the throngs, scattering them, and giving plenty of work for ambulances.

About 2 a.m. on the same night, as a group of about 10 of us were standing in a bar discussing the events, a Negro suddenly dashed in and through the place, out the back and over the rear fence on to God knows where. Not a word was spoken. A few minutes later a mob of about 15 or 20 whites, led by two policemen and a white man covered with blood, suddenly crashed into the doorway. The police demanded to know if we had seen a fleeing Negro. Certainly we had not. After a cursory search and a surly command that all

---

[282] *Indianapolis Freeman* July 9, 1910.
[283] *Indianapolis Freeman* July 9, 1910.

of us Negroes go home the entire bunch left. We Negroes remained where we were, drinking and laughing.'[284]

Black poet, Waring Cuney, wrote a poem about the Johnson victory: *O, my Lord what a morning, O, my Lord what a feeling, When Jack Johnson turned Jim Jeffries', Snow white face, to the ceiling.*

I actually cashed in from Johnson's victory over Jeffries in a small way. Jim Stewart, the big white heavyweight I had trained, and I, boxed a reenactment of the Johnson-Jeffries fight to fans live at the American League Park, or Hilltop Park as it was also called because it was on the Hilltop of Manhattan Island.[285] Stewart, whose real name was Henry Loerch, was from Brooklyn, New York, and was a big heavyweight at well over six-foot in height and 200 pounds. We boxed every round as soon as they were completed in Reno. The results came in via wire. The "Dixie Kid" and "Kid" Williams also boxed a reenactment at the Olympia Field after a baseball game, and Joe Bernstein and "Kid" Griffo boxed a reenactment at the Open Air Hippodrome. Hilltop Park was located in the Washington Heights section of New York City. It was the home of the New York Yankees when they were still called the Highlanders. The park had seats for sixteen thousand fans with standing room for another ten thousand. At this time, fans were actually allowed to stand on the field outside of the foul lines to watch the ballgame once all of the seats were sold. We had a large crowd on hand to witness our reenactment.

Our exhibition was recorded by the Empire Film Company using a moving picture camera. Unbeknownst to us, after the reenactment was complete the film company went around trying to sell the exhibition as the real fight! William Morris purchased a copy of the film to show at his American Music Hall without first reviewing the film. After much advertisement the hall was filled to capacity with fans waiting to view the bout which was to be narrated by former heavyweight champ James J. Corbett. After a two-hour delay the film was run and as soon as the film started both Morris and the paying audience immediately recognized it as a fake. The audience was in an uproar and the film had to be stopped and refunds given.

After another win and draw I traveled back up to Boston to face the "Tar Baby," Sam Langford again. Langford was in the same boat as me. We knew we were the top contenders of the division and yet we had to stand by and watch Johnson fight lesser-deserving white opponents.

Langford was small, not more than five-foot six-inches. He had a terrific reach of seventy-two inches and he was a master at using distance and range. I was used to boxing taller men and slipping under their punches. Boxing Langford created problems for me because I always seemed to slip

---

[284] *Negro* by Nancy Cunard pg. 119.
[285] *Fight Pictures: A History of Boxing and Early Cinema* by Dan Streible.

into his punches.

Sam took the fifteen round decision on September 6, 1910, at the Armory A.C. in Boston. He was defending the colored heavyweight title he now held. Dan felt the loss to Langford might be a good thing. He said that Johnson did not want to get in the ring with Sam but losing to Sam may get Johnson to believe that I was slipping and not as dangerous as I used to be. I was now 31-years-old, Langford was 27, and Johnson was 32.

I must have still been feeling Sam's punches a few weeks later because on the 29th of September I had an accident with a coal wagon while driving my car down Spring Street in West Hoboken. The accident was minor. I only suffered damage to my automobile's headlamps.[286]

On September 30 an article came out discussing my durability. In the article, Dan gave the following statement: *"Joe takes the heart out of his opponents by getting up after being knocked down. He is invariably slow in the early rounds. Langford always gets the best of the early sessions, but Joe is coming fast at the end."*[287] Jack Johnson stated in the article that I was the toughest man he ever fought and the hardest to hurt. He was also quoted in the article as saying: *"Why the more I hit that man the stronger he got. No wonder he beat Sam McVey in a finish battle."*[288]

That night I took on Morris Harris at the National Sporting Club of America in New York City. The *New York Tribune* described the match: *Jeannette held Harris in the hollow of his hand, so to speak, and loafed and stalled along for more than half the distance. He allowed the Philadelphian to lead and drew away enough to allow the blow to miss and then pumped his left into the latter's face, drawing blood from the nose and mouth and cutting both eyes. Jeannette dropped his man in the fifth round with a left to the face and repeated the dose in the eighth round with a similar punch. The bell saved Harris from a knockout several times. Jeannette did not use his right until the sixth round.*[289]

The *New York Times* also reported on the contest: *It was a highly colored show that Tom O'Rourke staged at the National Sporting Club last night. In other words, all of the bouts were between Negro fighters, and they furnished enough excitement for two shows. So pleased was an occupant of one of the boxes at the ringside that he presented Morris Harris, whom Joe Jeannette beat almost to a pulp in the final bout, with a $100 bill.*

While Harris was outclassed from start to finish, he gamely took his medicine, and only retreated or covered up when it became too hot for human endurance. He was unsightly at the finish, and was practically out, with just about enough consciousness left to hang on and wait for the bell. The two men shaped well in comparison, as they stood together in the ring, ready to start the bout.

---

[286] *Jersey Journal* September 30, 1910.
[287] *Jersey Journal* September 30, 1910.
[288] *Jersey Journal* September 30, 1910.
[289] *New York Tribune* October 1, 1910.

Jeannette opened the session by poking his left glove into Harris' face. Harris started to clinch early, and both were a bit wild. Jeannette slipped once on a missed left swing and went to his knees. Harris was inclined to force the pace and made Joe cover up toward the end of the round.

Harris continued his wild work in the second round and Jeannette was not any too accurate, but Harris is a hard man to get at, and it was easily seen that Joe only needed a little time to get his proper poise. This he did as the round drew near its close, and as Harris rushed pell-mell at him Joe planted both gloves about where he pleased.

Harris used all of his knowledge of boxing to land on Jeannette, and Joe ran around the ring, letting Harris follow. For this carelessness Jeannette caught a stinger on the side of the head and then went after Harris. He landed his left repeatedly on Harris' face and ear, but he missed several that had the most force behind them.

Joe contended himself with jabbing Harris in the face and on the body in the fourth round and the latter was very wild. He couldn't get a square blow in to save his life. The fifth round still found Harris persistent, but he missed nearly everything he tried. Jeannette didn't take very much advantage of his opportunities and contented himself with showing how far superior he was to Harris in a boxing sense.

Harris didn't land a fair blow during the entire sixth round. On the other hand Joe kept planting his left straight into the face and body. Once Harris rushed Joe to the ropes and it looked a bit bad for the latter, but he squirmed out of a tight hole and swung on Harris as he danced away. Harris showed a flash of good fighting in the fore part of the seventh round and roughed Joe in the clinches. In the last 30 seconds they swapped punches, and Jeannette wound the session up with a stiff uppercut, which caught Harris on the chin.

Harris started to get gay as the eighth period opened and Joe deceptively wobbled his head, indicating that he was tired. Harris walked into the trap, and as he came in Jeannette caught him with a straight left on the chin which plumped him on the floor. This blow took nearly all of the fight out of Harris, and he was hanging on desperately when the bell rang. The sound of the gong at the end of the ninth was the most welcome sound Harris heard during the whole round. Joe started the period by piling into his opponent, and pounded him on every part of his body above the belt. Harris got his bumps for fair in this round. His two eyes were swollen, his nose was bleeding, and his mouth must have been all cut up inside by the way he expectorated blood.

Only because of the peculiar tactics adopted by Harris in the last round was Jeannette unable to put his man away. Harris, hung on, hugged, covered up, and fought back. He was game to the backbone, and tried every way he knew to stay out the bout. In this he succeeded. It was the only balm he had had out of the encounter, if one accepts the handout by the fan at the ringside.[290]

On October 15 the "Michigan Assassin" Stanley Ketchel was shot to death. His manager, Wilson Mizner, upon hearing of the death, said if they would have started to count over Ketchel's body he would have gotten up.

---

[290] *New York Times* October 1, 1910.

That was a testament to Ketchel's heart and courage.

On November 10, 1910, at Long Acres A.C. in New York I faced "Black" Bill again. The contest was set for ten rounds and I was going to give the crowd a good show and not dispatch of "Black." Unfortunately the show got off to a late start. Between the fourth and fifth rounds a friend of mine leaned through the ropes and reminded me that we had plans for later on in the evening and that we would miss the dinner with our wives if the fight went much longer. "Black" had become a friend of mine so I wanted to tip him off to the fact that his night would be ending early. At the start of the fifth round when we met in the center of the ring I reached out my hand to shake Bill's. Bill looked at my glove and stated: *"Why, this isn't the last round, Joe."* My reply was: *"That's all right. It's the last round for you."* With that I proceeded to knock Bill out. After that day several other fighters copied what I had done that night. I did not intend to demean "Black." I just wanted to give him a heads up that I was turning the heat up. You know, give him a chance to protect himself from serious injury.

On Christmas Eve 1910 word got out that Jack Johnson had beaten his girlfriend Etta Duryea severely. Johnson tried to blame his driver, Gaston Le Fort, for beating Etta. The beating caused Duryea to be hospitalized with two black eyes and an even bigger black eye for all colored boxers looking to succeed in the sport.

After the "Black" Bill fight Addie forced me to take a rest. I had been suffering with a throat ailment for several weeks. I was forced to cancel a match with Sam Langford at the Armory A.A. My wife refused to let me fight Langford until my throat healed.[291] On December 27th I talked Addie into letting me fight Jeff Clark in Newark. I was still recovered from the infection and should have listened to Addie and rested more. The Clark match was ruled a draw. I ended 1910 with fifty-seven professional fights.

---

[291] *Boston Journal* December 8, 1910.

Chapter 15
A Tour of the South 1911

I started 1911 with another trip up to Boston to face Langford on January 10. Sam still held the colored title and once again Langford gave me fits as I got caught early in the first round and never fully recovered. Sam took the twelve round fight on points. I was one of only two boxers who had stopped Sam up to this point in his career; he retired after eight rounds of fighting on our Christmas Day 1905 match. His other stoppage loss was to "Young" Peter Jackson in June of 1906. I continued to have problems early in the matches with Sam's in and out style. He constantly kept me off balance. I was dropped three times in the losing affair. He most definitely was the toughest man I ever faced. Sam broke my nose in the contest and my septum was pushed all the way over to one end, which affected my breathing. After the fight I reeled off five more wins with two draws.

I went to a hospital in New York to get the nose reset on February 8. Addie was very worried but I told her I was fine and joked around a lot to show her I was okay. Mel Cooke, who booked me fights along with Dan, visited me and stood with me after Addie had left the hospital. The resetting of my nose had gone well and a bandage was placed over it to keep it in place. Mel told me it was too bad that my nose was damaged because he had a fight for me in Philly that night for five hundred dollars against Jim Barry. We both knew that Barry was no match for me. I told Mel I would take the fight. Mel looked at me and said: *"You've got to be kidding."* *"Absolutely not,"* I replied. *"What about your nose? Forget your nose, what about Addie? I don't think she would like it, Joe."* *"Don't worry, Mel, we'll take the train right back tonight. She will never know I was gone."*[292]

I jumped out of the hospital bed and we hopped a train to Philly where I fought a draw with Barry in a six rounder. I kept my chin tucked in and slipped to the side to avoid getting hit directly on the nose.[293] I was worried about my nose and I wound up breaking Barry's nose in the fight.[294] For the first time in Philadelphia fight history women were allowed to attend the fights. A Philadelphia newspaper described the presence of the "society women" as a: *"disgusting incident."*[295] After the bout I returned to the hospital five hundred dollars richer.

The next morning I was awoken by Addie, who entered the hospital room screaming, with a newspaper in her hand: *"Joe someone's been fighting in Philadelphia under your name. We are going to have to file suit!"* *"I don't think so,"* I

---

[292] *Brooklyn NY Daily Eagle* February 10, 1935.
[293] *Brooklyn NY Daily Eagle* February 10, 1935.
[294] *Macon Telegraph* February 19,1911.
[295] *Macon Telegraph* February 19,1911.

replied. *"Well it certainly wasn't you, Joe."*[296] I realized I couldn't hide the truth any longer. *"Yes it was, girlie, and I can prove it."*[297] I reached under the pillow and withdrew the five hundred dollar purse. At first I thought she was going to explode in anger but after a few quiet moments she burst out in laughter which caused me to start laughing too. A few seconds later she stopped and said: *"I hope you didn't damage the nose, Joe. The doctor will be really mad."* *"I didn't get hit once on the button,"* I replied.

On February 24, Jack Johnson announced if he did not receive thirty thousand dollars to defend his title he would retire. He also said: *"And when I retire, I'll stay retired. There will be no getting me to come back to regain the supremacy for the black race."*[298] Obviously this comment insulted every black heavyweight. I didn't understand his thinking when he made such comments. He refused to give other black boxers a chance at his title yet he proclaimed that no other black was capable of winning the championship.

Johnson had been writing weekly stories about his boxing career in *La Vie au Grand Air*. On March 4, he wrote the following about our many meetings, as well as his meeting with Langford: *"In July this year (1905), I fought four times, meeting with Morris Harris and Black Bill on the same day, July 15th. In all, thirteen times I fought that year. The last was a disputed six rounder on December 2nd against Joe Jeannette in Philadelphia, without a decision. In 1906 I met Joe Jeannette four times. Joe and I met so often that it became a game for us and we took much pleasure in our meetings. In our second meeting, which was six rounds, it was very serious and we both had much knowledge of each other, I was beaten on a foul in the second round.*

"Later in the season, we met again in Baltimore, and I won a fifteen round decision. I reckon that was one of the best fights of Jeannette's life. In April 1906, Langford and I found ourselves together for a fifteen rounder in Chelsea (Mass.). I found him one of the toughest opponents I have ever met in the ring. I weighed 190 pounds and Langford was only 138. In the second round, the little Negro hit me with a terrible blow to the right jaw, and I dropped like I was hit by a cannonball. Throughout my boxing career, not before, nor after, did I ever receive a blow that struck me with such force. I did all I could do to barely get back on my feet when the referee was counting 'Ten!' I succeeded but I assure you that I felt this blow for the rest of the match. I realized then that against a man like Langford, I should not discover that blow again and I used all of my knowledge to avoid it. In the fifteenth round, I was declared winner on points.

"In May of that year, I went to Gloucester (Mass.) and sent to the land of dreams Charlie Haghey with a few strokes. One-round was enough to prove to him and his friends that he had better choose another profession. Then I returned to Philadelphia, where I had a match of six-rounds, a no-decision, with Joe Jeannette. Jeannette was definitely my favorite opponent. We gave the spectacle of a beautiful encounter for the

[296] *Brooklyn NY Daily Eagle* February 10, 1935.
[297] *Brooklyn NY Daily Eagle* February 10, 1935.
[298] *Washington D.C. Evening Star* February 25, 1911.

pious people of Portland (Maine), those ten rounds ended in a draw."²⁹⁹

On March 16, I faced Jim Barry for the second time in two months. The following is the bout as described by the press: *Joe Jeannette, the Negro heavyweight, had all the better of a 10 round bout at New York with Jim Barry last night. There were no knockdowns. Jeannette used left and right jabs with effect, interspersed with heavy body blows and right uppercuts.*

Barry swung wildly for Jeannette's body throughout the fight, but few of the swings landed. In the ninth round Barry's lips were cut and bleeding, and at the final bell he was dazed and weak. Opinion at the ringside was that another round would have seen Barry knocked out. Barry and Jeannette will sail for Europe tomorrow, the former to meet all comers and the later to fight the winner of the Langford-McVey bout at Paris.³⁰⁰

Barry and I would go on to become close friends. Once again I was finding it hard to stay motivated in the ring. I didn't want to become one of those boxers that just showed up for a payday. I had always taken pride in my boxing abilities but it was just so hard to find a motivator other than money now. I had already won and lost the colored title. The most I had made in my career in one fight was three thousand dollars. A championship fight with Johnson could easily bring me five times that amount. All that money to box someone I already fought seven times. Money was the only motivator I could find to keep me boxing now.

On April 23, Sam Langford gave the following interview: *"It may sound funny but it is a fact. I fought Gans when I was much lighter, but that boy could hit like a mule kicking, and what is more, he knew how to hit and get all his strength with the blows. Gans was a wonderful fighter in every way, for he could hit and had great cleverness. If he had been a white man he would have been an idol. Joe Walcott was also a hard hitter, but he was wild and could not time his punches like Gans.*

"Stanley Ketchel was a terrific hitter, but he, too, was wild with his swings, and therefore could not be classed with Gans. I have read where I said that Ketchel was the hardest hitter of all, but that is not true. Ketchel never hurt me in that six round bout in Philadelphia, but he made some terrific swings, which, had they landed, might have done some damage. However, I always thought Stanley would be sure meat for me anytime we met, and I do not want to take credit from the boy, who is now dead, but it must also be borne in mind that Ketchel was far from his best when he met me.

"Joe Jeannette to my way of thinking, was the toughest man in the ring, not barring Joe Grimm. That Nig could certainly take the gaff, but he could not hit hard himself. If he could, he would have been a champion. They say I do not like his game. Well, anytime they can show me the dough little Samuel will be there with bells on and ready to take down the coin.

"As for Jack Johnson, I want to say that I do not consider him a hard hitter, and I am waiting for the chance when he can show me how hard he can hit. Johnson did not show his hitting when he met Jim Jeffries, for I would have stopped Jeff sooner than he did and

²⁹⁹ *La Vie Au Grand Air* March 4, 1911 "Mes Combats" by Jack Johnson.
³⁰⁰ *Springfield Daily Republican* March 17, 1911.

*so would other heavyweights I could mention: for Jeffries was not himself by a long ways.
If he had been, Jack Johnson would not be champion today. Johnson is a wonderful
blocker, and a marvelous defensive fighter and no one can take that away from him, but
just the same I do not think he is a hard enough hitter to stop me, and the only way he
can convince me to that effect is to put me down for the ten count. If he can do so I will
then say he is the greatest fighter in the world."*[301]

On May 30, the Indianapolis 500, a 500-mile car race, debuted. The race
was held on Memorial Day. Ray Harroun piloted his Marmon "Wasp" to
victory. His vehicle was outfitted with his new invention: the rear view
mirror. My passion for motorized vehicles was growing. These new
automobiles were so fast and attractive looking. Upon retirement from
boxing I planned on pursuing my passion of working with automobiles.

On June 3, Governor Woodrow Wilson came to West Hoboken to help
commemorate the city's fifty-year anniversary. Addie and I took the kids for
a walk to listen to the Governor's speech. The day before, we took the kids
to see the anniversary parade of decorated floats, wagons, and automobiles
that started on Hudson Boulevard and ran south on Spring Street to
Paterson Plank Road. Wilson would go on to become President of the
United States. When he was elected he was very open about his racist
beliefs. Wilson, when President of Princeton, discouraged blacks from
applying to the university and as Governor he refused to hire blacks in his
administration.[302] When he became President he allowed the segregation of
federal employees. He stated: *"Segregation is not humiliating but a benefit."*[303]

A few weeks later, Addie's sister Mary came over to our house very
excited. She told us that she met the vaudeville team of Victor Moore and
Emma Littlefield while working up at the Hudson Theater.[304] The couple
asked her to travel with them, to be a nanny for their baby son Victor Jr.
Mary was thrilled that she was going to travel the country. Victor and
Emma performed a comedy act called "Change your Act," which was about
a vaudeville team that needed to find a better act. Victor would go on to
perform in fifty-one movies and twenty-one plays in his acting career.

Dan asked me to train Carl Morris for Carl's manager Frank B. Ufer. Carl
was a big strong Oklahoma fighter but he did not possess much boxing
experience or skill. He was, however, a heavyweight, and more importantly,
he was white. It was an opportunity for me to earn some extra coin in
between fights.

Agnes and Joie loved to go to Goldstein's candy store at 207 Summit Ave.
in West Hoboken. After every boxing trip I would take them to the store

---

[301] *Elmira NY Telegram* April 23, 1911.
[302] "The Road to the Whitehouse" by Arthur Link pg.502.
[303] "Josephus Daniels to Franklin D. Roosevelt" June 10, 1933; *New York Times* November 13, 1914.
[304] Conversations with Charlie Hartleib, Ada Atzingen's nephew.

for a toy or I would take them to the Pastime Picture Theater at 607 Spring Street, also in West Hoboken. On special occasions Addie and I would take the kids up to the German run Schuetzen Park, which means Shooting Park in English. The Park had a rifle range, ten bowling alleys, and three dance pavilions. One spring day, Addie came in the house after walking with the kids on Bergenline Avenue in Union Hill. She did not seem herself. When I pressed her to tell me what was wrong she began crying. When she calmed down she told me the story. She was shopping on the avenue and the kids wanted ice cream. She stopped in an ice cream parlor. While she was standing in line a woman told her how cute the Negro children were that she was watching. The woman asked how much she charged to watch children. My wife explained to the woman that she was not babysitting. The children were her own. The woman gave Addie a horrific look. The woman then turned around to another woman she was with and whispered to her as they looked at Addie and the kids. Addie cried to me: *"How can people be so mean and cruel!"* After she calmed down I reminded her that we both knew how difficult an interracial relationship would be, not only for us, but for our children. I tried to remind her that for every cruel person that she met how many more people did she meet that were kind. Addie told me that every time someone gave her an angry look or made a comment under their breath she felt like a little piece of her soul was being ripped out.

I tried to keep my mind off of these things by diving deeper into boxing. Besides boxing myself I was now training several fighters. I decided if they wouldn't give me a shot at the title I would train my own white fighter to get a shot. I agreed to train Carl Morris and headed out to his Oklahoma training camp. A sports reporter named Robert Edgren came to camp and asked me what I thought of Carl and if he was a fake white hope. I was training Carl for his upcoming bout with Fireman Jim Flynn. My reply was: *"No indeed. Carl Morris isn't a lemon. Morris is a fine big fellow… He has only been at it for eight or nine months. Before he started training for fights he was a railroad engineer, not a fireman, running west to San Francisco, and he weighed 315 pounds… Morris isn't a clever boxer yet of course, but he has everything to make a good fighter and he is improving very fast. He thinks quickly and it is easy for him to learn… For instance I told him that Flynn holds his hands in a certain position when he rushes in, and showed him how to shoot his right through with an uppercut. I told him to try it the first time he saw me in that position. We went on boxing fast, and after a little, I tried it. He shot that right through so quick it surprised me… Of course he wouldn't stand a chance with Johnson now, and it will take a lot of fighting to teach him all he'll need for a championship fight…*

"The first day we boxed I made Morris chase me around and didn't let him put a glove on me. Then I stood and let him hit me in the stomach. When he didn't put me down he couldn't understand it, but you know. I can hold my hands up and let Langford wallop me as hard as he can hit. I told him to punch me on the jaw, and I just let my head roll with the smashes and stood up to them. He couldn't understand that either. But I just

206

said: *If you knew as much about these things as I do there wouldn't be any use in sending for me to teach you, would there? He saw the point and settled down to hard work.... At first when I punched him hard in the stomach he winced and showed that he was hurt. I made him lie on his back and go through all the stunts I use to harden my body. It was tough work for him, but he stuck and after a while he didn't mind being hit.*'[305]

I wrote an editorial to the *Evening Telegram* trying to entice Sam Langford back into the ring: *"For the first time in my career as a boxer I am writing a letter to the press and if you see fit to print it you will do me a great favor. The object is to make a match with Sam Langford. It has been repeated around town for several weeks that a number of efforts have been made to bring us together. This is a fact, and while I am willing and am anxious to fight, my manager Dan McKetrick had an idea that eventually we would get Langford to agree to a fight of twenty rounds or more. This now seems to be an utter impossibility, for Langford is going to Australia, not to France, to meet me there.*

"I went to Sam's dressing room after a recent fight and asked him if it was a fact that he was signed for Australia. He said he was, and that he didn't intend to meet me in France. His reply was exactly in these words: 'You ain't human. I won't fight you over ten rounds, because I intend to fight for a long while yet.' This means that if I want a fight it must be for ten rounds, and I am now prepared to make the match and fight inside of three weeks and McKetrick is prepared to sign the articles. So the annihilator of 'white hopes' can get busy as quickly as he wants to.

"I for one do not believe he is the bearcat that people give him credit for. He has been whipping a lot of boys who have not the class that he has. Smith, a newcomer and a middleweight; O'Brien, only a flash of his own self, and Ross: well, Samuel slipped a 'K.O.' on him once before. Ross got a little reputation by going ten rounds with me while my right arm was in a bandage and my left practically useless. Sam Langford and I fought five times, and when you figure out the dope the shade is with me. When we fought the six round bout in New York some two years ago Sam gave me a good walloping for three rounds, but what did he do toward the end? Stalled, because one punch to the body hurt him. When we fought in Lawrence, Massachusetts he deliberately hit me after the bell of the sixth round and cut my mouth from end to end. He had to go six more rounds that night, but didn't he deliberately quit in the eighth. That is, he refused to answer the bell for the ninth session. He can't say he wasn't good then, for it was three months after his fifteen round fight with 'Jack' Johnson.

"Then we were rematched in Boston, and I was given a draw at the end of twelve rounds. Every newspaper man that wrote the story said that I was robbed and earned the verdict with plenty to spare. We have fought twice since, and he has gained the decision in both fights. I admit he won, and he got me early in the fights, but toward the end he was running. In the last fight he broke my nose and smashed the two frontal bones with the very first punch and dropped me for a count of nine. Charlie White knows who was the best man when the twelfth round came. I honestly believe he would have done the

[305] *St. Louis Post* June 7, 1911 pg. 6.

Lawrence trick in the last fight had any referee but White been in the ring, for he deliberately bent down in the ninth round without being struck, and had White counting over him. He would have stayed there, but White walked over and said, 'Get up Sam'. He did, for he didn't want it said he quit. He won twice, got a draw which he didn't deserve and quit once, which makes it two for each, and as quit means it practically was a knockout. I am more than evened up and I am ready to fight it out with him, and I think I can repeat the Lawrence trick.'[306]

After the newspaper editorial, Dan got Langford's manager to agree to a match for September 5 at New York City's Madison Square Garden. I begged Dan to get me a twenty round match as I knew Sam was a fast starter but I had much more endurance. I also knew that Sam did not want to fight me more than ten rounds, so I would have a psychological advantage. As expected, Sam refused to fight me more than ten rounds.

Jack Johnson's problems with the law were continuing. After defeating James Jeffries on July 4, 1910, his fifth straight defense, he would not fight again for another two years. Some blacks looked at Johnson as a strong figure who would not bow to the white man, but others looked at him: *as a disreputable, irresponsible, dangerous embarrassment particularly because of his hankering with white women and prostitutes.*[307] After Johnson's eventual arrest on charges of violating the Mann Act, the black-run *Philadelphia Tribune* published a headline that read: *Jack Johnson, Dangerously Ill, Victim of White Fever.*[308]

I returned home from Oklahoma. On July 25, I took on Al Kubiak for the second time in three months. I had knocked out Kubiak in nine rounds in April. It took me just seven minutes and forty-seconds to knock him out in the rematch. When I entered the ring Kubiak wasn't there. Johnny Flynn, who was introducing the fighters, stated: *"Kubiak will be here in a couple of minutes, he is a little late in arriving."* Someone in the rear of the hall shouted back, *"Well he'll leave early!"*

Finally Kubiak arrived. After Referee White read the instructions, we went right to work. I took the first two rounds easily. I was much too fast for Kubiak. In the third round, Al hit me with a good left hook and followed it with three hard body shots. We clinched and when we separated I landed a hard right to the jaw that dropped Al hard, like a log. Kubiak stumbled to his feet and pushed the referee, who was standing over him, away. Al charged me and I ripped him with a right-left combo to the head, I followed it with a hard right hand that dropped Al again. Al rose on unsteady legs, grabbed me, and held on for dear life. I broke free and ripped several hard punches to the body. Kubiak staggered away and I walked him down and let loose a right hand that barely grazed his jaw. Al fell to his

---

Evening Telegram date unknown.
Interracial Intimacies by Randall Kennedy pg. 82.
Interracial Intimacies by Randall Kennedy p. 83.

knees. The referee picked up the count as Al was shaking his head. A ringside observer yelled: *"That's good for him it will clear his head."* The referee counted eight, nine, Al tried in vain to get up but he couldn't get his knee off of the floor when the referee hit ten. I won by third round knockout.[309]

On July 26 the Frawley Act was passed, which legalized professional boxing in New York State, thus the New York State Athletic Commission was created.

The assault by the press against Johnson was reaching a fever pitch. A sportswriter for the *National Police Gazette* called Johnson: *The vilest, most despicable creature that lives.*[310] An editorial for the Texas *Beaumont Journal* suggested that Jack's: *Obnoxious stunts... are not only worthy of but demand an overgrown dose of Southern hospitality.*[311] By which of course they meant lynching. The governors of Virginia, New York, and South Carolina also came out against Johnson's interracial marriage. Representative Seaborn A. Roddenberry of Georgia proposed a constitutional amendment stipulating that marriage between: *"persons of color and Caucasians... (be) forever prohibited."* Roddenberry also stated that: *"this slavery of white women to black beasts will bring this nation to a conflict as fatal and as bloody as ever reddened the soil of Virginia or crimsoned the mountain paths of Pennsylvania."* Roddenberry urged his colleagues in Congress to: *"uproot and exterminate now this debasing, ultra demoralizing, un-American, and inhuman leprosy."* He also proposed the "one drop rule" which meant if you had one drop of colored blood you would be barred from marrying a white person.

Anger against interracial marriages was growing. Addie and I were never more uncertain of our future. I recalled a boxer I trained with, who was Armenian, who told me of the massacre of his people in 1909 at Adana. Between fifteen and thirty thousand Armenians were massacred in April of that year and no one in the world seemed to care. Could the same fate befall those of us who were engaged in interracial marriages in the United States?

On August 27 an article came out in the *New York Times* which spoke of how Jack Johnson got around racial segregation in a London hotel: *The manager of the Piccadilly Hotel was in a quandary this week when Jack Johnson, the colored pugilist, who is booked to fight "Bombardier" Wells, the English champion, on October 2nd in London for the championship of the world, accompanied by his white wife, arrived at the hotel and occupied a suite of rooms booked for him by his white valet some days previously.*

It appears that toward the end of last week the valet went to the hotel and booked the rooms in the name of J. Johnson, paying for them in advance. Although that action was somewhat unusual, the management had no idea who the guest was until the colored

---

[309] *Indianapolis Freeman* August 12, 1911.
[310] *National Police Gazette* date unknown.
[311] *Beaumont Journal* date unknown.

champion arrived, and then it was too late to do anything.[312]

I was matched with Langford on September 5 at Madison Square Garden for the colored heavyweight championship of the world. There was some question as to whether the bout would come off, because the new chairman of the New York Boxing Commission, James Sullivan, abruptly resigned his position. The new Frawley Act was in effect for our bout. Willie pleaded with me not to take the fight because I was not in top condition due to the fact I was spending most of my energy training Carl. I appreciated Willie's concern but I went ahead with the match. Seven thousand people passed through the turnstiles to watch the fight. I was defeated by Langford over ten rounds. I was knocked down three times in the contest. I swore to myself I would never neglect training for a bout again.

The papers called the Langford bout "a savage fight" with the decision going to Sam "by a shade." By the time the bout started at ten o'clock, five thousand people were outside the Garden, in addition to the seven thousand who were lucky enough to get tickets. Before the bout, Langford was asked what it was like to fight me. Sam stated: *"Jeannette ain't human. I'd rather fight Johnson twenty rounds then Jeannette ten."*[313]

The following is a round-by-round description of the Langford bout: *Round One- They went to close quarters with short arm blows, with honors even. Jeannette slipped to the floor but was up in a moment. A light left hook sent Jeannette to the mat for a second. Langford worried him to the end of the round, which was the Boston man's. Round Two- Jeannette was quick when the gong rang and after a few rapid exchanges, sent Langford down for two seconds with a left and right to the face. Jeannette forced matters and sent five straight lefts and rights over with Langford using body blows at close range. This was Jeannette's round. Round Three- Langford kept rushing, but Jeannette's rapid footwork bothered the Boston man. Sam then sent lefts and rights to the face with Jeannette breaking ground. At long range there were several wicked exchanges, but Langford's heavy left hooks to neck and body gave him the round. Round Four- Langford forces Joe around the ring, but misses half a dozen swings and hooks. After a rapid exchange of body blows Langford hooked his left to the jaw and Jeannette went down for the count of eight. On arising he stalled off the smaller man until the bell rang. Langford's round. Round Five- Langford was the aggressor, playing for the body, while Jeannette vainly tried backhand swings. Langford had the best of the infighting and had the round easily on points. Round Six- Jeannette jabbed Langford with a stiff left but suffered for it by Langford's hooks to body and neck, and a left smash over the right eye. Both were cautioned for holding. Langford's round. Round Seven- Langford with left and right smashes, forced Jeannette into a neutral corner. Jeannette broke ground and made Langford miss several swings. They exchanged several heavy lefts and rights on the head. Jeannette stood up gamely and outfought Langford. Jeannette's round. Round Eight- Jeannette led, landing two lefts on the head. Langford sent a hard left to the body, but*

[312] *New York Times* August 27, 1911.
[313] *Oswego Daily Times* September 2, 1911.

missed two swings to the head. At close quarters Langford got to the body heavily, but was beaten off again by lefts and rights to the head. Jeannette's round. Round Nine-Langford forced the pace, but Jeannette put a couple of stiff lefts to the face. Langford jarred the big fellow with a hard left to the head. It was Langford's round. Round Ten-Langford rushed like a demon, trying hard for a knockout. He forced the pace and sent Jeannette down for a count of three with a left smash on the jaw. Langford took a couple of hard punches in the wind, but sent back lefts and rights with fierce force. He outfought Jeannette to the end and had the round and the fight.[314]

Langford came out hard for the last round as though he thought he was behind on the scorecards. I knew after the bout that I couldn't neglect my training to help other fighters anymore, especially if I was fighting someone of Sam's caliber. After the fight, I was changing in my dressing room when Langford walked in to rub in his victory. I chided Langford: " *'Well I beat you tonight and made you look like a monkey.' 'Beat nothing,' retorted Langford. 'How about the fourth round when you flopped?' 'How about that time I made you quit?' I handed back. Langford let loose some sarcasm and in a moment I was up from the couch. Grabbing Langford and hurrying him to the door I yelled, 'There's nobody in the house now, come down to that ring and we'll fight it out.' Langford laughed. 'I'm paid for my fighting.' McKetrick and I chased him out and down the stairs.'[315]*

On September 15, Carl Morris lost to Jim Flynn at Madison Square Garden. Carl was 7-0 going into the fight, with all his wins by knockout. The more experienced Flynn, who was originally from Hoboken N.J., battered Carl around the ring for ten rounds. He deserved the decision. Carl's left eye was completely closed by the third round and we had to lance the lump under the eye. He also suffered a swollen jaw and a large bruise that covered his temple to his lower jaw. Before the fight there was much controversy over the fact that Frank Ufer managed both Flynn and Morris. Bat Masterson, the famous gunslinger, was in town for the fight and he accused Ufer of paying Flynn to "lie down" for Morris. Ufer responded by stating that Masterson had: *"made his reputation by shooting drunken Mexicans and Indians in the back.'[316]* Masterson sued the *New York Globe and Commercial Advertiser*, who published Ufer's remarks. Masterson was later awarded thirty-five hundred dollars in damages by a jury.

Sam McVea left Paris after nearly five years of living in that country. In September he reached Melbourne, Australia with his wife and his manager Billy McClain. McVea was interviewed in Melbourne: *"I had a fine trip,"* he said, *"and was treated real well aboard that packet. The captain and officers are right fine men, and they recognized me as a sailor. You know I put in many years of my life at sea, and the last time I was in Melbourne I was on a sailing ship, the Melindo from San Francisco. I am meeting (Jack) Lester on the 30th in Sydney, and I am going to try and*

[314] *Watertown Daily Times* September 6, 1911.
[315] *Syracuse Journal* September 13, 1911.
[316] "Benjamin Cardoza Meets Gunslinger Bat Masterson" by William H. Manz.

win. You can't always say you will win, because you don't know until it is all over how you stand. You can bet he is going in to win too, and there is going to be some collisions about it. It takes a new beginner to beat an old timer, and I don't know Lester, never having met him, so I will say no more about him.

"I want to beat Jack Johnson. He is well entitled to the championship and a good man, one of the best I have seen in my life. He has a method of his own. I have fought him three times, and I have most of his best punches off by heart. I meet Johnson in Sydney on Boxing Day. But there is one thing certain, if I don't beat him in the ring I am going to beat him on my motor, I have two cars, one of them a racer, and I reckon Jack can't sight me when I start in it." "Guess he'll want an aeroplane," interposed Mrs. McVea. "Guess he will," responded her husband, "and a fine one too."

"Jack and I have arranged the match, and he is to bring three cars out with him. I hope to enter in some races while I am here to get into form. But I didn't tell you that I steered the Argylishire into the harbor at Adelaide, and through the heads here. All the way out I took my trick at the wheel from noon to 4pm each day. Captain Chicken, he knew me for a sailor as soon as I put my hands on the spokes." "You are good enough on a ship Sam but how about the Aeroplane?" asked Mrs. McVea. McVea showed a mouthful of white teeth. "Oh, the aeroplane," he said, "I only had one trip in that. It was enough. It is too dangerous for me. I will let "Lil" Arthur' (Jack Johnson) have that all to himself. There ain't no aeroplane contest on the bill. There can't be any ten second count out with aeroplanes. You just drop, and it's off to the cemetery."[317]

In another article Sam stated: *"I have been walloped by Johnson three times,"* said McVea, *"but don't forget I was a tenderfoot in those days. Jack will find that I know just as much about the game as he does. You see, Jack has been getting no better fast, while I've not been going back. Jack is big and flabby, and will have to sweat some to get down to decent fighting weight, and that sort of game's no good. I have nothing like that to bother me, and I am right now to fight anybody that walks. If you are having a bet on the fight on December 26th, don't forget to have your bet on me."* Sam would stay in Australia for the next three years, fighting thirteen times. The bout with Jack Johnson never materialized, as Jack refused to fight him.

On November 21, the following opinion by Dan McKetrick was published by newspapers nationwide: *"With the positive announcement of Jack Johnson that he has retired, and from other sources that contribute a verification of this fact, it is clear that the world's heavyweight championship is in default. Every sporting editor appreciates that the logical candidates to succeed the retired champion are Joe Jeannette and Sam Langford. Honors between this pair are pretty even but the last meeting between these two men was, according to the best authorities, in Jeannette's favor.*

"Once before, as the records show, Jeannette showed his superiority over Langford, at Lawrence, Mass., Langford throwing up the sponge in the ninth round of a twelve round contest. Again in Boston Jeannette was given a newspaper decision over Langford in twelve rounds, and also a draw. In New York Jeannette was given a newspaper decision

---

[317] *Australian Mercury* September 18, 1911.

over Langford. All this is a matter of record, nor do I dispute the record which gives some decisions to Langford. In the last bout between the pair at Madison Square Garden, Jeannette used different tactics employing science and judgment, and his cleverness put Langford to a disadvantage. Langford was clearly out boxed, outfought, and outgeneraled. It was almost a unanimous verdict with the sporting authorities, that Jeannette was the winner, by a large margin.

"All bets followed these decisions, and the contest has gone on record as a win for Jeannette. Langford and his manager have not dared to dispute this, in fact, have verified it by deliberately avoiding a new issue; for a long distance battle. I make the direct charge that Langford was spirited out of this country to avoid another meeting with Jeannette. When he sustained defeat at Madison Square Garden it was made evident to him that Jeannette was his master over a distance. To gain time for a getaway, Langford's manager negotiated for a new match with Jeannette, as different club managers can attest, but without a moment's notice he jumped out of the country, and for no other reason than to dodge the match. These are incontrovertible facts, and, according to all precedents, Langford has forfeited all consideration for a chance at the vacated title.

"Speaking by the book, Jeannette stands out as the man rightfully entitled to the heavyweight title, and he is open to fight any man in the world for the distinction, and the money that will go with it. I shall keep after Langford, although I despair of ever getting him in the ring with my man, but I state that Jeannette is open to fight any man in the world for the championship, and in support of this he will go all over this country, fighting all the white and black hopes, and make every effort to gain a clear title to the world's championship.

"As a brother newspaper man, and a dispenser of sports news, I make an appeal to you, with the above facts, and particularly mentioning Langford's making a match to fight Jeannette before Jim Coffroth's club, which he disgracefully repudiated, and jumped to Australia, and his also repudiating a match he made to fight Jeannette in Paris last April after signing articles. On behalf of Jeannette I announce that my man challenges the world for the heavyweight title, and if Langford can be drawn into a match, he can have one on his own terms."[318]

On December 6, a newspaper headline read: "Joe Jeannette wants chance for Heavyweight Title." The article, which was orchestrated by Dan, stated that Jack Johnson should be taken at his word for recent comments that he was retiring from the ring. The article also stated that Sam Langford and I were next in line for shots at the title. The article further stated that Langford broke an agreement to fight me on the Pacific Coast, and instead opted to sail to Australia for some easy wins. Dan was doing everything in his power to force the public to demand a title shot for me.

Dan told me he had an easy four-fight offer in some Southern states. He said the ten-day trip would bring us some quick, easy cash. All the bouts would be against colored boxers as mixed race bouts were illegal in most

---

[318] *Seattle Daily Times* November 21, 1911.

Southern states. I went home to discuss this with Addie, and to no surprise, she was very upset. She told me she didn't want me to go. She was worried about the current racial climate. I explained to her my stepfather told me numerous stories about the South and I would be fine, as Dan was going with me. I reminded her that many Northern black boxers fought down South without incident.

She reminded me of the nightmares I had been having since I was a child about being on a train that accidentally headed south. She said she would let me go only under one circumstance, if she went with me. After much discussion I finally agreed to let her come, but now I had the added worry of my wife's safety. My stepfather had told me that the South's treatment of Negroes had gotten worse after the Civil War ended and from what I read in the papers it continued to grow worse. On December 6, in a town called Clifton, Tennessee, a colored father and his two daughters were killed. Ben Pettigrew was driving his wagon load of cotton from Clifton to Savannah, Tennessee, with his daughters, when he was stopped by four white men. The men were part of a group of "white caps," who were white farmers who banded together to stop black farmers from succeeding in their businesses. The "white caps" shot Pettigrew in the chest, killing him. His two daughters were sitting on the cotton load. As they screamed for their father they were dragged from the wagon and hanged from a nearby tree. Mr. Pettigrew and his daughters were then placed on top of the cotton load and were set on fire. It was impossible to push these types of incidents out of my mind as we headed south. Addie and I wept when we heard of this cowardly crime.

My first fight was set in Memphis, Tennessee, which was only 150 miles away from the murders. I told Addie there was no way I would allow her to bring the children on the trip. We made arrangements for Addie's brother Joseph and his wife Emma to watch the kids. We left on December 8 and took a train south through Pennsylvania, West Virginia, and Virginia. The train had "white" and "colored" coaches and dining cars.

I agreed with Dan's idea to let Addie stay in a separate Pullman sleeping car for the ride south. This would help us to avoid the trouble of Southerners seeing a black man staying in the same room with a white woman. As we passed the "Mason-Dixon Line" from "the North" to "the South" the conductors came through the cars advising all colored people to move to the last car on the train. I felt humiliated as I walked to the back. Addie wanted to go with me but I explained that it might create more of a problem if she was seen in the rear with me.

When we arrived in Memphis I noticed the waiting areas and the bathrooms at the train station were segregated. I saw the words written large in bold letters: "COLORED" and "WHITES." I stood staring at the signs for some time thinking back to my stepfather's Sunday lessons on the South.

I was reminded by Dan that many states in the South had enacted laws not only forbidding interracial marriages, but several states like South Carolina, Mississippi, and Alabama refused to recognize any interracial marriages no matter what state they were consummated in. Mississippi even made the offense punishable by life in jail!

We were undecided as to which hotel we should book for our stay in Memphis. Dan wanted to stay in the Peabody but it was whites only. If we stayed in a black hotel, however, people would know something was wrong. We decided to act as if I was the driver for Dan and Addie. When we checked into the Peabody the desk clerk told Dan I would have to sleep in the shed out back or find a room in a colored hotel. I decided to sleep that night in the shed but Addie refused to let me sleep alone. Around midnight she came outside to join me. Strange as it may seem, that was one of the more memorable nights we had together. The next night we found a colored hotel to stay in.

On December 11 I boxed "Young" Jack Johnson of Boston. I knocked Johnson out in four rounds, after carrying him a few rounds for the fans. We left the next morning from Memphis and headed to Chattanooga, where I was scheduled to box on the 15th against Nat Dewey, who was a home-town boy.

We decided again to stay in a colored hotel. We found a small one on the edge of town. The next morning we went to a local diner for breakfast. Addie noticed I was not given a place set. I could see she was upset. I told Addie it was just an oversight on the waitresses' part. When Addie pointed this out to the waitress a place set was brought over. We ordered our drinks. Addie and Dan were given their drinks but I did not recieve my drink. When Addie questioned the waitress on my drink the waitress sounded sincere when she said she forgot the drink and would bring it right away. The waitress returned without the drink and asked if we were ready to order. Addie stood up and said: *"We will not be ready to order until my husband recieves his juice."* The waitress walked away, came back, and slammed the juice down in front of me. We looked at eachother stunned. Dan threw a few dollars down on the table and said: *"I've had enough. I wouldn't eat here if you paid me. Joe, Addie lets go."* We were very careful where we ate after that.

If Dan had to meet with a promoter, Addie and I remained in the hotel room. Whenever we ate or went out for walks we did it as a group. It's sad to think that I could walk freely in public with my wife in another country like France without a problem, but I could not walk safely with my wife in my own country. I had to walk in the street while my wife walked on the sidewalk with Dan. On the only occasion that Addie and I walked alone, a group of white boys saw us and threw rocks at us. We had to run back to our hotel.[319]

I beat Nat Dewey by decision over eight rounds and dropped him in the final round with a short uppercut when he was trying to clinch with me.

On December 18 my manager Dan McKetrick wrote an editorial to Eddie McBride, the sports editor of the *Buffalo Enquirer.* *"I have arranged to bring Jeannette to your city for a contest with Jack 'Twin' Sullivan. Now, Eddie, you have never seen this big Indian of mine in action. On the square, he is the logical heavyweight champion of the world. I have always contended he is as good a man as Jack Johnson: in fact, I firmly believe that he can whip Johnson without any trouble in a long fight. Jeannette is not a short distance boxer, but likes the marathon route, and has never been shaded in a long contest.*

"I would like to have you come and look Jeannette over in his contest with Jack 'Twin' Sullivan, and then give me your honest opinion of what you think of him. I am sure that you will agree with me that he is a world's champion. A little dope on what Jeannette has done may be of interest to you, and you might want to publish it.

"Jeannette started boxing as a welterweight, and his first few fights were all won with knockouts. He then jumped into the middleweight class, and as a middleweight fought Langford and Johnson. The first fight he had with Johnson was in Philadelphia, where Johnson was signed to meet two men at three rounds apiece. The first fellow Johnson stopped in two rounds, and he then took on Jeannette, and instead of stopping Jeannette the latter gave Johnson a prize walloping in three rounds. At this time Jeannette weighed 155 pounds.

"A month later they fought a six-round bout, and again Jeannette won the popular verdict, the Philadelphia papers being unanimous in declaring Jeannette the winner. They boxed three more times in Philadelphia, and every contest was won by Jeannette. Between these fights he went to Lawrence to fight Langford, and they went twelve rounds to a draw. They fought again and Jeannette made him quit in eight rounds, Langford deliberately refusing to leave his corner for the ninth session. They have fought many fights since, and in every instance Jeannette was winning before the end: in fact, in the last fight Jeannette gave Langford a good thrashing.

"I contend that Langford will never fight Jeannette a route, and here is the reason why: Langford agreed to fight Jeannette in Paris and was guaranteed by Victor Breyer $5,000 for his end. A week later, Langford told Breyer that the fight was off unless he was given $7,500. Breyer jumped to London and signed articles of agreement with Langford on those terms. Two weeks later Langford sent word to Breyer that his father was dying in Nova Scotia and jumped on a boat for America, even leaving behind his manager, Jim Woodward.

"In repudiating his contract with Breyer he has cancelled his chance of ever getting another match in France; in fact, he will never be able to go back to that country, for all contracts are made there on government paper, and if you violate them the government holds you responsible, which means the government will attend to Mr. Langford if he ever

[319] Interview with JoAnn Flannery-Mostaccio Joe Jennette's great-niece.

goes back. Now, here is another instance that Jeannette beat Langford. He was offered a fight in California by Jim Coffroth. Once more Langford accepted and we were getting ready to go to the coast when we learned that Langford has suddenly gone in another direction, and the next thing we knew he was on a boat for Australia. Now, surely this is proof positive that he did not want nor will not fight Jeannette 20 rounds. Such being the case, what right has he to fight for the championship?

"In my opinion the next best man to Johnson and Jeannette is Sam McVea. This Negro, last spring, fought a 20-round draw with Langford in Paris. At that time I believed McVea was entitled to the decision. However, McVea and Langford fight it out on Xmas, and I think that McVea will be returned the winner. That Jeannette is a better man than McVea was proved when he whipped McVea in a 49-round bout in Paris. Shortly before Johnson sailed for England he was interviewed by Robert Edgren of the Evening World. Edgren asked Johnson why he did not fight Langford, and Johnson's reply was: 'Will you show or tell me what club ever offered us a date?' To this Edgren had to agree, and then Johnson went on and told Edgren that in his opinion Langford was not in the same class with Jeannette in a fight of 20 rounds. 'I believe,' said Johnson, 'that Jeannette will stop Langford or make him quit if they ever go over 10 rounds, for I think that Jeannette is the greatest man in the world in a finish fight.'

"That Johnson believes this is now certain, being that he was offered $35,000 to fight Jeannette to a finish in Paris next June, the night of the Grand Prix. Tom O'Rourke also cabled Johnson an offer of $25,000 to fight Jeannette in this city, and Johnson's reply was that he was out of the game. It is on the above ground that I claim the championship for Jeannette if Johnson has retired, and I intend to post $5,000 to fight for the title, this sum of $5,000 to go as a side bet on the result. If Johnson does not accept, I will claim the title and then stand ready to let Jeannette fight any man in the world for that side stake.

"At present I am sending Jeannette around the country meeting all comers. In the last two weeks he has had six fights, five of which he won by knockout inside of four rounds. Tonight he boxes in Chattanooga a chap called Al Mitchell, a 230-pound giant from Oklahoma. He then goes to New Orleans on Friday night to battle 'Topeka' Jack Johnson, and will immediately return and go to Buffalo for the Jack 'Twin' Sullivan fight. All the training he has been able to have for these fights has been done on trains, because he has been continually on the road, and this goes to show what a remarkable man he is.

"You can rest assured that you will see a remarkable fighter when you see him, and I wish that you would favor me by coming to the fight, for, as before, I want your candid opinion of him."[320]

I wrapped up the Southern trip with knockout wins over Al Mitchell in Memphis on the 18th, and "Topeka" Jack Johnson in New Orleans on the 21st. When I returned from the South I helped put the final touches on Tom Kennedy for his upcoming bout with Carl Morris. I had worked with

---

[320] *Springfield Daily News* December 23, 1911.

Carl previously, but now I was working with Tom. Tom was fighting Morris on December 27 at the Empire A.C. in New York. Morris won the fight by a ten round newspaper decision. Kennedy would go on to have a successful acting career after he retired from boxing.

On December 26, in Australia, Sam McVea defeated Sam Langford by decision in a twenty round bout. McVea won the colored heavyweight and Australian heavyweight titles with the win.

On December 26 at the Convention Hall in Buffalo, New York, I defeated Jack "Twin" Sullivan via ten round decision. Three thousand people were on hand. Sullivan did a lot of running and holding in the bout. The *Cleveland Plain Dealer* wrote: *Jack "Twin" Sullivan took as much of a beating as a man can without being knocked out, from Joe Jeannette last week.*[321]

On December 27 my manager McKetrick wrote a letter to Jack Johnson, by way of the press, trying to force Jack to fight me: *"Friend Johnson, as you have denied the cable reports of your announced retirement from the ring and state that you are prepared to make a match with any of the eligible heavyweights, I again renew my request for a match for Joe Jeannette for the title. Your statement is that you are still the heavyweight champion, ready to defend that title, and will fight any man living. It is this very candid statement that induces me to write you this letter.*

"Joe Jeannette is not only willing but anxious for a match with you. You will appreciate that Sam Langford is removed from the field, having been beaten by Jeannette in a ten round contest last November, and afterward defaulting after making a new match to fight Jeannette before Jim Coffroth's club. He simply ran out of the match and made a hurried departure for Australia, evading the issue at a distance. This leaves Jeannette the only logical man to contend with you for the title. You appreciate that there is no white hope in sight that the public has any confidence in or would go to see you fight. Under the impression that you are sincere in your last statement, I am going to appeal to your fairness to give proper consideration to my request for a match. It is not necessary to enter into a wide range of unnecessary monologue or oratory and a lot of messy technicality to evade if your statement is to be accepted at par. We want the match and we want it badly, and in support of this assertion I am ready to prove that I am earnest by posting $5,000 with any newspaper you name.

"The terms of the match can be such as you may fairly exact under the Queensberry Rules. The one essential point is to make the match, and the details of the match can then be reached. Like you, we are anxious for the best financial inducements, but they are only secondary with us. What we particularly want is the match. You understand conditions, etc., having experienced many obstacles and having to make many concessions to secure an opportunity. It is the same kind of opportunity which you so long sought that we are after.

"In support of my insistence for a match for Jeannette, you know that my man has long asked for a meeting at a distance with you, and I ask you to recall some of your bouts with him. They were meritorious to warrant your stating, just prior to your sailing to

[321] *Cleveland Plain Dealer* December 31, 1911.

England, that you believed Jeannette to be the best man in the world as a pugilist, outside of yourself, particularly for a long fight.

"It is with this in mind that I present a claim for a match in a businesslike way, and not hampered with needless or abusive language. To this I add that it is eighteen months since you fought for the title, and under the rules and precedents it is 'time' that you defend that title with a challenge from a sincere and logical rival."[322]

---

[322] *Baltimore Sun* December 31, 1911.

Chapter 16
The Offer and Arthur Accepts 1912

On January 4, 1912, Jack Johnson advised the *New York Times* that he would defend his title two more times and then retire. One bout would be against Sam McVea and the other against Jim Flynn. His proposed bout with McVea was to take place on June 23. I had sacrificed so much to win the finish fight against McVea so I could receive a title shot. Now Johnson was going to fight McVea, the loser, and not me. Jack stated he would not fight me because such a bout would not generate enough purse money. That was ridiculous because he would not make a penny more against McVea. In the same *New York Times* article the Empire A.C. gave an offer to Johnson of fifteen thousand dollars to box me ten rounds in New York City. A representative for the Empire A.C. stated that: *Jeanette... no doubt is the next best man to Johnson in the heavyweight line*. I had just returned from Utica, New York, where on January 19 I knocked out Griff Jones in three rounds. Once again I was forced to play the waiting game.

On February 5, my manager, Dan McKetrick, took heavyweight Frank Moran "The Pittsburgh Dentist," to London to box Fred Storbeck. The match took place at The Ring, at Blackfriars in London. It was supposed to be an easy win for Moran, so he did not train very hard for the fight. I believe Dan McKetrick was the greatest manager and second. He helped me win many fights with his strategies. I'll let famous boxing referee Eugene Corri describe the Moran-Storbeck fight and how important McKetrick was in the outcome: *"The fight at The Ring between Fred Storbeck, the Boer blacksmith, and Frank Moran of Pittsburg, the great fighting dentist, is still fresh in my memory. If ever a boxer had his second to thank for winning a fight, Moran had on this occasion. The dentist was seconded by Dan McKetrick, who afterwards became Young Ahearn's manager. It was a twenty round contest, and ended in the (twelfth) round, when Storbeck was stopped, to the amazement of everybody. Two rounds before the surprising finish Storbeck had won easily on points, and Moran looked as if he couldn't have knocked over a tailor's dummy. The dentist, I believe, was going to stop, when his shrewd second called out to him: 'Walk round, Frank, walk round. He's awful tired; like to drop.'*

"Storbeck tired! The Boer was going as strong as a springbok. But Moran was too far gone to see this, so he believed McKetrick and took heart again. The ruse of this ingenious second succeeded. Moran walked round and round the ring, keeping out of Storbeck's way and gathering his wind. After the minute's interval he came up for the (eleventh) round a new man. In the (twelfth) round Storbeck's seconds 'threw the towel in' literally. I said to McKetrick: 'That fight was won by you and nobody else.' He looked at me as much as to say: 'I know it was, and who had a better right?'

"There have been few greater managers or seconds than this same McKetrick, who studied the men in his care till he knew what they could do better than they knew

220

themselves. The boxer who has found a good manager, like the man who has found a good wife, is decidedly in luck's way. "[323]

On April 1 I faced Griff Jones again, at the Olympia A.C. in New York City. The *New York Times* described the bout: *The action of the referee saved Jones from a sure knockout, as he was completely outclassed in every way by Jeannette and did not have a chance. Jones weighed 174 pounds and Jeannette tipped the beam at 189 pounds just before entering the ring. The only entertainment the bout afforded was furnished by Jeannette. During the second and third round he raised his guard four times and allowed Jones to punch as much as he cared to, Jeannette remained perfectly still until Jones had stopped. Then Joe began to box Jones with his left hand only, shooting in punches by the dozen without getting a return. In the third round Jeannette started in as if to finish the bout quickly and the crowd called for one more round. Joe acceded to the popular demand and assumed the defensive, finishing the last half of this round without allowing Jones to hit him. Early in the fourth round Jeannette floored Jones twice with lefts to the stomach, and, though Jones protested that he would continue, Referee (Dan) Tone ended the bout.*[324]

On April 12 Sam McVea suffered a serious injury to his right hand in Australia: *While overhauling his motor car at his residence at Double Bay, Sam McVey had his right hand crushed in the machinery and the forefinger was so badly injured that it was found necessary to amputate the top joint. McVey's manager Billy McClain, says his charge will require a long rest, and that for a month training will be out of the question.*[325]

On April 15 the news broke that the RMS Titanic had sunk. The loss of life was enormous. We held our collective breaths as we awaited the survivors' arrival into New York Harbor. Adelaide was always nervous about me traveling by ship after the incident. On April 18 the Carpathia arrived in New York Harbor with the survivors.

One of the residents of my hometown in West Hoboken was a victim on the Titanic. His name was John Ashby, 57-years-old, and he was the father-in-law of Greenwood Robinson, who was the proprietor of the Colonial Theater on DeMott Street. Mr. Ashby had been on a trip to England to visit relatives and he was returning on the Titanic. The entire town knew Mr. Ashby and his family and we were all very upset about his loss as well as all the others who lost their lives on that voyage. His body was thought to have been recovered on April 22 by the cable ship MacKay-Bennett, which was in the area of the sinking searching for bodies, but it was a mistaken identity and his body was never found.

Also on the ill-fated ship was Miss Elizabeth Dowdell, 30-years-old, of 215 Park Avenue, Union Hill. Miss Dowdell was lucky enough to get into one of the life boats and was saved by the Carpathia. Her relatives went to

---

[323] *Thirty Years a Boxing Referee* by Eugene Corri pgs. 222-3.
[324] *New York Times* April 2, 1912.
[325] *Kalgoorlie Western Argus* April 16, 1912 pg. 39.

the Carpathia's arrival in New York and were saddened when they did not see her name on the survivors list. They boarded the 14th Street trolley car in Manhattan to return back to New Jersey. To their amazement Elizabeth came aboard the trolley a few passengers later. There was a great reunion and celebration.[326]

On April 21, the *Atlanta Constitution* published an article by former world's champion James J. Corbett. The article read: *"On the eve of departure for Paris, where he hopes to utilize Fred Storbeck, the South African champion as a means of replenishing his dwindling bank account, Joe Jeannette the Negro boxer, usually a person of great reserve and taciturnity, grabbed his trusty fountain pen and let loose a few hundred words about the attitude of one J. Arthur Johnson, heavyweight champion of the world. I take it from the tenor of Joe's maiden effort as a letter writer that he can hardly be classed as an ardent admirer of the present title holder.*

"Joe is peeved. In sooth, it is no wonder he feels vexed. Willing to box anybody, no color or creed barred, he finds it a difficult task to land an occasional job; this applies to the entire bunch of heavies from Johnson down to the most hopeless of the hopes. The champion in particular refuses to give him a tumble at all, and that's what gets Joseph's goat. Therefore, it is at the Johnson person (no less), that the Hoboken scrapper slings his bunch of libelous language.

"Angry that none of the boxers in this country, with or without a 'rep' wants his game, and because he finds it necessary to hike to Europe to earn a piece of money, Jeannette in his arraignment of the champion, lands some damaging blows to the already tottering reputation of Jeffries' conqueror. He charges Johnson with cowardice, dubs him a 'moving picture' fighter, a 'four-flusher' and other names that indicate great affection for the accused; asserts he is champion only through a 'lucky break,' that he is stalling to avoid meeting Langford or himself (Jeannette), and knows he will surely be licked if he boxes either. He brands Jack as an overrated champion, concluding with the declaration that he made Johnson quit in their match in Philadelphia, and offering to bet $5,000 he can do the trick over again. Outside of these few failings the champion is alright, according to Joe.

"Fight followers who doubt Jeannette's right to challenge for the title need only peruse the record books to convince themselves of his eligibility. If the match with Langford arranged for Los Angeles in July goes through and he emerges a victor over the doughty 'tar baby,' Joe declares he will force Johnson to give him battle or lay down his hand and retire from the game."[327]

The following was my letter which was printed by several newspapers nationwide: *"For the past year both my manager and myself have tried to obtain a contest with Jack Johnson. We have repeatedly sent him challenges, all of which he has ignored. This 'moving picture' champion, who by a lucky break at Reno became the world's champion, now refuses to defend that title. I hereby defy him to meet me. I further add that this refusal to fight me is due to cowardice. He knows that he will lose his title if he ever meets either Langford or myself. He is now stalling about meeting Langford, but*

---

[326] *Jersey Journal* April 20, 1912.
[327] *Atlanta Constitution* April 21, 1912.

really wants to pick on Jim Flynn or Al Palzer, and he knows right well that Palzer is a novice but these are the kind of men he would fight. I have whipped him decisively several times in Philadelphia, and he deliberately quit on me in one contest over there. I say 'quit' because when I had him bad he maliciously fouled me to save himself from defeat. He has been offered $10,000 to box me six rounds in Philadelphia and $10,000 to fight me in this city (New York), but both these offers he has ignored. If he can get up enough courage to box me twenty rounds I will bet him $5,000 that I will stop him. I will not say 'knock him out' for he has not enough courage to stand up and fight and be knocked out. I sail for Europe this week and will return on the next ship if Johnson has enough nerve to accept my defy. I know that I can beat him and I know that the public would like to see the title change hands. Now, Mr. Johnson, are you a fighter or a 'four-flusher'. Your answer to this letter will decide the question."[328]

Willie Lewis sailed to Europe with Dan and I on May 18. Willie was to box Georges Carpentier for the EUB European world middleweight title on May 23 at the Palais de Sports in Paris. I was to box George Rodel in Plymouth, Devon, England on May 24. Willie put up a good scrap but lost a twenty round decision to the kid he helped teach how to fight. Willie's fight with Carpentier was described by Paul Hamelle: "*At 10pm the two great athletes made their way into the ring. And the stentorian voice of Max presented to the public 'Willie Lewis, American 71 kilos 530 grams; Carpentier, French, 71 kilos 950 grams.' They advanced towards each other, exchanging the hand shaking ritual. Here they were opposite one another, in the bright lights cruelly greening, which broke down their faces, lending to the scene something indescribably fantastic.*

"*Willie Lewis, more saddle, very straight, was bearing in half open, Carpentier, more nervous, back in a defensive posture. They appeared perfectly balanced, beautifully matched. And the duel would, although briefly, allow us to follow this adventure. During the first five rounds Carpentier dominated slightly. In the sixth round, the battle came alive and became violent, without a clear benefit. In the seventh round, Lewis was driven into the ropes. The battle was becoming increasingly fierce, crosses, uppercuts, direct exchanges with a generous abundance. The Frenchman, who continued to attack, failed to break the spirit of the American, who also continued to attack. And then in the eighth round, catastrophically, the heart of the French beat a second of anxiety.*

"*It was toward the end of the hard fought round that Carpentier became a bit disjointed. With an electric trigger, the American managed to hit the jaw of Carpentier with a right. The blow made a popping noise which was followed by silence. Under the shock, flexed our champion, stunned, and though he did not quite fall, he had to 'take' a knee and rest awhile in that position, his eyes haggard. Would he recover? Would the American have enough time to finish him? Carpentier got up and at that very moment the gong sounded which saved him. If delivered a moment earlier what would have been the result of this terrible blow? The crowd anxiously asked, and after the minute interval that followed, we found that the favorite was strong enough to withstand the Yankee*

---

[328] *Detroit Free Press* April 28, 1912.

attack.

"And indeed during the ninth, tenth, eleventh, and twelfth rounds, the American clearly dominated, but he did not succeed in placing the decisive blow that would turn his advantage into victory. Little by little, and perhaps better than all his achievements, Carpentier overcame his failure, recovered from the shock, so much so that-oh! pleasant surprise in the thirteenth round, he, in turn, took the offensive. It seemed that his game was gaining speed, accuracy. His shots were coming driving in. And the packed crowd gave an ovation. They fought with him...

"In the fourteenth and fifteenth rounds, Lewis was spent; he used his head or leaned down during the clinches to avoid separation. He was bleeding from the mouth. In the sixteenth round, Carpentier seemed to coast for a moment. Though brief. The attacks started to increase. The men expended all their energy. In the following three rounds, seventeenth, eighteenth, and nineteenth, the fighting got fiercer, without ceasing, and for that you can thank both sides. Carpentier strove to regain the lost points, and Lewis to retain the advantage that he had gained earlier. And here came the twentieth round; a whirlwind. We did not see the shots, we just saw Carpentier, who drew from his youth, his will to win, the delirium of the crowd, a burst of energy, his opponent stunned by the sudden hail of blows. Before the judge, the public stood in a unanimous gesture of enthusiasm. Carpentier declared the winner!"[329] The next day, May 24, I knocked out George Rodel in eleven rounds.

On May 26, Johnson arrived in Las Vegas to prepare for his fight with Flynn. Johnson and Jack Curley, the promoter, had wanted the Flynn affair to take place in Madison Square Garden. Frank O'Neill, the New York State Boxing Commissioner, publicly announced he would never allow Johnson to box in his state. Johnson gave a statement on the Commissions' actions: *"I guess that's discrimination for you. As an American citizen why have I not the right to box in New York as anyone else?"[330]*

Sam Langford and I were allowed to box in New York, which angered Johnson even more. The commission obviously was not discriminating against Johnson because of his color. It was personal. I was also in an interracial marriage, so that was not the issue either.

On June 12, I heard more bad news for poor Sam McVea in Australia. Sam's wife: *and three other ladies were motoring near Manly... when the car struck a tramway pole. The driver of the vehicle was trying to avoid some cyclist. All the occupants of the car were thrown onto the roadway, and were picked up in a semi-conscious condition. Mrs. McVey sustained a concussion of the brain and severe bruises, but the others escaped serious injury. The car was badly damaged. Mr. Sam McVey and a friend, motoring along the same road, came across the wrecked car.[331]* Sam's wife would recover from the accident.

On June 15, 1912, I faced "Black" Bill for the eighth time. The fight was

[329] *Le Sport Universal Illustre* 1912 by Paul Hamelle.
[330] *Unforgivable Blackness* by Geoffrey C. Ward pg. 279.
[331] *The Register* June 4, 1912 pg. 14.

at the Royal Athletic Club in Brooklyn. I weighed 196 1/2 pounds to Bill's 197 1/2 pounds. I decided to use my jab and let the fight go a few rounds for the fans. Bill rushed me at the opening bell like he was John L. Sullivan. I landed some solid rights and lefts in the round as he lunged in. Round after round I landed the jab on Bill's head. He seemed to be getting agitated that I was landing my jabs more effectively than I did in our previous battles. I stepped inside and scored with hard left hooks and right crosses. In the fifth round Bill tried to wrestle me to the ground and even attempted to trip me to get me off of my feet. In the sixth round Bill continued his ugly tactics and even threw me into the referee a few times as he tried to wrestle me through the ropes. Twice during the round Bill pushed me, the referee, and even himself through the ropes. The crowd was booing loudly and the announcer entered the ring and stated that the referee gave the decision to me. The referee, after hearing this, re-entered the ring and stated that he had made no such decision. Instead the ref proclaimed that "Black" Bill was disqualified. It was one of the dirtiest fights of my career.

"Bombardier" Wells, an English heavyweight, came to the United States in June seeking big money fights. He lost a match against Al Palzer on June 28 in the Garden via third round knockout. His Manager, Jem Maloney, commented on Wells' future plans: *"Well's came here seeking a fight with Jack Johnson. But, of course, that is out of the question since Palzer has beaten my man. If Wells defeats Kennedy, however, we will gladly box Jeanette, who in our opinion is at least the equal of Johnson."*[332]

An article published on July 1 nationwide, was titled: "Jack Johnson's Peer, Jeannette?"[333] In the article the reporter explained that if Jack wanted to take part in a real fight when he finished with Jim Flynn he would fight me. It mentioned that Victor Breyer had offered Jack thirty thousand dollars to meet me in a thirty round bout in Paris in October. Johnson repeatedly stated that he would meet any man if his price of thirty thousand dollars was met. Breyer had met that demand. I was willing to make the match on any terms whatsoever. The article stated: *Joe Jeannette is probably the least appreciated pugilist in the ring today, considering his merits. Although his real worth is well recognized by close followers of boxing, the majority of those only casually interested in the ring fail to appreciate his ability to the full extent. Of all the men who covet Johnson's title, none looks to have a better chance of defeating the champion than the Hoboken Negro. Johnson himself is fully aware of this, and studiously avoids mentioning Jeannette's name when discussing future matches. Another good point about Jeannette is that he always tries to win as decisively as possible, instead of saving his opponents up for another match. And, opponents are mighty scarce and hard to find.*

Jeannette returned from a trip from Paris and England about a week or so ago. He was forced to go abroad because he could find no more heavyweights who would risk a meeting

---

[332] *Watertown Daily Times* July 18, 1912.
[333] *New Orleans Times-Picayune* July 1, 1912

with him. On the other side he had no better success, for none of Europe's big men were feeling belligerent when Jeannette hove in sight. He did manage to get a match at Plymouth, England, and Glasgow, Scotland, but in each place his opponent was of no standing. He knocked them both out easily. Jeannette is a superbly built athlete. He does not tend to take on fat and is always as hard as a marble statue, even when out of training. When in perfect condition it is worth the price of admission merely to watch the play of his muscles as he moves about the ring.

He can absorb punishment even more amazingly than he deals it out. One of his favorite tricks when feeling in a humorous mood is to drop his hands and allow his opponent to swing both hands at his stomach. In attack he is lightning fast. His left jabs shoot to the mark with speed that would be envied by a featherweight. His right crosses and uppercuts are only surpassed by those of Sam Langford. Jeannette is particularly anxious to meet Langford in a twenty round bout, but the Boston Negro evidently prefers the easier game in Australia. Twice Sam has found his way out of matches with Jeannette in California by making himself scarce when fight time came around.

Jeannette is, of course, delighted in the prospect of meeting Johnson in the fall, but he says he has his doubts whether Johnson will sign articles. In the meanwhile he would like to keep his hand in by taking on all comers.[334]

On July 3, Dan McKetrick sent Jack Johnson a telegram. In the telegram Dan stated that a Paris boxing club had guaranteed Johnson thirty thousand dollars if he boxed me thirty rounds. Johnson never replied to the telegram.

The Flynn fight took place in Albuquerque, New Mexico, on July 4, 1912. It was a one-sided massacre with Johnson carrying Flynn while Flynn tried desperately to head-butt Johnson. When a reporter asked me what I thought of the fight I told him Johnson had turned into a: *"motion picture fighter."* I made the statement because Jack carried Flynn just to make money from the newsreel sales.

In New York on July 5 the Garden A.C.'s manager Gibson sent a telegram to Jack Johnson: *"Have signed Jeannette to fight you. What are your terms?"*[335] Up until July 11 Gibson had not received a reply even though he had received confirmation that Johnson indeed received the telegram.

Sam Fitzpatrick, who managed Johnson when he faced me several times in 1905 and 1906, admitted that I was Johnson's master in more than one bout. Due to the inability to get Jack into the ring, Dan was working on fights with either Luther McCarty or the winner of the upcoming Bombardier Wells-Tom Kennedy contest in the Garden.

On July 9 the *New York World* and the *New York Tribune* carried an article titled "Joe Jeannette is the Next Hope." The article was as follows: *Billy Gibson, manager of the Garden Athletic Club, yesterday signed Joe Jeannette to articles of agreement for a ten round bout with Jack Johnson, providing the latter is anxious to fight here. Gibson denied a report that the Garden Athletic Club had offered a purse for*

---

334 Untitled newspaper article July 1, 1912.
335 *Trenton Evening Times* July 11, 1912.

a fight between Johnson and Al Palzer. He stated that in his opinion Palzer would be no match for Johnson; neither would Luther McCarty nor any of the other present day white hopes. But in the view of the fact that Jeannette had held his own with Johnson on four separate occasions, he believes a match between Johnson and Jeannette would be popular here. [336]

On July 12 the *Washington Post* printed the following: *Victor Breyer of Paris, has made Jack Johnson an authentic offer of 150,000 francs ($30,000) for his end to fight Jeanette thirty rounds in France, says the Evening World. Before making this offer Breyer succeeded in getting permission from the authorities to put on Jeannette and Johnson in a thirty round battle, although the usual police regulations limit all bouts to twenty rounds.*

Breyer offers to post Johnson's end ($30,000) in advance. The only stipulation he insists upon is that Johnson must post in the hands of some responsible party a forfeit of $10,000 to guarantee his appearance. This Breyer considers a necessary factor in the match, as Johnson might take it into his head to "run out" at the last moment unless he had up a big forfeit.

Johnson has steadily refused to meet Jeannette in a long fight. He has met Joe half a dozen times or more in short contests, and knows that the more Jeannette is punched the stronger he grows and the harder he fights... Another offer to Johnson and no doubt as good as Breyer's, is that of McIntosh, who wants Johnson to take a trip to Australia. He offers the champion $45,000 to meet McVey and Langford in Australia...

Billy Gibson, of this city, has sent Johnson a very substantial offer for a match with Jeannette in the Garden. Such a match would pack New York's famous arena until the last one would have to climb the rafters to see the ring. But Johnson answers: "Nothing doing. I might box Palzer ten rounds in New York for $30,000."

The champion won't take a chance with a man he knows to be a crack boxer and a fighter too. He knows Palzer is practically a novice- big, strong, game- but a novice without knowledge enough of the game to do Jack any damage in ten rounds. [337]

A possible fight with Johnson was triggering a frenzy of newspaper coverage. Dan sent a letter to the New York papers that was printed on July 13. In the letter Dan stated: *"Why does Jack Johnson refuse to recognize Joe Jeannette's right to a contest for the world's championship? Is it because he fears the issue or that he believes he has a perpetual claim on the title? For two years I have tried by all manner and means to induce Johnson to meet Jeannette. He has not only ignored all challenges, but every offer as well for a battle.*

"He has been offered $20,000 to meet Jeannette for ten rounds in this city. He hasn't had the decency to reply to these offers. Without mentioning Jeannette's name, he tells the world he will fight anyone for a guarantee of $30,000. That is another method of dodging Jeannette, but what he believed would scare promoters has acted as a boomerang for Victor Breyer of Paris has made Johnson the following offer: A guarantee of $30,000 for his end to meet Jeannette in a contest of thirty rounds or more. This offer has been sent to

---

[336] *New York World* July 9, 1912.
[337] *Washington Post* July 12, 1912.

Johnson by Breyer and his New York representative.

"*The above offer is a bona fide one, under the Marquis of Queensbury rules a champion must defend his title when challenged. Unless Johnson agrees to a contest within thirty days, I will claim the heavyweight championship of the world for Joe Jeannette and he will be ready to defend it against all comers.*

"*Jeannette's claim has a solid backing, for unlike the white hopes, his caliber has been tested and found A-1. Jeannette holds the heavyweight championship of Europe, winning it from Sam McVea, whom he stopped in forty-nine rounds and later whipped in thirty rounds. He has the only knock out to his credit that was ever scored against Langford, and only this month Langford repudiated a contest calling for a match with Jeannette at the McCarey club in Los Angeles. Besides he has whipped Johnson four different times decisively. Perhaps that is why Johnson refuses to meet him.*"[338]

The reporter who wrote the article injected his own opinion after Dan's letter: *Your communication has been received and filed, Mr. McKetrick. Really we don't know why Mr. Johnson should be dodging your bronze currency chaser. Maybe he dodges in deadly fear- maybe he's drawn the 'color line'. One can't get a good line on any of 'them' champions. If Mr. Jeannette is as good as you say he is one could hardly blame the popular Chicago café director for dodging. Champions as a rule are not hunting defeat and according to your dope John Arthur would stand no more chance in a battle with Joe Jeannette than Jim Flynn would have in a Newport Cotillion. But keep on offering the gigantic 'burr head' $30,000 and someday when the bankroll is light he will take the bait. They all 'come through' some time.*[339]

On July 18 "Bombardier" Wells knocked out Tom Kennedy at Madison Square Garden in the eighth round. On July 19 I boxed a draw with "Battling" Jim Johnson at the Olympia A.A. in Philadelphia. Johnson was out of shape and looked it, with his paunchy stomach. The *Boston Daily Globe* reported that I took it easy on Jim: *Joe did little or nothing to prevent the over fat Johnson from remaining upright in the ring from gong to gong.*[340] What the papers didn't understand was we needed each other to make a living. If I destroyed everyone I fought I wouldn't be able to support my family. It was getting nearly impossible for me to find fights.

On July 25 I boxed two boxers on the same night at the New Bedford A.C. in New Bedford, Massachusetts. First I fought Mickey McDonough, stopping him in two rounds. Jeff Madden was next, I knocked him out in the fourth round.[341]

Also on July 25 Johnson had announced, via long distance telephone from Chicago, that he was ready to sign for a match with me on Labor Day, at Madison Square Garden, if he could get his price of thirty thousand

---

[338] *Washington Post* July 12, 1912.
[339] *Washington Post* July 12, 1912.
[340] *Boston Daily Globe* July 20, 1912.
[341] *Boston Journal* July 16, 1912.

dollars.[342] The champion refused a twenty thousand dollar offer. Johnson spoke to Billy Gibson, manager of the Garden Athletic Club. Johnson stated: *"You'll have to act quickly because I would want to begin training on Monday."*[343] Gibson informed Johnson that he would have to confer with Dan McKetrick before making a decision.

On July 28 the *New York Times* also reported that Johnson would not box me unless he received the guaranteed thirty thousand dollars. The Garden Athletic club offer of twenty thousand dollars was unacceptable to him.

I was on a roll. I had won sixteen straight fights from January to the end of July and 23 straight going back to September 5, 1911, when I lost a decision to Sam Langford. According to a reporter from the *New York Times: Johnson was afraid to take a chance with the other (Jeannette) black gladiator.*[344]

William Poth, head of the syndicate that runs the Garden, accompanied Dan and Gibson to Chicago to make an in-person offer to Johnson. The offer was on the table from the 28th until the 29th at two o'clock when it would be pulled. I prayed hard that night. On July 31 the United States Congress passed a law banning all interstate shipment of prizefighting films. The passing of the bill was sparked by the Johnson-Flynn fight. Some said that Congress was trying to stop Johnson from making money. Others said it was to prevent the violent outbursts that occurred when people viewed the mixed-race bouts.

An August 7 newspaper article stated that I was the new heavyweight champion because Johnson had failed to defend his title against a worthy challenger and thereby deserted his claim to the throne. In the article, which I cut out and saved in my scrapbook, Dan McKetrick stated: *"Joe Jeannette, the heavyweight champion of the world, is going to start on a tour across the continent, meeting all comers, with no color line drawn."* The reporter commented: *You've got to hand it to Danny. He's made first grab at the title, deserted by Lil' Artha', and anybody that can get it from McKetrick- well, it can't be done, that's all.*[345]

McKetrick told the press that I forced Johnson into retirement. Dan said: *"There is no doubt that Jeannette forced Johnson into retirement for when Breyer guaranteed Johnson $30,000 (when the latter said he would fight anybody for that amount) Johnson came out with the announcement of quitting the game. Gibson, when in Chicago, offered Johnson $20,000 to box Jeannette ten rounds in the Garden. Before the promoter reached New York Johnson sent out another retirement notice, fearing that Gibson would accept the latter's terms. Jeannette now stands ready to defend the title, and if Tommy Burns is sincere in his desire to return to the ring he can fight Jeannette for the heavyweight title."*

On August 13 the *Indiana Star* reported: *Dan McKetrick, manager for Joe*

---

[342] *Boston Daily Globe* July 26, 1912.
[343] *Olympia Record* July 26, 1912.
[344] *New York Times* July 28, 1912.
[345] *International News Service* August 7, 1912.

Jeannette, claimant to the world's heavyweight title, announced tonight that he had refused an offer of $15,000 from Hugh McIntosh for the 'champion' to go to Australia to fight for him. McKetrick said he had signed Jeannette to fight Sam Langford in Los Angeles, and moreover, he did not want his new champion to absent himself from the United States for so long a trip, since he might be called upon to defend his 'title' here. He said Jeannette is ready to meet Tommy Burns or any other white hope.[346]

I guess the article got a lot of attention, especially Johnson's, because on August 13, 1912, the *New York Times* reported that Johnson stated he would fight me in New York City.[347] The McMahon brothers of the St. Nicholas Club of New York traveled to Chicago to finalize the deal and get Johnson to sign the contract. I had already signed the contract. The fight would be scheduled for late September.

Johnson stated he was only taking the fight to please his wife and that he would retire immediately afterwards. I didn't care why he was fighting as long as I finally got my title shot. Against all prudence I dared to dream about winning the title. Johnson was to get twenty-five thousand dollars with a privilege of fifty percent of the first fifty thousand dollars in receipts and thirty-five percent of all gate receipts over that. Johnson was also to get half of the motion picture returns. Dan told me he was still negotiating my purse. I told him I would fight for free if I got my shot at the title. That's how confident I was that I would beat Jack.

Johnson was feeling the heat of being stripped of his title, as described by an *L.A. Times* article: *Declaring the stories printed recently, giving the fact that he was 'all in' as a champion as the reason for his retirement had caused his wife to demand that he vindicate himself and eventually forced him back into the fighting game, Jack Johnson today opened negotiations with the McMahon brothers of New York for a battle with Joe Jeannette.*

"I expect to sign the papers tomorrow for the fight with Jeannette," said Johnson. "Money is not the consideration, but, of course, I'll get all I can. When I announced recently I was through, I meant it, but critics write I was retiring because I was 'all in,' and now I will prove to the contrary. I am going to give Jeannette the worst beating in his career, and will get down to training just the minute I sign the articles."[348]

The *New York Times* wrote: *After the government this afternoon dismissed the prosecution of Jack Johnson, champion heavyweight pugilist, on charges of intimidating a government witness in the smuggling indictment against him and his wife, Etta Johnson, the champion immediately announced that he had rescinded his decision made a short time ago to quit the prize ring, and will accept a challenge to fight Joe Jeannette in New York City...*

Johnson declared that he was going to fight only once more, in order to appease his wife, who has been insisting that she wants to see him add laurels of another battle to his

---

[346] *Indiana Star* August 13, 1912.
[347] *New York Times* August 13, 1912.
[348] *Los Angeles Times* August 13, 1912.

pugilistic career.

"I expect to sign papers that will close the arrangements for a ten round fight with Jeannette in New York City," said Johnson. "I have decided to fight this battle for the sake of my wife only. When I announced recently that I had withdrawn from the ring for good, I meant it, but my wife persuaded me to make one more fight. I won't fight when I am through with Jeannette. I am then going to quit the ring and retire to private life."[349]

The charges of intimidating a witness were related to Johnson and his wife having been charged with smuggling a diamond necklace into the country.[350] On August 14, Johnson signed a contract to fight me on September 25, at St. Nicholas Athletic Club in New York.[351]

On the same day Johnson signed the contract a reporter came to my home at 522 Clinton Avenue in West Hoboken to interview me: *After many months of challenging and weary waiting with but scant encouragement, Joe Jeannette the West Hoboken nemesis of Jack Johnson, at last sees his hopes to be realized. Jeannette declares that he will need but twelve days of work to prepare for the bout with Johnson. "I never work more than twelve days for a fight," he explained in discussing the match. "I trained twelve days for Langford when we met in that last go at the Garden, and, if you remember, I was in fine shape. In fact, I think I was a little too fine. I weigh 189 pounds now but by the night of the fight, I'll weigh about 192. You know most fellows drop a lot of weight while training but it affects me differently, for I always gain, and fall off when I am doing nothing."*

Jeannette is a quiet spoken, unassuming fellow who is well liked by everyone with whom he comes in contact. His features are more of the Hindu or North American type than the full blooded Negro. His skin is a rich nut brown and when he is in perfect condition it glows with health, which together with his wonderful muscular structure, makes him a sight worth more than a second glance. In or out of condition he never carries any fat to speak of. Although he averages about 190 pounds, he is only 5 feet 10 inches in height, facts which indicate that his bones are extra large.

He has the peculiarity of being very deceptive in regards to his height. When seen in the ring he creates an impression that he is close to six feet, and it is only when standing by his side that one is undeceived. He called attention to this fact himself and said that it was a mistake that was constantly being made. Jeannette is always diffident about criticizing his opponents. He is very sensitive and fearful of being thought boastful. However, repeated questions induced him to discuss his chances of defeating Johnson at some length.

"Jack and I haven't got much for each other," he said. "We have had some tough fights and they have created a lot of hard feelings. I am always willing to forget what happens in the ring and be friends, but Johnson is not built that way. Whenever we have happened to meet he has always tried to avoid me without speaking. I know I can give him a good fight and I hope to outpoint him at least. He never had much on me in our other fights.

[349] *New York Times* August 13, 1912.
[350] *Unforgivable Blackness* Geoffrey C. Ward pg. 287.
[351] *Hartford Courant* August 15, 1912.

"I could always hit him without much trouble and once I cut him up pretty badly. I only weighed about 165 when I fought him last, now I am twenty-five pounds heavier, and Jack is getting old and fat. I think he showed in his bout with Flynn that he is losing his punch. If Flynn was butting him, as they say, from what I know of Jack he certainly would have cut loose unless he was afraid of getting tired.

"I'll go up after his body because I think that is his weakest spot now and besides body punching is my long suit. It was a body blow I got in that made him foul me that time in Philadelphia. I caught him with a right uppercut in the pit of the stomach and it made him gasp. Right after that he began hitting low. He hit me with a right that landed below the belt and the crowd began to hiss. I was hurt pretty badly, but I kept my feet and he deliberately struck me again with the same punch. When I woke up I was in the hospital. Johnson was arrested and they wanted me to press charges against him, but I didn't want to do that."

"How do you think Johnson intends to fight you this time?" Jeannette was asked. "Well, I shouldn't be surprised if he intends to stall as much as possible. He probably figures he can go along without doing much and not take any chances. Of course it takes two to make a good fight, but it won't be my fault if there is not plenty of action. He never could hold my arms like he did with Flynn and Tommy Burns. I only hope he reaches out to grab me, because if he does something is going to happen."

Jennette brought out a scrapbook full of newspaper clippings to substantiate his remarks regarding his different bouts with Johnson. He also exhibited a series of photographs taken during his battle with Sam McVey in Paris, showing himself, taking the count in all sorts of curious positions at different times during the contest in which he was floored twenty-one times and yet won out in the end. Jeannette looked them over with a curious smile, remarking, "Johnson admitted when he was in Paris that I could beat him in a finish fight. I hope I can do it in ten."[352]

On August 18, reporter Virginia Brunswick Smith of the *Hudson Dispatch* came to my home to interview me: *'Jeanette, Prize Fighter, Tells How he became a Pugilist.' Can you lower yourself down to the floor on one leg, keeping the other perfectly straight and then get up again, without bending the other knee? Can you lie prone on the floor and with your back perfectly straight, alternately raise and lower yourself, only your toes and hands touching the ground and your arms acting as hinges? Can you grasp the upper edge of a door or doorway and by the strength in your arms alone raise yourself up until you can 'chin' the top? If you can do any of the foregoing stunts I take my hat off to you in a sweeping salutation of obeisance and admiration. You amount to something in this world, and I frankly envy you. Ever since my interview with 'Joe Jeannette' the other day I have spent a large part of my leisure time practicing the aforesaid stunts with no further results at the present writing than the realization that there are concealed in the intricate mazes of my anatomy possibilities in the way of aches and sprains hitherto undreamed of. While as for my muscular control- it seems to be a quality as elusively baffling as the Irishman's flea- when you put your finger on it, it isn't there. However,*

---

[352] *The Freeman* August 31, 1912. Source Unpublished Manuscript "Square Joe" by Gregory Speciale.

I'm still practicing, and if the door will only hold out another six months I am confident of ultimate victory.

That any good thing- even the negligible virtue of a half-apologetic emulation of a gymnastic stunt- should have been the outcome of that interview is in itself scarcely less than a miracle. About pugilism I knew little and cared less and try as I could, not a particle of enthusiasm or even cold-storage curiosity could I evoke when the name of the colored prize-fighter, who by the retirement of Jack Johnson from the ring now claims the championship of the world, was suggested as the subject of an interview. "What do men see in prize-fighting?" was my disgusted ejaculation when the matter was first broached to me. "That's for you to find out," came the incisive reply.

So waiting only long enough to arrange for a suitable convoy, I hurried to the home of the redoubtable 'Joe' to find out. (By thus running them to earth beneath their own vines and fog-trees you can get at the true inwardnesses of them far more thoroughly than by summonsing them before you.)

So hostile in my aversion to pugilism that I had not even taken the trouble to formulate any theories beforehand as to the personality of the pugilists themselves or the aspect of the airs to which they retreat when their bouts are over, but if any such foregone conclusions had encumbered my mind they would have been something on this order: That the men themselves must be considerably lower than the brutes. That their dispositions without a doubt were utterly ferocious and savage. That little decency might have lurked in the recesses of their characters in the beginning must have long since evaporated by reason of their degrading occupation. While as for their domestic living, a cross between a Spanish bull fight and a Fenian riot best describes my mental picture of a pugilist's home life. And from the fact that Jeannette was hailed as the champion heavyweight of the world by default, I argued that in all these harrowing particulars he must be the greatest miscreant of them all. These things being true, the interview with Jeannette, turned out to be quite speck-making so far as the revision of my own ideas is concerned.

'Joe' himself was the first surprise. Knowing how susceptible is the average African head to inordinate swelling at the slightest hint of notoriety, I had confidently expected to find in him an over-garrulous, unbearably conceited and anything but respectful type, whose head had been long since turned by his successes to such an extent that I should need all the self control I could muster to endure him at all.

What I did find was a splendidly formed well-favored colored man, whose face shone with good nature and honesty, and whose manner was as respectful and unaffected as the most carping one could exact. 'Joe' has the characteristics of his race in that his forehead is low, his nose rather flat and his lips thicker than those of the Caucasian, while his hair, of course, is kinky, but between his comely, kindly, countenance, beaming with good wisdom, good nature, and that of the repulsive, brutal looking Sam McVey- otherwise an African- and his greatest opponent in the prize fighting world- there is as much difference as there is between 'Joe's' racial type and the Caucasian type itself. An anthropoid ape is a veritable Adonis compared to the picture of the Californian Negro whose picture I saw now and again, in juxtaposition to Jeannette's in numerous newspaper clippings which he brought out for my perusal.

'Joe' is as far from being garrulous and it was no easy matter to get from him the

233

necessary facts to fill out an interview. There is not a vestige of boastfulness about him. Notwithstanding the fanfares of applause that greet him wherever he goes from the sporting fraternity, and the praises of his exploits that fill the sporting columns, the Negro has kept his head with commendable judgment, and is today the same simple, unspoiled, unassuming good nature as when he used to drive the coal trucks of Jagels & Bellis, long before the idea of the ring ever entered his head...

His own age, weight and height I discovered to be respectively 32 years, 192 pounds, and five feet nine and a half inches. He was born in Homestead, New Jersey, as were all the rest of his family. "How many brothers and sisters have you?" I asked at this point. "Dunno. I'll have to stop and count 'em up'," replied Joe with a chuckle. After a moment's cogitation he announced the number as "two brothers and five sisters, ma'am." "And what are your other measurements?" I asked. According to Bernard McFadden, a professional athlete would know down to a hair's breadth the variation in his chest expansion, the exact circumference of his biceps, and just how the girth of his waist fluctuated from day to-day. Not so the dusky specimen before me, however. "Gosh, I don't know," was the cheerful response. "I don't never have none of my measurements taken. All I ever do is jump on and off the scales."

"How long have you been er-contesting for pugilistic renown?" I proceeded in some embarrassment. I wasn't sure just how freely one might presume to call a spade a spade in the presence of a spade. "How long I been fighting?" revised Joe, to my vest relief. "I started in the latter end of 1904. I was a truck driver for Jagels and Bellis then, you know." "And what made you think you could-er box,- I mean fight?" "Oh it wasn't me, ma'am, it was a passel of my friends. They kept all the time gettin' after me, and persuadin' me into it, and then this feller Dickerson came along; he was a prize fighter for fair." "Colonel Dickinson do you mean?" I asked with interest. Dickinson was a name noteworthy on some account, I knew, but in what particular-line I no longer remembered. "No'm', this was a colored gentleman over in Jersey City named Arthur Dickinson. He was a professional prize fighter. Well, Dickinson, he thought he wanted to fight me, and a lot of my friends, they thought I could lick him, so that's how come I got into the ring."

"And were your friend's right about your superior ability?" "Well he didn't lick me," answered Joe, showing two rows of excellent teeth, adding half apologetically; "It was along of my friends talking me into that I first went into the ring, though. I didn't want to start the game myself." "But now that you're in, you haven't much to regret," remarked the Convoy, who had sat silently through the preliminary skirmish, but now showed signs of animation. "Deed I haven't" acknowledged Joe, heartily. "I don't have to work nothing like as hard as I used to, and I gets just about," a chuckle finished the sentence. "The pecuniary compensation has increased appreciably, you mean?" suggested the Convoy. "It sure has," seconded Joe, showing every tooth in his head.

"But isn't the training very irksome?" I wanted to know, "and don't you have to give up pretty nearly everything that makes life worth living in the way of food and drink?" "Certainly you have to train," answered Joe, "before you goes into a fight, but you don't have to give up much eating. You eats whatever you can get. And I never did drink, no how, so it aint nothing to me to go without that." "Do you mean that you don't use

234

alcoholic beverages at all?" I asked in amazement. "Why I thought all prize fighters were-- that is that." "You mean you thought they were regular tanks?" the Convoy helped me out, obligingly. I thanked him gratefully.

"Why yes," I admitted. "I took it for granted that when they weren't fighting they were carousing. And I've certainly been told that the reason why a retired pugilist never has a cent, in spite of the fact that his fights have brought him in fabulous sums, is because he wastes it all in dissipation." "A lot of 'em does," said Joe at this point, gravely. "Look at Young Corbett. He's the guy that licked McGovern, you know." "Terry McGovern, the pugilist," put in the Convoy, soto voce, noting my widening eyes, and guessing rightly that concern for the good Recorder of the Hoboken Police Court was responsible for my alarm.

"I a'pose that man has went through his weight in gold, and all along of drinking and dissipating," Joe was continuing his dissertation. "That's what puts them on the blink. Even some of the best fighters goes groggy long before their time because they don't know how to put on the brakes."

"Don't you smoke, either?" I inquired, much impressed by Joe's unexpected temperance lecture. "No ma'am. I used to smoke, but I gave that up when I went into the ring. And I can't recollect I ever took an intoxicating drink over the bar in my whole life. Not that I don't sometimes take a beer with my dinner on a right warm day, but not often, and never anything stronger." "That's how Joe gets his wonderful endurance," here explained the Convoy. "He's famous all over the sporting world for his enduring qualities, you know."

I turned to look with renewed interest at the well knit frame. Novice that I was I could not fail to observe how symmetrically the Negro was developed. There were no evidences of the development of one set of muscles at the expense of the other. From head to foot Joe Jeannette gave the impression of boundless reserve force and power. He was clad in the short-sleeved, knit jersey of the running track, so that the muscles of his arms and neck were in full view.

"Can you wink your biceps?" I asked him expectantly. "We once had an office boy who could do that. Not a finger or joint would move, all the rest of his arm would be motionless, except for those muscles of the upper arm. They would jump back and forth in the most fascinating way. Won't you make yours do it?" "Sorry ma'am, but I can't oblige you. I never could get the hang of that trick." Both the Convoy and the pugilist laughed unrestrainedly at my disappointed countenance. "It's only a small matter," comforted the Convoy. "It doesn't indicate any special muscular development."

"The things that count in the ring," went on the Convoy, in pitying cognizance of my ignorance, "are endurance, foot work, the ability to take a punch as well as deliver one, and, of course, powerful muscles. In all of these essentials Joe is way up. Why look at what he took from McVey over in Paris. Joe, tell her about that fight, will you?" Joe grinned. "It was 49 rounds, and I got knocked down 24 times." "And how many times did you knock him down?" "Only once," laughed Joe, exchanging a meaning glance with the Convoy. "But I thought the newspaper clippings spoke of you as being the winner," I demurred hazily. "Yet you got knocked out 24 times." "Knocked down," corrected the Convoy. "Knocked out is quite another thing. That was where McVey got his- and he

was 30 pounds heavier than Joe, too." Light began to break. "Oh, I see, it really means that although McVey kept knocking him down he couldn't really gain anything because of Joe's endurance, and it was his endurance that wore out his opponent and won him the fight in the end." The thought grew upon me.

Think of getting knocked down 24 times in succession and still having the grit to keep on fighting. Why even fate isn't quite so relentless in her assault and battery of humanity. She does allow us to get in an occasional upper cut between her whacks. And think of not only bobbing up serenely each time, but standing it for forty-nine rounds and then winning out! "Pretty game, wasn't it?" seconded the Convoy, with enthusiasm, while Joe squirmed about in his chair uneasily, and but for his dusky hue would doubtless have blushed outright. "Joe," pursued the Convoy, "where's that medal they gave you over in France. Can't you show it to the lady?" Joe allowed that he could and disappeared in quest of the trinket.

During his absence a chocolate-colored youngster attired in the habiliments of an Indian brave entered the room followed by a little girl several years his junior. She was a bright mulatto with more than her share of childish good looks. The two peeped at us from behind their father's big easy chair, but were apparently tongue less. The return of their father, however, disclosed these necessary members, to be in good working order. "Soap water," demanded the little girl, displaying a small clay pipe. "Pappy, make us some soap water," supplemented the boy. "Presently," answered Joe, as he handed me a watch chain to which a gold enameled medal was affixed, and at the same time took the little girl on his knee. "Where's my medal?" came an aggrieved childish treble at this juncture, and the small Indian brave came at his father in an attitude which I afterward learned represented a 'crouch.'

With a delightful grip, Joe drew from a small leather case a medal which was a diminutive replica of his own. "He got that when we were out there," he explained. "He wasn't but two and a half years old. They thought it would be something he'd like to have when he was growed up." Pride beamed in the Negro's face, but it was pride in his offspring rather than his own achievements.

'Presented to Joe Jeannette, Jr., to record his father's great fight in Paris, April 17, 1909,' was inscribed on one side of the little medal. On the other, beneath an enameled figure representing a pugilist, was engraved, 'May he grow up as straight and as game.' Joe Junior during my examination of his medal was seconding his sister's pleadings for soap water. It was easy to see that the big Negro was the play fellow of his children, and that romps with them consumed a large part of his spare time. Turning my attention to the larger medal I read: 'Presented to Joe Jeannette by the S.P.B.A. Paris championship of Europe. Joe Jeannette beat Sam McVey, 3 h. 15 m. 49 rounds. April 17, 1909.'

"A 49 round fight! Why that's the event of the century, in itself!" exclaimed the Convoy inspecting the medal attentively. "It must be awful!" I shuddered. "How does it make you feel to go into a fight, I mean?" Joe scratched his head with Joe Junior's medal and grinned, "I feel just the same way I do now," came the reply. "Don't you feel nervous?" "No'm, I don't never feel nervous. Most times they has to wake me up when it comes time for me to go into a fight. I generally falls asleep in the dressing room." "There's a case of power through repose for you," commented the Convoy. "But doesn't the outcome,

your possible defeat, even worry you?" I pressed. "I don't never worry 'bout nothin',"
came the response. "I'll tell you how I figure it out. I figures I've got to fight anyhow. If a
better man than me comes along, he'll beat me, and that's all there is to it." A flash of
white teeth accompanied this disquisition upon the philosophy of a prize fight.

"But you've been a lucky man so far," observed the Convoy. "Yes, I surely am," mused
Joe. "Aint never been knocked out yet." "Aint you never goin' to make us that soap
water?" asked a plaintive voice from under his chair as the Indian brave, flat on his
stomach, assayed to 'scalp' his father. "You go an' ask yoh mammy to make you that
soap water," advised Joe. "I did, and she won't," complained the little girl, shinning up
her father's broad back as he leaned forward in the chair. "She says she's busy, she said
ask you. N' we tole her we did ast you'n you said no." Joe chuckled and plucking the
small wheedler from his shoulders, held her up at arm's length, while she squealed in glee.
"Well, pappy'll say yes presently. You wait a while." Protesting that they had already
waited several whiles the two children nevertheless betook themselves to a corner and were
temporarily quiet.

During the colloquy the Convoy had been pouring over the big scrapbook full of
newspaper clippings. From every English speaking country on the globe, there were
accounts of Joe's battles and glowing accounts of his unexampled powers of endurance and
pugilistic cleverness. Thrown down together in wild disorder in the back of the book were
extracts from European newspapers' in French, Italian, Spanish, and German. Many of
them showed pictures of the big Negro, while one and all the tale they told was the same,
that of a man physically as near perfect as the human frame can be made, with the rugged
endurance that comes only through health and temperate living, and whose capacity and
temper had repeatedly made him an easy vanquisher of men less expert in these respects.

"How did you manage to get into such splendid form in the first place?" I asked, more
and more impressed over the articles, with the man's physical fitness, and abounding
health. "Reckon I was born that way in the beginning," laughed Joe. "Then it's like I
told you. I've always lived temperate and got enough to eat. When you talk about
trainin'- why I don't never train more than eight or nine days before a fight. That's along
of my keeping myself in good condition all the time. A heap of them fellers after they've
made one fight loafs around drinking and putting on weight until they has to work for
two or three months getting it off again when they want to get ready for another fight.
With me I actually puts on weight when I'm in training. I aint been in a fight now for
three months, and the other day I stepped on the scale and I weighed 2 pounds less than
when I was fighting."

"What do I do for exercise? Well. I gets out and works on my automobile. I looks after
that myself, altogether, and foolin' around with that thing, cleaning it up and polishin' it
keeps me tolerable busy. Punchin' the bag is an exercise I keep up, too. And then the
Public Service people across here at the car barns have rigged me up a little gym over there
and I work over there considerable. There's one or two other stunts I aim to do regular.
They limber a feller up and keep his muscles right."

It was then that I had demonstrated for my edification the fascinating stunts referred to
in the opening paragraph of this article, and with such deceptive ease were the feats
performed by the accommodating Negro that not until I got home and tried them in the

237

privacy of my own room, did I realize the skill and practice that they entail. When Joe did it there it looked as simple as rolling off a log. When I attempted them, especially the stunt of rising from the floor without bending but one leg, well try it yourself, if you want to know what happened!

"When I'm in regular training," continued Joe, "I box with some of the fellow's everyday and get out and run five or six miles. Skipping rope is another thing. Sometimes I skip eight or nine hundred times without stopping. That's to get endurance." "You get ready to say 'yes' yet?" a voice from the corner besought wistfully. "You said you'd say yes an make some soap water presently two or three hours." Without a trace of impatience Joe took up the soap water controversy where he had left it half an hour before. "You go get a teeny bit of soap in a cup and pour some water on it an' stir it around," he instructed, "Pappy'll help you if it doesn't work." A stampede in the direction of the kitchen ensued, whereat Joe smiled expansively. There is no doubt whatever about the softness of his heart, his profession notwithstanding.

"You don't have anything to do with the business ends of the fights, do you?" I asked, prompted by the Convoy. The question would never have occurred to me unassisted. "No'm. All I has to do is train and fight. Mr. McKetrick does all the rest. I wisht I'd had Mr. McKetrick two years sooner. I'd have been champion of the world." "But aren't you champion now?" I inquired in some bewilderment. "They told me that Johnson had refused to fight you and that by so doing he had forfeited his title to the championship." Joe's ivories were again in evidence. "Well, speaking technically, I guess I became champion when Johnson retired; but I'm not going to dwell on technicalities. Of course, I'd rather have a finish fight, but ten rounds may be enough, after all, to make me the real champion of the world."

"My manager had about prepared a trip around the world, and challenged all comers. I guess we'll start down in Pennsylvania, and then work west." "And will you come home after each fight to get over the results?" was my inquiry. Jeannette chuckled. "N'om. I don't hardly guess I'll be done up as bad as all that. It ain't my first tour, you know, ma'am. I've been down through the South once. We'd have to make a 200 or 250 mile trip every night between the places we was booked for, the fights came so near together. One time I had seven fights in one month." "And what was the result?" "Oh they didn't give me no trouble. Five of 'em knocked out and the other two I won points." "I didn't mean that," I explained hastily, "I mean what bruises did you have to show for it? And how long did it take you to recuperate?" "Oh that?" Joe seemed genuinely surprised. "It don't never take me more'n a couple of days or so to get over a fight. I ain't never been mussed up much." "And how do the other fellows look?" here put in the Convoy meaningly. Joe laughed, but declined to commit himself. "It isn't so much of a hardship to fight, after all," was my wondering comment as the comparative ease of Joe's conquests was borne in upon my mind. "The way I looks at it, it ain't no kind of hardship," grinned Joe. "Getting three or four hundred dollars for thirty minutes work looks good to me." "Goodness, do prize-fighters get as much as that!" My eyes were fairly bulging out of my head. "What in the world do they do then, to go through their fortunes so quickly?" Joe shrugged his shoulders expressively.

"Carousin' around can eat it up in no time," he said. "But gee, I'd like to get one of

them fortunes together once. I'll bet it wouldn't get away from me like that." "You haven't got much kick coming, Joe," reproved the Convoy. "You own your little home, here, and you've got your automobile." "That's right, too," assented Joe with easy acquiescence. "'An' if I had a mint of money I don't guess I'd do much different than I do now. The kids would get the benefit of it though." "How about the automobiles?" I quizzed, remembering Jack Johnson's weakness. "Would you go in for many racing cars and speed records?" "By the way, Joe," put in the Convoy with a sly wink in my direction, "How many times have you and Jack Johnson been arrested for speeding." "Never been arrested- and don't intend to." Joe laughed in appreciation of the question, "I don't try to keep up with Jack Johnson's troubles," he said, "but I ain't never been arrested for speeding myself, never been arrested for anything and don't intend to be."

With these noble sentiments the interview ended. "There's as fine a type of darky as I've ever seen," was the Convoy's contribution on our homeward journey. "He keeps his head-doesn't let success make a fool of him, takes pride in his home, and is devoted to his wife and family. Sometimes up here at New Town Hall where he plays basketball for the Club, a lot of toughs try to josh him and pick a quarrel with him. But he takes it all good naturedly and never lets anything rattle him. He's certainly as straight and as game as they make 'em. I hope he'll be acknowledged as champion." "If a colored man has got to have it, so do I," I agreed with a cordiality that still surprises me.

I don't yet want to countenance such a brutal pastime as prize-fighting, but I do begin to understand what men see in it. 'Gameness' is a quality that no one can help admiring, and Joe Jeannette is certainly game.[353]

On August 21 Jack Johnson gave the following statement to a reporter when asked if he would fight me: *"Joe Jeanette is a tough fighting proposition. I'm not afraid to face him in a ring, but I would much rather fight Sam Langford or Sam McVey. It's because I regard Jeanette as the next best fighter to myself in the world that I'm sticking out for $30,000. He is a tough man- the hardest scrapper in this or any other country to defeat. If you knock down most fighters you have them practically whipped. Not so with Jeanette. You can knock him down time and again and he keeps coming up for more. Friends of mine who saw him fight Sam Langford in Madison Square Garden say that he trimmed Sam plenty and then some. That is why I say I'd rather meet Langford or McVey than Jeanette."*[354]

The article went on to state how Jack had signed to fight me for twenty-five thousand dollars and fifty percent of the gate and fifty percent of the moving picture privileges. Everything was looking up for me. I was finally getting my title shot and the recognition that goes with it. Everything looked great until August 19. The newspaper headlines read: "Looks Bad for Johnson in New York,"[355] referring to my scheduled fight with Jack there. Johnson was on a list of boxers that were barred from fighting in New York. The article stated: *It is more than probable that Jack Johnson and Joe*

---

[353] *Hudson Dispatch* August 19, 1912.
[354] *Kalamazoo Gazette* August 21, 1912.
[355] *International News Service* August 19, 1912.

Jeannette will not settle any argument as to fistic superiority in this city. The McMahon Brothers are going ahead with the work of preparing for the match, but the wise ones believe it is a certainty that Johnson will never collect a cent of that $25,000, not next month anyway.

The state athletic commission has a rule in indelible ink in the big book up in Albany, absolutely barring Jack Johnson from boxing in the state of New York. This banishment is due partly to Johnson's annoying way of seeking publicity in New York, partly to the fact that Governor Dix has noted the fact that practically every time Johnson had appeared in the ring there was trouble of some kind after the affair, also to the fact that assurances were given the governor when he signed the Frawley bill that no prize fights would be staged in the state.

At that time Johnson's name was put on the list of undesirables. There has been no official notice from the state athletic commission, but that body will meet the later part of this week. The rule is a part of the state statutes and put in the book to stay.

Three heavyweight battles of ten rounds each will be decided in Madison Square Garden tonight. Joe Jeannette, who is believed to have a chance to whip Jack Johnson if it should happen that they come together here next month, will meet Jeff Madden, a Boston heavyweight, who has convinced many ring judges that he possesses natural fighting ability. Madden weighs 210 pounds, while Jeannette scales 195.[356]

That night I faced a big but unskilled Irishman from Boston named Jeff Madden at Madison Square Garden. I had beaten Madden by knockout in the fourth round on July 15 at New Bedford, Massachusetts, and I could see the fear in Madden's eyes as we awaited the opening bell. I decided I would make quick work of Madden to get home to Addie and the kids. After the bell rang I wasted no time in attacking Madden with lefts and rights. My blows landed with precision. Madden fell into a clinch with me to stave off my attack. The round was less than thirty-seconds old when I heard a young fan yell from the upper decks: *"Wait a second Joe, I just come in!"* I positioned Madden so I could look up at the gallery fan and I smiled to him. After the break, I boxed Madden the rest of the round. About halfway through the second round the same fan yelled out: *"Let's go, Joe, What da ya say!"* I hauled back and smashed Madden right on the tip of the jaw knocking him out cold. It took thirty minutes to revive him, and when he came to, he said he thought that the roof of the building had fallen on him. He refused to believe that I had knocked him out again.[357] The *New York Herald* described the contest: *Jeannette, who likes to play to the gallery, toyed with his man in the first round and did not try to hit him hard. In the second, to show why he should be considered a fit contender for Johnson's title, he began to pound Madden viciously. Madden dropped four times, and it looked as though it was as much from terror as from the punches he received.*[358] Two of my close friends and sparring

---

[356] *International News Service* August 19, 1912.
[357] "Palookas & Plutocrats" by Henry W. Clune
[358] *New York Herald* August 19, 1912.

partners, Luther McCarthy and Tom Kennedy, lost on the same card. McCarthy was upset by Oklahoma cowboy Jesse Willard, who took the ten round decision. Kennedy was stopped by Jim Savage when the referee, Billy Joh, called a halt to the fight due to both of Tom's eyes being closed from punches.[359]

The following day I fought two boxers on the same card: "Battling" Jack Brooks and the six-foot six-inch "Big" Bill Tate. Brooks was a sparring partner of mine who did more damage to the air than to his opponents. I took it easy with him when I was sparring, but he started believing that he was actually my master. Worse than that, Brooks was going around telling people that he had floored me several times in practice. I talked promoter Joe McNulty into letting me fight both Brooks and Tate on the same day. The show took place at Morris Park in Newark, NJ. First I fought a scheduled six rounder against Brooks. I toyed with Brooks for a round. When the bell rang for the second round I held my hand out to Brooks. A sickly pallor came over his face. *"This ain't the last round, Joe,"* he said with quaking knees. *"It is for you,"* I replied and within twenty seconds Brooks was rendered a minus quantity for the remainder of the evening. I wound up fighting Brooks two more times in 1915 to help him make a few paydays.

My second match was against "Big" Bill Tate. Tate was huge and had some boxing experience down South, though none of it was recorded. I knocked Tate out in the second round.

On August 20, an article was printed that further discussed the proposed Johnson bout: *When Jack Johnson, heavyweight champion of the world meets Joe Jeannette before St. Nicholas Athletic Club on the night of September 25th, it will be the eighth meeting between the two boxers, who are old ring rivals. Johnson is guaranteed $25,000, with a privilege of 50 percent of the first $50,000 of gate receipts and 35 percent of all over that amount. Jeannette will receive 10 percent of the gross receipts... Dan McKetrick, manager for Joe Jeannette, was surprised when he heard that Johnson had signed. "I didn't think he would," said McKetrick, "for I know he is afraid of Jeannette."*[360]

Because of reports stating the New York Commission would not allow Jack to fight there, Johnson, who was in Chicago, made the following statement to the press about beginning his training for the bout: *"I don' care about doing all that hard work for nothing,"* Johnson said. *"The MacMahon brothers will have to show me a letter from the commission before I will go into training. When the match was made the promoters told me they had everything 'fixed' with the commission, but according to reports from the east there is a screw loose somewhere.*

"In fact I don't care about fighting. I was forced into this match by my wife and I will be only too glad to call it off. It is beginning to look as if I got my money in just the right

---

[359] *Denver Post* August 20, 1912.
[360] Untitled newspaper article August 20, 1912.

time. I honestly don't believe I ever will be allowed to fight in this country again. Whenever my name is mentioned in connection with a fight in any part of the country the ministers and reformers immediately get busy with the governor, with the result that there will be nothing doing for Jack Johnson. Take it from me, I will not start training until I am shown my fight with Jeannette can take place as scheduled."[361]

On August 22 the McMahon brothers, who were the promoters for the September 25 title fight between Johnson and I, met with the New York State Athletic Commission. After the meeting Edward McMahon spoke: *"There has been adverse criticism about this match and the commissioners apparently do not want it to be held. That is why we are calling it off. For the betterment of the sport the commissioners do not want Jack Johnson to appear in a match in New York City."*[362]

I was devastated. I was so close to finally getting my title shot. Now it wasn't Johnson who was stopping me. It was the state boxing commission, which through its hatred of Johnson, was denying me my title shot. State Commissioner O'Neil stated: *"The commission decided some time ago that Jack Johnson would not be permitted to fight here. We believe now and we did then, that the presence of Johnson in a ring contest in this state would be inimical to the best interests of boxing, the status of which has been greatly improved under the Frawley Law."*

On September 2 Dan and I took a train across New Jersey and Pennsylvania to Pittsburgh. You could never imagine just how long Pennsylvania is until you have to cross that state. I took on Jeff Clark, a colored boxer from Joplin, Missouri in an open-air bout. It was the first open-air bout held in Pittsburgh. I weighed in at 196 pounds to Clark's 163 pounds. The bout was scheduled for six rounds. The "Joplin Ghost," as he was called, stood five-feet eleven-inches and was 26-years-old. I was now 33-years-old. We arrived in Pittsburgh the night before the bout and my legs were still stiff from the long train ride when I entered the ring the following day. The Johnson situation exhausted me both physically and mentally. I should have never taken the Clark bout. The first round was about even and I had the better of the second round. In the third and fourth sessions Clark stepped in and out with quick combinations. I just couldn't get my punches off. I don't know if it was the Johnson fight being cancelled, the long ride, or I was just having an off day. In the fifth round I landed a solid left to Clark's jaw and I battered him around the ring for the rest of the round. In the sixth and final round Clark fell to his knees when we were in close quarters to avoid being hit by an uppercut. When he got up I tried to land several hard body shots under his elbows but he blocked them. Clark finished the fight landing combinations to my head while the crowd yelled its applause. The local newspapers awarded Clark the fight in the no-decision bout.

---

[361] *Milwaukee Journal* August 20, 1912.
[362] Untitled newspaper article August 23, 1912.

On September 9 I took on Tony Ross of Newcastle, Pennsylvania, at Madison Square Garden. I was winning the ten round bout easily when Ross was disqualified in the seventh for repeated low blows.

On September 11 Jack Johnson's wife Etta Duryea committed suicide with a revolver. She had been beaten several times by Johnson and was suffering from depression. Etta was disowned by white America and black American females loathed her as well. Every time they looked at Etta's face they would sneer and some would even spit at her.[363] Colored women claimed that Etta had contaminated the minds of colored men, who had begun to follow the example of Johnson, seeking out white women for sex partners.[364] Before her death she had lamented: *"I am a white woman and tired of being a social outcast. All my misery comes through marrying a black man. Even the Negroes don't respect me. They hate me."*[365]

She committed suicide by shooting herself in her room above Johnson's Café de Champion. Rumor had it she killed herself because Jack was fooling around with one of the colored singers in his club named Adah Banks. That rumor was confirmed when Jack brought another white woman to town named Lucille Cameron. Banks got into a fight with Cameron after which Banks shot Johnson in the leg. Johnson didn't press charges but his club was closed. He later married Cameron. Johnson stated to the press that his wife Etta killed herself because of all the pressure that white America was putting on her husband. He was quoted as saying: *"She was murdered by the hatred and prejudice that is trying to murder me and may the Lord have mercy on your souls."*[366]

On September 13, the *New York Times* printed an article explaining the deal that H.D. McIntosh was trying to piece together. McIntosh sent a representative named W.C.J. Kelly to Chicago to pitch the deal to Jack Johnson. McIntosh was offering Johnson sixty thousand dollars to go to Australia and fight Sam Langford, Sam McVea and myself. The sum would be split into three purses. Thirty thousand for Johnson to fight Langford and fifteen thousand apiece for him to fight McVea and I. I don't think anyone was really sure if or when Jack would fight again due to his personal problems.

The September 14 issue of the *National Police Gazette* published an article titled: "Johnson and Jeannette may fight in Paris." In the article, French promoter Victor Breyer offered Johnson thirty thousand dollars to fight me thirty rounds in Paris or Monte Carlo. Chicago sports writer George Pardy asserted: *"Nobody knows better than the champion himself what a bad proposition he is called upon to solve when he meets Jeannette and, despite the golden lure advanced by*

---

[363] *The Big Black Fire* by Robert H. DeCoy pg. 129.
[364] *The Big Black Fire* by Robert H. DeCoy pg. 131.
[365] *Interracial Intimacies* by Randall Kennedy pgs. 80-81.
[366] *The Heavyweight Championship* by Stanley Weston pgs. 77-78.

the French promoter, it is quite possible that he may back pedal on his agreement between now and the time set for the battle. Victory for (Jeannette) would leave the heavyweight championship crown still in possession of a Negro, but a change of ownership would liven things up a bit. Of two evils, one naturally chooses the least, and even among the denizens of the black belt the popular opinion holds that the reign of a Jeannette would be preferable to that of a Johnson."

Public support for a match between Johnson and myself was starting to grow. Sam McVea was interviewed in Australia and gave these thoughts on Jack Johnson: *"The champion is 'an awfully good man.' And the greatest boxer, perhaps, the world has ever seen. To beat Johnson one must be a defensive fighter, defensive and quick, too, in order to get out of the way of uppercuts and all else that is in the armory of the man who beat Jeffries."*[367]

I was in Philadelphia resting for another bout with "Battling" Jim Johnson. I had to block out thoughts of a possible Johnson championship match and prepare for the bout that evening. No matter how hard a boxer trains and how good he looks in sparring he never knows what he will have that night until the bell rings. Now I had to work extra hard to motivate myself. Boxing for a few hundred dollars when I might lose the opportunity to earn thousands could distract even the most focused individual. I defeated Jim Johnson via six round decision.

On October 14, former President Theodore Roosevelt was shot at a political rally in Milwaukee, Wisconsin. Roosevelt was a big boxing fan. He had stated that: *"the only wise, honorable, and Christian thing to do is to treat each black man and each white man strictly on his merits as a man."* This type of speech gave the black communities much needed hope.

Roosevelt also oversaw one of the worst events involving black Americans in the early 1900s. Many black Americans blamed him for not treating black men of the 25th Infantry fairly after an incident in Texas in 1906. The troops were blamed for the shooting death of a white man and one hundred sixty-seven of the black soldiers were dishonorably discharged without even the benefit of a hearing.

In Australia, Sam Langford and Sam McVea met each other five times over an eleven-month period. Langford won four bouts, two by stoppage, and there was one draw. McVea quit in one fight on October 9 because he claimed Langford was not fighting fairly. McVea stated: *"He fights for fouls. Three times he hit me in a delicate place... Why didn't you see him hit the referee in the seventh round. He was hitting all the time after the word break. When the referee let him hit me three times where I told you. I thought it time to quit."*[368]

McVea and Langford weren't always angry with each other. One night in Sidney at the Princess Theatre the two Sams actually performed a song together to benefit the Sidney hospital. McVea sang "Love Me and the

---

[367] *Kalgoorlie Western Argus* October 1, 1912 pgs. 20-21.
[368] *Kalgoorlie Western Argus* October 15, 1912 pg. 32.

World is Mine" while Langford accompanied him on the piano. After the song, both boxers performed a boxing exhibition.[369] McVea performed and sang onstage often while in Australia.

On October 29 in New York City Dan McKetrick signed a promotional contract on my behalf with W.C.J. Kelly, who was representing Hugh McIntosh. The contract called for me to fight five times in Australia. Dan said it was the right move because Johnson did not want to fight us, and even if he did, no commission would approve him. The first fight in Australia was to be against Sam Langford and the second against Sam McVea. McIntosh agreed to give me twenty-five thousand dollars with the privilege of twenty-five percent of the gate, and five round-trip tickets for Dan, three sparring partners, and myself. We were to sail from San Francisco in late November. McIntosh would also donate a gold belt emblematic of the world's heavyweight championship to the winner of the tournament. The Australian fights were to be a tournament to decide who would succeed Jack Johnson as heavyweight champion as Johnson was so inactive. However, the tournament would later be scrapped because of a lack of funds.

On October 30, I was matched against journeyman "Battling" Jim Johnson of East Orange, N.J.[370] The bout took place at the 44th Street Sports Club in Manhattan. After overcoming a first round flash knockdown, I out-boxed "Battling" Jim over the next nine rounds. The bout was marred by fouls. "Battling" Jim used head butts, low blows, thumbs, and any other dirty tactic he could think of. I had to be especially careful when infighting him. When we were in a clinch in the fourth round, he hooked his left arm around my right arm and turned to his left with all his weight. The move twisted and ripped my right arm out towards my back. The pain was excruciating. There is no doubt in my mind that the move was purposely committed.

Willie Lewis also fought on the card, knocking out Dia Thomas of England in the third round with a right to the jaw. Thomas outweighed Willie by twenty-one pounds, 178 pounds to 157. A year later on December 19, Jack Johnson fought "Battling" Jim in Paris and Jim fractured Jack's left arm in the contest. I often wondered if "Battling" Jim used the same foul move on Jack as he did on me.

Johnson's fight with Flynn was his only bout in two years. Where was the outcry from the public? Didn't they want to see the best boxers face each other? Why were they only concerned with a white boxer beating Johnson? If they wanted Jack beaten so badly they would demand that he fight me or Langford. But no, they were only interested in a white boxer facing Johnson.

---

[369] *New York Clipper* February 3, 1912 pg. 23.
[370] *Washington Post* October 31, 1912.

Dan spoke with me about publicizing that my mother was from Bavaria. He said that might help us make the Johnson match. I didn't think it would make much difference. The public had tunnel vision and wanted Johnson beaten by a white boxer. Dan said: *"If the public knows your mother is white maybe they'll support your title quest."* *"As long as I have brown skin,"* I said, *"the public couldn't care less how much white blood I have. They want Jack beaten by a man with white skin."*

Dan also believed, as I did, that Johnson was motivated by the coin. He wanted to make as much money as possible. Actually, the public's demand that Johnson fight white boxers was playing right into his hands. He was being forced to box less dangerous opponents for more money. He was laughing all the way to the bank. I don't blame the public as much as I do Jack. He kept saying that he wanted to be the only black heavyweight champion. What right did he have to exclude his own race from the same opportunities that he was given?

Our family suffered a tragedy on December 23 when Addie's mother Josephine died. She was only 49 years of age.

Joe Jennette portrait Memphis, Tennessee, December 1911.

Joe Jennette portrait Memphis, Tennessee, December 1911.

L to R: Dan McKetrick, Willie Lewis, Frank Moran, and Sammy Smith, on board the Adriatic enroute to France, March 24, 1911.

Jennette & family on cover of Paris magazine, January 7, 1914.

Jim Pratt & Joe Jennette play spar, circa 1913.

Joe Jennette training Paris, France 1913

Joe Jennette sparring with Otto Flint.

Joe Jennette promotional pose.

Joe Jennette promotional poses.

Joe Jennette training Paris, France 1913

Joe Jennette in fighting stance.

Striking the light bag.

Striking the heavy bag.

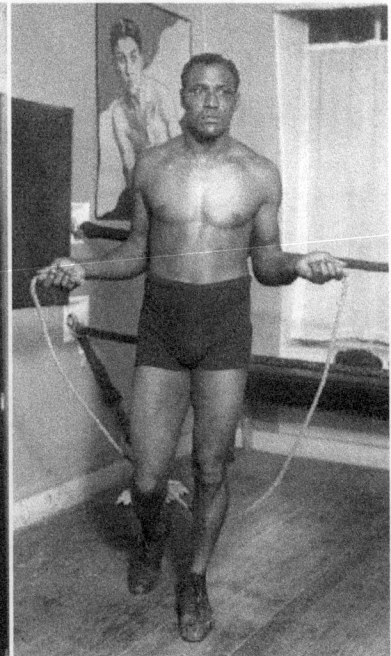

Jumping the rope.

Training camp L to R; Johnny Gabigan, George Gunther, Gus Wilson, Unknown, Albert Lurie, Auguste DeGand, Joe Jennette, unknown, & Otto Flint, Paris, France, circa 1913.

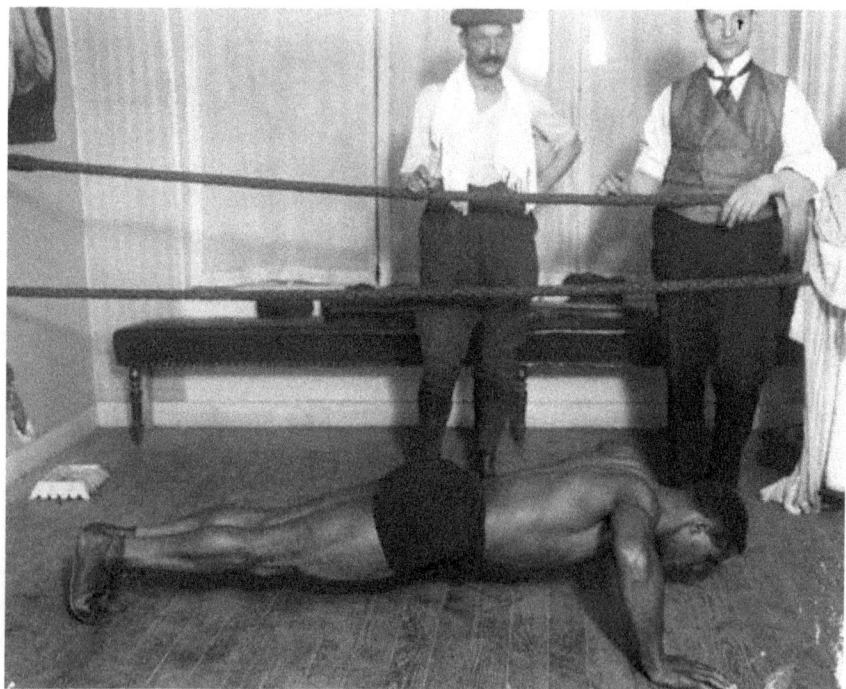

Joe Jennette exercising in training camp, Gus Wilson on right, Paris, France, circa 1913.

"The Black Quartet" by Dessin de Jean Bouttier. From left; Johnson, McVea, Jennette, & Langford.

Advertisement for Jennette-Langford bout December 20, 1913.

Joe Jennette & Sam Langford trade punches Paris, France, December 20, 1913.

Jennette jabs to Sam Langford's body Paris, France, December 20, 1913.

Jennette & trainer cool down after Sam Langford bout Paris, France, December 20, 1913.

Jennette family traveling to France, circa 1913.

Joe Jennette & his two children, Joe Jr., & Agnes, circa 1913.

Newspaper ad for March 21, 1914 bout between Georges Carpentier & Joe Jennette.

Jennette & Carpentier shake hands after signing contract for March 21 bout.
Jim Pratt standing to left of Carpentier, Dan McKetrick on far right.

Jennette rips body shots while Carpentier crouches in defense, March 21, 1914, Luna Park, Paris, France.

Jennette & Carpentier clinch, March 21, 1914, Luna Park, Paris, France.

Georges Carpentier and Joe Jennette facing off during bout, March 21, 1914.

Georges Carpentier attempts a right hand while Joe Jennette counters with a left hook.

Jennette slips a Carpentier right cross, March 21, 1914.

Artist Dessin de A. Berrere's rendering of Georges Carpentier
versus Joe Jennette, circa 1914.

Jennette helps Carpentier to his feet after he slipped to the canvas in the 10th round. Ringside reporters likened it to a father helping his son up.

Artist rendering of Joe Jennette landing a left hook on Georges Carpentier, circa 1914.

Joe Jennette & protégé Carl Morris.

Georgianna & Daniel Jennette.

Agnes & Joe Jr.

Joe, Ada, Joe Jr., & Agnes Jennette
steaming to France, circa 1913.

Joe Jennette with children Agnes
& Joe Jr., circa 1913.

Selection of Joe Jennette cartoons

Fire hose at 49-round fight.

Speaking of knockout string.

Frustrations on getting Jack Johnson in the ring.

Speaking of knockdowns in 49-round fight.

Selection of Joe Jennette cartoons

Jennette teaching Carl Morris, Jim Stewart, Tom Kennedy, & Frank Moran.

Sam Langford as a bull & Joe Jennette as a tiger.

Joe Jennette chasing Johnson for a match.

Joe Jennette training Carl Morris, circa 1911.

Chapter 17
A New Champion 1913-1917

On New Year's Day 1913 I took on "Battling" Jim Johnson at the Irving Athletic Club in Brooklyn. The bout was scheduled for ten rounds. I weighed 194 1/2 pounds to Johnson's 210. In the opening round I was dropped by a stinging right hand. It was a flash knockdown and I was madder at myself for letting Jim reach my jaw than I was hurt. I jumped up at the count of one and Johnson tried to capitalize on his luck. He forced me into the ropes where he landed another right hand, this time to my neck. I clinched and cleared my head. When the referee broke us I jabbed and moved for the rest of the round. For the remainder of the fight, I easily out-boxed Jim. I was very cautious, though, not to get lackadaisical again like I had in the first round.

A January article in the *Washington Post* talked about how some managers and their fighters were "pals." The article spoke of several managers who were good friends with their fighters, such as Dan Morgan with "Knockout" Brown and Billy Nolan with Willie Ritchie. The article also stated: *Another good pal of a manager is Dan McKetrick, who made Willie Lewis a fortune. McKetrick also has Joe Jeannette, the great Negro heavy, and Jack Denning. McKetrick's boxers have a wholesome respect for him and he for them.*[371]

Several years earlier I started my own semi-pro basketball team. It was called Joe Jeanette's Jersey City Basketball Team. Everyone knew me as Jeanette, and so as not to confuse people I spelled the team's name that way. On January 10, 1913, I traveled with my team up to South Manchester, Connecticut, to play the South Manchester G Team at the Armory.[372] Our team was managed by Steve Fallon. The *Hartford Courant* newspaper called me: *one of the fastest basketball players in the country.*[373]

Colored basketball players were not given an opportunity to play professional basketball at the time. On the team with me was fellow boxer Al Benedict, also from West Hoboken, who was a journeyman heavyweight. The rest of the lineup included John Atkins, C. Bruggy, Harry Wallum, and Ed Roach. In 1912 we came in second in the State of New Jersey, losing in the championship match to Paterson 20-19. This season we defeated Troy, NY, and Johnston, Pa.

I also played center for the Olympia A.C. Five of Union Hill. We practiced at the Olympia Athletic Club, which was located adjacent to Union Hill's city hall. We held scrimmages at the Turn Hall on New York Avenue and Lewis Street. A newspaper reported: *Although practically new at the game,*

---

[371] *Washington Post* January 5, 1913.
[372] *Hartford Courant* January 10, 1913.
[373] *Hartford Courant* January 10, 1913

Jeannette has developed into one of the best players in the country. He is noted for his speed and ability to jump, and, when it comes to basket shooting, he is on the job all the time.[374]

On February 5, 1913 the New York State Athletic Commission banned bouts between whites and blacks. In early March, Dan brought Frank Moran in from Pittsburgh for me to train. Dan was trying to sign Moran to a management contract. I trained Frank at the Olympia up in Union Hill. Moran was a dentist back in Pittsburgh.[375]

On March 8, the NAACP sent a letter to the Wisconsin state legislature.[376] The letter, written by Oswald Garrison and W.E.B. DuBois, denounced the so-called Jack Johnson bill which forbade interracial marriage. The letter stated that the NAACP: *earnestly protests against the bill forbidding intermarriage between the races.* The letter went on to assure that the NAACP's opposition to the bill was not to be misconstrued that they advocated interracial marriages. DuBois' opposition to the bill did not reflect his personal view on Jack Johnson's marriage to a white woman. DuBois opposed Johnson's marriage because he felt that racial pride and love of one's race were essential to the advancement of the black race.[377] He also felt that if intermarriage alienated blacks from progressing as a people, then interracial relations should be avoided for the betterment of the race. While Johnson was a source of pride for most blacks, for some he was an embarrassment to black society.

In May 1913, Jack Johnson was convicted of violating the Mann Act. On June 4, he was sentenced. Judge Carpenter who passed the sentence stated: *"This defendant is one of the best known of his race, and his example has been far reaching. The court, therefore, is bound to consider the position he occupies among his people. In view of these facts, this case calls for more than just a fine. John Arthur Johnson, I sentence you to serve one year and one day in the state prison at Joliet, Illinois, and to pay a fine of one thousand dollars."*[378]

Jack's conviction sent shockwaves and confusion throughout the boxing world. Would he be stripped of his title? Would he appeal the conviction? The answers were not immediately apparent. What was apparent was that he had no plans of fighting Sam Langford or myself.

On May 24, Luther McCarty was killed by a blow thrown by Arthur Pelky at Tommy Burns Arena in Calgary, Alberta, Canada. Luther, or Lute as I called him, was a very close friend. The fans in attendance thought the fight was a "throw down," or fix, until they realized McCarty was dead. Some at ringside never saw a punch landed. This was yet another reminder of just

---

[374] Untitled article from Joe Jennette scrapbook. Courtesy Ben Hawes collection.
[375] *The Fight Game* by James & Frank Butler pg. 29.
[376] *Interracial Intimacies* by Randall Kennedy pg. 257.
[377] *Beyond The Ring* by Jeffrey T. Sammons pg. 42.
[378] *The Heavyweight Championship* by Stanley Weston pgs. 79-80.

how dangerous this profession can be. Luther had been a professional fighter for only twenty-eight months but was on the fast track up the heavyweight ladder until he fell off of a horse.[379]

The events leading up to Luther's death were very eerie. As the crowd filtered into the arena, the rain poured down on that dark and dreary day. Before the bout got underway, a clergyman asked for permission to speak to the crowd to ask for donations to his parish. The audience was well-to-do, as the tickets for the fight cost one thousand dollars each. The minister asked for help, and seeing that the crowd was not giving him their full attention, he pleaded loudly: *"Who knows what will happen to any of us? Here before you stand two wonderful athletes, each in the flower of youth, each trained to the highest perfection, marvelous physical specimens of American manhood. Who among us dare say that the Great Referee will not count out one or both of these men within the next year, the next month, the next day, nay, the very next hour, if He so will it?"*[380] After listening for a few moments the crowd started ignoring the preacher again, not one of them coming forward to donate. McCarty shook the pastor's hand and said to him: *"I guess it didn't work, pastor. But don't let it bother you. We'll think of some other way."*[381] McCarty then turned to his manager and said: *"That's a hell of an audience. They didn't understand a word he said. Now, remember, I want you to give the pastor some dough for me."*[382]

Luther's manager thought it strange that Luther asked him to make a donation on his behalf. Why couldn't Luther do it himself after the match? While Luther was being counted out on the floor the rain stopped and the sun broke through the clouds. There was a hole in the arena roof and a ray of sunlight beamed through the crack and shone directly on Luther's prostrate form.[383] When the referee finished counting over him, Luther's manager entered the ring and immediately knew his fighter was gone. The coroner stated Luther died of a brain hemorrhage from a previous injury. Some at ringside thought it was a blow to the heart that did him in. Others thought it was related to his recent fall from a horse. Luther had fought four boxers that I trained: Frank Moran, Jim Barry, Jim Stewart, and Carl Morris. Jim Stewart was the only one who beat Luther. The day after the tragedy, an arsonist burned the arena to the ground.

On June 6, Jack Johnson escaped to Montreal. He snuck out of the country with a colored baseball team. Johnson steamed for France on the Corinthia and he arrived in Paris on July 10.

On Wednesday June 18, an article was written by T.S. Andrews in the *Racine Journal-News* about me. The title of the article was "Joe Jeannette,

---

379 *Champions of the Ring* by Gerald Suster pg. 66.
380 *Bill Stern's Boxing Stories* pgs. 34-37.
381 *Bill Stern's Boxing Stories* pgs. 34-37.
382 *Bill Stern's Boxing Stories* pgs. 34-37.
383 *The Fireside Book of Boxing* by W.C. Heinz pg. 35.

Who Claims Title, Not Full Blooded Negro." The topic of the article, besides my being one of the leading contenders to the heavyweight throne, was the fact that my mother was a white woman of German ancestry and my father was partly Arabic. My father's Arabic blood was deduced by our family physician, who stated so from my father's bone structure. The article stated that I should not be denied a title shot because of Johnson's antics. I knew that Dan was behind the article. He was trying everything he could to get public support for me. If it took claiming I was part Arabic, so be it. I did not want to disown my heritage, but I went along with the idea because I was desperate for a title shot.

In mid-June, I traveled to Memphis, Tennessee, to take on Jeff Clark, the "Joplin Ghost," again. Clark was a fast, clever, and very tough fighter. Clark was born in Morrisville, N.J. but he was living and fighting out of Joplin, Missouri. The fight took place on June 23 at the Phoenix A.C. The day before the bout, a local reporter met up with me for an interview. Of course the topic was Jack Johnson: *That Jack Johnson is too "fresh," and that his head has been turned by money, was the statement of Joe Jeanette, the only Negro prize fighter that ever whipped Jack Johnson, in a fair ring fight. Johnson since, however, has been whipped by law, baggage men, and a few other things that have comparatively stripped him of money, jewels, and a right to live in the United States.*

Jeanette arrived in the city yesterday to stage a fight against a local boy, and with an unassuming air went into training immediately upon his arrival. Neither did he breeze into a fashionable hotel and sputter because the apartments were for whites only, nor did he have a fight with a Pullman conductor, owing to the fact that he desired to mingle with the whites in the observation car. In fact, Jeanette has firmly stood on the best testimonial he has ever received during his time in or out of the prize ring. "He's a white man's nigger," said the proverbial Southern coronel, and since that time Jeanette unlike the man that he gave such a drubbing, has conducted himself with regard to the compliment.

"Yes, I know Johnson pretty well," he admitted to the direct question. "Among his own people he's all right, except a bit too fresh." Continuing, he stated that he was never exactly a 'running mate' for the black who recently skipped the country, but had met him professionally several times. "Money's turned his head," he continued under pressure, "and about white folks, I think that he's too fresh. He tries to mix with them when they don't want him. He won't act like he ought to." Jeanette denied that he knew anything of Johnson's matrimonial affairs, and condemned them in the strongest terms. "It's not right for him to act that way," he continued, "he gets the rest of us in bad."[384]

When I read the article I was fuming. I was a white man's nigger! The reporter also tried to make me out to be a racist against my own people. He used me. He tried to talk to me in the dressing room before the Clark fight, but I had Dan kick him out.

Clark came into the bout weighing around 166 pounds to my 190 pounds.

---

[384] Undated article from Joe Jennette's scrapbook. Courtesy Ben Hawes collection.

I knocked Clark down in the second, sixth, and seventh rounds, but he was very tough and kept on fighting. I admired his courage. He reminded me of myself. When I knocked Jeff down early in the seventh round, I decided that since I had the fight easily won I wouldn't take any chances. I would just cruise the rest of the fight. I was spending the round moving around and jabbing when the referee Billy Haack, who was also the promoter, jumped in between us and stopped the fight. Haack stated that he was stopping the contest because it was "a fake." The fight was ruled a no-contest. After getting dressed, I met with reporters and issued a statement about the fight: *"I may not have tried as hard as I should have but I refused to take advantage of my opponent who was conceding many pounds in weight. I just wanted to give the crowd a run for the money."*

Two weeks after the bout an article was written about the fake fight allegations. In the article it was questioned whether Haack stopped the contest because we weren't trying or because he wanted to withhold our purses for himself: *Joe Jeannette was accused of faking his contest with Jeff Clark at Memphis the other night. Jeannette has been boxing a good many years and this is the first time he has been accused of deliberately withholding his best efforts.*

Billy Haack, who promoted the contest, also acted as referee, and in the final minute of the bout stopped it, declaring that Jeannette was not doing his best. This is strange, in view of the fact that Jeannette had put Clark down for the count in the second, sixth, and seventh rounds. The peculiar part of it all is that Haack allowed the men to go on until the last minute of the contest, and when he did stop it, refused to return the fans their admissions.

Jimmy Bronson, who is manager of Clark, has quite a few things to say concerning the affair at Memphis. "This Clark," says Bronson, "has been fighting for many years- has met men weighing over 40 pounds heavier than himself- has been beaten but twice, but this is the first time that anyone has accused him of deliberately faking. Billy Haack is the referee- the matchmaker- and the manager of that club in Memphis and after pulling that raw deal he not only failed to refund the admission fees to the patrons, but he refused to give us our guarantees."

Dan McKetrick, who is handling Joe Jeannette, is hot on the trail of Haack. "That was one of the rawest things I saw pulled," says McKetrick, in speaking of Haack's action. "I don't care so much for the money he failed to give, as promised, but I'm going to see that Jeannette is vindicated." Both managers will seek the aid of the law.[385]

On June 27, I traveled to Joplin, Missouri, and took on my basketball teammate Al Benedict. Al was also from West Hoboken and trained with me. Our fight was scheduled for fifteen rounds. In the first round I drew blood from Al with a blow to his mouth. For the rest of the fight his mouth bled profusely. In the third round I landed a right hook to Al's jaw and he went down for a nine-count. When he got back up I floored him again. Al

---

[385] *New Orleans Item* July 6, 1913.

was very courageous and staggered to his feet again, but thank goodness the referee waved the fight off. On July 21, Benedict would fight and lose a ten round decision to another friend of mine, Tom Kennedy.

At the end of July I was booked to perform boxing exhibitions for a week at the Lafayette Theater in Harlem against Frank Moran. Our Monday, July 28 exhibition was described as follows: *At the last performance Monday evening the fighters boxed but two rounds and a fraction, there being a hitch in arrangements. Joe Jeannette was responsible for the stage waits between the two heavyweights, as he accidentally uncorked a claret punch that caused a claret to gush from a gash over Moran's eye like oil from an oil well.*

This piece of acting, which was not down on the program, occurred in the second round. While Moran retired to the wings for temporary repairs, Joe Jeannette sat in his corner and the orchestra began to play: "You Made Me Love You." Then somebody remarked that Jeannette ought to get up and sing a parody on the song, the title of which should be: "You Made Me Hit You, But I Didn't Mean To Do It." But the Hoboken fighter sat in his corner and took up the time explaining to his manager, Dan McKetrick, that he had no aspirations to make Moran look gory.

Moran pluckily returned to finish the third round after Dan McKetrick had announced that the white fighter would be unable to finish the contest. When hostilities were resumed it was apparent to the onlookers as are the objects under a diaphanous skirt, that Jeannette was loathe to do any mixing up. He did not allow Moran to hit him, but he did not hit Moran. The only punching done was when Moran hit the atmosphere hitting at Jeannette. The one-sided boxing exhibitions staged this week at the Lafayette Theater by Jeannette and Moran show what a pronounced advantage the colored heavyweights have over the white heavyweights of to-day.

Moran is regarded as one of the most hopeful of "white hopes," but were he and Jeannette to be turned loose in a ring and instructed to try to break the speed limit there would be work for the coroner the next day, and Jeannette would be present to testify. Maybe the Boxing Commission has been prompted to draw the color line from a humane standpoint. But with the ban put on colored and white fighters meeting in the ring in many cities in this country and elsewhere I find myself wondering when the white race ever expects to win back the heavyweight championship title.

In his contests with Moran, Joe Jeannette gives evidence of being very pert and agile on his feet. For a big man he not only ducks quickly but gracefully. Monday evening in the first round the two contestants exchanged a few blows, but Jeannette appeared to be more intent on keeping Moran from hitting him than he was to tapping the "white hope."[386]

On September 26, the *Auburn Citizen* announced that Dan had reached an agreement with Theodore Vienne to bring five boxers over to France for prearranged matches later in the year. The fighters would consist of heavyweight Frank Moran, Barney Williams- a middleweight from Philly, Young Ahearn- a welterweight from Albany, Mickey Dunn- a bantam-

---

[386] *New York Age* July 31, 1913.

weight, and myself. Williams and Ahern were actually Dan Morgan's fighters, but he loaned them to McKetrick, who was his partner, for the trip. I was promised two fights on the trip with one possibly being against Jack Johnson. Moran was set to take on Britain's "Bombardier" Wells.

On October 3, I met Sam Langford at Madison Square Garden in what was being promoted as an elimination bout to see who would face Jack Johnson in Paris in December for the world's heavyweight championship. The Langford bout would be ten rounds for the colored heavyweight championship. Langford refused to fight me more than ten rounds. The ten round limit worried both Dan and I. Langford was a quick starter and I, known for my great endurance, was unfortunately a slow starter. I stepped up my training for the bout and sparred at a faster pace because of the reduced rounds. I was 34-years-old and realized that I did not have much time left for a title shot.

There was an estimated two thousand five hundred fans in attendance and the gate receipts totaled sixteen thousand dollars. At the weigh-in, Sam looked heavy and out of shape. He weighed 199 1/2 to my 195 pounds. Remember, Sam was only five-foot six-inches to my five-foot nine-and-a-half-inch frame. Sam was known to have drastic weight fluctuations between bouts. My game plan was to utilize the jab and keep Sam at bay. I always had difficulty when Sam got in close because he was smaller than me. On the inside I liked to work the body and follow with uppercuts. With Sam that was difficult because in order to reach his body I had to bend extra low which put me right in Sam's range for his uppercuts and overhand rights.

I decided to fight Sam tall this time. For the first three rounds my plan was effective, as I kept Sam at the end of my stinging jabs. In the fourth round Sam realized he had to take some chances to get in close. Sam rushed me and landed some heavy rights and lefts which forced me to fall into clinches with him. I knew that Sam was using extra energy to force the fight in close, and if I could just survive this round, I felt he would start tiring. The bell seemed to take forever, but it finally rang.

In the corner, Dan and Willie were screaming at me to stay away and use my jab until Sam tired more. In the fifth round, Sam again forced his way inside and we both ripped devastating body blows in the session. In the sixth, I easily out-boxed Sam. His punches felt weaker and weaker. Sam tried to land some haymaker overhand rights in the sixth but I easily slipped them. The crowd started booing during the sixth round because it expected more action. After the round, Dan yelled at me to disregard the booing. Dan told me to remember the saying: *"Stick the jab and move away, live to see another day."*

For the next four rounds, I boxed Sam's ears off. On the few occasions that Sam did get close and land a few desperate right hands, I took the sting out of them by rolling with the punches. After the bout, the crowd was mixed with boos and cheers. Many of the boxing insiders praised me for my smart fight and the exceptional boxing skills I displayed. Unfortunately, the *New York Times* called the bout a draw.

The *Atlanta Constitution* reported that I had won the bout. Sportswriter Ed Curley reported: *Tis a short tale of a nasty left-handed glove that swashed steadily across the ebony jaw of Tham Langford aided and abetted by a persistent right, that constantly sunk into Tham's ombongpong, and this combination of circumstances gathered Joseph Jeanette a victory over Tham Langford last night in the ten round battle held at Madison Square Garden... Jeannette started after Langford the moment Referee Billy Joh gave the boys the high sign. He slapped with the left, he punched with the left, he jabbed with the left, then he walloped with the left.*

Now, when a husky battler does all those things, they certainly help to slow up a gent built on the lines of a pork barrel. Tham tried to crash over those deadly rights in the opening rounds, but Joe absolutely refused to receive them on his map. He just turned his head sideways and the gloves slid over the bag. In the opening rounds Tham gave an exhibition of his old-time stuff, but three rounds of this was all he shone in. That Jeannette left had changed a smile into a frown and Tham is some frowner.

After the third everybody sat back and realizing that all Jeannette had to do was to snap those gloves on Langford to win in a walk. Jeannette lived up to the dope. When the fifth round reached the homestretch Tham was slightly weary. His wallops were lacking the old power, which delighted Jeanette, who started in to sway wallops with his old side kick.

From the sixth to the final Tham blossomed for a minute in each round and then died. In the interim, as they say, Jeanette didn't stop annoying him with pesky gloves. The final round found Jeanette crashing rights steadily against that Langford jaw and making the Langford head do the 'bobbing up and down' act. Some of the gentlemen that patronize the sport didn't seem to be pleased with the bout. That's all in the game. Joe Jeanette doesn't care. He won; that's good enough for him.[387] I was hopeful that my performance would force Johnson to feel the pressure to fight me, but no contract was offered and no great media pressure followed.

On October 13, Harry Lewis was seriously injured in a bout in Philadelphia. Harry, who held the welterweight championship from 1908 to 1912, was knocked out by Joe Borrell in the fifth round of their scheduled six round bout. Lewis had been involved in a serious car accident several months prior, and was trying to resume his career. Lewis collapsed in the ring after receiving a blow to his jaw. It was said he suffered a blood clot. He was near death for several days. Harry miraculously recovered, but never fought again. Harry Lewis was yet another sober reminder of how dangerous and deadly boxing can be.

On November 26, I traveled with my basketball team to Buffalo, New York, where we took on the Buffalo German team. The *Watertown Daily*

---

[387] Indianapolis Freeman November 8, 1913

Times described the upcoming game: *The local management went to a big expense and have secured the Jersey City basketball team, one of the best in the country. In the lineup is Joe Jeanette, the heavyweight boxer who is booked to sail for Australia immediately after the game here. Jeanette is a clever player and a great admirer of basketball for he says, "The reason I and every fighter ought to play basketball is that it quickens the eye and develops the muscles around the shoulders and the arms. It is a grand game."*[388]

Dan and I steamed again to Paris with Moran, Ahearn, and Dunn. I took my wife and two children along for the trip. Around noon on December 18, the day we arrived, Dan and I walked to a local cafe to talk to reporters about my upcoming bout with Sam Langford on the 20th at Luna Park in Paris. Langford was there, as well as "Battling" Jim Johnson, who was scheduled to box Jack Johnson on the 19th at the Velodrome d' Hiver in Paris. Johnson had arrived in Paris after first fleeing to Canada to avoid arrest in the United States. Johnson was treated like a hero in Paris despite his fugitive status in the States.

Most of the fancy hotels, though, turned Johnson and his entourage away. They were turned off by Johnson's wild nightly receptions that would cause hotel guests to complain of the noise. Finally, the St. Lazare Terminus Hotel rented Johnson rooms. Parisians were pressuring Johnson to fight Langford or myself. The French Boxing Federation declared the world's heavyweight title vacant. Its director, Paris promoter Theodore Vienne, stated that Johnson was being stripped because he had been sentenced to prison in the United States and more importantly because he was refusing to box the top contenders like Langford or myself. I was feeling weak after the cross Atlantic trip because the seas were extremely rough on the journey.

The Jack Johnson versus Jim Johnson bout would be the first time Jack would box a colored boxer as champion, and would be the last time two colored boxers would box for the heavyweight title for twenty-five years, until Joe Louis defeated light heavyweight champ John Henry Lewis in 1939. For our upcoming bouts, Jack, Sam Langford, Jim Johnson, and I were all interviewed by the local papers. Jack Johnson walked into the press conference dressed to the nines. He held a silver-headed walking stick, shoes made of soft doeskin and crocodile leather, with a biscuit-colored silk suit and a pale soft golden hat. A silk bandana adorned his upper jacket pocket and an orchid hung from his lapel.

After my interview, I put my coat and hat on and was preparing to leave with Dan. Johnson came over to me and asked to speak to me alone. I was surprised because Jack hadn't spoken to me in six years. I nodded to Dan to go on without me, and I followed Jack through a back room in the cafe out

---

[388] *Watertown Daily Times* November 5, 1913.

onto the streets of Paris. There were no reporters or cameras, no wives or entourages, just me and Jack Johnson. We walked for several minutes in silence and I was starting to feel uncomfortable. Finally we reached a park bench by the Seine River. Jack sat down and motioned me to do the same. Jack stared down at his shoes and in a trembling voice said: *"These white folk will never understand what we have to go through as black men. I was forced to walk the 'coon walk' as a kid. Had to walk in the street like a dog.*[389]*I had to start my boxing career at the Royal Sporting Club of Galveston in 'Battle Royals' where five other black boys and me were thrown together in a ring to beat each other until only one was standing while the white men called us all kinds of names.*[390] *After the fights some whites would throw pennies and nickels at us. Some would take a match to a penny to get the metal real hot and then throw it at us to burn our skin. Or the times I 'rode the rails' as a child and saw white men, called 'yard-dicks,' taking a black hobo they caught and throwing him underneath the rolling wheels of a train, to kill or dismember him.*[391] *This was the price a nigger would pay when and if they caught him. I will never forget those memories. Now I feel like the whole world is closing in on me. I can't take it anymore. I just can't. I never suffered from that famous nigger disease called 'white folks fear' but I am afraid.*[392] *Afraid they are going to arrest me at any moment."*

I didn't know how to respond to him. Here was the world's heavyweight champion, the cockiest man in the world, and the guy who was denying me a shot at the title, and he was looking to me for sympathy. He didn't appear cocky at all now. Although his apparel exuded confidence, inside he was frail and brittle. He looked very unsure of himself and his situation.

I patted him on his shoulder. Although I was frustrated with him not giving me a title fight, we were both more similar than different. We both suffered from racism and we both had to deal with the pain of being in interracial marriages. Jack took a deep breath and said: *"How do you handle the pressure so well, Joe? It never seems to bother you? You're the only Negro boxer I know who doesn't take refuge with alcohol or women. How come it doesn't get to you?"* *"Of course it gets to me, Jack,"* I replied. *"You don't think it bothers me when I take my wife out to a nice restaurant and they seat us in the back by the kitchen and we are purposely given horrible service. When my wife is out with my children and people treat her like she is babysitting 'colored' kids. When we go for Sunday drives and we have to avoid stopping at out of the way diners or gas stations to avoid problems. I'll bet an entire fight purse that my family's food has been spit in more than once."*

Jack looked at me and wiped the tears from his eyes. *"I loved her, Joe. I miss Etta very much. She was my best friend. I treated her horribly and I feel so guilty. I didn't understand the pain she was going through being in an interracial marriage."* Etta Duryea was Jack's former wife who committed suicide in September of

---

[389] *The 100 Greatest Boxers of All Time* by Bert Randolph Sugar pg. 48.
[390] *The Big Black Fire* by Robert H. DeCoy pg. 33.
[391] *The Big Black Fire* by Robert H. DeCoy pg. 21.
[392] *The Big Black Fire* by Robert H. DeCoy pg. 25.

1912. He continued: *"I cheated on her all the time. I was so foolish." "Jack,"* I said, *"There is nothing you can do to change the past. She knew you loved her. She just fell into a deep depression and couldn't fight her way out of it. My wife struggles with the same pressures every day."* Jack replied: *"But your wife is still here for you, Joe. I love Lucille but I need Etta now more than ever. I miss her and I love her. She is the only one who made me feel safe. I felt that in Etta I had found a love that would continue uninterrupted. I wanted her to bear my children but she wouldn't. She would tell me: 'You can't even protect me from what I have to go through. How do you think you could protect the children we'd have?'"* [393]

I could see just how fragile Jack was at this moment. *"Then don't let her struggles be in vain, Jack. Help people to learn to accept interracial relationships by your life and actions. As champion of the world you have the power to bring attention to the dangers of depression."* Jack replied: *"You're right, Joe. I am going to build a sanitarium for neurasthenic people. I want to make sure no one has to suffer like my Etta did."* We sat on that bench for almost two hours. We cried, we laughed, and we cried again. Here we were, two of the toughest men in the world, yet we were both so fragile. Jack went on: *"I guess I owe the coon walk most everything. If it wasn't for the walk and what it stood for I would have been happy in Galveston and maybe I never would have left."* [394] Then the fighter returned. A stern, focused look came over Jack's face as he continued: *"I know the horror of being hunted and haunted.* [395] *I'm black and they never let me forget it. I'm black alright! I'll never let them forget it!* [396]

We walked back to the cafe and back into the circus life we were living. Jack thanked me for listening to him. One week later, a famous French showgirl named Mistinguette was proclaiming how she recently sampled Jack and found him: *"formidable."* [397] The affair became so torrid that the French press and journals echoed the sentiments of England's Winston Churchill, urging that Jack Johnson be expelled from: *"not only Paris, but the soil of France."* [398] A December 14 newspaper article came out in New York. The headline read "Heavyweight Bout in Paris to be for the Title." Mr. Vienne, the director of the Society for the Propagation of English Boxing in France, stated his reasons for proclaiming that my match with Langford was to be for the heavyweight title: *"The title held by Jack Johnson is declared vacant because it is not admissible in sport for a man to legitimately hold all his life, or at least as long as he pleases, a title which he obstinately refuses to defend against qualified aspirants. Nobody can contest that principle. Now, I have repeatedly offered Jack Johnson an opportunity of defending this title in Paris under the usual conditions of a*

---

[393] *The Big Black Fire* by Robert H. DeCoy pg. 134.
[394] *The Heavyweight Champions* by Stanley Weston pg. 71.
[395] "Jack Johnson-Rebel Sojourner" by Theresa Runstedtler pg. 132.
[396] "Yesternow" A Tribute to Jack Johnson by Miles Davis 1971.
[397] *Champions of the Ring* by Gerald Suster pg. 67.
[398] *The Big Black Fire* by Robert H. DeCoy pg. 192.

participation in the receipts with a guarantee of $25,000 then $30,000. Jack Johnson has always refused. In an interview Jack Johnson had in Paris with Victor Breyer, then my associate, then later with Leon See, director of boxing, he made the same public declaration which remains still without denial, that 'I will not box again even for a million.'

"Since coming to Paris, Johnson made an engagement to meet me. He did not come himself, but his representative came, only to declare to me that Johnson did not wish to really box a capable adversary to maintain his title, but only adversaries of a second class. Under those conditions no one can be expected to submit to Johnson's fantastic demands. The sporting world has every right to rebel and to place open for public competition a title which the holder because it is too much trouble, does not wish to have to defend."[399]

At 34-years-old, I was unsure how many ring wars I had left. The aches and pains of boxing were taking their toll on my body. Although the weather was cold, Addie and I still took the kids on the many attractions in Luna Park. The park was a literal wonderland for children. There were rides such as the Bridge of Brooklyn Ride, the Water Chute, the Scenic Railway, the Mysterious Underground River, the Chatoullieur, and the Devilish Wheels. The Scenic Railway was much like a roller coaster ride without the big dips. The Water Chute was similar to a log flume type ride.

While I was with my family, Dan was working out the final details of the matches. Willie Lewis could usually be found in one of the Paris bars, such as the Hotel Lotti, where he talked up his boxing career to anyone who would listen, especially the women. The French Boxing Federation had stripped Johnson of his title and they billed my fight with Langford as being for the heavyweight championship of the world. I didn't understand how France could see the injustice of Johnson avoiding the best contenders for the title but my own country could not. The only thing America was concerned with was having a white heavyweight champion, not the best heavyweight champion.

The upcoming bout with Langford was the buzz of Paris. Famous playwright George Bernard Shaw visited both camps. Shaw was a big boxing fan. He wrote a book on boxing in 1886 called *Cashel Byron's Profession,* which was about a runaway boy who became a famous boxer. Rumors spread that Langford and Shaw were very close and that Langford was actually play sparring with the 57-year-old Shaw. Dan was careful not to let Shaw see any of the moves we were working on for Langford. This contest would be twenty rounds. Dan and I believed twenty rounds would be to my advantage because of my stamina. Unfortunately for me, I had suffered from sea-sickness again on the ship coming over. The bout was fought only two days after I arrived. I definitely was not a hundred percent for the bout.

---

[399] *Cleveland Leader* December 15, 1913.

On December 20, 1913, I met Sam Langford at Luna Park in Paris. I arrived at ringside with my seconds Dan McKetrick, Willie Lewis, and "Young" Ahearn. Langford arrived with his manager Billy Woodman, veteran trainer Bob Armstrong, and several other cornermen.

Jacques Mortane described the Jack Johnson fight, as well as my fight with Langford: *He (Jack Johnson) believed he could easily defeat his opponent (Jim Johnson) but his breath fled him. He was himself for the first three rounds. In the fifth round he fractured an arm that for two years was used more for wearing jewelry than boxing gloves. He went into the tenth round with the hopes that the best that could happen for him was a draw. It is the only result that would have been correct. And it upsets me... that the thought that over 2,000 spectators went to this humorous event and that the boxing record of Jack Johnson now bears the defect: 'Draw with Jim Johnson' an indelible stain. Those who claim we had been wrong to say the title should be withdrawn from Jack Johnson are now in fits...*

But enough of this grisly subject. Let us move on to the championship of the world that was fought last Saturday at Luna Park between Sam Langford and Joe Jeannette under the auspices of Wonderland and the arbitration of Frank Reichel...

Negroes will not give a good fight against themselves, say the ignorant, for whom the sport is nothing but a vague commercial. We have never attended a battle twenty times more stressful, more exciting. From start to finish, all spectators passed through the phases of the most varied and exciting. Rich in twist, such as a dramatic masterpiece, this championship will go down in the annals of pugilism. It can be summarized as follows: Initially, the fight is equal. Joe Jeannette concentrates on the body to exhaust his rival, who aims for the jaw and the sides. Joe Jeannette piles up the points. The match goes far to his advantage. The twelfth round comes without any change to this aspect.

Then it was the thirteenth round that was the fateful number, so cruel to him. Jeannette continues to tabulate points, without trying to knock out a man who seems un knock-out-able, when suddenly, a short hook that certainly carried no more than six inches of momentum, struck the jaw of Jeannette by Langford. Jeannette goes down. To many, Jeannette would not get up. They were wrong, they do not know the tremendous energy resources of this true hero. At eight, Jeannette shakes his head to revive his senses and recovers, ready for battle. He is unsteady on his legs but he will not admit defeat. Langford, his fists as hard as a hammer, struck the same spot and Jeannette goes down again. This time we believed the fight over. Not at all! Jeannette rises at nine in front of his little opponent. He barley has the strength to raise his arms and shield the attack which still finds its way to his face! He was just trying to avoid the shot to the jaw that would have been the 'coup de grace.' As soon as Langford threw his fists, Jeannette turned his face and looked away so the punches would land where they would be least effective. But he cannot always avoid them, again he goes down to the floor, his arms crossed. The room yells in excited encouragement for the unfortunate knock down and for a few seconds you could not hear from the noise. And at the count of nine, when we believed the end was near, he again stands back on his legs, which no longer seem to have the strength to bear his weight. The bell rang and it was a relief for everyone, who really feared the punishment that the man had endured.

279

He is the toughest and bravest we have seen in the ring. The fourteenth round allows Jeannette to recuperate. Langford cannot find the openings. In the fifteenth round from the middle to the last, we see the best demonstration of heroism and endurance. Jeannette recovered from his knockdown and does not stay on the defensive. He wants to attack, he wants to catch up... he led the fight brilliantly. He had seemingly recovered and some were astonished, considering the possibility of a draw, forgetting now the thirteenth round, when we arrive at the second minute of the twentieth round. Langford feels the current sympathy for his opponent, he's afraid of the decision; he wanted to make a definite advantage. He then attacked with all his might, using his last reserve of energy. He threw incredible hooks to the jaw. He bloodied the face of his rival who looked so sad and painful that I could not describe, it was too painful to see. He would prefer to be killed, and he would not descend until the end and when the gong sounded he was liberated, Jeannette was always in front of his opponent and would only be beaten by points in the most admirable battle of both their careers. Langford is the new heavyweight champion and he bravely bears the weight of these heavy and enviable laurels and is the proud successor to Sullivan, Corbett, Fitzsimmons, and Jeffries. He seems superior to Johnson and Tommy Burns. But if we praise the value of this great boxer, this ring phenomenon, given his small size, do not forget the scientific Jeannette, so brilliant and especially so brave. The loser and the worthy winner deserve the highest praise that could be addressed to both Jeannette and Langford.[400]

The French magazine *Le Plein Air* described the fight as follows: *Is Jack Johnson still worthy of the title of boxing world champion?... For us it is proven... the black Langford, who brilliantly beat the other black fighter Joe Jeannette, is quite worthy of the title of world's boxing champion... Organizers should seek to establish in the shortest time possible, a Jack Johnson-Langford meeting, and this time definitely for the title. If Johnson avoids fighting such a competitor, Langford should be proclaimed the world's champion. Langford has undoubtedly defeated Joe Jeannette magnificently... Yet the unfortunate Jeannette gave us the same beautiful ring fighting that he had in his first trip to Paris. We know he is a beautiful boxer, a true virtuoso of the fist, with a perfect knowledge of boxing with courage and a passion for battle like no other. But Saturday Joe Jeannette found himself in front of a wall. A man who had no regard for the blows he received, a fellow concerned only with the blows he was landing and God only knows how he and Jeannette both absorbed these punches.*

Despite his fine fighting spirit and his great desire to win, Jeannette was almost always dominated by Langford... Jeannette was down three times in the thirteenth round, and he was almost asleep, and in the twentieth round, before our very eyes he displayed truly miraculous energy to escape the indignity of a knockout. The courageous Jeannette was unbelievable, the man never ceased to attack, even stunned he still struggled to fight, even in the face of a terrible beating he kept the hope of winning. It was sincerely one of the finest fights, and perhaps the best that was ever offered to sportsmen in Paris.[401] The magazine went on to voice its disgust with the Jack Johnson versus Jim

---

[400] *La Vie Au Grand Air* December 27, 1913.
[401] *Le Plein Air* December 25, 1913.

Johnson match. The paper called the match: *A big disappointment.*

On December 30, 1913, Robert Fitzsimmons was denied a license to box by the NY State Athletic Commission because he was 51-years-old. Many boxers were worried that they would also be stripped of fighting because of their age. Fitzsimmons filed suit and the court ruled that allowing Fitzsimmons to box would risk serious injury to him, the sport, and society.[402]

In early January 1914, Dan advised me that Jacques Mortane of the French magazine *Vie Au Grand Air* wanted me to come to his office at 90 Champs-Elysees Avenue in Paris for an interview. The magazine was preparing to put out a special boxing issue. Besides myself, they invited Sam Langford, Joe Woodman, Georges Carpentier, Willie Lewis, and Francois DesCamps.

Woodman discussed the origins of boxing, Carpentier talked about his career, Langford discussed proper training techniques, DesCamps discussed managing boxers, and I was asked to discuss Negroes in boxing. Dan asked me to be careful not to say anything that might be received negatively back in the States. My entire career I had kept inside what I felt about the way blacks were treated in boxing. Today I was going to let my real feelings be heard.

The following is a portion of my article as told to Jacques Mortane of *La Vie Au Grand Air*. *'The Negroes in Boxing' by Joe Jeannette. 'It is not without some satisfaction that I recognize the gains made by blacks in boxing since 1791, but since Bill Richmond first took part in boxing it has been a struggle.*

"I know that in America Negroes are not loved, but that reason is independent of the issue of sports. Among the boxers from my race, there are those who have found this unpleasant, certainly, but among whites, there are many who have shown that their feelings were not exactly those that we are accustomed to seeing from men of integrity and loyalty. I respond to an accusation often carried against pugilists of color: certain whites pretend that we lack courage. Look at this example, Big Peter Jackson: while he was on the decline he was game for 61 rounds against Jim Corbett; then there is George Godfrey, the first champion of true color in America, and Frank Craig and today Sam Langford, Jack Johnson, Sam McVea and myself.

"I do not believe that anyone can say that one of these boxers lack courage... I will speak especially of the glorious black trio composed of George Dixon, Joe Gans and Joe Walcott who were all three champions of the world before Jack Johnson and Sam Langford. Dixon was the first one having obtained the worlds championship in the Bantam and Featherweights. Gans was champion of the world in the lightweight class and Joe Walcott, champion of the world at welterweight.

"Dixon, although black, acquired an extraordinary popularity in America. He was certainly a wonderful artist in the ring...'[403]

Also in January, I was invited to a photo session by *La Boxe & Les Boxeurs,*

---

[402] *Beyond The Ring* by Jeffrey T. Sammons pgs. 64-65.
[403] *La Vie au Grand Air*-Boxing Special Issue 1914.

which was another French boxing magazine. The magazine wanted a picture of my family and I, to put on the cover of their January 7 issue.[404] The kids were excited, as was Addie. Back in the States a picture of an interracial family on the cover of a magazine was unheard of. I think partly the French wanted to show the U.S. how much more open they were in regards to interracial relationships.

On March 21, 1914, I met the French champion, Georges Carpentier, at the Cirque de Paris. At the weigh-in, Carpentier joked about how he and DesCamps could not get passes to see me box Sam McVea in 1909. The promoter, who they fought for on the previous night, refused to give them passes. Georges said they waited for hours outside the Cirque de Paris, as the crowd cheered inside, waiting for the verdict. I joked back that he would now have the best seat in the house, and I would work very hard to make sure he would not have to wait long for the results. I was much heavier than Carpentier, 184 pounds to Georges' 168 pounds.

Unlike my fight with McVea, this time I was going to fight the real "Idol of Paris." McVea had many supporters in France when I fought him but Carpentier was a home-grown product. Several newspaper reporters supported Georges, such as Leon See of *La Boxe & Les Boxeurs*, who wrote:

Why, I have been asked, can he (Carpentier) beat a man like Jeannette, who in the ring will outweigh him by 10 pounds, whose strength is such that Sam Langford himself could not incapacitate, whose stamina is so fantastic that he could sicken a colossus like Sam McVea, and finally one whose meetings could not be more honorable, on several occasions, against Jack Johnson himself?

To predict a Carpentier victory would be like saying that the champion from Lens is better than the champion of the world. Obviously these opinions seem valid at first, but my opinion nevertheless is very clear, 'Carpentier defeats Jeannette decisively.' I'll tell you the reason for my paradoxical view. First of all I've never had an exaggerated confidence in Jeannette, in my view, when he met McVea, he was knocked out. I myself saw with my own eyes, how he repeatedly was on the ground for more than ten seconds, and if the arbitrator had not had an exaggerated slowness, the fight would have been lost, if I remember correctly, five or six times... On the other hand Joe is not a terribly good hitter, if you look at his record even a few years ago, when he was at full strength, Sandy Ferguson stood with him for twenty rounds, Sid Russell fifteen rounds, and Jim Smith a no-decision for ten rounds, Tommy Ross did the same as well as many other men of second and third class, in front of the honorable mulatto.

Now we have to say things as they are, Jeannette is no longer a young man, he is well into his thirties and those who have recently seen him in the ring have noticed a slip in the beautiful bronze statue's fine feline movements, which were so admired. Jeannette is thicker, heavier, and has slowed down considerably. Do not forget that he committed, under penalty of 5,000 francs, to get down to 84 kilos two hours before the fight, on the

[404] *La Boxe & Les Boxeurs* January 7, 1914.

day of the battle. He weighs nearly 90 kilos now and it is unlikely that he will want to give a gift of one thousand dollars to Carpentier, but it is highly unlikely he will reach this limit. It will be at the expense of his strength and his punch, which is not already very frightening...

Carpentier, on the other hand, is weight free, trusting his record victory over Bombardier Wells, his hands are in good condition, he's in full possession of his speed and is comfortably in his twenties, he has gifted footwork which is incomparably faster and will be surprised himself if he cannot take advantage of this...

Here is how I expect the meeting; Carpentier dominates his foe, he lands hard with his left and before the sixth round Jeannette will hit the ground several times. He will continue this up until the tenth round. The pace will slow down. Carpentier, fearing damage to his hands, will become reluctant to land heavy shots. The advantage of the weight is beginning to be felt and his opponent will end the fight with the last rounds slightly in his favor, but beaten widely on points. Now, needless to say the odds are fragile, but he has a great chance, of reigning supreme in the ring but that result can change completely with one punch.[405] Obviously Leon was not a supporter of mine with that prediction. Leon See would later go on to manage heavyweight champion Primo Carnera.

I was weak going into the contest because I had to dry out for seven days to make the contract weight. My diet for that week consisted of three glasses of tomato juice a day and nothing else. It was a diet that Willie Lewis had used for a few bouts. I had to lose the weight because in the contract if I didn't get to within 16 pounds of Georges I would forfeit one thousand dollars. Not long after this bout, I began losing my hair at a rapid pace. Without a doubt, I believe drying out for the Carpentier bout was the cause of my hair loss. I didn't sleep much the week of the fight. I continuously had acid coming up in my throat from the tomato juice. I did, however, make the contracted weight.

The *New York Times* described the upcoming Carpentier bout: *No event in French boxing history has aroused as much interest as the contest between Joe Jeannette and Georges Carpentier, which takes place at Luna Park, Paris, just before midnight tomorrow. It is expected that nearly 6,000 people will be at ringside, and it is estimated that the receipts for admission will reach $30,000. Hundreds of tickets have been sold at $25 each, so Carpentier and Jeannette, who have agreed to box for a percentage- 25 percent to the winner and 20 percent to the loser- are practically assured of a small fortune each. Jeannette hints that his share will enable him to retire even if beaten. There is the keenest speculation as to who will win. Carpentier never yet has suffered a knockout, and has met many big men of repute. One of Jeannette's supporters declared today that nothing short of a crowbar could force Jeannette to give in.*

Jeannette himself is not inclined to 'talk fight.' Questioned today he said, "I should win, I believe, and will win- but there, let's talk about something else." Jeannette leads such a

---

[405] *La Boxe & Les Boxeurs* March 18, 1914.

clean life that he never requires much training, but he has been in strict training for the last few weeks, and will have the advantage in weight. The articles governing the match stipulate that he must not weigh more than 187 pounds, ringside, but it is believed he will have to forfeit $1,000 for overweight. Carpentier will not weigh more than 168 pounds.[406]

Jacques Mortane described the outcome of the fight: *Joe Jeannette defeated Georges Carpentier on points last Saturday at Luna Park, over 15 rounds. That is the brutal fact. The Frenchman's reputation has grown considerably from this defeat. Carpentier fought the best fight we could have imagined, exceeding the expectations of all those who were impartial... Carpentier was more accurate than the marvelous scientific Joe Jeannette, he was faster and showed courage and resiliency, the qualities which one needs to become a champion. I repeat what I wrote: military service will be the greatest good. For three years he will live a healthy life, he can continue training to maintain his speed and skill, he may fight from time to time, he probably will gain the 10 pounds that he is lacking, and in his return he can easily become a world champion in all categories. What is lacking at the present time is weight. He is too light...*

That said, however, we find the French supporters so blinded by bias, that there could be no discussion of the verdict with them. Our colleague Frantz Reichel, who arbitrated with the skill that no one can challenge, returned the only verdict that could be imposed under the circumstances. Carpentier himself, after the first excited moments, must be satisfied. Besides the protests were not very numerous, but they are unfortunate because they were raised by a few notables... Being barely beaten by Joe Jeannette is a considerable success and he has no need to be sullied by injustice. Carpentier has proven that he is one of the top five current heavyweights, even though he is a small heavyweight... Currently the only present contenders for the title: Sam Langford, Joe Jeannette, Georges Carpentier, 'Gunboat' Smith, and the title holder Jack Johnson. The youngest and the lightest is our champion!

I do not see a thrilling battle for the moment except a revenge match between Jeannette and Carpentier. Oh what an exciting meeting! The prospect would be scary! This time, it would not be 15 but 20 rounds. I am convinced that if Saturday had 5 more rounds Joe Jeannette would have won even more clearly and without an argument of doubt. I am not alone in this view: the fight would have been a repeat of the Carpentier versus Billy Papke fight... There were 180,000 francs of receipts the other night; we could reach 200,000 francs, as the sportsmen would be assured of attending a night of excitement... The weight loss suffered by Jeannette, we must not forget, was a serious handicap for the mulatto last Saturday, perhaps more serious than Carpentier being 16 pounds lighter. He was troubled by exhaustion. So by adding weight we might not get the result that we desire.[407]

Georges surprised me by coming out aggressively in the match. There were many close rounds in the fight. I was awarded the decision after fifteen rounds of boxing. Georges was the most popular boxer in France at the time so when several spectators disagreed with the decision it was not a

---

[406] *New York Times* March 21, 1914.
[407] *La Vie Au Grand Air* March 28, 1914.

shock to me. I know the fight was close because I felt very weak from the weight loss. I asked Willie if he thought I deserved the decision. Willie gave me a surprised look. He asked me how many times I was robbed in my career. Without waiting for an answer he continued: *"Joe I'll take a win any way I can get it, decision, knockout, or a gift!"*

Willie was right. Why should I feel guilty about winning a close fight when I was on the losing end of several terrible decisions. During one of the many times I made Georges miss wildly in the fight, he fell onto the canvas. I reached down to help him up and the crowd roared its approval. A reporter later wrote I was like a father helping up his son.

Leon See, a huge Carpentier supporter, wrote: *In my opinion Carpentier had merited the decision... Jeannette from the beginning of the meeting had sought to exhaust his opponent by infighting with body blows and uppercuts to the chin. During the first round Carpentier was being dominated by the mulatto... when suddenly... Carpentier lands a wonderful right hook and Jeannette went to the ground... It was a moment of mad excitement in the room and one could already foresee the French victory by K.O. but, in the second round, the smiling Jeannette resumed his work and anxiety came back strong in their hearts. Would Carpentier get exhausted from the infighting? Holding the hard shots to the pit of the stomach of a man who, in the ring must have weighed over 186 pounds? Once again Carpentier was up to the task in front of him, he immediately adapted to the circumstances, accepting to confront Jeannette's tactics... Holding his head against the mulatto he began infighting and dominated the body blows ten to one.*

Carpentier finished with a bloody, swollen face, but it was by far his prettiest work to date. He descended on Jeannette in the first round and was shaken repeatedly by perfect classic left hooks and finally he succeeded, in the end to take advantage of the infighting, to penetrate the inside of his opponent. And this is what is called a victory.

It was argued that Carpentier finished the fight completely exhausted, while his opponent was still very fresh. 'Carpentier could not do one more round,' said many spectators. That argument is absolutely worthless. The fight was over 15 rounds not 16 or 20; Carpentier gave his full effort over the fifteen rounds, if the meeting had been longer, he would have conserved his energy and would have ended well.

The decision of 'Jeannette winner' was greeted with amazement by all in attendance. The referee once more was not clearly involved and showed his inexperience. It is really unfortunate that even today, after the excellent results achieved by the application of the three judge system, we continue to organize fights with a single arbitrator... It is permissible to say that if the Carpentier-Jeannette match had been arbitrated by three judges, the champion of Europe would have been declared the winner.[408]

The opinions of the press were varied. Another Paris reporter wrote: *"The French public is overly chauvinistic. It does not want to admit that it's idol was beaten."*[409]

After the bout, several beautiful women approached me and offered to

---

[408] *La Boxe & Les Boxeurs* March 25, 1914.
[409] "Jack Johnson-Rebel Sojourner" by Theresa Runstedtler pg. 187.

help me celebrate my victory. I thanked them for their generous offer but told them the Missus was awaiting my arrival back at the hotel.[410] While McKetrick was bragging to the girls of how successful he was and how much money he had, I grabbed my cloth cap and bade McKetrick and the girls good night. Georges, who was not far away, approached me and stated: *"Joe, you sure are made from a different mold."* Carpentier would later say: *"It was then that I decided that marriage could never mar boxers- rather it made them."*[411]

Georges and I would become fast friends after the contest. I would later help train him for his million-dollar bout against Jack Dempsey. I was asked my thoughts about Carpentier after the fight: *"I admit that Carpentier surprised me. I went into this fight as one that I could easily control as I could not believe a fighter weighing a dozen kilos or less could stay in a fight with me. I didn't think the battle would take more than seven or eight rounds. Carpentier strikes extremely hard and holds a better punch than I thought. For his age, he is actually amazing. My tactic first of all was to exhaust him with blows to the body but he had remarkably adapted to my game. I then tried to pressure him at close range with uppercuts but he negated my shots by deftly placing his arm in the right location. Carpentier is very dangerous and he is a man who can beat the best."*[412]

Carpentier gave his thoughts on the match: *"I've been beaten by Jeannette. If I thought that I deserved the defeat I'd be the first to say that. When I was defeated by Klause and Papke and others, I never invoked the slightest excuse or discussion of the decision. But today, truthfully, without boasting, I think I won. From the first, I felt that Jeannette's shots weren't strong, I was surprised and I stayed inside working the body, and I accepted the game plan that my opponent was imposing on me, eh well, the blows that Jeannette hit me with did not do anything. My abdominal wall is very hard and I felt nothing. I wanted to show Jeannette that I could beat him at his own tactics. The only shot that disfigured me was a shot that made my nose bleed, but that did not harm me and at no time did I feel I was losing.*

"In the later rounds I did all of the forcing as I continuously attacked the body, however, much that counted for points. It seems to me that over the distance my speed was much greater. And if someone was on the ground it was not me. Jeannette used many tricks against me that are not allowed in the ring. He was often holding and hitting and the referee did not see it. When Reichel was on one side of us Jeannette held me with his other arm and hit me with his arm that was facing the referee. When he changed his location Jeannette switched to the other arm. I am very annoyed at this decision which I did not deserve, but I am glad that I did well against a powerful opponent, that his blows did not hurt me, while my blows were effective, even to a man of his weight."[413]

Gus Wilson worked my corner for the Carpentier bout. Wilson relayed a

---

[410] *Seattle Sunday Times* April 4, 1920.
[411] "Why Boxers Should Marry" By Georges Carpentier Undated.
[412] *La Boxe & Les Boxeurs* March 25, 1914.
[413] *La Boxe & Les Boxeurs* March 25, 1914.

comical story about the fight: *"Jeannette settled down in a little cottage with his wife in a Paris suburb and trained hard for the match. He was a very fine man and devoted to his little lady, who couldn't do any of the housework while Joe was around. He'd just take the mop, or whatever she was using, away from her and do it himself. I have reason for mentioning this.*

"Well just before the fight I gave Joe his instructions. Only one thing, I told him to keep his guard high. 'Don't give him a clean shot at your chin with his right,' I said, 'and you have nothing to worry about.' Joe nodded, the bell rang, and he shuffled out. I leaned down to put the water bottle under my stool. When I looked up, there was Jeannette, flat on his back. A right hand.

"Joe struggled up at nine. With more experience, Carpentier would have finished him right there. But Georges came in wildly, throwing right hands all over the place. For an interminable period of three or four rounds, Jeannette took a fearful beating. But sheer instinct kept him bobbing just enough to spoil Carpentier's aim. Joe was still out between the fourth and fifth rounds. He said, 'Let me take that broom, Baby.' He thought he was home sweeping the kitchen." [414]

In April 1914, black newspaper reporter Ernest Stevens visited Jack Johnson in Paris. Stevens was investigating the buzz that colored people were treated much better in France than they were back in the United States. After the interview, Stevens wrote that both Johnson's and his advice to colored people in the United States was: *"to remain in their own country where they can become better citizens and get a hundred cents worth out of every dollar they spend."* Stevens also stated, *"I have not seen many Afro-Americans and I would not advise anyone to come here looking to better their financial condition as there are very few avenues of employment open to them. The only exception, perhaps are theatrical folks and prizefighters, and even the latter is not advisable, Paris having been overrun with fistic aspirants of every shade and kind... there is only one Afro-American in Paris who can say that he is happy and that is Jack Johnson."* [415] Stevens stated Johnson was the only happy black man in Paris because he had a fine residence and several first-class cars at his disposal. Stevens also mentioned that he felt colored people were treated better in Germany than in England.

Addie, the kids, and I arrived back in the States on May 12 aboard the Kronprinzessin Cecilie. When we stepped ashore in New York City, a *New York Times* reporter was standing by to interview me on the pier. The reporter asked me how I performed on my seven-month journey to Europe and I replied: *"I won five and lost one against Balla the Australian who is some fighter, believe me."* I was then asked what I thought of Frank Moran's chances against Jack Johnson in their upcoming battle: *"Well I tell you it's just this way. If all them stories that's going around about the way he (Johnson) has gone to pieces through drink and other kinds of dissipation are true it ought to be easy for Moran to whip him. But on the other hand if them stories ain't true Frank Moran will not*

[414] *Brooklyn NY Daily Eagle* September 6, 1945.
[415] *Chicago Defender* April 25, 1914.

I did the best I could to make Moran look competitive without going overboard. I didn't think Frank had a chance, but Dan was Frank's manager and he asked me to do the favor for him. Dan was also the promoter for the Moran-Johnson fight under the corporate title of *La Societe pour la Propagation de la Boxe Francaise*. Moran had a solid right hand that he called the "Old Mary Ann."

Dan was very upset with the French sportswriters. He had distributed three thousand six hundred dollars in "press money" for the reporters to drum up excitement for the bout. The reporters instead wrote that the bout would be a blowout. Dan was furious. He asked me for more help with the press, but I refused. I wanted my shot at the title. I gave one statement supporting the fight and I wouldn't do another. Dan had to give away hundreds of free tickets to the fight and even that didn't help because instead of attending the fight, the people who were given free tickets wound up selling them at a cut-rate price, which hurt the ticket sales at the box office.

Johnson must have read my remarks on his condition, because he changed his habits for the Moran fight. He sent his wife Lucy to Spain and he followed a strict diet of eggs, vegetables, and lean steak. Jack also had a special mixture he called "Texas Juice." Jack gave the recipe as follows: *"Texas Juice was made of three parts buttermilk, one part whole cream, one-half part sweet butter and four parts gin."* I cannot see how that mixture could help a fighter, but as they say, ninety-percent of it is in your mind. If Jack thought the elixir worked then I guess for him it did.

On June 1, I was again asked my thoughts on who would win the Johnson-Moran fight. Moran was giving Dan a hard time and was acting like he was a superstar. Moran refused to sign with Dan. Dan was livid after all he went through to get Moran the fight with Johnson.

I told the reporter, who was visiting me in my West Hoboken home, that even if Johnson entered the ring on crutches he would still slaughter Moran inside a few rounds. I said that I would like nothing better than to see Moran annihilated. During the interview I spoke of how I picked plenty of kale while in Paris, which meant I earned a big bankroll. I introduced the reporter to my wife and two children and I showed him my new car. I told him: *"This, my fourth trip across the big waters, was the most enjoyable. As you already know I engaged in six battles and won all but that close decision Sam Langford got. I received decisions over Carpentier, Alf Langford, and Kid Jackson in Paris, and trimmed easily Con Bell of Australia and Andrew Johnson at London. Carpentier is a tough kid, and you can quote me as saying that he can beat fellows like Gunboat Smith and a lot of the white hopes around New York. Some people in Paris say Carpentier must serve*

---

⁴¹⁶ *Ithaca Daily News* May 14, 1914.

in the army, and others claim that it will be fixed for him to duck army service and remain in the prize ring. I don't know how true the latter statement is. Of course you know that Jack Johnson is a French subject now, and the ruling in that country is that every man under thirty-five years of age must enroll. Well Jack just celebrated his thirty-sixth birthday, so they can't make him do military duty. They're very strict about it. When he enters the ring with Moran he will wear the French colors on his belt. Is he coming back to America? Search me." The reporter then asked me: *"They say on the other side that Moran stands an awfully good chance of beating Johnson. What's your opinion?"*[417]

I became enraged. Moran was lucky to be getting a title shot. Now he was going around telling everyone what a great fighter he was. The only reason he was getting the shot at the title was because of Dan. I replied: *"That ungrateful cuss. He'll lick Johnson no more than my little Joe. I'm through with him. If he can't appreciate a good thing he ought to lie low and keep his mouth shut. But no, he wants to tell the world what a great fighter he is, whereas if it hadn't been for the untiring work of little Danny McKetrick, as fine a fellow as ever lived, you would never have heard of him. I saw Johnson at Wonderland on May 5th, the day I left for home, and he looks great. He told me he weighs about 210 pounds, 25 more than he scaled when he knocked out Jeffries. But believe me, he'll be in the best of shape when he battles Moran and I'll miss my guess if he doesn't knock him out in no time, Moran doesn't sit with him. I don't blame McKetrick for asking Moran to sign a contract with him. Ever since the match was talked of Moran has gone clean nutty. What did he ever lick to deserve a swelled head? He caught the tottering Al Palzer when he was ready to fall and managed to stop him. Where in his record are there any victories worthwhile? None. He is a foolish boy.*

"McKetrick knew something was up when Moran quit him in Paris and came here, and he made up his mind that he was not going to lose the $1,000 that he paid out in expenses for Moran's living on the other side, when he was loafing and doing nothing. You've got to spank a boy like Moran to keep him in line. I've been with McKetrick for six years and we never had words. When he took me to the other side the first time he had me sign a contract for six months because he didn't know me. Three days out on the ship he came to me and said: 'Joe, see this piece of paper, a so-called contract? Well here she goes' and Dan tore it up and threw it overboard. Do you know Moran tried three or four times to double cross me in exhibition tours? After he whipped Palzer, Dan put us on the stage, and I remember well how he attempted to beat me up on the stage. But I didn't let him get away with it.

"During our week's stay in Boston I had to lay off one Friday night because I had to box Sam Langford in the Garden the next night. I went through a tough battle and returned to stage work the next night. Well you should have seen Moran pile into me, when I told him my arms were in bad shape. I got onto him and made up my mind to give him a good thrashing, even if I had to lose my hands for good. And, believe me, he

---

[417] *Auburn Citizen* May 26, 1914.

got a licking he didn't forget for some little time. That's the only way to handle fellows like that. I could go on and recount thousands and thousands of other little things about this ingrate, but what's the use?'[418]

A couple of years later Dan McKetrick wrote to the papers describing how the Johnson-Moran fight came to be: *"Joe Jeannette is responsible in more ways than one for the success of Frank Moran. When Moran first came to New York and placed himself under my management I turned him over to Jeannette. The latter schooled him for several years and after Moran's defeat of Palzer, I took him abroad with Joe Jeannette and Young Ahearn.*

"Moran jumped into fame by his fight against Jack Johnson and it came about in this manner. When Billy Gibson was manager at Madison Square Garden, he signed Jack Johnson to an agreement to meet Jeannette. After signing articles and upon Gibson's return to New York, Johnson repudiated the agreement and announced his retirement. Shortly afterwards he made his getaway to Paris. When I reached Paris I told Johnson he would have to box Jeannette and advanced this argument: 'Jeannette is popular here by reason of his knockout over Sam McVey and his defeat over Carpentier. The public will demand this bout and unless you agree to fight him, I will make things miserable for you.'

"Johnson stalled me for several weeks, and then finally came to me and said: 'I do not want to box Jeannette, for I am quite satisfied that he will win the decision on points in a 20 round bout and I do not want to lose my title to another colored man. I want to be the only colored man to be heavyweight champion of the world. If you will agree to stop challenging me with Jeannette, I will agree to box Moran for you.'

"I put this up to Jeannette and he readily agreed. He felt that if Moran beat Johnson, that he would at least have the satisfaction of having developed the man who had taken the title from Johnson. This is how the Johnson-Moran fight was made, and which I promoted, and Moran's stand against Johnson was what made him the popular candidate for a Willard-Moran match when he returned to America. Jeannette has beaten Johnson several times in no-decision contests some seven years ago and Johnson always realized that Jeannette was the best man in the country."[419]

There was one thing that Dan left out of the letter. He promised me that if Moran defeated Johnson, I would be his first title defense. I had no choice but to go along with the deal because Johnson was not going to fight me. When Dan first told me that Johnson said he wanted to be the only black heavyweight champion I was furious. What right did he have to make that decision? Many black Americans looked to him as their idol. If they only knew that he was just as prejudiced against blacks succeeding as many white American's were, I am sure their love for him would have waned. There were some black folks who hated Jack much more than white folks did.[420] Jack's climbing in and out of white women's beds created a world of trouble for black Americans. Booker T. Washington said: *"Jack Johnson has*

---

[418] *Auburn Citizen* May 26, 1914.
[419] *Syracuse Journal* May 9, 1916.
[420] *The Big Black Fire* by Robert H. DeCoy pg. 11.

harmed rather than helped the (black) race. I wish to say emphatically that his actions do not meet my approval, and I'm sure they do not meet with the approval of the colored race.'[421]

Before I left France, Johnson asked me to send him eight pairs of American shoes.[422] I told the papers that I would send them even if I had to charter a special ship. After Dan told me of Jack's comments about wanting to be the only black heavyweight champion I thought twice about sending the shoes, but I sent them anyway.

When I arrived back home I set up training in the recreational area of the Public Service building on Clinton Avenue and Angelique Street in West Hoboken. The recreational area was set up for the drivers of the trolley cars when they took their breaks. It was on the second floor of the "car barn" as it was called. The huge brick building looked like a castle with its tapered conical brick spires. The recreational area had a lunch room, a bowling alley, and a pool table. The workers all supported my boxing career and they were more than happy to let me set up a small boxing gym in a back room.

Unfortunately, it didn't last very long. I was running my own jitney service with a partner named George Poeschel. We had four buses that we ran in North Hudson and business was very good. When the union boss at Public Service found out I was running the jitney buses he told me I couldn't train in the building anymore. He said it was for liability reasons, but I knew it was because I was running the jitneys.

On June 9 I took on the up-and-coming prospect Harry Wills of New Orleans in his hometown. It was the second time we faced each other. The press described the bout: *Joe Jeanette… and Harry Wills of New Orleans fought ten rounds to a draw here last night. Jeanette did the greater part of the leading, worrying Wills with a stiff right to the jaw frequently.*[423]

Johnson won the June 27 bout against Moran in Paris by a twenty round decision, even though he had an injured left arm from the bout with Jim Johnson. Moran missed his "Mary Anns" all night. When he finally landed one the crowd cheered. Jack stepped back and clapped his gloves together along with the crowd, showing the punch had no effect on him. Dan McKetrick stated that Moran only touched Johnson twice in the bout, when they touched gloves at the beginning of the match and again at the beginning of the twentieth round. Willie Lewis, who was very close to Moran, worked his corner. Moran gave strict instructions to the referee, Georges Carpentier, that no one was allowed to throw in the towel on his behalf except Lewis. Neither boxer would get paid for the fight, as the sixty-two thousand dollars the fight netted wound up getting frozen in a

---

[421] *The Big Black Fire* by Robert H. DeCoy pg. 15.
[422] *Auburn Citizen* May 26, 1914.
[423] *Elkhart Truth* June 10, 1914.

Paris bank due to the feud between Dan and Moran.[424] Dan never did get the money from the championship fight released. It would be the only time in heavyweight championship history that neither fighter received any compensation. Johnson looked flabby and sluggish in the bout. Jack would complain to me, every time he saw me after that fight, of how Dan beat him for his purse.

A reporter asked me who would win in the upcoming battle between "Gunboat" Smith and Georges Carpentier: *"I think that Carpentier has a good chance. He is a good boxer and has a very good punch. Can he stand punishment well? Yes, he is game enough. In a match I had with him, Carpentier stood up, although his face was swollen to an awful size and he could hardly see, but he fought on. I think that he has a good chance to beat Smith."*[425] I finished by telling the reporter I had no immediate plans for the future. Carpentier defeated Smith by six round disqualification on July 16 in London.

On the same day at the Stadium A.C. in New York I fought a ten round draw with "Battling" Jim Johnson. There was a bit of controversy in the match because I was hit with a low blow and was knocked down, but the referee Billy Joh never saw the errant blow. I was given three minutes to recover, which at the time was unheard of.[426]

On August 5, 1914, I faced "Battling" Jim again at the Stadium A.C. I outpointed Johnson, although "Battling" Jim made a good rally in the sixth. Johnson weighed 223 pounds to my 197. I jabbed Jim at will. The fight was described by the *NY Times*: *Johnson started several vicious blows, and after turning them loose trusted to luck that they would land somewhere. Oftentimes he had no luck at all and the swipes did nothing more than churn up the atmosphere in the immediate vicinity of referee Billy Joh. Jeannette landed a right swing on Johnson's jaw in the second round that staggered the big fellow.*[427]

At the end of 1914, F. Hurdman Lucas, of the London newspaper publication *Boxing*, asked me to write a few paragraphs about my life and boxing career. The following article titled, "That World's Title," was published in the year-end annual edition of the paper: *"Although fighting is more in my line of goods than writing, it is with pleasure that I accede to Mr. Lucas' desire that I should 'put together' a few words for Boxing Annual. The pen is mightier than the sword, I have heard it said, but I might add that I find it a mighty difficult thing to handle properly. Being more used to the manipulation of gloves- 4 oz. ones by preference- I seem to get 'k.o.d' when it comes to expressing myself in black and white.*

"Nevertheless, as I don't believe in taking the full count, even in the matter of writing an article, I guess I had better set about it at once, and get the matter over. I always believed Mr. Lucas was a friend of mine until he sprung this stunt on me. Just a few

[424] *New York Post* January 29, 1936.
[425] *Indiana Freeman* May 30, 1914.
[426] *New York Times* July 16, 1914.
[427] *New York Times* August 6, 1914.

lines, you know, Joe, for readers of Boxing.' He knows perfectly well that I would sooner meet Jack Johnson any day than make a goat of myself with pen and ink. Had I only known at the beginning of my ring career that such a calamity as the present one was in store for me, I might have saved myself- and others- many hard knocks.

'Never let that fellow Lucas come to me again with his smooth-tongue for a 'few words.' They have cost me many sleepless nights, but- well, it's a terribly difficult thing to talk or write about oneself and feel modest.

'Writing of Jack Johnson reminds me that I have met him seven times. Not in the street, but in a ring. Four no-decision bouts in Philadelphia; fifteen round decision in Baltimore, which I lost; a ten round draw at Portland, Maine; and a win for me on a foul in two rounds.

'I hope I may be further allowed to state that the newspapers were unanimous in naming me as winner of the no-decision bouts, clippings of which I shall be pleased to show anybody who may doubt this statement. There is a little story attached to the ten round draw at Portland, which, in the face of Johnson's present attitude, I should like to relate. Although Johnson had accepted all conditions of the match, he refused to enter the ring on the night of the fight unless it should be declared a draw if we were both on our feet at the end. It was a case of take it or leave it, or Hobson's choice, so a draw it duly was. At the time I weighed 167lbs., but today 195lbs.

'It was only last year that Monsieur Breyer came to New York with an offer for Johnson to box me in Paris. This offer was no less than a substantial percentage of the gate, with a guarantee of $30,000. Johnson accepted, and at last I saw the possibility of putting in a bid for that well-nursed world's title. What was my horror later to find that instead of meeting me Johnson announced his retirement from the ring! Now, according to all precedents, Johnson has forfeited his title, but even then I refrained from claiming it, as my desire was, and is, to win it legitimately in a contest. My manager, Dan McKetrick, was of this opinion; but we surely could not wait until our hair turned grey. We therefore came to Paris once more, with the hope of finally inducing Johnson to meet me in the ring. But that gentleman seems to prefer wrestling and dancing to boxing.

'Perhaps the secret of this persistent refusal on Johnson's part to enter a ring may be gathered from the following incident: When in New York, Johnson was offered $25,000 to meet me in a ten round no-decision at Madison Square Garden. Surely this was a 'soft' thing for a world's champion; but again the offer was turned down, and we all gasped. It appears that Johnson told a friend later the reason for his refusal in the following words: 'I intend to go down in history as the only undefeated champion of the world.' Need any more be said? No; Monsieur Vienne again offered him a 125,000 francs guarantee to box me; and although Johnson accepted the sum it was with the stipulation that his opponent was to be a third rater, and that he barred both Langford and me. When it was urged upon this passive world's champion that I should be his opponent, he 'cried off.' If all this does not entitle me to the mundane title, does it not at least prove that Johnson thinks me capable of wrestling it from him?

'Langford has had the same difficulty with Johnson; that is why the International Union determined to put an end to an intolerable state of things, and dispossess the latter of his crown, after a too inactive and autocratic reign. If it had been my good fortune to

beat Langford for the title, I should have been prepared to defend it against all comers.

"Having bored my readers with all this dry stuff, it may interest them to know a trifle about my private life. Although I have been called a Canadian, I was born in (West) Hoboken, N.J., of a white mother. I am the happy father of two children... I am proud of being the only colored member of the Troy's and Olympia athletic clubs, playing center on the former's Eastern States champion basketball team.

"I started life breaking in young horses for a large coal company, but my mind was centered on being a veterinary surgeon. The small salary I was earning at the time stood in the way of my studies. So, always being fond of boxing, I determined to scrape up the necessary money in the ring. There happened to be a boxer named Johnny Carroll about, against whom my employer backed me. This was my first fight, but I knocked out my opponent in two rounds, and he fell clean into his father's arms.

"This started my ring career, and my fifth contest was against the man I have been after so long- Jack Johnson. He had undertaken to knock out two men, one of whom happened to be little Joe Jeannette. Having disposed of No. 1 in two rounds, he evidently looked upon No. 2 as equally soft. What was his consternation, when I outpointed him in those memorable six rounds! This performance brought me into some prominence. I gave up all ideas of doctoring horses in favor of doping men with the aid of boxing gloves.

"For the benefit of young boxers I may state that I lead a regular life, early in bed and early out; have never touched alcohol of any kind in my life; and could not tell you what tobacco tastes like. The secret of health is good living, the secret of success lies in good health. I feel better today than I ever did in my life- and thank the stars this is finished!"[428]

On August 28, I held a picnic for the Joe Jeannette Association at Greenville, Schuetzen Park.[429] Many black families attended the fundraiser. Top fighters from the area attended, as well as local politicians.

Dan McKetrick was a fine manager, but he definitely was no saint. On February 13, 1915, Dan got an idea to fight Willie Lewis in Havana, Cuba. Willie was 31-years-old and he had been boxing professionally for fourteen years, since he was seventeen. Willie had been knocked out in five rounds by Al McCoy four months prior, and he did not have the desire to box anymore. Willie was working as a bartender and he drank almost as much as he served. In fact, he drank so much that when Dan went looking for him to offer him the fight, Willie was in the hospital, on what some say was his death bed. He was emaciated and his skin was grey. Dan offered Willie a fight with Jacob Woodward, who was better known as "Young" Ahearn. Dan managed both Ahearn and Lewis so he stood to collect on both ends. I had traveled to Paris with Ahearn in 1913 and gave him pointers while we were training together in New York. Ahearn, when interviewed later, gave the following statement: *"If I am really a good fighter today,"* concluded Ahearn, *"thank Joe Jeanette. He boxed with me almost every day for more than a year and told*

---

[428] *Boxing* annual 1914 "That World's Title" by Joe Jeannette pgs. 42-43.
[429] *Jersey Journal* August 29, 1914.

me everything he knew. I think and always did think he was the greatest heavyweight of the day. Finally I got so I could hold my own with him, and every once in a while I'd catch him on an off day and get a shade on the day's work. Then I said to myself that if I could hold my own with Joe Jeanette I could beat any white man in the world and most of the black ones. And that spirit is with me now whenever I put on the gloves. I bet my own money I can beat any white man in the world. I care a lot for money, too."[430] The purse was two thousand dollars for the twenty round contest. Dan pulled Willie out of his death bed, over the doctor's protest, and brought him to Havana, Cuba. The promoter in Havana was under the impression that Willie was in top fighting shape. Willie looked horrible and was knocked out in two rounds. Rumor is Dan was lucky to get out of Havana alive after that fiasco.

I fought eleven times in 1915, winning nine, losing one newspaper decision, with one draw. On April 5, 1915, Johnson lost his title to Jess Willard in Havana, Cuba, in the twenty-sixth round of a scheduled forty-five round fight. It was a brutally hot day with temperatures reaching over one hundred degrees. The weather and the six-foot six-inch Willard were too much for the 37-year-old Johnson to handle. Jack would later say he threw the fight and he was covering his eyes from the sun. If you look at the film you can clearly see that Jack threw his arms up over his face out of defensive reflex when he was dropped. At the time of the knockout Jack had won eighteen of the twenty-six rounds. Willard, when told that Johnson was claiming that he threw the fight, said: *"If Jack Johnson throwed that why did we haveta go twenty-six rounds? It was hotter than hell down there."*[431] After the loss Jack stated: *"Alone, at last they will leave me alone. The better man won. I have no kick coming."*[432]

On April 15, I beat Sam Langford for the colored title over twelve rounds in Boston. The *Boston Journal* described the contest: *Sturdy "Old Black Joe" Jeannette won a decision over his also sturdy old fellow colored opponent, Sam Langford, in the main bout of the opening show of the Atlas A.A. last night. "Old Black Joe" received the decision because he outboxed the Tar Baby practically all the way through the contest. Again it was stiff left jabbing that made Langford the second best man in the ring. There was absolutely no question about the award. It was right, and also popular. In fact, the goodly sized crowd in attendance was with Jeannette, at least those who were rooting were, and it seemed to please them to see the "local bonecrusher" outboxed.*[433]

I fought to a draw with Sam McVea in Boston on April 27. The *Springfield Union* described that bout: *Sam McVea and Joe Jeannette, the big colored heavyweights, battled for 12 rounds at the Atlas A.A. last night and Young Donahue, the referee, could see no better decision than a draw. It was not a bad one at that, though*

---

[430] *Auburn Citizen* March 8, 1915.
[431] *Champions of the Ring* by Gerald Suster pg. 69.
[432] *Champions of the Ring* by Gerald Suster pg. 70.
[433] *Boston Journal* April 14, 1915.

some of the fans believed that McVea had won and others figured Jeannette should have got the award. It was McVea's first appearance in this city and the fans liked the way he worked at times.[434]

On April 21, Georges Carpentier was interviewed about stomach exercises, and he gave the following statement: *"I was first made aware of the necessity of developing the stomach muscles by an unusual incident. It was when Joe Jeannette was training to box Sam McVea that I paid a visit to his quarters. Although a mere stripling at the time, I remember being tremendously impressed by the body developing exercises, which consisted, first, on lying on the back and slowly bringing the legs up to the head; secondly, by sitting on a chair with the feet held, while Jeannette threw his head and body backward as far as he could. It was after these performances that this boxer used to invite anybody to punch him in the stomach as hard as they could, just to show how impervious that part of his body was to blows. I actually watched several heavy men follow his bidding with no other consequence than a smile from Jeannette. So astounded was I with what had taken place that I forthwith determined to acquire something like the same muscular assistance, that I might be able to permit people to punch me in the same manner. It was a tremendously irksome affair, for, being too young to possess the quality of tissue necessary to withstand such ill treatment, it took years. But I persevered and succeeded. And never forget that deep breathing exercises have a great deal to do with stomach hardening."*[435]

On May 7, 1915, the RMS Lusitania, on which I had sailed, was sunk off of the coast of Ireland. The Germans were behind the sinking of the ship, which had sailed out of New York. The United States had secretly stored ammunitions on the ship being sent to the British, which was why the Germans targeted the vessel. The 1,924 passengers aboard the vessel had no knowledge of the cargo being transported. 1,119 passengers perished when the ship sank.

In June of 1915, I spoke with Addie about us looking into buying cemetery plots for ourselves. We drove to a cemetery and went in to speak about prices. Immediately I noticed the look that the salesman was giving me. I tried to ignore it, but I could tell Addie also noticed it, and she was not as reserved as me. Finally he came out and said: *"I really don't think this cemetery is for you, sir. I apologize."* We walked out of the office numb. Not only were we to be tortured with racism throughout our lives but we would also have to deal with it in death as well.[436] I was snapped back into reality from my wife running back into the office and telling off the curator of the cemetery: *"I wouldn't be buried here if you paid me!"* The drive home was quiet until Addie said: *"Don't worry Joe we'll find a much nicer place. We don't want to be buried there anyway."* We both looked at each other and broke out laughing at the same time. *"You're right, Addie,"* I said. *"I don't want to be buried at all!"*

---

[434] *Springfield Union* April 28, 1915.
[435] *Los Angeles Times* April 21, 1915.
[436] *Marriage Beyond Black & White* by Barbara & David Douglas pg. 126.

My only loss in 1915, a newspaper decision, was to "Battling" Jim Johnson, whom I had defeated five times previously. The bout took place at Sohmer Park in Montreal, Canada, on May 10. Near the end of the third round Johnson hit me low, sending me to the canvas. I could have taken the bout on a foul but I insisted on continuing the fight.[437]

On September 3 I decided to take my mind off of boxing and have some fun. Addie and I drove over to the Buschatzke Terminal Casino at North Beach to partake in their annual cakewalk contest. Seven hundred people were in the casino when the contest was started by casino manager Tom Kelly just before midnight. The *Brooklyn Daily Star* described the event: *Joe Jeannette, heavyweight boxer, his six feet of ebony blackness encased in a suit of vivid red with gold trimmings, and set off by a smile which ran from ear-to-ear, led off the contestants... Every couple gave its own particular conception of the possibilities of the cake walk, and then retired to the side lines under the marshalship of "Misto" Jeannette. Time and time again he "could not make his feet behave" and "jest had to get in the play" with the contestants.*[438] Addie and I didn't win the contest but we had loads of fun.

Jess Willard made several statements that he would not fight colored fighters. I was so disgusted, I decided to retire as a fighter. On September 11, 1915, I issued a press release: *"Willard has drawn the color line, and that about lets me out. There is no one for me to fight anymore and so I have quit the ring game for good."*[439]

On February 6, 1916, I sat down and wrote another press release: *"Willard has drawn the color line. In this he was wise and perhaps his decision will benefit the game. I would like to make one more fight but feel it would be unfair to the public to ask for a match with any of the present crop of hopes. With no one to box, my fighting days are over, so I will devote all my time to business. I want to thank the public for years of support and I quit, knowing that I have always tried my best and was on the square."*[440]

My heart just wasn't in the fight game anymore. When a boxer doesn't have the desire to train, or the focus and determination, he can risk serious injury. I knew that I didn't have that competitive fire any longer. Unfortunately for me, I didn't listen to the gut feeling for long, and I returned to the ring nineteen days later for a payday.

Colored boxers won a small victory on February 10, when the New York State Athletic Commission announced it would end its ban on mixed bouts. I was contacted by a reporter, who asked me my thoughts on the new ruling: *"The color line left my field somewhat limited. Langford and McVey were the only opponents I could hope to meet and these I have met so often that the public could scarcely take serious that kind of competition. Harry Wills, the New Orleans Negro, has*

[437] *Boston Daily Globe* May 11, 1915.
[438] *Brooklyn NY Daily Star* September 4, 1915.
[439] *Washington Post* September 12, 1915.
[440] *Seattle Daily Times* February 7, 1916.

made a great reputation around here. I would have tackled him before, but there was no use. I could not have gone anywhere even with a victory, for that would have eliminated my last meal ticket. Things are different now with the bar removed. Nothing would please me better than to take on Wills. I beat him twice within the last two years at New Orleans and he knows it, though he got a draw from the referee the first time. I will bet Wills $5,000 on the side anytime he agrees to face me. The same offer goes to Frank Moran. My ambition is to clean up with all the Negro heavies and force some of the white fighters to give action to the local fight public.'[441]

The article mentioned that I was an exceptionally clean liver that was prepared to meet any heavyweight at a moment's notice. The article also made mention that I was a devoted handball player since childhood. I sharpened up my handball game against former world's handball champion Mike Egan. Egan was a terrific athlete who sparred with Bob Fitzsimmons, Jim Jeffries, Jim Corbett, as well as myself.

It appeared as though most of white America would rather have the heavyweight championship be held by a mediocre white fighter than by the best fighter, if that fighter happened to be black.[442] I returned to action on February 25, 1916, in Montreal, Canada, where I knocked out Silas Green in six rounds.

On March 20 Dan McKetrick took Frank Moran to court. Dan's complaint alleged that Moran owed him $1,400 that Dan had lent to Moran before the Jack Johnson fight in 1914. Moran had to take a day off from training to attend the court proceedings. Frank was in training for his fight against heavyweight champion Jess Willard. The *Philadelphia Inquirer* described the event: *Moran wasted another day, or rather added more care and worry to his well-filled cup, by first getting a decisive victory over Dan McKetrick in a court action, then being forced to interfere to protect his friend from bodily injury when a fist fight started in a downtown café, where Moran had gone to eat his luncheon. Moran did not land any blows in the fight, but rather acted as a peacemaker, but the notoriety and excitement did him no good as far as preparing for his mill with Willard is concerned.*

Moran's exciting few minutes began in the City Court before Judge Lynch and terminated for the time being at a restaurant on Fulton Street. In the courtroom Moran heard a jury exonerate him from blame in an action brought by McKetrick in which McKetrick alleges Moran owed him $1,400 advanced before the Johnson-Moran fight in Paris. Moran did not deny this advancement, but he testified that McKetrick had collected most of the money that came from the fight and also held notes discounted since, making more than the amount asked for. The jury, in five minutes, found for Moran.

The finding of the jury was not to the liking of McKetrick, and when he entered White's establishment, accompanied by Harry Pollock a few minutes afterwards, and discovered Moran seated with Willie Lewis, his trainer, and Frank O'Neill, his attorney, he opened a verbal assault against Mr. O'Neill. According to Mr. O'Neill, McKetrick

---

[441] *Grand Forks Herald* February 12, 1916.
[442] *Beyond The Ring* by Jeffrey T. Sammons, pg. 51.

followed up his remarks by landing two smart blows to Mr. O'Neill's face. Lewis went to O'Neill's assistance, and when Pollock arose to help McKetrick, Moran grabbed Pollock by the arm. This kept Moran and Pollock out of the proceedings.

Waiters entered into the affair quickly and tried to quite the combatants, but before order was restored several more blows were exchanged and a bowl of soup was spilled on Moran. O'Neill, after taking stock of the damage done him, thought that the papers in the court action had disappeared, but Moran was sitting on these. Moran and his party quickly disappeared toward the Bronx. An immense crowd was attracted to the scene of the struggle, and at first it seemed that it would be necessary to call out police reserves, but Moran exhibited wisdom by climbing into his automobile and driving away.

McKetrick, who allowed everyone present to know that he used to be Moran's manager, was still vowing vengeance when Moran and his party were traveling up Fifth Avenue at a good rate of speed. This mixture of words, punches and worry was about the only exercise indulged in by Moran during the day.[443]

I decided to continue fighting, and on March 24, I was scheduled to meet Cleve Hawkins, the Montreal Tar Baby, at the East New York A.C. in Brooklyn. Hawkins pulled out of the fight because of a fractured rib he suffered in sparring. Jake Ahearn, the manager of the club, told Dan he had an able substitute named Joe "Kid" Cotton of Philadelphia. The six-foot three-inch, 217-pound Cotton, wasn't much of a fill-in. I sent him to dreamland in the second round.

On March 25 Jess Willard defeated Frank Moran via ten round newspaper decision at Madison Square Garden. Willard would not fight again for three years.

Besides managing Willie Lewis and I, Dan McKetrick managed several other world class boxers including Brooklyn middleweight Jakob Bartfeldt, better known as "Soldier" Bartfield. A newspaper reported some of Dan's experiences with the frugal Bartfield: *Daniel had Bartfield fighting upstate. When the money was handed over there was still $51.04 coming to Bartfield. McKetrick, the next morning, peeled off $51 and gave it to Bartfield, slipping the rest of his million-dollar roll back into his pocket. "Hey!" yelled Bartfield, as McKetrick turned away. "Come back here. Haven't you forgotten something?" "What's up now?" queried Daniel indignantly. "Where's my four-cents?" whooped Bartfield.*

On another time the Soldier wanted to mail a letter home to Austria. McKetrick gave him three two-cent stamps. Bartfield put two on and was about to drop the letter into the box. "Hold on," said McKetrick. "You can't short-change the government! Put that other stamp on." "Won't they take it for four-cents?" demanded Bartfield. "No. Put the other stamp on." "I will not," said the Soldier. "I won't put on six-cents for five-cents postage. I will go to my cousin's on Rivington Street and get him to trade me two ones for this two." And he did it.[444]

On May 12, 1916, I met Sam Langford for the thirteenth time. One of my

[443] *Philadelphia Inquirer* March 21, 1916.
[444] *Washington Post* May 5, 1916.

proudest achievements in boxing was never having been knocked out by the hard-punching Langford. Our bout would take place at the Arena in Syracuse, New York. Once again the colored heavyweight title was on the line. I had never knocked out Langford, although I did get him to quit in one of our bouts. When I arrived for the weigh-in, I immediately noticed how overweight and out of shape Sam appeared. We both weighed in at 198 pounds, but I held a three inch reach and a three-and-a-half inch height advantage on Langford. I had easily outboxed Sam in our last bout and I saw a golden opportunity to finally knock him out. The bout was scheduled for ten rounds. The following is a newspaper account of the fight: *Sam Langford of Boston knocked out Joe Jeannette of New York in the seventh round of a scheduled ten round boxing contest at the arena last night. Langford sent Jeannette to the floor with a crashing left hook flush on the point of his jaw and the Gotham battler was unable when referee Cawley counted off the fatal ten, although he managed to get to his feet before the echo of the referee's voice had died away in the babel of voices that filled the vast auditorium. The finish was tragic. For three rounds Jeannette stood his rival off with a lightning left jab and flashy right hook. Langford could not penetrate the dazzling defense of his rival and was plainly worried when he came up for the fourth session. Early in the fourth, however, he hooked his left to Jeannette's midsection and from that time to the finish the New Yorker never fully recovered.*

In the fifth and sixth Langford punished Jeannette severely with a volley of left hooks to the body and powerful right crosses to the face. In the clinches Langford worked both hands to his opponent's body and occasionally shot his right across to the point of Jeannette's jaw. The finish came with an abruptness that startled the crowd. Jeannette, back against the ropes in his own corner, took a swinging left hook flush to the jaw and as his knees sagged Langford sent home another blow to the same place.[445]

I will let Sam explain his version of events: *"Those who don't think miracles can happen can read this. Up to 1916, I had fought Joe Jeanette eleven different times and I never was able to knock that boy out. I had started boxing him way back in 1905, and I just couldn't drop that boy for 'Ten.' Sometimes he would win the decision, sometimes I'd win it. Then it would be a draw. Every time up to 1916, I went into that ring, hoping I could knock him loose from his hair. I hit him with about 100,000 punches and I hit him with everything but the referee's necktie but I never could put Joe away.*

"Along in 1916, came a chance to fight Joe again, this time in Syracuse. I had gotten out of the idea that I could ever put him out. And anyway, after that Syracuse bout had been made, we were offered another fight somewhere else for a couple of weeks later. So, not wishing to knock us out of that fight, even if I could, and feeling I just couldn't flatten Joe anyway, I never trained a single minute for that fight. Joe saw I was out of shape when I climbed through the ropes. And right there I guess he decided he'd do what he was wanting to do for eleven years, and that was to knock me out.

"He came tearing at me like a wild man and pounded me all around the ring. He got

[445] *Post Standard Syracuse NY* May 13, 1916.

awfully, awfully rough. That Joe is a lovely boy, except when he gets rough. Then he's bad. And bad boys just must be spanked. So I began mixing it with Joe, and I was puffing like a freight engine and pretty soon Joe was puffing too. And then Joe slowed up and I was so tired I first didn't know if it was Syracuse we were fighting in or Chicago, or where it was.

'We were to go 10 rounds. We had gone 6. Joe knew by that time that he couldn't stop me. And I was sure that even if I hit Joe on the chin with a shovel I couldn't put him away. But the customers had paid to see ten rounds not six or seven. They wanted a little action the rest of the way. Joe was still willing and he came in nasty like in the seventh, even though he had about fought himself out. I had to do something to make it look good to the crowd. So I began throwing a lot of those haymakers and when I'd throw and Joe would jump back, the customers just laughed themselves sick.

'Then something happened. I took a right hand off my knee and I closed my eyes, playful like, and I let it fly, thinking it would miss Joe by about a foot. But what does that Joe do except in some way or other decides to rush me at that particular moment. The crazy swing catches Joe Jeanette squarely on the point of his chin, and the thing I had tried to do with 100,000 serious punches had been done with a joke swing. I saw Joe stagger. I saw his knees bend. I thought there was some trick in it, and that Joe was trying to fake me into a trap and then maybe knock me dead. But no! Joe crumpled to the floor and was counted out and of all the surprised people in the place I was the most surprised of all.

'Joe had gone out so dead, cold out, that it was about ten minutes before he really came back to life and his handlers weren't sure his neck wasn't broken. If that knockout wasn't a miracle, what are those miracles?'[446]

Sam left out the fact, which he himself stated to the press, that I was on my feet before the referee counted ten and I was more than willing and able to continue. The *Cincinnati Inquirer* reported: *Referee Tom Cowler declared he had counted ten over Jeannette, although Jeannette was on his feet. Tommy Ryan and Charlie Huck, owners of the club, both said Jeannette was on his feet. Langford was of the same opinion.[447]*

I'll let Dan McKetrick describe how it happened: *" 'If I am ever knocked out I will retire from the ring.' For years Joe Jeanette has told me and after his bout with Sam Langford, he brought up the subject again. 'I was not stopped, Dan, for I was on my feet before the referee said 'ten'. He made the mistake of his life and I want you to get another match for me with Langford.' The above covers exactly what I want to say.*

'Jeannette, like myself, and many who witnessed the bout, feel that referee Cowler made a grave error of judgment. I told Cowler immediately after the fight that he was in the wrong, and had placed against Jeannette's record a knockout that should not be there. Jeannette was down for the count 34 times in his bout with McVey. Nevertheless, he finally stopped McVey. In a contest several years ago at Lawrence Mass. with Sam Langford, the latter had Jeannette down several times, and the bout ended in the eighth

---

[446] *Jersey Journal* September 12, 1924 "My Fighting Life" by Sam Langford.
[447] *Cincinnati Inquirer* May 13, 1916.

round with Langford refusing to leave his corner.

"At Boston, Jeannette had his nose and two frontal bones broken in the first round, and was down five times in that round. Charlie White refereed that contest, and despite the fact that Jeannette was reeling, did not stop it for the reason that Jeannette is never out until he is flat on his back with a count of ten over him. In this fight, Jeannette won the decision. Jeannette wants to box Langford again and I would like to have the match held at Syracuse, where Jeannette can prove to the fans that Langford is not his master."[448]

The referee of the contest, Thomas Cawley, wrote to the press to defend his decision: *"After the recent Langford-Jeannette contest Dan McKetrick, manager of Joe Jeannette, wired a story to the New York World and other papers that I, the referee, counted Jeannette out after he had risen to his feet before the expiration of ten seconds. This story has circulated throughout the country and has given the sporting world a wrong impression of my honesty as a referee. I wish to state through your newspaper that I am too old a man in the boxing game to show any favoritism and seek to do nothing but what is honest and fair.*

"Rule no. 21 of the State commission rules reads if a contestant falls through weakness or is knocked down he must get up unassisted, ten seconds being given him to do so, I think yourself and a large majority of the spectators who witnessed the contest will agree that Jeannette had not risen within the prescribed time."[449]

In July, we received terrible news from Addie's sister Mary in Pennsylvania. Somehow Mary's two-year-old daughter Adelaide Hartlieb wandered into a water-well and drowned. The family was devastated. Mary took the tragedy especially hard. The baby was brought back to Hudson County and buried with Addie's mother Josephine at Holy Name Cemetery in Jersey City. After the burial, Mary and her husband Oswald moved back to New Jersey and opened a farm in North Bergen. They ran a dairy farm on their seven-acre property. They also raised pigs, rabbits, and Guinea pigs.

In late June 1916, I received a call from my old sparring partner and friend Carl Morris. I had trained Carl for several fights when we were in camp together. Carl asked me to train him for an upcoming bout against Frank Moran. Both boxers were top-ranked heavyweights. I never forgot how Moran had treated McKetrick, so I was focused on preparing Carl properly for the match. I arrived in Morris' Kansas City camp and set out to prepare him for the coming match. Carl was a big heavyweight, standing six-foot four-inches and weighing in at around 235 pounds. One July day during training, a young boxer who called himself Harry came into camp and offered his services as a sparring partner.[450] We looked him over but he appeared too small for Carl. He was six-foot one-inches but he was only around 170 pounds. The kid convinced us to use him because he explained

[448] *Watertown NY Daily Times* May 18, 1916.
[449] *Syracuse Herald* May 21, 1916.
[450] *Dempsey* by Jack Dempsey with Barbara Piattelli Dempsey pgs. 52-53.

that his speed would help us deal with Moran. Eventually, the fight with Moran was called off. We told the kid we wouldn't be needing his sparring anymore. I never thought I would here from that kid Harry again. Little did I know it at the time, but we would meet again. Harry's real name was William Dempsey, but he would be known to the world as Jack Dempsey, the "Manassa Mauler."

The United States entered the First World War on April 6, 1917. Under the command of General John J. Pershing, more than two million U.S. soldiers fought on the battlefields of France.

On July 6, I took on the "Tango Kid" of Brooklyn at the Vanderbilt A.C. in New York City. I pounded the Kid around until the fifth round, when I landed a right hand to the jaw that sent the Kid down for the full count.

On July 20, I decisioned Andre Anderson over ten rounds at the Vanderbilt A.C. in Brooklyn. I outpointed Andre over the first eight rounds. In the ninth, I floored Andre with a left to the jaw. The bell saved him from being counted out. He survived to the final bell by holding.

On September 14, 1917, Sam Langford was awarded a newspaper decision over me in Toledo, Ohio. Langford was defending his colored version of the heavyweight title in the twelve round bout. I injured my right arm in the eleventh round. I felt as though I clearly outpointed Langford.

Chapter 18
The Jack Dempsey Affair 1918-20

In January 1918, Dan and I thought of an idea on how to drum up publicity for a fight with heavyweight champion Jess Willard. I offered to meet Frank Moran, Fred Fulton, or Carl Morris for any number of rounds, with the proceeds of my entire purse going to the Red Cross. Furthermore, I offered to wager one thousand dollars that I would knock out any one of these fighters within ten rounds, with this side bet also going to the Red Cross. When I finished with this preliminary test, I was willing to face Willard with my entire purse for that fight also to be donated to the Red Cross. The only stipulation I had was that the Willard fight must be twenty rounds to a decision, not a no-decision bout. I offered to fight two bouts against world-class opposition for free. The press thought I deserved a shot at the title but that it was unlikely that Willard would give me one.

The heavyweight picture looked bleak. Since Jess Willard won the title by knocking out Jack Johnson on April 5, 1915 he had only defended it once. That was a ten round newspaper decision victory over Frank Moran on March 25, 1916. That bout had originally been scheduled for March 8th but had to be rescheduled because Willard claimed he was battling a throat ailment. Some in boxing circles thought Willard was stalling to give himself more time to prepare for Moran.[451]

The lack of movement in the heavyweight division coupled with the appearance that the champion Willard had lost his desire to fight was causing more athletes to try their luck in the squared circle. Early in 1918 while I was training several of my boxers at the Spring A.C. Dan McKetrick stopped by. He was very excited and said he was approached with a great opportunity for me. He said that a popular baseball player was thinking of quitting the sport and taking up boxing. I asked him who the player was and Dan replied: *"Babe Ruth."*[452] I had always loved baseball and I was thrilled to get the chance to train the Boston Red Sox pitcher. Ruth, 22-years-old, was one of the rising stars in baseball. He had won 23 games in 1916 and 24 in 1917. Ruth played an important part on the 1916 Boston Red Sox World Series championship team. We decided to keep Ruth's boxing training a secret. This would help keep the press away and give Ruth the opportunity to concentrate on boxing while also giving me the ability to teach him in a distraction free environment.

Ruth started training in January. He sat with me and explained the reason why he was considering leaving baseball. He stated he wasn't making enough money and he was thinking of either changing teams or trying his

---

[451] *Trenton Evening Times* February 16, 1916.
[452] *Untitled New York Newspaper* January 22, 1932.

luck at boxing. Ruth thought, like many others, that Willard lacked the desire to box anymore. Ruth had good size at six-foot two-inches and 210 pounds. He was a strong lefty, which was rare in boxing at the time. The plan was to build up Ruth quickly with increasingly tougher opponents. Within a year we were going to pursue a match with "Gunboat" Smith. The 30-year-old Smith was slipping. He had won only one fight in his last five bouts and that win was against Frank Moran.

After a few weeks of training I started to spar with Ruth. I got the feeling almost immediately that he did not like getting hit. He also looked frustrated that he was not picking up the technique quickly enough. Ruth needed to shed some pounds so he could move around the ring more easily. When I mentioned that he should go on a diet Ruth looked at me like I was crazy. After another month of training Ruth and I both decided that he should return to baseball. During the 1918 season Ruth continued his discontentment with playing for the Red Sox. He regularly fought with the team's manager Ed Barrow and he threatened to leave the team several times to play for the Delaware River Shipbuilding League.[453] At the end of the 1919 season Ruth demanded twenty thousand dollars a year or he would quit baseball.[454] On December 26, 1919 Ruth was sold to the New York Yankees. During the 1919 and 1920 seasons Ruth again thought about trying his luck in the boxing ring but ultimately decided against it.

By the fall of 1918, the Great War was nearing its end. A new war had begun with the deadly outbreak of a strong strain of the influenza virus called "Spanish Influenza." Between 1918 and 1919 the virus would claim close to fifty-million lives. Twenty-percent of the world's population would be infected. President Woodrow Wilson was infected with the virus early in 1918. The flu was most dangerous for people between the ages of twenty and forty, unlike the usual flu, which was more dangerous for younger and older people. Nearly 675,000 Americans would die from the virus, including one of my stable-mates and a boxer I had groomed named Jim Stewart. Jim died on September 26, 1918. Jim was a big six-foot four-inch white heavyweight who had the strength to match his size. Another boxer who succumbed to the flu was "Battling" Jim Johnson. I had faced Johnson ten times in my career. Johnson was big and strong at six-foot three-inches. He died on November 6, 1918. It was a very scary time. Many healthy, athletic people died from the flu. One day a person would be walking around fine and the next day they were dead.

Stewart had retired as a boxer because of eye sight problems and he was the athletic director at the Camp Dix Y.M.C.A.[455] Stewart had contracted the flu only three days before his death. Jim was a dear friend. He was a

453 *Philadelphia Inquirer* July 5th, 1918.
454 *New York Times* December 25, 1919.
455 *Syracuse Journal* September 28, 1918, *Brooklyn NY Daily Eagle* September 27, 1918.

very generous person. He joined the National Athletic Club in Brooklyn as a youth and took up high jumping. It was also at the club that Jim was introduced to boxing. He never made excuses like so many boxers do when they lose fights. Jim was unable to join the armed services because he had been blinded in one eye from his boxing career.[456]

The public health department issued gauze masks for people to wear in public. Department stores were ordered to cancel their sales price advertising in hopes of avoiding large gatherings of people in one place. Street-car conductors would not allow passengers on the trolley cars if they did not have a mask on, and police officers were issuing summonses to those who did not follow these restrictions. It was so bad that there was a shortage of coffins and grave diggers. Public funerals were banned in many communities for fear of spreading the virus. It was recommended that to avoid the flu, one should breathe in fresh air, drink plenty of fluids, and get plenty of sleep. Some doctors recommended Vick's Vapo-Rub and atropine capsules to combat the flu, along with bundling up to sweat. Some used whiskey and opiates, while others ate red onions with coffee as a combatant. None of these treatments seemed to work against the virus.

On October 8, 1918, a *Hudson Dispatch* reporter came to watch me train for my upcoming bout with "Kid" Norfolk. The flu outbreak did not stop my many fans from coming out to watch me train. The title of the article was 'Jennette Trains in Presence of Admiring Mob': *"You can say for me that I will be in the best condition of my life when I meet Kid Norfolk at the Spring A.C. next Friday night," said Joe Jennette, after finishing a vigorous workout last night at a local gymnasium. Quite a few fans witnessed Joe in action against an able corps of sparring partners. The veteran displayed his old-time speed and skill in ten fast rounds of boxing.*

The Jennette-Norfolk fight is the biggest and best card offered yet by the Spring A.C. Both men, two of the best in the heavyweight division, furnished a sensational eight round bout at the Jersey City ball park recently. The fighting was so intense throughout that there was a wide difference of opinion as to the winner among the sporting writers, who sat at ringside. None, if any, North Hudson fans will be absent when the men take their corners. Jennette is by far the most popular fighter in this state and has a personal following second to none in the game.[457]

On October 10, the state of New Jersey banned all public gatherings in an effort to combat the virus. Theaters and boxing promoters suffered immensely. The Schuetzen Amusement Park in Union Hill was closed down. Dead bodies were accumulating everywhere. The rate of virus contraction finally started to decline in November.

On the same day as the ban, over two hundred fans came out to watch me as I went through my pre-fight training routine at a local gymnasium.[458]

---

[456] *Atlanta Constitution* September 1, 1918.
[457] *Hudson Dispatch* October 8, 1918.
[458] *Hudson Dispatch* October 10, 1918.

Upwards of 1,800 fans disregarded the ban and flu scare and came out to watch my bout with "Kid" Norfolk, the "Panama Flash," at the Spring Street A.C. in West Hoboken on the 11th.[459] I defeated Norfolk by decision over eight rounds. It was my second decision win over Norfolk in three months. The five-foot nine-inch Norfolk was a young 25-years-old compared to my 39 years. I outweighed Norfolk by 5 pounds. I weighed in at 191 pounds to his 186 1/2. I also held a small height advantage over Norfolk. A local paper dubbed the event "Jennette Night." I wore my customary gray trunks and was accompanied into the ring by Dan. Most in attendance gave me seven of the eight rounds with the first round even. In the seventh stanza I nearly dropped Norfolk with a quick left-right combination, but Norfolk clinched as his manager Leo P. Flynn screamed: *"Hold on!"*

Reporter Hyatt Daab wrote of the Norfolk battle: *Clean living and strict attention to his profession for more than a decade have rewarded for Joe Jeannette, the veteran Negro heavyweight of West Hoboken. His victory over Kid Norfolk, one of the best Negro heavyweights of the day, in their recent match over in New Jersey lifts Jeannette again up near the fistic pinnacle. It was his second defeat of the "Panama Flash."*

Joe Jeannette is by long odds the most popular heavyweight in New Jersey. He has been boxing the best men in his division for more than ten years; has fought them all, including the Johnson's and the Langford's, and the best of the white men too, but while his rivals have fallen before the assault of increasing years, Joe has held his course on the upper trail, and today we see him defeating Kid Norfolk, a youthful, ambitious, highly skillful Negro whose chief claim to fistic fame is his defeat of Billy Miske in a twelve round bout in Boston several months ago.[460]

In mid-October I was approached by James W. Coffroth in regards to volunteering to box at a war-drive fundraiser. I told him I would love to do so. I offered to box the world's champion Jess Willard or the top contender to the crown, Jack Dempsey. Coffroth said he would get back to me. After several days, I received a call that a match with either Dempsey or Willard would not be possible because they refused to box me. Coffroth apologized and said he would have loved to match me with either of the heavyweights, but they simply did not want to fight colored fighters. I couldn't believe that at 40 years of age, the 34-year-old Willard and the 23-year-old Dempsey were ducking me and using the "color line" as an excuse. I decided to write a letter to my friend Fred Hawthorne, who was the sports editor of the *New York Tribune*. The letter was as follows: *"Would you permit me to offer a suggestion which I believe if carried out would add a good many thousand dollars to the United War Work Council Fund? I have offered to fight, gratis, any of the leading heavyweights for any war charity. I now propose to request Mr. James W.*

[459] *Hudson Dispatch* October 12, 1918.
[460] *Evening Telegram-New York* October 13, 1918.

Coffroth to match me with Jack Dempsey or Jess Willard. They cannot honestly advance the worn out excuse of 'color line,' for the money earned by this fight will be used by these wonderful organizations to help, amuse and succor our gallant fighters, irrespective of race, color, or creed.

"The fact that I am supremely confident of beating Willard or Dempsey is not my reason for wanting to meet them. They may claim that I want a chance to win the world's championship. That title means nothing to me. I am so sure of beating either of this pair that I will sign an agreement to immediately retire and turn over the championship to the United States Army or Navy, with the understanding that they can offer the title to be fought for between men in the service, for that is where the heavyweight championship of the world rightly belongs. They are the real champions; we of the padded mitts are more or less boxers.

"Willard won his title from a colored man- one whom he never had any personal or physical regard for. Jack Johnson admitted in Paris that he would not fight me, as he wanted to be the only colored man to be the world's champion. I never was hysterical over Willard's ability. A 'champion' who could not beat Frank Moran decisively was a poor champion. As for Dempsey, he may be a great fighter. However, I have noticed in the papers where he repudiated two matches with one Kid Norfolk, whom I have twice defeated.

"I would like to get some action soon for I shortly go on the road for the Commission on Training Camp Activities. My duties will take me to the various camps where I am to instruct and have charge of the colored troops' physical welfare. My challenge to Willard and Dempsey is for a fight for a good cause, and it can be staged for eight, ten, or twenty rounds or to a finish. Yours Respectfully, Joe Jeannette."[461]

A *New York Evening Telegram* article by Hyatt Daab described Dempsey's feelings on boxing me: *The addition of Jack Dempsey, foremost contender for the heavyweight championship of the world, in the program for the boxing carnival at Madison Square Garden next Saturday night for the benefit of the United War Work Fund, assures the success of what promises to be one of the greatest fistic tournaments ever held in this city. Dempsey has consented to box any man the committee may select. It is likely his opponent may be named today. Although Dempsey in the past had asserted he did not object to boxing Negro pugilists, it is understood that he has declined to meet Joe Jeannette in the Garden because such a match would establish a precedent he has no desire to set. In other words, Dempsey had drawn the color line, and at present there is a meager chance of his altering his stand.*

Jeannette had been clamoring for a chance to meet the conqueror of Fred Fulton. The West Hoboken Negro, in fact, has refused to box Kid Norfolk, whom he has twice defeated, and if the committee won't match him with Dempsey, as he desires, Joe probably will not appear on the Garden program. "I have offered to box Dempsey any number of rounds, but he pays no attention to me," declared Jeannette. "I am confident I can beat him, and unless the committee will let me box him I shall refuse to appear in the show

---

[461] *New York Tribune* November 1, 1918.

next Saturday night. They don't have to look very far for a suitable opponent for Dempsey."

But in view of Dempsey's feelings concerning the color line it is altogether doubtful he will meet Jeannette, even if the committee should fail to procure a suitable white opponent to meet him. Charlie Harvey and his associates on the committee in charge of arrangements for the show are scurrying about today in an eleventh hour effort to obtain a topnotch heavyweight to meet the Utah boy, but good heavyweights who are willing to clash with Dempsey are almost as extinct today as the well known do-do.[462]

The event was allowed, even though New York had banned gatherings of ten or more people just months prior. The United War Work Fund was started by President Wilson to help raise money for the Army and Navy. The boxing event brought together seven different organizations to help raise money for the fund. The crowd was large, despite the recent influenza outbreak.

The event was held at Madison Square Garden, a beautiful arena built in 1890, replacing the first garden. Both were located at 26th and Madison Avenue. This new Garden was New York City's second tallest building, rising thirty-two stories high.

I agreed to box "Kid" Norfolk again. Norfolk was a tough customer from New York City. He boxed mostly in the light heavyweight division. Jack Dempsey, "The Manassa Mauler," wound up agreeing to face a white Midwestern boxer named Joe Bonds. Bonds had been managed in the past by Jack Kearns, who was Dempsey's current manager.

Several days before the show, Norfolk pulled out. I decided to take a fight at the Fourth Regiment Armory in Jersey City on Saturday night instead of going to the fundraiser in New York. I finished my bout at the Armory and was dressing to go home when a friend of Dan's walked into the dressing room. He told me that Bonds was a no-show and Dempsey agreed to box me. I quickly changed into my street clothes, hopped in my car, and made haste for New York. I changed in a dressing room and was led out to the ring wearing my trunks and a robe. I was seated in the front row. I took a nap during the preliminary bouts. I was awoken by the crowd's roar as Dempsey made his way into the ring.

The 23-year-old Dempsey was vying for the title held by Jess Willard. Dempsey was surrounded by fans and reporters. It brought back memories of early in my career when Jack Johnson received all of the adulation, while I was invisible behind the shadow he cast. Dempsey's camp was prepared to use Bond's no-show act as a publicity stunt to build up their fighter in the New York media. "Dempsey Sends His Opponent Fleeing the Building" would be the headline.

Dan motioned to me after Dempsey climbed into the ring. This would be

---

[462] *Evening Telegram-New York* November 13, 1918.

a great opportunity for me to get my name back into the headlines as a contender. He pulled the hood of my robe up over my head and we made our way up into the opposing corner. The announcer handed the microphone to Dempsey's manager Jack Kearns, who brazenly proclaimed that Jack Dempsey would: *"box any man in the world."*

Kearns was just beginning to explain to the crowd how Dempsey's opponent did not show when I pulled my robe off and the crowd erupted. Kearns looked around and covered the microphone as he asked the promoter what was going on. Kearns walked up to me and asked me why I was in the ring. I replied that I was here to box Dempsey. Dan approached Kearns and told him I had volunteered to fill in for Bonds and box Jack. Kearns said he had never agreed to such a match. He walked over and huddled with Dempsey and his trainer Jimmy De Forest in their corner. Then I heard Dan screaming and cursing. I knew it wasn't good. Did they want money for the match? Less rounds than six? Dan walked over to me with a beet red face. *"Joe,"* he said, *"Dempsey has refused to box you."*

I stood there and felt my skin chill over. My legs felt lighter than they had from any blow to the temple I received in all of my years in the ring. I was humiliated. This was more degrading than all of the racist words that had been hurled at me during my boxing career. Then Dan continued: *"Dempsey said he refuses to box you because you are black."* Dan continued to explain how Dempsey was lying and that he was drawing the "color line" because he was just plain scared, but his voice was trailing off. I saw Dan's lips moving, but I could not hear his words. My head was buzzing, not the buzzing of a cobweb-clearing punch. This was a buzzing from my blood pressure boiling over with anger. My entire career I had been passed over for big paydays because of my skin color. I was forced to stay in separate hotels from other boxers when I traveled for bouts. I had endured the shouts of coon, darky, shine, and nigger throughout my career. My parents, my brothers and sisters, my wife, and my children all suffered from racism. I had had enough. I was not going to step back into the shadow this time.

The eight thousand fans that filled the arena were sensing something was amiss. Their grumblings turned into jeers. I leaned back into the ropes by my corner and stared at Dempsey. I purposely gave a mocking grin to taunt him into trading leather with me. Someone from the crowd yelled up: *"Dempsey's yellow!"* Another: *"Yellow dog! Big Bum."*[463] Still another: *"Quitter!"* I turned to the crowd to plead my case. I raised my hands up over and over, inciting the crowd to demand a match. They responded with loud chants of: *"We want a fight! We want a fight!"* I walked over to where Dempsey was standing with De Forest. I taunted him face to face but still he refused to budge.

---

[463] "They Called Me a Bum" by Jack Dempsey September 1925 as told to John B. Kennedy.

There was nothing left for me to do. I had made my point. I was walking back towards the ropes when the fans, realizing that I was going to exit the ring, shouted up: *"Stay there Joe!"* I stopped in my tracks. I turned and smiled to the crowd. They were right. If Dempsey didn't want to box me, he could leave the ring first. I took a seat on my stool in the corner, and just as they had done throughout my career the crowd energized me into action. I rose from my stool and crossed the ring to where Dempsey and his entourage were planning their exit. I issued a straight dare to him, face to face. This was the same dare given to me fourteen long years earlier by my friends in Jersey City when I first strapped on the leather mittens. Dempsey looked at De Forest to his left and Kearns to his right to save him. Kearns yelled: *"Get him out, for we will not meet a Negro! Sit tight Jack. Box Bond or nobody."*[464]

The scene inside of the ring exploded. "Kid" Norfolk and Leo P. Flynn jumped into the ring followed by a half dozen other black and white boxers along with their seconds, managers, the announcer, and several sponsors. The tension was rising to a boil. The shouting was growing and people were being pulled apart. Dempsey spoke softly: *"I'll fight any white man they put on but I didn't agree to fight a colored boy."*[465] After order was finally restored, Jack Britton offered to box Dempsey three rounds. Another person yelled that Bonds had arrived at the arena but he was nowhere to be seen. It was probably only a distraction to calm the tension.

Dempsey, standing in his fighting trunks, announced he would not box at all. I had made my point and I exited the ring. The crowd's applause for me was the most memorable of my career, and I didn't even throw a punch. Twenty minutes of screaming and hissing ensued.[466] Then Dempsey, head bowed, was led away. I left the arena. In the dressing room Dan Morgan and Jack Kearns almost came to blows over the incident. They even pulled out revolvers on each other.[467] I cried uncontrollably on the ride home. I could not stop. Was my skin color to forever bar me from success? A lifetime of racism flashed before me all at once. I thought of all the years of boxing the most dangerous opponents in the world and being denied a title opportunity while lesser-deserving white boxers received shot after shot. All of the long trips for short money while white boxers made ten times my purses.

Would my children suffer the same painful humiliation? Would they be denied opportunities because of their skin color? Why did my wife want to endure the pain of marrying a black man? What type of pain had my father and his father endured? My thoughts came back to my children. I would protect them, if I could do nothing for myself. I would fight for them when

---

464 "They Called Me a Bum" by Jack Dempsey September 1925 as told to John B. Kennedy.
465 "They Called Me a Bum" by Jack Dempsey September 1925 as told to John B. Kennedy.
466 "They Called Me a Bum" by Jack Dempsey September 1925 as told to John B. Kennedy.
467 *Schenectady Gazette* December 10, 1918.

I could no longer fight for myself.

Dempsey's manager would later say that I set the whole thing up, that I was responsible for Bonds not showing up. That couldn't be further from the truth. I never spoke to Bonds. It was also being said that "Dumb" Dan Morgan and my manager Dan McKetrick were responsible for setting up Dempsey because they wanted revenge for Dempsey knocking out "Battling" Levinsky several weeks prior. Rumor had it Morgan wouldn't let Levinsky into the ring until he received a promise from Dempsey that he wouldn't knock Levinsky out. A right cross to the jaw in the third round of the bout broke that promise. Dan was very close to Kearns, and some called him Kearns' rep on the East Coast. Dan would never two-time Kearns, but this was boxing.

Dempsey, to his credit, had contributed five hundred dollars to the War Fund. When a local reporter asked me what had happened, I replied: *"I first boxed at the Fourth Regiment Armory in Jersey City Saturday night and as I was dressing a certain gentleman approached me and said, 'Come Joe, you're going to fight Dempsey. Everything is fixed.' I never imagined there was anything wrong, but I did think that perhaps Bonds was sick and could not go through with his agreement.*

"Arriving at the Garden I was met by a few more fellows. One grabbed my grip and the others hustled me into the building. I was tickled to death to think that I was going to battle Dempsey as everybody knows I challenged him repeatedly. I lost no time in jumping into my fighting togs and before the third bout went on I walked into the arena and planted myself in a ringside box beside Mrs. Freddie Welsh and a party of friends. Then I fell asleep, but you can bet I never dreamed that Dempsey was being 'framed'.

"I was awakened by the salvo of cheers that greeted Dempsey's arrival at the ring. I took this as a cue to take my corner. I wasn't sitting there a minute before Jack Kearns dashed over and demanded what I wanted. I assured him I was there for no other purpose than to fight his man Dempsey. 'But we didn't agree to fight you!' roared Kearns. It was these words that gave me the first thought that there was something wrong somewhere. Seeing that Dempsey made no move to strip for action I became suspicious and going over to his corner I said: 'What's the matter, Jack? Don't you want to fight?' 'You'll have to see my manager,' he replied.

"It was after having a talk with Kearns that I realized Dempsey was being tricked and that I was being made the scapegoat of the whole rotten affair. I have been fighting for many years and this is the first time I have ever been accused of framing anybody. As much as I want to fight Dempsey I certainly would not have allowed myself to be forced on him Saturday night. I have always been on the level and intend to play the game fair until I lay away the gloves."[468]

The reporter who interviewed me wrote: *Dempsey had a golden opportunity to make himself solid with the boxing fans but he didn't have the common sense to take advantage of it. When Bonds refused to go through with his bout Jack should have taken*

---

[468] *Hudson Dispatch* November 19, 1918.

Joe Jennette just to show the thousands assembled that he feared no man. If he is the real champ he is cracked up to be he would not only have went through six rounds with the 'Old Master,' but also succeeded in rendering the efforts of the plotters to belittle him in the eyes of the public worthless. When a man of Jack's repute ducks a no-decision bout with a veteran like Jennette he places himself in a very bad light... In view of the gallantry of the American Negroes under General Pershing in France, the sporting public no longer recognizes the drawing of the color line in pugilism. Dempsey volunteered his services for the United War Work Campaign, which doesn't discriminate between white and black fighters in our victorious Expeditionary Force. Subsequently Dempsey's refusal to box Jennette because of the latter's color didn't appeal to the crowd that went to the Garden to help the war charities.[469]

The reporter ended his article by saying that even if I never get the chance to meet Dempsey, I had the satisfaction of knowing that I was in the same ring with him stripped for battle.

Hyatt Daab also reported on the incident: *There is no place today in boxing for the pugilist who draws the 'color' line. With Negroes doing their bit just as heroically as white soldiers and sailors to make the world safe for the generations to come, it behooves no boxer, whether title holder or near champion, to employ the 'color' line as a defensive barrier against formidable Negro challengers.*

Whether Jack Dempsey declined to meet Joe Jeannette when that hoary veteran challenged him to fight before more than eight thousand fans in Madison Square Garden Saturday night because he feared to meet the group of efficient Negro heavyweights who have been stalking his trail is problematical...

Regardless what impelled Dempsey's ill-timed refusal to meet the Negro on Saturday night, however, his popularity will wane altogether should he continue to maintain his present attitude toward Negro challengers... By what peculiar line of reasoning then did Dempsey decide to draw the 'color' line?

He is still but a challenger himself. It is a matter of record that he has fought Negroes, not once, but on numerous occasions... But it is difficult to believe such a splendid fighter as Dempsey has shown himself to be such that he should seek refuge behind the weak kneed... There is one thing for Dempsey to do if he desires to reestablish himself in the esteem of the thousands who acclaimed him. That is to erase the 'color' line and meet all comers. Persons who profess to know assert that personally Dempsey had no objection to boxing Negroes, and that had it not been for Jack Kearns, his manager, he would have boxed Jeannette Saturday night. All of which may be true.

The public, however, is interested only in Jack Dempsey. Should he persist in observing the 'color' line the public will condemn him as he deserves. The deluge of catcalls and jeers that swept the Garden as he and his retinue slunk out of the arena last Saturday night should be sufficient warning.[470]

Dan Morgan was interviewed and stated the following: *"I went to Joe Bond's dressing room with Bill Brown, who was to have refereed the contest. Bond's said he had*

[469] *Hudson Dispatch* November 19, 1918.
[470] *Evening Telegram-New York* December 2, 1918.

received a bruise on his head while playing football and while he was in no condition to fight he would go on and take a beating. Bill Brown said he wouldn't referee any such bout. Then I suggested to Brown that Jeannette would fight Dempsey. Brown replied that such a contest would be worthwhile, so I told Jeannette to go in the ring.

"In justice to Dempsey I wish to say that I believe in my heart that he would have gone on with Jeannette had not his manager, Jack Kearns, refuse to permit him to do so. I figured that Dempsey would have wiped up Bonds so quickly that it would be a blow to the game. I was only trying to protect the game when I sent Jeannette into the ring."[471]

On Thursday, December 12, 1918, I volunteered to box an exhibition bout at Camp Merritt for the soldiers returning home from the war.[472] The show was sponsored by the Knights of Columbus and the Ded Drop Inn Club of Jersey City. Also helping out with the benefit was "Big" Jim Coffrey. It appeared as though the influenza outbreak had finally passed. I helped transport volunteers to the event in my limousine.

On February 9, an article came out in the *Philadelphia Inquirer* which spoke about a match I had against Jeff Madden on July 15, 1912. Sam Langford was Madden's trainer for that bout: *Well, one day while Sam was training in a gymnasium he discovered a boxer whom he thought was a wonder. He went to (Joe) Woodman and asked him to secure a bout for his newly found prodigy and Woodman agreed to do so. The fighter was matched with Joe Jeanette, and that was not putting him in easy. Langford's pupil was on the floor twice in the first round, three times in the second, and four times in the fourth. Langford acted as chief adviser to his pupil and when the fighter returned to his corner at the end of the fourth round Langford said: 'Man, you're slipping; rub your feet in the rosin.' The fighter looked up at Sam and replied: 'There ain't no rosin that will keep me up from what I'm getting- throw in the sponge.[473]*

On July 4, 1919, at Bay View Park Arena in Toledo, Ohio, Jack Dempsey became the new heavyweight champion of the world when he knocked Jess Willard out in the third round. The new champion garnered public favor by playing on the race question.[474] Dempsey told the fighting public that under no circumstances would he box a black man. White America rejoiced at hearing this, as they still held hatred for Jack Johnson, for both his preference of white women, and his dominance over white fighters.

On August 7 I broke my training camp to accompany Tom Cassidy to Clason Point in the Bronx. The purpose of the journey was to take part in an exhibition bout for the entertainment of over 500 orphaned children at the Christian Brothers' Asylum. The kids thoroughly enjoyed the show. Frankie Burns, Johnny Duff, "Soldier" Roberts, and Frankie Nelson also

---

[471] *Brooklyn NY Standard Union* November 18, 1918.

[472] *Hudson Dispatch* December 10, 1918.

[473] *Philadelphia Inquirer* February 9, 1919.

[474] *Beyond The Ring* by Jeffrey T. Sammons pg. 73.

performed on the show.[475]

On August 20, 1919, I helped to organize a benefit for the ailing Sam Langford. It was held at Fletcher's Field in Fairview N.J. The main exhibition was Joe Borrell versus "Battling" Siki. "Philadelphia" Joe Jackson and "Mexican" Jack Rivas also competed, as well as a local West Hoboken boy named Jimmy Francis.

On October 20 I returned to the ring once again to take on the up-and-coming colored prospect, Harry Wills. Wills was considered one of the rising stars in boxing. We fought at the Fourth Regiment Armory in Jersey City. It was the third time we faced each other in the ring. The first two bouts were ruled draws. Wills weighed 209 pounds to my 204. Wills, 31 years of age, was nine years younger than me. As much as I tried, I just couldn't keep up with the younger and quicker Wills. He won an eight round newspaper decision. After the fight, I realized that my fighting days were coming to a close.

On Thanksgiving Day in 1919, the towns of West Hoboken and Union Hill held a football game between the towns' high schools. Both of the schools principals were against the game because they were fearful it would magnify tensions between the two border-town schools. West Hoboken's Emerson High School Bulldogs and Union Hill High School's Hillers played to an exciting 0-0 game in the first of what would become a heated rivalry over the years. The game was played at Woodcliff Lake Park in North Bergen. Years later the park would be re-named after one of the boxers I had trained, Jimmy Braddock.

Late in 1919, I was approached by a friend named Fred Wolpmann. He asked me if I was interested in investing money in a new amusement park that was being built at Hudson Boulevard in North Bergen, across from Schuetzen Park. The group was called the Columbia Amusement Park Company. The park, which company president Otto Aeschbach stated was going to rival Coney Island Amusement Park, opened on May 30, 1920. The park included a dancing palace, a swimming pool that could hold six thousand bathers, a roller skating rink, basketball courts, boxing, an ice skating rink, bowling alleys, a shooting range, three restaurants, a banquet hall, a Ferris wheel, roller coasters, a pony track, a merry-go-round, a scenic railway, and fifty concession stands.

On January 22, 1920 I made an announcement that I was going to retire from the fight game. I told the press that it appeared as though: *"The day of the colored boxer has passed."*[476] I made the statement because it appeared as though the boxing public was not interested in having a colored fighter box for the heavyweight championship. Jack Dempsey held the title, he drew the "color line," and boxing fans accepted this.

---

[475] *Jersey Journal* August 8, 1919.
[476] *Atlanta Constitution* January 23, 1920.

On January 26, I received terrible news. My former stable-mate and cornerman Willie Lewis had been rushed to the hospital the night before, after having been shot several times.[477] I went to the hospital and the doctors there stated they did not think he would survive his wounds. Willie had always lived his life on the edge, and it appeared as though his lifestyle had finally caught up with him. Willie was the manager of the Chateau Thierry, a basement cabaret located at 42 East Fourteenth Street in Manhattan. That is where the shooting took place. Willie had invited Addie and I to the club and we visited him there several weeks prior. Addie and I were both uncomfortable with the crowd and the fact that they were serving alcohol, which was illegal due to prohibition. After chatting with Willie for about an hour, Addie and I made an excuse for having to leave. Later that week, Willie got arrested for dealing in illegal alcohol. We assumed that his shooting was related to his illegal liquor involvement.

I met Willie's wife Tillie and his mother Maggie at St. Vincent's hospital. At around nine o'clock on the 25th, with the cabaret fairly filled, Willie had entered the phone booth at the entrance of the club to make a call. Two men walked in and went to the back of the club looking for Willie. After being told that Willie was in the phone booth, the men turned their ulster collars up over their faces and pulled their soft hats down over their eyes as they approached the booth. They jerked open the booth's door and began firing pistols. Willie attempted to punch one of the gunmen but was shot two more times and fell to the floor. At the hospital Willie told Doctor Tierney: *"I don't know who they are or why they did it."* I knew Willie was a tough customer, and I was not surprised when he fully recovered from his wounds. I sat with him in the hospital several days later and told him he needed to change his ways. He agreed.

Dan came up to visit Willie and we sat and talked of the old times. I asked Willie which one of his fights was the toughest. Willie replied: *"Joe, the hardest fight I ever had in my life was the night you and Sam McVea fought that terrific forty-nine round battle in Paris."* Willie was referring to the forty-nine trips he had to take up and down the stairs between rounds.

On July 20, 1920, Jack Johnson entered the United States and surrendered to Federal Agents at the Mexican border town of Tijuana. After being allowed to visit his ailing mother he was sent to Leavenworth Prison to serve his year sentence.

In the fall of 1920 I was working with Georges Carpentier. He had asked me to help him prepare for his upcoming light heavyweight championship bout against "Battling" Levinsky. We had a camp set up in Summit, New Jersey, at a Knights of Columbus Hall. I returned home to my family in West Hoboken for the weekends.

---

[477] *New York Times* January 26, 1920.

One Saturday I was sitting home with Addie when there was a knock on our door. I opened the door and a small fellow in his mid-forties was standing there. He asked to speak to Mr. Jennette. I told him that I was Joe Jennette. He introduced himself by saying: *"I am Harry Houdini and was wondering if I could have a minute of your time."* I knew he looked familiar. I couldn't believe Harry Houdini was actually at my home! I invited him in. Addie was just as excited as I was to have Houdini in our living room. I called Joe Junior and Agnes into the room to introduce them to the great Houdini. After things simmered down I asked him what he was doing in West Hoboken. He responded by saying that he had quietly opened up a warehouse on 216 Weehawken Street. He told me that he created many of his props in the warehouse and he was also using it as his headquarters for his Film Developing Corporation Company. Harry told me he was in France at the same time I was over there boxing in 1909. He was making a movie titled *The Adventures of Houdini in Paris.* I asked Houdini how I could help him. Harry told me he had heard that I was the man to see for strength and conditioning exercises. He was interested in learning how to make his stomach muscles stronger because he was having fans hit his abdomen as a show of strength. I showed Harry how I used to lean back off of a chair and let boxers hit my stomach to build strength. I told him it was important to breathe out slowly, through the nostrils, while tightening the stomach muscles during the exercise. I gave him some special sit-up exercises to strengthen the upper and lower stomach muscles. I explained that after a couple of weeks of practice he would be able to withstand the hardest of punches from the strongest men. Harry was very excited and thanked me for my time. I told him to stop by anytime he needed help.

On October 12, 1920, Georges won the light heavyweight championship of the world when he knocked out "Battling" Levinsky in the fourth round at Westside Ballpark in Jersey City. I worked Georges corner in the bout. Georges didn't even have the belt tied around his waist when he hinted that he wanted to challenge Jack Dempsey for the heavyweight title. Aside from the money the fight would bring, Georges knew of the incident that transpired between Dempsey and I, and he wanted to help me exact my revenge. On November 5, 1920 Georges signed a contract to fight Dempsey for the heavyweight championship of the world. The date and location of the bout would be forthcoming.

In December, Sam McVea sat down with James J. Corbett and gave the following interview: *Sam McVey opines that he'll retire from active ring warfare in another year or so. "I'm getting rather old," sighed the dusky heavyweight. "Been fighting nigh onto twenty years now and the old legs and the old arms aren't doing all the work that is needed for a man who wants to continue as a topnotch ringman."*

And then Sam sighed again. "I ain't ever had much good luck in this fight business and I certainly am having a tough break now," he said. "Just when the game is getting good and there are a lot of opponents to fight and the purse offerings have jumped to about twenty times what they were when I broke into the game, and nearly triple what they were at any other time. I get slow and old and a little bit fat, and will have to quit. Now, I ask you. Isn't that tough luck?"

"Who gave you the toughest fight of your career?" McVey was asked. The Negro scratched his head in reflective manner for a few moments then replied: "Well, I guess it's a toss-up between Sam Langford and Joe Jeanette." That boy Langford certainly fought me some fights when he was going good, and I think that he was one of the toughest men that ever lived. Couldn't seem to hurt him and every time he hit, it made me think that an express train had rammed into me."

"But I think that the hardest fight that I ever figured in was against Jeanette in Paris. That happened in 1909 and I reckon that things happened in that battle that haven't happened in any affair in ring history. The battle went 49 rounds. I knocked down Joe Jeanette 36 times during that fight- and every knockdown came as the result of a wallop smashed to the face or body. Each new time I dropped him everybody around the ringside thought that he was through. But Joe would get up and someway and somehow save himself from the fatal count of ten.

"Yes sir, I knocked down Jeanette 36 times in that fight, never was knocked off my feet once and yet I lost the fight in the 49th round with the records saying that I lost it by a knockout. You see, it was this way. I wasn't in wonderful shape when I went into that fight and didn't expect Joe to give me as tough a battle as he put up. When you knock a fellow down 36 times it seems you've got to put something into at least 36 of those smashes. I put everything I had into each one of mine, but Joe wouldn't stay down. I beat him up something awful, but I am not denying that Joe didn't wallop me good and plenty. It was a toss-up as the 49th began as to which of us was in the worst shape.

"As we came into the center of the ring my legs began to buckle under me. I got dizzy and I could hardly see anything. About the only thing that my eyes could uncover was Joe wobbling around in front of me brandishing his gloved fists. I heard him say: 'Come on in here boy- we're going to do some more fighting and I'll knock the tar out of you yet.'

" 'No.' I said to Joe as I began to turn my back on him and walk back to my corner. 'You've done everything you could do to me this evening. I'm human and I can't stand this any longer. You can win this old fight if you want to but you forgot that I knocked you down so often that it will take you a month to figure it up.'

"I got to my corner and flopped into my chair. The referee asked me to go out and continue the battle. I told him I was through for the evening- that I didn't dislike Joe so much that I wouldn't fight him again. So he gave the fight to Jeanette and it took me about a week to recover somewhat from what happened in the 49 rounds. Yes sir, that was a tough fight."[478]

---

[478] *Illinois State Register* December 23, 1920.

Chapter 19
The First Million Dollar Gate 1921

Georges Carpentier and Jack Dempsey agreed to fight on July 2, 1921, at Boyle's Thirty Acres in Jersey City. This would be the first boxing match broadcast live via the radio. After I defeated Georges in 1914, he and I had become good friends. I had worked with him for several of his bouts in the United States including the Levinsky title fight. He asked me to work with him as his chief sparring partner and assistant trainer for his bout with Dempsey. I was more than happy to oblige him. Georges' arrived in New York on May 16 on the steamer La Savoy. He opened up his training camp in Manhasset, Long Island on May 20. Georges' head trainer was Gus Wilson. Wilson was fluent in French and English and could communicate well with both Carpentier and DesCamps.

I still felt the sting of what Dempsey did to me in the ring back in 1918. He not only disrespected me, he disrespected all black Americans. I never felt he drew the "color line" with me because of race. He drew the "color line" with me because of fear. He just used racism as a cover to hide his fear. Using racism as an excuse to me was just as improper as being a racist. He feared losing to a 40-year-old black boxer in the Garden, and he feared losing his heavyweight title opportunity, the same opportunity I was denied because of my skin color.

On my first day in camp, I decided to bring my wife and kids along to see Georges. I drove to the training camp in one of my work limousines. When we pulled up out front, a slew of reporters ran up to the car, snapping photographs. The reporters had thought that it was some superstar celebrity that had arrived. My wife and kids thought it was the funniest thing. When we went inside of Georges' house, my daughter Agnes spotted a piano and asked if she could play. She played several French songs that her piano teacher taught her. Georges was amazed that Agnes knew French songs. Georges sang along to the French tunes.[479] My son loved music so much that he would later perform in an orchestra. I taught myself how to play piano. I played by ear.[480] I passed on my love of music to my children.

I helped Georges get into the best shape of his life. We sparred dozens of rounds and ran together every morning. I taught Georges all the tricks of the trade I had learned from sixteen years of professional boxing. I knew that Georges had heart, a big right hand, and he was a very good boxer. My only worry was his size and the fact that he cut easily. Another big worry was an injury that Georges suffered while training for the bout. He injured his right hand while sparring with me and he was forced to end his sparring

---

[479] *Dallas Morning News* June 29, 1921.
[480] Interview with JoAnn Flannery-Mostaccio Joe Jennette's great-niece.

a week earlier than we wanted. We tried to get Georges to postpone the bout but he refused. He needed the money. Georges spent most of his career in the middleweight and light heavyweight divisions. He would have to use his speed and footwork to offset Dempsey's size. Dempsey was very quick, which made our strategy more of a challenge. I tried my best to imitate Dempsey's style. I led with my right hand often, as Dempsey did. We worked on Georges' boxing and footwork because we knew he would not be able to stand toe to toe with the bigger and stronger Dempsey.

On June 1, Sam McVea stopped into camp. We talked of the old times and compared our right arms. We both suffered injuries to our right arms during our boxing careers, which is why we both utilized our left hands so often when we fought.[481]

Georges and I both knew that Dempsey thought I was too much for him in 1918, so we decided to use the press to try to intimidate Dempsey. We waited until a full contingent of reporters was on hand for one of our sparring sessions. I let Georges hit me with a right hand and down I went. The reporters fell for it hook, line, and sinker. The next day's headlines throughout the country spoke of how Georges' vaunted right hand dropped the great Joe Jennette.[482]

"Philadelphia" Jack O'Brien dropped into camp. O'Brien told Georges he had some advice that might help Georges in his fight with Dempsey. Gus Wilson agreed to let O'Brien see Georges. O'Brien told Georges that hitting Dempsey on the chin or in the body would do no good. He told Georges that Dempsey had only one vulnerable spot, the throat. O'Brien then opened his hand with his thumb extended and proceeded to poke Georges in the throat hard. Georges gasped for air and coughed. When Georges straightened up O'Brien repeated the foul. Georges let out another gasp and doubled over.[483]

Gus and I rushed in and asked what was going on. O'Brien stated that he was just giving advice on how to beat Dempsey. I chased O'Brien out of the training complex. For two days, Georges' throat was in so much pain he couldn't sleep. It was later discovered that O'Brien was good friends with Dempsey's manager, Jack Kearns, and he injured Georges on purpose.

Many celebrities stopped by during training camp. It was surprising to see how much American support Georges had. The steady stream of well-wishers was so large that we had to post a police officer at the camps entrance. Occasionally I would take Georges for an hour long ride in my car so he could relax away from the media and fans. Tennis star Vincent Richards stopped by to show his support. One of the visitors who stopped by a few days before the match was my old pupil Babe Ruth. I considered

---

[481] *New York Times* June 2, 1921.
[482] *Boston Daily Globe* June 8, 1921.
[483] *Bill Stern's Boxing Stories* pgs. 215-216.

Babe a star when I trained him in 1918 but now he was a superstar. He had shattered baseballs homerun record two years in a row with twenty-nine and fifty-four home runs for his new team the New York Yankees. The Bambino was nicknamed the "Sultan of Swat" for his homerun prowess. The Babe was given a kings welcome when he arrived at the camp. Ruth engulfed me with one of his signature bear hugs. I introduced him to Georges. *"Hello Georges,"* began Babe, *"My name is George too; hope you get a homerun Saturday." "Same to you,"* replied Georges through my translation.[484] I had become fluent in French from my many journeys to the country.

On one of the media days, reporters' Damon Runyon, Grantland Rice, Jack Lawrence, Ring Lardner, and Cullen Cain stopped by to interview Carpentier. Cain reported the following: *While we waited for the Frenchman to appear I noticed a tall, impressive looking Negro standing by. Grant Rice told me he was Joe Jeanette, a real contender for the title in his prime... Carpentier's manager had called him to coach the Frenchman on American ring craft and especially the art of infighting, in which Carpentier was most deficient. I figured here was the man who could give me the best line on the Frenchman and his chances.*

I found Jeanette to be a friendly, soft-spoken person, and he surely knew all about the fight game. "That Frenchman is a real fighter," he assured me. "He is fast and clever, and his right cross is a knockout punch. Yes, I coached him on infighting, but it's hard to learn an old fighter new tricks. The worst trouble with him is he comes up to his man in a crouch. He crouches too low. I can't break him out of it. You know what a wild fighter Dempsey is when he gets stung, and he is liable to batter that Frenchman about the head and even the back of his neck."

"But the 'rabbit punch' is barred," I told him. "Yes," replied Jeanette, "but how can the referee be sure about it in a wild mix-up?"

When the French fighter appeared he tripped across the grass, started up the steps to the ring and did a somersault over the ropes. Then he skipped the rope with a grace and speed and skill that was amazing. I remarked on it to Runyon, but he coldly replied, "Yes, but can he skip Dempsey's left hook?"[485]

Besides being the first live radio boxing match, another important first was to take place for this bout. For the first time, a sanctioning body, the National Boxing Association, would be sanctioning the championship bout. It would also publish lists of outstanding challengers, and would withdraw titular recognition if needed. Up until this point, the New York State Athletic Commission wielded the most influence in the boxing world, in regard to sanctioning championship bouts. Both organizations would crown their own champions, leading to confusion, but this was better than one group having total control over the sport's champions and challengers.

Obviously had there been a sanctioning body fifteen years prior, it may have forced Johnson to fight the top contenders. This might have helped

---

[484] *Augusta Chronicle* June 29, 1921.
[485] *Miami News* February 2, 1952.

Sam Langford and I get a crack at the title.

Most people don't remember that Dempsey was not the fan favorite going into the Carpentier match. He was considered a draft dodger. The Jersey City crowd was pro Carpentier. Even though he was French, he had served valiantly in the Great War and was a hero to most in the United States. Dempsey stated that he avoided the draft because he had to work to support his mother and siblings. I cannot and will not judge Dempsey on this issue, but the promoter used the war hero versus draft dodger angle to help sell tickets for the fight. The fight was promoted by Tex Rickard, and he billed the show as "The French War Hero" against the "Manassa Mauler."

Willie Lewis was asked who he thought would win the match: *"Here's my dope. Dempsey never whipped anybody; he can't take punishment; he can't go the distance, and he hasn't any grey matter... Carpentier will outthink him. He won't stand up like Willard did and take everything he's got. He'll figure out a defense and he'll work it before the rounds over. He's got a terrific punch and he's strong as a horse..."*[486]

When asked my thoughts on the bout I opined: *"Carpentier is too smart a fighter to lose this bout. He will be away when Dempsey hits and the champion will not be able to see his right hand, it will be that fast."*[487]

The bout was titled "The Battle of The Century." It was the first million-dollar gate in ring history. Instead of driving from Long Island to Jersey City for the fight, Georges wanted to sail over on a yacht. The morning of the fight we sailed across Long Island Sound into the Hudson River and on to Jersey City.[488] Over eighty thousand people were in attendance for the contest. In all of my ring battles I had never earned more than three thousand dollars in one contest. In this match both fighters would earn much more. Dempsey received three hundred thousand dollars and Georges took home two hundred thousand.

The list of dignitaries who attended the event included Jersey City Mayor Frank Hague, New Jersey Governor Edward I. Edwards, John D. Rockefeller, William H. Vanderbilt, Vincent Astor, Henry Ford, Al Jolson, and George M. Cohen. Back in 1909 Cohen had supported Jeffries against Johnson and he publicly stated he would bet one thousand dollars on "The Boilermaker."[489]

We arrived at the stadium and went to our dressing room area. The sky was full of war clouds. There were rumors that the main event was going to be cancelled because of rain. During one of the preliminary bouts between my friend Frankie Burns and Packy O'Gatty, it started raining. Tex Rickard feared that the fans would leave if they thought the main event was going to

---

[486] *Trenton Evening Times* March 28, 1920.
[487] *Idaho Statesman* July 1, 1921.
[488] *Jersey Journal* June 30, 1921.
[489] "Unforgivable Blackness" by Geoffrey C. Ward pg. 149.

be cancelled. Rickard had radiophone announcer J. Andrew White go on the air and announce: *"It is drizzling rain while Packy O'Gatty and Frankie Burns are battling. It is the eighth and last round and Tex Rickard has just announced that Jack Dempsey and Georges Carpentier will fight at 3 p.m., rain or shine for the world's championship."*[490]

The sky eventually cleared up. At the last minute, just before we were to leave the dressing room, Georges pulled me to the side. He had a terribly sad look on his face. I told him to cheer up, that he would feel more comfortable once the bell rang. Georges explained to me that it wasn't the fight that was bothering him. He said that DesCamps was pressuring him to use all Frenchmen in his corner. I stopped in my tracks. I was shocked. After all the time we spent in camp preparing for the bout. No one understood the game plan or could get Georges to follow it like I could. He explained he didn't know how to tell me in the dressing room. He begged me to understand. I told him not to worry. I wanted Georges to be as focused on Dempsey as possible. I whispered into Georges' ear: *"For the love of Mike box him! Just fool him and you will get him for sure."* Georges replied: *"Joe, I am going to fight with all I have. Even if I am killed."*[491]

I looked around and the only empty seat I could find was by Dempsey's corner. I sat in a press seat directly behind the north section. I will never really know why DesCamps made this decision but there were two possible reasons. Not working the corner meant that I would not receive a piece of the ten-percent cut that trainers and cornermen usually split. The other reason was a quote that was attributed to me that was printed on the day of the fight. The quote was printed in an article by Joe Vila. Vila stated that he received my quote from an anonymous "reliable Jerseyman" who overheard a conversation between myself and boxing Commissioner Charles McNair. Vila printed the following: *Commissioner Charles R. McNair visited Manhasset the other day and after a hard work-out by Carpentier he called Joe Jeannette aside. Revealing his identity, the Commissioner asked Jeannette to give him an honest opinion of the coming battle. Jeannette replied: "Carpentier is fast, but Dempsey is, too. Jack is the harder hitter, though, and should win easily. I wish that, old as I am, I could be in Dempsey's shoes on July 2."*[492]

DesCamps either pulled a fast one to pocket more coin or he was upset over the newspaper quote, a quote that I never made. Georges looked at me several times before the opening bell. I motioned him to stick to boxing and moving. He looked very relaxed, maybe too relaxed. It is usually better for a fighter to have that anxious look. It prevents him from being caught cold early in a fight. I gave Georges a confident thumbs-up, but inside, my stomach was churning. Helping to train a boxer is so much different from

[490] *Jersey Journal* February 9, 1960.
[491] *Melbourne Argus* January 6, 1934.
[492] *Philadelphia Inquirer* July 1, 1921.

getting in the ring yourself. When you are boxing you know what moves you want to make, but when you are watching your boxer compete, you are relegated to biting your nails and hoping that your charge sees the same openings and punches coming that you do.

A band was playing songs in between the bouts. Before the Dempsey bout the band played the Irish ballad "Sweet Peggy O'Neil." When the band got to the chorus part of the song almost the entire eighty thousand fans in attendance joined in and sang the chorus:

If her eyes are blue as sky, that's Peggy O'Neil,
If she's smiling all the while, that's Peggy O'Neil,
If she walks like a sly little rogue, if she talks with a cute little brogue,
Sweet personality, Full of rascality, that's Peggy O'Neil.[493]

When Carpentier entered the ring the band played the French national anthem *La Marseillaise*. The crowd cheered loudly for Carpentier, which seemed to anger Dempsey. The boxers refused to shake hands. The opening round was won by Dempsey, highlighted by a swooping overhand right. It was the same type of right hand I was throwing at Georges in training. Georges came out attacking in the second. The "Orchard Man," as Georges was called, staggered Dempsey in the second session. The crowd was alive and electrified with excitement. At the start of the third round the crowd was cheering on Georges to continue his aggression. Dempsey would have no part of it and he used his superior size and strength to land several hard rights to the head along with a devastating right to the midsection that turned the tide back in his favor. Dempsey finished the round with several more hard blows to the body. I screamed at Georges to follow the game plan, to use his jab and move. The fourth round began with Dempsey again charging across the ring. Georges covered up for what he thought was a right hand coming to the head. Dempsey landed a hard left hook to the body that dropped Georges for a nine count. The large throng of blood thirsty fans roared in approval. The pine bleachers shook and swayed when the fans jumped to their feet.[494] When Georges rose, Dempsey dropped him again with a right to the jaw and Georges was counted out. The fight was over and Dempsey, the same Jack Dempsey who refused to box a 40-year-old black man, the man who drew the "color line" when it suited him, would go on to become an American icon. I wept after the bout.[495]

Georges gave this description of the contest: *"I almost flew from my corner when the gong went, and at once drove a left hand to the champion's unshaven face. It was a blow that had much weight in it, the kind of blow by which I had brought stars into the eyes of Beckett. But, to my amazement, Dempsey no more than sniffed. Dempsey rather*

---

[493] *Miami News* February 2, 1952.
[494] *Hudson Dispatch* July 2, 1971.
[495] *Brooklyn NY Daily Eagle* July 3, 1921.

than retreating as I expected, came after me like some bear who had been stung. I shot out three straight lefts that landed in the neighborhood of his snub nose. But it was like pouring water on a duck's back. He crashed his way to close quarters, and with his right, left me doubtful whether he had smashed my ribs.

"Then as I ducked and dodged to escape the full force of his onslaught he hit me on the top of the head, and for a moment I feared that my spine had been broken. Why I did not go down and out under the awful force of that blow I shall never be able to explain. To me Dempsey was as some monster, and I now readily make the confession that it was only instinct that helped me to continue. I did not lose my fighting wits. I could see and think straight and I managed to hit him with my right to his jaw.

"Dempsey, however, merely shook his black head, and by his clever footwork he left me to beat the air, and pinning me with my back to the ropes he drove sledge-hammer blows to my body, to knock me almost through the ropes. Only the bell saved me.

"DesCamps, Gus Wilson, and Charlie Ledoux worked upon me so furiously that I felt I was near to normal when I set out to begin the second round. Feinting with my left, I smashed my right hand full to Dempsey's jaw, shaking him from head to foot. His long arms, as he stood with his back to the ropes, hung loosely about his hips, he rocked and swayed as will a man who is tottering to defeat. There he was, inviting to be knocked out. Joe Benjamin, one of his seconds, shrieked, "Grab him, Jack!" Kearns (Dempsey's manager) reached for smelling salts.

"A hundred thousand people jumped to their feet expecting to see the champion dethroned, but I missed the greatest opportunity of my life. In trying a second right-hander, I missed the swaying chin of Dempsey, and he clutched and hugged me tight, so that I was helpless to complete the work I had begun. Dempsey at the end of that round went to his corner without showing traces of the greatest blow I have ever delivered. My reaction was terrible. Not only that, but I had broken a bone in my right hand.

" 'Francois,' I confided to DesCamps, 'It is impossible. This Dempsey is invincible.' The champion, so untroubled did he seem to be as he entered upon the third round might never have been in a fight. At once he came after me, and by his colossal strength insisted that the fight should be at close quarters. How he rattled and nearly caved in my ribs. He pounded me with right and left uppercuts, but I refused to believe that I could be beaten. The crowd screamed 'Dempsey!' So great was the uproar that it was almost impossible to hear the signal for the end of the round.

"I was terribly conscious as I sat in my corner, that my doom was sealed. My right hand was useless; my face was cut and bruised. My sides ached so that I suffered excruciating pain; my head swam. DesCamps, as he splashed me over with ice-water, cried 'You will win mon cheri, two more rounds finis!' He knew he lied for there was Dempsey as fresh as paint.

"How sick and weary I was when I went into the third round it is beyond me to say. Not even the merciless thrashing that I took from Frank Klaus and Billy Papke before the war left me in such a woeful condition. And yet, with the hope born of desperation that I might turn the tide, I held to my heart. I pumped new life into my weary legs, and sought to make every use of the ring, so that I might lure Dempsey into a false position and with my left- my only hand- do damage.

325

"But whatever I did was all in vain. He fooled me so it seemed, to a given spot, and punished me almost to the point of senselessness. But I would not give in easily. I said to myself, 'will I be beaten when I am left all stretched out.' My determination helped me survive the third round. It was as much as I could do to scramble to my feet to begin the fourth and what proved to be the last round. I was left with little of my strength. I was but a shell of my real self.

"Dempsey at once forced me to the ropes, but though I dodged his right hand, he ripped his left into my body. One, two, three, four blows he rammed into my almost broken ribs and down I went doubled up. How I managed it I shall never be able to tell, but at the count of nine I pulled myself to my feet. Now, however, it was child's play for Dempsey. With a right-hander he sent me to the floor of the ring, and though I had not been robbed of my mental faculties, and would have fought on, it was impossible for me to rise."[496]

I had done my utmost to give Georges the best strategy I could. I wasn't able to work his corner, so I had no idea what he was being told leading up to and during the fight. I sensed Georges felt very uncomfortable that I wasn't able to be in his corner. I explained my feelings to a local paper: *"It wouldn't have happened if he (Carpentier) had done what I told him."[497]* I was grief stricken at the outcome. When I was asked why I was not in Carpentier's corner, I stated: *"There was no use in having a crowd around him."[498]*

Cullen Cain described meeting me after the match: *In the Frenchman's dressing room after the fight I met Jeanette again. He shook his head as he sadly reminded me, "What did I tell you about that crouch? It must have been a rabbit punch that ruined him. He (Carpentier) told me he remembered nothing about that mix-up in the third round." Memory of the scenes and incidents of that famous fight will remain with me always, but somehow I best recall when the band played 'Sweet Peggy O'Neil' how the 90,000 people in that amphitheater joined in and sang the chorus. And how the Frenchman came up in that crouch in that third round and Joe Jeanette's gloom and his sad voice in the dressing room when he told me that all he feared had come to pass.[499]*

I had learned many years ago that having too many people screaming instructions in a corner can be detrimental to a fighter. This was the excuse I gave to the reporter to cover up DesCamps' last-minute money-saving move to replace me. I knew DesCamps never thought Georges had a shot at winning. He wanted to make as much money as possible just in case Georges was seriously hurt in the fight. A local reporter stated: *The fact that... the Frenchman's chief sparring partner and mentor, should not be with him in the hour of dire need caused no little comment among fans at the ringside who noticed Joe sitting in the crowd.[500]*

When pressed by the reporter I stated: *"I never like to reveal state secrets but*

---

[496] *Melbourne Argus* January 6, 1934.
[497] *Hudson Dispatch* July 4, 1921.
[498] *Hudson Dispatch* July 4, 1921.
[499] *Miami News* February 2, 1952.
[500] *Hudson Dispatch* July 4, 1921.

I'm fit to be tied. He didn't fight like we had planned at all. I told him and pleaded with him right along not to in-fight Dempsey for I foresaw the disaster if such plan of battle were adopted. It was very plain that if Georges had stood off and boxed him he would have beaten him to a pulp. Whoever sent him in to do anything other than to box scientifically sent him to his doom. If I were in his corner we would have never attempted such foolish tactics. I don't think he lost his head because he was apparently as cool and collected when bordering on the verge of defeat as he was when he entered the ring and bowed to the plaudits of his thousands of well-wishers. I'm sorry for him because I not only trained him for this fight, but took the interest in him that a devoted father would to a son. It broke my heart to see him go down, but there is some consolation in knowing that he went down with colors flying.'[501]

The *Philadelphia* Inquirer reported: *Joe Jeannette, a veteran colored heavyweight, who helped Georges Carpentier train for his losing battle with the world champion, Jack Dempsey, in Jersey City last Saturday, partially blames Manager Francois DesCamps for the defeat of the Frenchman. When Carpentier had been counted out by Referee Ertle in the fourth round, Jeanette exclaimed to a prominent fight expert: "I could not tell them anything. They knew it all. I think I could have made Carpentier win or at least stay twelve rounds. It was bad handling all the way."*

Jeannette, a first-class boxer, wasn't invited to act as one of Carpentier's seconds, although he knew more about Dempsey than did DesCamps and the latter's aides. Jeannette didn't sit near the Frenchman's corner. Instead, he saw the fight from the opposite side of the ring, not far from Dempsey's chair.

In the opinion of Jeannette and other competent judges of ring tactics, DesCamps made a fatal mistake when he sent Carpentier out in the first and second rounds with one idea in mind- to get his right hand over to the world champion's jaw.

Had DesCamps ordered Carpentier to stay away as long as possible, instead of carrying the fight to Dempsey immediately after the first gong, it's a reasonably sure thing that the fight would have been prolonged and the Frenchman would have received credit for a much better showing.

Carpentier's footwork created the impression among competent observers that he should have boxed the world champion at long range. At that style of milling it cannot be denied that the Frenchman made Dempsey look comparatively slow and even awkward. But when it came to mixing, Dempsey's superior weight, strength and stamina, coupled with tremendously powerful blows, proved too much for the pugilistic idol of Europe.[502]

On July 14, I drove Georges to the Chelsea Pier in one of my limousines. He left on the steamship *La Savoie* to go back to France. We drove past the Chelsea Village on West 16th Street and the area was aflutter with the tri-colors of France. A large crowd turned out to see Georges off. The day he was leaving also happened to be Bastille Day, the French version of the Fourth of July. On hand and heading back to France with Georges was Francois DesCamps, Paul Journee, Frank Moran, and Jack Curley. After we

[501] *Hudson Dispatch* July 4, 1921.
[502] *Philadelphia Inquirer* July 6, 1921.

shook hands and embraced, Georges handed me a wallet inscribed with the initials "G.C. to J.J." When I opened the wallet, to my surprise, it was filled with gold coins.[503] I tried to thank him, yelling in French to him as he was walking up the gangplank but I stumbled trying to find the right French words to say. Georges had paid me from his own cut. That's the kind of person he was.

On July 9, 1921, Jack Johnson was released from prison. Upon his release Jack was given a hero's parade in Harlem on July 22nd. The *Harrisburg Patriot* described Johnson's arrival: *Jack Johnson arrived in New York today and was welcomed in Harlem with much ado by several thousand Negroes. Two brass bands blared forth as the pugilist stepped from a train from Chicago. A parade was immediately started up Lennox Avenue. Johnson being accompanied by Sam McVey and Joe Jeannette.*[504] When asked of his thoughts on current champion Jack Dempsey, Johnson flashed his gold teeth smile and replied: *"Jack Dempsey? He's just a caretaker champion."*

Dempsey would be offered two hundred thousand dollars to defend his title against the 43-year-old Johnson, but to no one's surprise, Dempsey and his manager Kearns declined the offer.

---

[503] *Chicago Daily Tribune* July 15, 1921.
[504] *Harrisburg Patriot* July 23, 1921.

Jennette family & friends at Atlantic City beach, circa 1915.

Joie & Agnes Jennette.

Ada, Joe, Agnes, & Ada's sister Mary.

Joe & Agnes Jennette.

Agnes, Joie, & friend of Agnes'.

Joe Jennette in Atlantic City.

Agnes Jennette dressed as an Indian.

Agnes & friend at the beach.

Agnes Jennette poses at the beach.

Agnes Jennette on porch of Union City home.

Selection of Joe Jennette's Opponents

Jim Barry

Colin Bell

Jeff Clark

Yg. Peter Jackson

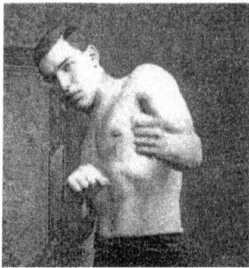
Al Benedict

Jim Coffey

Morris Harris

Black Bill

John Lester Johnson

Cleve Hawkins

Battling Jim Johnson

Al Kubiak

Bartley Madden

Kid Norfolk

Hank Griffin

George Cole

Carpentier & Jennette sparring for Levinsky fight, Summit N.J. circa 1920.

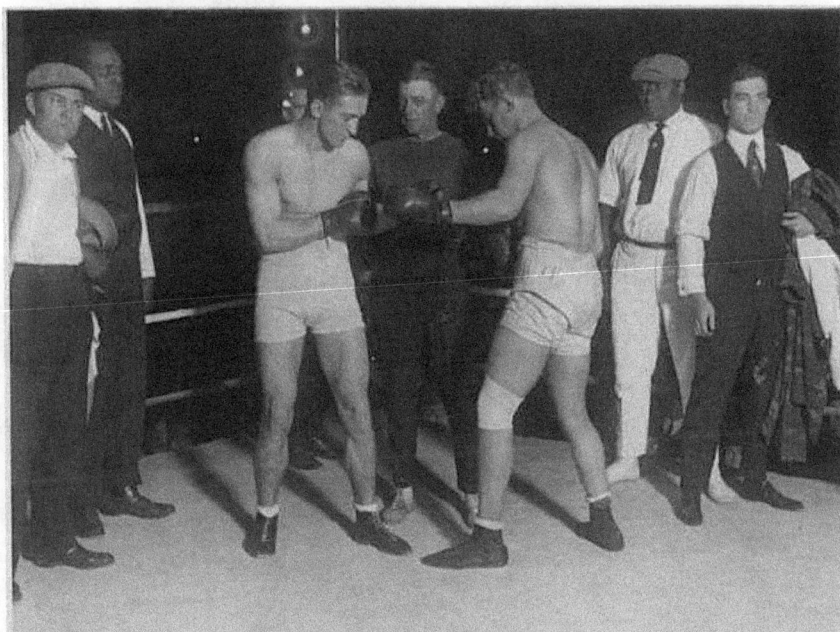

Georges Carpentier (L) versus Battling Levinsky October 12, 1920 at Westside Ballpark, Jersey City, N.J. Trainer Joe Jennette to left of Carpentier standing next to DesCamps. Carpentier won by KO, 4th round.

Georges Carpentier & Joe Jennette sparring Manhasset L.I., circa 1921.

Georges Carpentier training camp, Manhasset L.I. June 16, 1921; Carpentier sitting on
banister in black, Joe Jennette is standing to Carpentier's left, Gus Wilson sitting to
Carpentier's left, Sam McVea is fourth from right, Paul Journee second from right.

Sam McVea, Georges Carpentier, & Joe Jennette
at Manhasset L.I. training camp, June 16, 1921.

Georges Carpentier & Agnes Hartlieb
at Manhasset L.I. training camp.

Georges Carpentier & Babe Ruth at Manhasset L.I. June 28, 1921.

Joe Jennette & Georges Carpentier sparring at Manhasset L.I. June, 1921.

Carpentier & Dempsey shake hands before July 2, 1921 bout.

Georges Carpentier versus Jack Dempsey at Boyles Thirty Acres Jersey City N.J., July 2, 1921.

Georges Carpentier waves as he steams back to France, circa 1921.

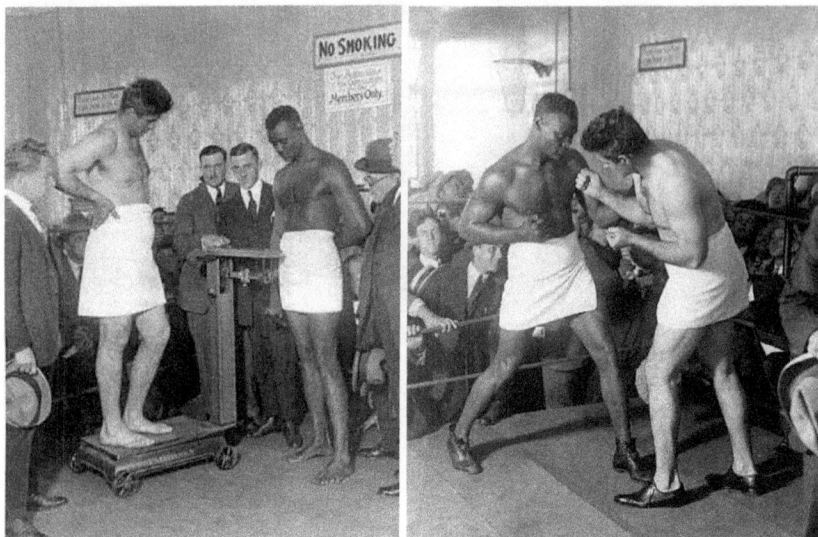

First ever open public boxing weigh-in held at Joe Jennette's boxing gym, West Hoboken, N.J. Joe Jennette is directly behind Firpo in left photo, September 11, 1924. In left photo boxing inspector Cesar Walter is standing behind scale next to Wills.

Marcella Jennette.

Agnes & Joie Jennette swimming in lake.

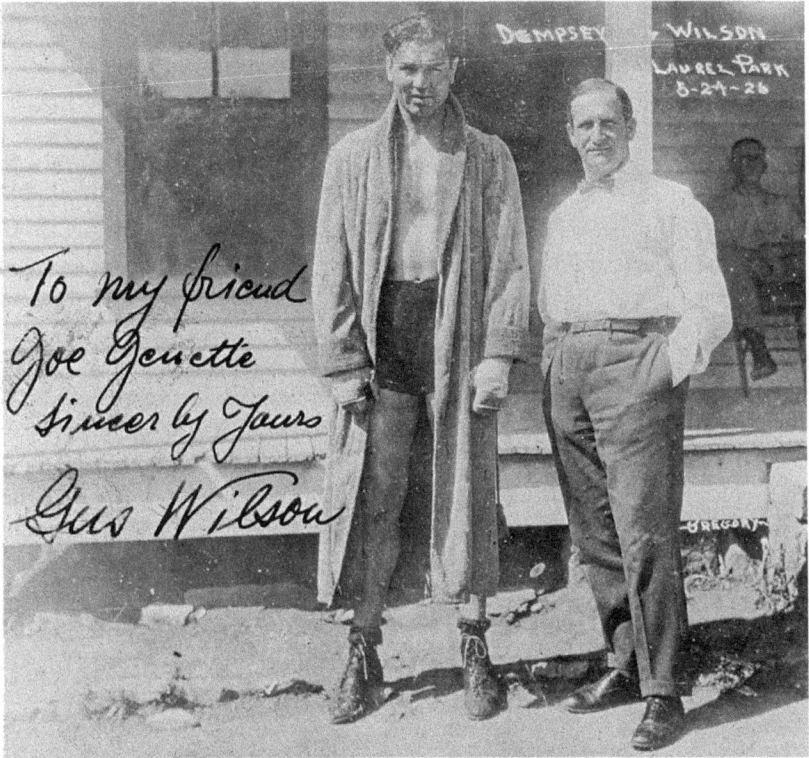

Gus Wilson autograph to Joe Jennette. Jack Dempsey on left.

From L to R; Joe's brother Daniel Jennette, his wife Georgianna, Joe's sister Grace, his daughter Agnes, wife Adelaide, son Joe Jr., unknown child and mother Sabina. Two small children in front left and center unknown. Child on right Agnes von Atzingen, circa 1921.

Chapter 20
Losing McVea and Hanging up the Gloves

Sam McVea was 37-years-old in 1921, but the toll of his many years of ring wars made him appear as though he was in his fifties. His eyebrows were covered with scar tissue that caused him to have a sad looking expression, as his brows drooped in from the outer corners. His speech was difficult to understand and at times it sounded as though he was speaking with marbles in his mouth. Sam was always upbeat, though, talking about the good times in the ring. He had taken up training young boxers. We last faced each other in 1915. He had fought Sam Langford eight times, Harry Wills four times, and Jack Johnson thrice. Sam and I had fought five times, with me winning twice, Sam winning one, and two contests being called draws.

I was preparing for Christmas on the 23rd of December when I learned that Sam had died in St. Claire's hospital just after midnight. He died from pneumonia. Sam was thin, frail, and weak-looking near the end. He had given every last ounce of his soul in his ring battles and he died penniless. I cried on Addie's shoulders when I learned of his passing. There is a certain personal connection that boxers have with each other when they have done battle. Our forty-nine round finish fight in Paris years earlier gave us a bond I will never be able to fully explain.

After Sam's death, I was told that a reporter, Henry Brown, had been visiting Sam just before he went into the hospital. Sam had promised the reporter to show him some keepsakes of his career. Brown was to meet Sam at two o'clock on the 22nd but Sam did not show up. Later that evening, Brown received a message to respond to St. Claire's Hospital. McVea, realizing how ill he was, had checked himself into the hospital. When Brown arrived at St. Claires, Sam apologized to him. *"I couldn't find a thing worth giving you, old man,"* he said. *"Perhaps I lost them,"* he continued, *"the gloves I fought Joe Jeannette with in Paris."*[505] Sam started sweating profusely as he turned his head from side to side. He kept repeating over and over: *"the gloves, the gloves, I can't find the gloves!"*

Sam McVea died that night still searching for the Tunmer gloves that he had so desperately wanted as a keepsake from our epic battle in Paris, twelve years earlier. They were his last remaining vestiges from our great battle. The last words he spoke on this earth were about our finish fight in Paris.

Sam McVea, the California rail splitter, was a talented and courageous boxer. He had the most lethal left hook that I was ever struck with. He was never intimidated by anyone, no matter how big the reputation or physique.

---

[505] *Chicago Defender* March 14, 1931.

Jack Johnson and McVea were close friends. Sam looked up to Jack. Jack heard of McVea's death and that he was to be buried in a potter's field because there wasn't any money for a burial. He wired money to pay for Sam's service. Jack arrived in New York soon after to guarantee the funeral expenses were paid.[506]

Langford loved to clown around with McVea. He would joke about McVea being the ugliest man on earth. Once, Langford handed McVea a key. He told McVea that someone had given him the key and told him if he should ever meet an uglier person than himself he should give that person the key. When Langford met McVea he shouted: *"That's him! Where's my key?"* Langford forced the key into McVea's hand and told him if he ever meets anyone uglier than himself he should give that person the key. Langford said: *"Golly, McVea, you'll have some trouble getting rid of that key."* McVea replied: *"Holy smoke! Mrs. McVea's son Sammy ain't never won any beauty contests. I guess I'll carry that piece to the grave."*[507] Every time Langford saw McVea after that he laughed: *"I know, I know, you still have the key."* A *Los Angeles Times* reporter once said that McVea: *"would scare back the rising moon."*[508] Trevor Wignall called McVea: *"the ugliest man I've ever met."*[509]

Langford was a big joker. Once, a fight club manager asked Sam why he had not brought up the subject of the referee for one of his matches. Sam replied: *"Ah carries mah own referee..."* The club manager said that the club always appointed the referee. Langford then said: *"He goes into the ring with me whenever ah fights. Here he is..."* Langford then lifted his fists and waived them under the nose of the club official.[510] Another time Sam saw one of his opponent's seconds cutting up orange slices for his fighter. Sam asked: *"What you doin' with all them oranges?"* The second replied that his fighter liked to suck on them between rounds. Sam replied: *"Man, you aint gonna' need them oranges."*[511] Sam knocked his orange-loving opponent out in the first round. During another match, a spectator urged Sam's opponent to hit him in the stomach: *"The niggers don't like them down there!"* The fan yelled. Langford yelled back to the fan: *"No they don't, and do you know any man who does?"*[512]

Of course, Langford also took his profession quite seriously. When interviewed by reporter Lud Shahbazian he gave these quotes: *"Always fight a boxer and box a fighter. Y'gotta be able to change and do what the other man don't want you to do. That's what you got to do."* Sam also stated: *"You have to be in condition at all times. You can sweat out the beer and you can sweat out the whiskey.*

506 *Trenton Evening Times* December 28, 1921.
507 *Sam Langford Boxing's Greatest Uncrowned Champion* by Clay Moyle pg. 94.
508 *Champions of the Ring* by Gerald Suster pg. 55.
509 *Ring Noir* by Claude Meunier pg. 30.
510 *The 100 Greatest Boxers of All Time* by Bert Randolph Sugar pg. 35.
511 *The 100 Greatest Boxers of All Time* by Bert Randolph Sugar pg. 35.
512 *Seconds Out* by Fred Dartnell pg. 173.

But you can't sweat out women.[513] From all my bouts with Langford I learned one very important thing: *"you had to be strong enough to keep him away, because if he ever got close, he'd kill you."*[514]

Most people think that boxers are illiterate and uneducated. Sam McVea was the perfect example of how untrue that is. Sam was an accomplished piano player who read sheet music. He also was a singer. He loved the arts and loved to visit museums. McVea and I shared many special times together in San Francisco and France but the most memorable time we spent together was on April 17, 1909, when we showed the boxing world what courageous fighters we both were. Jack Johnson was another example of an intelligent fighter. Although Jack had only a fifth-grade education he taught himself to read French, Italian, and Spanish, and he spoke seven languages, including German, Russian, and Portuguese.[515]

By the time 1922 rolled around, battling the aches and pains of seventeen years in the ring became an everyday challenge. After Sam McVea passed away I had a long talk with Addie about hanging up the gloves. Boxing is a wonderful sport for the young and those that are quick of reflex. But when your reaction time slows up, boxing can be a deadly and unforgiving sport. My knees were always aching from years of running with work boots. My hands were always sore from the fractures, especially my thumbs, which were dislocated several times in my career from body shots that hit opponent's elbow-bones.

One way you can tell a big puncher in boxing is when you shake his hand. If he shakes your hand softly he is usually a big puncher. His hands are fragile from all of the powerful shots that his arms and back deliver through those tiny hand bones.

Back pain is another ailment from which I have been suffering. A boxer must utilize his upper back and swivel on his lower back with his blows when bobbing and weaving. The strain of doing this hundreds of times in a bout and in training leaves its mark. My jaw has been displaced several times in my career. The pain is worse now then when I took the punches. The jaw bone in front of my ear where my jaw connects sometimes sends a sharp pain up the side of my head, followed by a numbing feeling which can cause dizziness. I have to be careful not to chew hard foods like bread, which can aggravate the problem and cause my jaw to click. We fought without protective gear when I boxed, so every time an uppercut hit my jaw there was no cushion between my teeth. The blows would smash the teeth together. Teeth smashing against each other was better, however, than getting caught with your mouth open, which could cause teeth loss, a broken jaw, or a severed tongue.

[513] *Hudson Dispatch* July 7, 1979.
[514] *Hudson Dispatch* July 7, 1979.
[515] *The Big Black Fire* by Robert H. DeCoy pg. 13.

My eardrums were perforated many times during bouts. My hearing comes and goes on occasion, which can cause me to lose my balance. I have had lacerated corneas from glove laces, thumbs, and rosin. A lacerated cornea is one of the most painful injuries. Every time you blink it feels like someone is scraping Emory cloth over your eyeball. Once in a while I will feel a sensation in one or both eyes from the injuries.

I boxed five times in 1919, but I did not box in 1920 or 1921. In February 1922 *The Ring* magazine printed its first issue. The cost of the magazine was twenty cents. The twenty-four page magazine was published by Nat Fleischer. The New York City based publisher started awarding championship belts beginning in 1922. The first recipient of the award was Jack Dempsey.

I was 43-years-old when I fought Harry Gibson in Orange, New Jersey, on June 1, 1922. We boxed to a six round draw. My skills had eroded immensely. I decided to retire permanently. I went home after the fight and cried. It was over. I would never have the opportunity to be heavyweight champion of the world. Over one hundred sixty documented fights with no title shot. Addie consoled me. She told me if I still had the passion for boxing I should become a full-time trainer or referee. I finished my professional career with a respectable official record of 79-9-6 with 66 KO's, 62 no-decisions, and 1 no contest.[516] Unofficially I boxed in well over four hundred contests.

Later in the year I performed an exhibition match at Sam Cohen's Hudson Burlesque Theater in Union Hill. Also performing that night was comedian Gracie Allen. George Burns was in the audience. He had come to watch Allen. After seeing her performance, Burns asked Allen to be his show partner.[517] She agreed. George took Gracie on a date not long after. Their first date was at the Hudson Theater, where I was boxing an exhibition with "Kid" Norfolk. Burns and Allen would go on to become a famous comedy team.

In 1921, I was asked to star in a movie called *Square Joe*. The all-black cast included Marion Moore, John Lester Johnson, Bob Slater, and Frederica Washington. Johnson was a former pro boxer whom I defeated twice. He would go on to play in many movies, including *Mr. Smith Goes to Washington* in 1939. He also played Bumbo in the Our Gang episode *The Kid from Borneo* in 1933. Fredi Washington was a beautiful light-skinned woman who had green eyes and fair skin. She was so light colored that Hollywood studio heads asked her to "pass" as white. They told her they could make her a bigger star than Greta Garbo and Joan Crawford. Fredi refused to disown her heritage. She went on to head the Negro Actors Guild. The following is a newspaper ad on the play: *Square Joe- Six Acts, A dramatic story of a square*

---

[516] International Boxing Hall of Fame
[517] *Gracie A Love Story* by George Burns pg. 40.

fighting champion, who always fought on the level, but is framed by his enemies, and accused of the death of a cop. Lester Johnson, who fights Jennette in this picture, is the only man who ever knocked out Jack Dempsey.

The movie debuted at the Roosevelt Theater in Harlem on June 18, 1922. The *New York Age* reported on the debut of the film: *"Square Joe," featuring Joe Jeannette and Marion Moore, and an all-star cast of colored actors, will have its first showing at the Roosevelt Theater on Sunday, Monday, and Tuesday, June 18, 19, and 20. This picture was taken in Harlem and the entire cast is composed of local actors.*

The story, an exceptionally good one written by J. Harrison Edwards, who also directed the picture, centers about the conviction and imprisonment of an innocent man, charged with shooting a policeman in a raid on a neighborhood gambling house. How the real murderer was captured and finally punished makes a story which thrills and holds the interest of the spectators from beginning to end. The prize fight between the hero and his opponent is done with vivid realism.

Joe Jeannette, the renowned pugilist, who trained Georges Carpentier for his fight with Jack Dempsey last year, takes the part of the innocent man who is convicted and imprisoned for shooting the policeman, and gives an exceptional performance. Ms. Marion Moore is well cast as the beautiful and winsome heroine, who gets the evidence that saves the convicted man... This is the first production of the Colored Feature Photoplay Company, which was organized for the purpose of producing a picture that will appeal to both young and old, and which is without any degrading or repulsive scenes. The management of the Roosevelt feels that in booking this picture they are not only showing the best colored production obtainable, but are also helping to establish a market for colored pictures and by doing so are opening up new opportunities for the race.[518]

On January 7, 1923, Willie Lewis was interviewed by George Underwood. Willie made the following statements: *"There is one man among all those whom I have gone into battle against, or gone into the ring behind, whom above all others I will take off my hat to. That is good old black faced, soft spoken, hard fisted, straight acting Joe Jeanette.*

"I met Joe the other day. I hadn't seen him in several months. He looks just like Uncle Tom. He has no more hair on the top of his head than the old Uncle Ned they used to sing about in the song. You remember how it went: 'There was an old darky, and his name was Uncle Ned. And he died long ago, long ago. He had no wool on the top of his head- the place where the wool ought to grow.'

"Joe Jeanette, ah, there was the fighter for you. There was the man! Joe Jeanette, of all the black faced crew, the whitest man I knew- the whitest man I ever knew, any way you want to take him. I never have met a man who had so many good traits or who inspired greater respect.'[519]

On February 24, 1923, the New York State Athletic Commission honored me by licensing me as the first black professional boxing judge and referee

---

[518] *New York Age* June 17, 1922.
[519] *Evening Telegram* January 7, 1923 pg. 9 Willie Lewis Interview.

in its history.[520] It was a great honor. New Jersey was to follow.

In 1924, Sam Langford had an emergency operation to save his eyesight. He had a detached retina in his only good eye, the right eye. Sam went to a French hospital and a surgeon named Dr. Smith performed a successful operation. Sam's eye troubles began back in 1917, when Fred Fulton landed dozens of hard blows onto both of Sam's eyes. At the end of the sixth round of that contest, both of Sam's eyes were shut, and he lost when the fight was stopped in the seventh round. Sam was hospitalized after the Boston battle. Sam fought on with the damaged eyes for seven more years before getting treatment. After the operation, Sam fought eight more times, and finally hung up the gloves for good on August 2, 1926. In Sam's final bout he was 43-years-old and blind. He needed to use the ropes to find his way around the ring. He was knocked out in the first round of that bout. Sam had said in 1922, when he fought for the Mexican title against "Kid" Savage, that he was completely blind in the left eye and was seeing only shadows in the right eye.

In mid-October 1923 I received a telephone call from Mrs. Lena Skelly, who was an elementary school teacher in Merchantville N.J. Mrs. Skelly explained to me that to help motivate her students she invited successful black American's into her home on Saturday's to speak to them. She said some of her guests included journalist Marcus Garvey, singer Marian Anderson, tap dancer Bill "Bojangles" Robinson, and boxer's Joe Gans and Sam Langford.[521] I told Lena I would help her anyway I could. She asked if I could find the time to come speak to her class. I told her I would be honored to do so. The following Saturday morning I arrived at Mrs. Skelly's home. I was greeted by dozens of nine and ten year old students who anxiously awaited my arrival outside Lena's home.

After I shook hands and hugged the students we made our way into the living room. The children sat on the floor as Lena introduced me as a successful boxer and businessman. After I spoke a little about myself I asked the children if they had any questions. One of the children asked: *"Were you a world champion?"* *"No I wasn't,"* I replied. *"Why not, did you lose?"* another student asked. Lena could see I was struggling with an answer so she jumped in to help me out. *"Mr. Jennette was a very famous boxer who defeated a lot of great fighters. He never had an opportunity to fight for a world championship but he did not let that stop him. He went on to open his own successful limousine business. He also trains young boxers."* One of the students, Arnold Cream, stood up and said: *"You fought my uncle, Jeff Clark."* *"Why yes, I most certainly did,"* I replied. *"Your uncle was a very good boxer."* Arnold continued, *"My uncle told me you beat Jack Johnson, is that true?"* *"Why yes it is, but now Jack and I are very good friends."* The children were very excited. *"Really? Could you ask him to come visit*

[520] *New York Times* February 25, 1923.
[521] *Oklahoma Daily Leader* July 28, 1985.

us?" a student asked. *"Why sure, I will call Mr. Johnson as soon as I get home."*

After I returned home I gave Jack a phone call and asked him if he wouldn't mind visiting Mrs. Skelly's students. Jack said he had a very busy schedule but I refused to take no for an answer. Finally he gave in. Years later Arnold Cream would describe Johnson's visit to a newspaper reporter: *"...it rained very hard. He was supposed to arrive at noon, but we kids all got there early, even though it was raining. He didn't show up until about three. We kids waited in the rain, like drowned rats, for him and he drove up in this fancy Stutz car with two big dogs inside. He drove past us without slowing down and sent mud splashing upon us. The dogs never let us get near him. He had them on a leash and when he got out of the car, he proceeded into the house without ever saying hello or talking to us kids. He ran through us with those dogs, scaring the hell out of us."* It was at this point in his story that tears came to (Arnold's) eyes and rolled down his cheeks. *"That was the day I told myself I would be heavyweight champion of the world one day, and I promised myself that when I became champ I would never do to kids what Johnson did to us."*[522]

Arnold Cream would later become a professional boxer. He would change his name to Joe Walcott, a boxer that he idolized. Arnold would be known to the world as "Jersey" Joe Walcott and he would go on to become heavyweight champion of the world.

On May 9, 1924, Addie and I purchased a plot of land at Angelique Street and Summit Avenue in West Hoboken. We purchased the lot from the Leuly Real Estate Company for nine thousand dollars.[523] I used the gold coins that Carpentier had given me to help pay for the land. I had saved them in the same wallet that he gave me after his fight with Dempsey.

Soon after we purchased the lot, Addie went to visit the site with her sisters Mary and Aloise. One of the neighbors approached her to introduce himself. The neighbor told her he was happy to meet her. He explained that he had heard a rumor that Negroes had purchased the lot and he was glad it was not true. Before Addie could reply, to her surprise, her sister Mary responded: *"My brother-in-law is a Negro and he is a finer man than you will ever be!"* Addie told me the man walked away without saying another word. After our home was built he came over and apologized to us. We became good friends.

We built a two-story home with an attached building. The attached building had a business on the first floor and space for me to have a boxing gym on the second floor. It cost us about thirty thousand dollars to erect the building. I spent my time building up my limousine service. I also had an Esso gas pump installed on the property to sell gasoline. The property was one block north of the old Hudson Consumers Brewery on Angelique Street. Prohibition had forced the brewery to go out of business. It was an

---

[522] *Oklahoma Daily Leader* July 28, 1985, *Daytona Beach Sunday News-Journal* August 1, 1971, *New York Times* July 25, 1985.
[523] *Pittsburgh Courier* May 10, 1924.

exciting time for Addie and I. We built our beautiful dream home from scratch. I installed a swinging saloon-type door from my home to the attached gym. I built a boxing ring one-foot off of the floor and I hung two punching bags and one light speed bag. I also installed a basketball hoop and a handball area for the other two sports I loved so much. I officially opened "Joe Jennette's World of Boxing" in August of 1924.

Addie was always supportive of me, and she wanted me to keep my attachment to the sport I loved. Wives of boxing trainers are sometimes called "boxing widows" because their husbands spend so much time away in the gym or at fights. I never imagined that running a boxing gym would be so much different from being a boxer. When the first boxer I trained made his way into the ring, I was more nervous for him than for any of my own fights. I felt helpless. I couldn't block or deliver blows. I had to sit outside the ring and hope that I trained my fighter well enough.

A major issue I was forced to deal with in running a gym was advice. Every trainer, family member, and boxer had advice for my boxers. I was constantly telling people not to give advice to my fighters. I was working with them on specific strategies, and along came all of these boxing sages who knew what was best for my fighters. It is very disrespectful to both the boxer and the trainer when someone speaks directly to the boxer about training techniques and strategy. Some do it to try to steal fighters, while others do it because they don't know better. Either way, when a boxer is told several different things, it confuses him. The last thing you want is a boxer who enters the ring confused and doubting what he should do. Another issue I had to deal with was people shouting instructions to my boxers during sparring. A boxer must be trained to hear one voice and one voice only, during training and fights. I would tell gym guests time and time again, if you feel the need to say something to my boxer, say it to me. I never had to deal with these issues when I fought. If anyone approached me with advice or offers I cut them right off and said: *"Go speak to my trainer or manager."* I gave the same advice to my fighters.

Another situation I never had to deal with as a fighter that became an issue when running a gym was the "traveling fighter." The traveling fighter is the boxer that moves from gym to gym blaming his poor technical skills and training habits on his trainers. When he loses he blames the trainer and moves to another gym. Every once in a while a kid like this walked into the gym. He could be coming from another gym or just starting out, but you have to identify and get rid of this type of fighter quickly. He will only spread his negativity like cancer in the gym.

Another mistake to avoid is not "cutting" a fighter. "Cutting" is a term used for taking your percentage of the fighters purse for your work with him. You always have to cut the fighter, from his first pro fight. A lot of guys feel bad cutting a fighter's purse when they first turn pro, because the kid isn't making a lot of money. Let me tell you, though, if you don't cut the kid right away you're going to have a big problem cutting him later. Another mistake some trainers make is not putting the kids on paper right away. Signing the kid to a contract helps to prevent any feelings of mistrust. If you tell a kid to sign a contract and he tells you: *"You can trust me, coach, I ain't going nowhere,"* be very wary. Boxers today don't have the loyalty they did when I fought. If your boxer is loyal, he'll sign the contract without thinking. You also have to watch what kind of coaches you bring into the gym. Unfortunately there are many guys out there who claim to be coaches but they are only cheerleaders. Have the new trainer show you what he knows by making him work with the new boxers. Let him prove himself by creating his own fighters. I always tell the promising fighters that everyone has advice for the kids with talent. Everyone wants to train kids who know how to fight already.

I was surprised at how quickly word spread of my gym's opening. Almost immediately the gym had the feel of having been open for years, with pros training side by side with new kids learning the trade. I charged twenty-five cents a day or a couple of dollars a month training dues, but I often overlooked the fees when kids came to me and said they didn't have any money to pay the dues. We were in the middle of the roaring twenties, but still, many families did not have enough money to feed and clothe their children.[524] When I looked into their eyes and saw their desire to box I just couldn't turn them away. It would break my heart. Addie used to complain to me that I was not a good businessman. She was the frugal one not me.[525] I would have spent all the money from my fights quickly if not for Addie.

Georges Carpentier sailed across the ocean and trained in my gym for his July 24, 1924 bout with Gene Tunney, a man who was a very good technical boxer. Tunney won the light heavyweight bout when Georges could not continue at the start of the fifteenth round, after receiving a brutal fourteen round beating.

On August 16, I participated in an exhibition bout to raise money for Sam Langford at the Lafayette Theater. I sparred three rounds with one of my boxing students.[526]

On September 11, 1924, at three p.m., I was honored to hold the weigh-in for the Luis Firpo-Harry Wills bout in my gym. The bout was being held that night at Boyle's Thirty Acres in Jersey City, the same location as the Dempsey-Carpentier fight. Addie came up with the idea to charge an entrance fee to see the weigh-in. I swept the gym clean in preparation for the event. Five hundred people jammed their way into the gym and another four thousand stood outside. Wills showed up early, at two p.m., but Firpo didn't arrive until three-fifteen p.m. by taxi. This was the first open public

---

[524] Interview with Nick Mastorelli, a Jennette gym member, 2011.
[525] Interview with JoAnn Flannery-Mostaccio, Joe Jennette's great-niece.
[526] *Pittsburgh Courier* August 23, 1924.

weigh-in in boxing history. Anyone who wanted to witness the weigh-in could enter. I let as many people in as possible, until we were at capacity. We charged a fifty-cent entrance fee and made over two hundred dollars! That was enough to pay a few installments on my mortgage. Boxing Inspector Cesar Walter and Dr. Mains did the weighing in and examination of the boxers. Firpo tipped the scale at 224 1/4 pounds and Wills weighed in at 217. The police on scene had to escort Firpo by motorcycle from the Plank Road to the gym. When Firpo exited the car, police officers had to form a wedge to get him through the crowd and into the gym.[527] No official verdict was rendered in the fight, as none was permitted under New Jersey ring law. Firpo was knocked down in the second round and nearly every round of the twelve round bout went in favor of Wills.

A boxing reporter approached me at the contest and asked me my thoughts on Jack Johnson's reign as champion. I gave the following statement: *"Jack was powerful and a wonderful boxer, but he didn't believe in overworking or taking chances. If you didn't hurt him, he didn't hurt you. I boxed him nine times and we could have made it nine times more with nobody getting hurt. Jack was afraid of Langford, though. He beat Sam once, when Sam was only a middleweight, but he wouldn't have anything to do with him when Sam got bigger and better."*[528]

I also told the reporter how I felt about Johnson not giving other worthy black boxers, myself included, a shot at the title: *"Jack forgot about his old friends after he became the champion and he drew the color line against his own people."*[529] I was also asked my thoughts on Sam Langford: *"Sam had everything. He was tough, strong, a fine boxer and a dangerous puncher. He could take you out with one punch. You couldn't get careless with him at any time. In all our fights, I got careless only once, and I learned my lesson."*[530]

I was so unimpressed with Firpo's performance against Will's I issued a challenge to the Wild Bull. I began working out daily in my gym in preparation for a possible Firpo bout.[531] Even though I was 45-years-old I felt great. Maybe I needed to get hit in the head to get the "comeback fever" out of my system. I was never taken up on my challenge and never did return to the ring.

[527] *Hudson Dispatch* September 12, 1924.
[528] *The Ring* "Last of the Big Four" September, 1958.
[529] *The Big Book of Boxing* "Joe Jeanette The Great Black Heavyweight Time Forgot" pg. 29.
[530] *The Ring* "Last of the Big Four" September, 1958.
[531] *New York Sun* October 9, 1924.

Chapter 21
The Bulldog of Bergen 1925-1933

On June 1, 1925, the New Jersey State Legislature approved the merger of West Hoboken, the town I lived in, and Union Hill, into one city called Union City. The merger was enacted on January 1, 1926. Most of the street names in both towns were changed due to the merger. The street that I lived on was changed from Angelique Street to 27th Street. The cross street, Summit Avenue, remained the same.

I started training Jack Sharkey in early June, 1925.[532] Jack had a record of 13-5 with 3 knockouts. Jack's real name was Paul Zukauskas. Jack had only won five out of his last nine fights. I was helping him brush up on his boxing skills. On July 2 Jack was scheduled to box four rounds on the Italian Fund Show at the Polo Grounds. Also on the card was Harry Wills taking on Charlie Weinert. We were going to fight the winner of that contest. The fight was cancelled and Sharkey's manager decided to find another trainer. Sharkey would later win the heavyweight championship of the world on June 21, 1932, when he defeated Max Schmeling by split decision.

I ran into Aaron Brown, the "Dixie Kid," in January 1926. The "Kid" had a long career as a boxer. He lost to Sam Langford twice. He fought Willie Lewis three times, winning one, losing one, with one fight ending in a draw. He beat Georges Carpentier by knockout in five rounds in 1911. He was down on his luck and asked me if he could help train fighters in my gym. I agreed to bring him on board. The "Kid" slept in a spare bedroom behind the gym.[533] The "Kid" had taken a lot of punches in his career, and the effects were starting to show. One afternoon, I walked into the gym after working a wedding with my limousine. I heard the Charleston coming from the player piano in the gym. When I stepped into the gymnasium I saw the "Kid" had all of the fighters doing the Charleston![534] I couldn't believe it. I asked the "Kid" what was going on. He told me that the Charleston was a much better exercise than jumping rope. He said that he was going to make all the boxers do the Charleston for twenty minutes instead of skipping rope. After about a month of Charlestoning, the fighters all started complaining that the gym was turning into a dance hall. I had to tell the "Kid" we needed to go back to jumping rope.

Georges Carpentier returned in 1926 for an April 21 bout against Eddie Hoffman. The bout was judged a draw. It was around that time that Georges contemplated retirement. Although he was only 32-years-old, he

---

[532] *New York Sun* June 30, 1925.
[533] *Baltimore Afro-American* January 9, 1926.
[534] *Baltimore Afro-American* February 27, 1926 pg. 8.

had been in many ring wars. He wound up hanging up the gloves for good in September after winning by knockout in Idaho over Rocco Stramaglia.

On April 26, the movie, *Square Joe*, played for a week at the Dixie Theater in Baltimore. At the end of April, a tall lanky 21-year-old light heavyweight walked into my gym. He had just begun his pro career, and his brother Joe, also a fighter, wanted him to train in a professional atmosphere. His name was Jimmy Braddock, and he was a quiet and respectable young man. His record was 1-0-1 when he arrived. His two professional fights gave him some extra money which he used to pay his gym dues. I helped him to snap his jab better in order to set up his powerful right cross.

Jimmy and I would sit and talk after training was completed. He would stare at my old fight photos and newspaper articles. He asked me questions about my career, and why I never fought for the title. I explained the barriers that colored boxers faced inside the ring as well as outside of it. I told him that hopefully in the future, boxers would be judged solely on how they performed in the ring and not by the color of their skin. We both agreed that someday the public would demand to see the best heavyweights in action regardless of their skin color. Unfortunately, now was not yet the time. I described to Jimmy how Jack Johnson, the former heavyweight champ, refused to give other top black boxers of his day a chance at making a decent payday by giving us a title shot. I told him how I was embarrassed by Jack Dempsey in Madison Square Garden when Dempsey refused to box me. Jimmy promised me that if he was ever in the position to give a black boxer a chance at a decent payday he would do so. I wanted to believe him, but I knew all too well that most up-and-coming boxers didn't control their own careers or who they fought.

I told Jimmy there were many great white boxers in my era such as Jim Jeffries, Bob Fitzsimmons, Jim Corbett, Tom Sharkey, and Marvin Hart. I also told him of the great black boxers such as Sam Langford, Sam McVea, and Harry Wills. I told him how I dreamed of a chance at the title. That dream was long gone now.

Jimmy dreamed of someday becoming the light heavyweight champion of the world. Obviously, if you're around the boxing game long enough, nearly every kid that walks into the gym thinks that they are going to be the champ. You just never know when that one in a million boxer will really walk into the gym. Reporter Lud Shahbazian later wrote about Braddock coming to my gym. He said: *The move turned out to be the most important of his (Braddock's) career.*[535]

In early June, 1926, Jimmy was 4-0-1 with 4 knockouts. It was still too early to tell what kind of world-class talent he had, but he could punch like a "mule kick." One late afternoon as Jimmy was weight training, the famous

---

[535] *Relief to Royalty* by Lud 1936 pg. 34.

magician John Scarne walked into the gym. Scarne started performing his card tricks for Jimmy, Bill Daly, Lew Diamond, Pete Reilly, and myself.[536] Daly, Diamond, and Reilly were fight managers who frequented my gym scouting young talent. While we were being entertained, a young manager named Joe Gould walked in. He paid the twenty-five cent, one-day dues for his boxer Harry Galfund to train. Galfund was a top-ranked middleweight, but Gould was trying to sell his contract to some local Hoboken beer barons because Galfund was a difficult fighter to handle. The Brooklyn fighter had a record of 32-12-6. The Hoboken beer barons were to pay twenty-five hundred dollars for the contract but they wanted to see Galfund work out first, to make sure he wasn't damaged goods. Gould and Galfund were to split the money if the deal went through. Galfund had just boxed on the 9th in Bayonne, knocking out Larry Estridge in eight rounds. After watching him hit the bag for a few rounds the potential buyers wanted to see Galfund box.

It was early evening and all of the boxers were gone except Jimmy Braddock. Jimmy was exercising with pulley weights.[537] Gould offered Jimmy five dollars to spar a few rounds with Galfund, which Jimmy readily accepted.[538] Gould didn't tell Braddock who Galfund was because Harry had just knocked out the tough Estridge, 50-9-2, and Gould was afraid that if Braddock knew who he was getting in the ring with he would have backed out. All parties waited as Jimmy and Galfund suited up for sparring. I took out my stop-watch and called time for the sparring to begin. The experienced Galfund rushed across the ring to impress the buyers. Jimmy kept sticking Harry with a long left jab and hard right hands to the body. Daly, Diamond, and Reilly watched with their mouths agape. At the sight of this, a look of panic overcame Joe Gould. He could see the twenty-five hundred dollars slipping right through his hands. Galfund walked straight into a left hand by Jimmy that sent him reeling backwards. Harry smiled to the potential buyers and rushed Jimmy again. He walked into a stiff right that stopped him dead in his tracks.

After the first round, I saw some openings and advised Jimmy how to proceed. In the opposite corner Gould was screaming at Galfund to stop playing and: *"Go in there and kill him. What the hell are you trying to do ruin the sale now?"*[539] Galfund replied: *"Listen Joe, this bird is tough and he hits like a mule. I'm not so sure about flattening him. He may flatten me if I'm not careful."*[540]

For the next two rounds, Jimmy beat Galfund worse than the first. After the sparring, Gould gave Jimmy ten dollars instead of five. After Galfund

[536] *The Odds Against Me* by John Scarne pg. 133.
[537] *New York Sun* December 6, 1928.
[538] *Relief to Royalty* by Lud 1936 pg. 36.
[539] *Relief to Royalty* by Lud 1936 pg. 36.
[540] *New York Sun* December 6, 1928.

and the Hoboken businessmen left, Gould stayed behind to talk to Jimmy, who had returned to working on the pulley weights. I figured Gould had liked what he saw and would try to sign Jimmy. The sparring cost Gould plenty, though, as the Hoboken sportsmen paid only twelve hundred dollars for Galfund's contract after the poor performance. Gould offered Jimmy a management contract. When Gould left the gym, Jimmy told me about the offer. He was ecstatic that Gould was interested in him. For the next two days, all he talked about was one day becoming light heavyweight champion. Jimmy promised to take me along on his road to the championship. I laughed and told him he would first have to make it to fighting ten rounders before having dreams that big. Jimmy asked me what I thought of Gould. I told Jimmy I didn't know much about him but I had heard that he was a front man for Owney "The Killer" Madden, the New York gangster.

Madden, a part-time fight promoter, owned several New York night clubs, including the Cotton Club and Club De Luxe, which he bought from Jack Johnson and turned into a "whites only" club with black entertainers. Madden had a piece of fighters Max Baer and Primo Carnera. Madden promoted fight cards with "Broadway" Bill Duffy and George "Big Frenchie" DeMange. I told Jimmy that having a manager with money and connections was important, but the gangster connections could be dangerous. That Saturday, Gould took over Jimmy's career as Joe Braddock, who didn't have the money or connections, gave up control. Jimmy's mother had to sign the contract because Jimmy was underage.[541] Gould's first order of business was to cut me out as trainer. Gould had his own plans for Jimmy. He brought Doc Robb in as trainer and eventually moved Jimmy's training to New York. Jimmy finished his first year as a pro at 14-0-2. I would have never guessed at that time that Braddock would accomplish what he did. As he climbed the ranks years later, I often wondered if he remembered our gym talks when he was starting out. Gould would later say that meeting Braddock that day in my gym was: "*the luckiest break of my life.*"[542]

On July 9, 1926, I returned to refereeing and I was the third man in the ring for the main event bout at Boyle's Thirty Acres in Jersey City. The lightweight bout was between Bayonne's Johnny Kochansky, 47-7-6, and Seattle's Tod Morgan, 57-6-20. Morgan was the reigning world's champion at junior lightweight. His title was not on the line in this fight. I had heard a lot about Morgan, that he was a very good fighter. The *Los Angeles Times* described the bout: *Tod Morgan can weave a lot of interesting stories about the fourteen fights for which he has made title poundage... One deals with a no-decision bout he had with Johnny Kochansky in Jersey City back in 1926. Joe Jeannette, the old*

---

541 *New York Sun* December 6, 1928.
542 *New York Sun* December 6, 1928.

fighter, was the referee. At the end of the sixth round Jeannette went to Morgan's corner. "Pep it up, kid, you can do better than that," he said.

Morgan figured he was winning handily, but he complied with Jeannette's command in the seventh round and stepped on the gas. He floored Kochansky just before the bell. Much to his amazement, Jeannette again stepped over to his corner between rounds. "That's better, now let's see what you can do next round." Morgan swarmed all over his man in the eighth, but did not floor him. Jeannette 'rode' him again. "Say, what does that guy want?" demanded Tod of his manager, Frank Churchill. "Guess he thinks you're not fighting," said Churchill. "You'll have to knock this guy out."

In the ninth Morgan again floored Kochansky with a left hook and had him reeling at the bell. Over came Jeannette. "This is the last round," he snapped. "Now show me that you're a real champion." Out went Morgan at the start of the round. Boom went a left hook. Down went Kochansky. Up he came at nine, and hung on desperately. Morgan wrestled and tugged, and Kochansky hugged till his head cleared. He raced around the ring with Morgan in pursuit. Finally Morgan cornered him. Boom went another left hook, and Kochansky reeled into the ropes. Morgan looked beseechingly at Jeannette to stop the bout. "Speed it up," snapped Jeannette.

Morgan surged to the attack again, and then providence in the form of a short bell saved a beaten foe. A merciful timekeeper shortened the round to two minutes. Jeannette came to Morgan's dressing room after the fight. "Say kid, you're a real fighter. I heard a lot about you, but I never saw you fight until tonight. You were beating that guy so easily I just wanted to see how much you had on the ball." Morgan says it was his best fight.[543]

It was after the Morgan fight that I realized that my heart and my passion were in fighting and teaching, not refereeing. I stopped refereeing a few years after. That night I also refereed Jimmy Braddock's knockout victory over Walter Westman.

On September 23, 1926, Gene Tunney shocked the boxing world when he moved up in weight and defeated Jack Dempsey to become the new heavyweight champion of the world. Dempsey had been inactive since 1923 and was enjoying all of the financial rewards that being world's champion brought with it. The bout was held in Philadelphia and Tunney gave Dempsey a boxing lesson over ten rounds. Tunney would only defend the title twice, retiring in 1928.

On October 31, 1926, I received terrible news. Harry Houdini died in Detroit, Michigan from peritonitis brought on by a ruptured appendix. Part of his act was letting fans hit him in his stomach to show his superhuman strength. While Harry was in his dressing room reading mail, two fans came into the room. After asking Harry about his ability to withstand body punches, one of the fans, J. Gordon Whitehead, hit Harry in the stomach several times. Harry was sitting in a chair when the young man hit him. He didn't have an opportunity to harden his stomach muscles. Harry's wife

---

[543] *Los Angeles Times* April 4, 1929.

Bess said that Harry had been having stomach pains from appendicitis prior to the stomach blows. Harry was only 52-years-old.

On January 19, 1927, at the Walker A.C. in New York City a benefit boxing show was held for Sam Langford. More than five thousand dollars was raised to help the nearly blind Sam. The *Boston Daily Globe* described Sam's entrance: *Sam was led into the ring on the arm of Joe Jeannette before the final bout, with a shade over his eyes. Sam and Joe, you know, fought 18 times and there was a tear in Jeannette's eye as he stepped forth. Sam was too overcome to make a speech and asked others to thank the packed house for what they had done for him.*[544]

The spring of 1927 brought back memories of my childhood that I thought I would never relive. My daughter Agnes was 18-years-old and had recently started dating. She was very concerned about her looks and she used to cry to Addie that her hair was unmanageable and too curly. She would scream: *"Why can't I have straight hair like everyone else?"* I gave my sister Grace a call and asked her to come over to speak to Agnes. Grace took Agnes into her bedroom and explained to her how she had felt about herself when she was a child: *"I hated my skin color when I was a child because it was different then all the other kids in school."* Agnes replied: *"But Auntie your skin is beautiful."* Grace continued: *"Yes, I know that now, but back when I was young I didn't realize this. Now I see how everyone wants to sit in the sun to tan their skin. Trust me, a lot of girls wish they had your hair. You can leave it curly or you can straighten it out. You are very lucky. That is why you are so special."*

My daughter never complained about her hair again. A few months later, Agnes could not stop talking about a boy named Robert that she wanted Addie and me to meet. This boy, Robert, must have really gotten her attention because she was more concerned about her looks and the way she dressed than ever before. Agnes is a beautiful girl, not just because she is my daughter. She has light brown hair with brown eyes and copper-tone skin that looks like a perfect permanent sun tan.

One night in early June after I had closed up the gym, Agnes brought Robert over to meet us. I was sitting in the living room with Addie having a cup of coffee and Agnes walked in all loud and excited. She entered the living room and smiled at both Addie and I. Right behind her walked in a tall, thin Caucasian boy. He smiled at my wife as Agnes introduced her. Agnes then pointed in my direction and stated: *"This is my dad."*

I could see the look on this boy's face change as his cheeks turned red. He did not say a word but only nodded. He turned back to Agnes and said: *"Nice to meet you all."* There was silence for a few seconds which was broken by Agnes saying: *"We've got to go, Robert's taking me to the movies."* I don't believe Agnes realized the uncomfortable feeling that both her mother and I felt at that moment. A feeling we experienced many times in our life

---

[544] *Boston Daily Globe* January 20, 1927.

together. Needless to say, Robert never returned to our home. Nor did Agnes mention him again.

I remembered when I was a child, my sister Annie had experienced the same rejection. It is the price you must pay when you are a child born of a mixed marriage and your appearance is much more favored to one color than the other. I felt a chill deep inside of me. Several days later, Agnes refused to eat or leave the house. Addie gave me a signal that she would talk to her. I retired to my bedroom and I could hear Agnes crying loudly to her mother: *"Why do I have to live like this? Why can't anyone understand that I have a normal family like everyone else?"*

The memories all flooded back to when I met Addie and we talked about getting married and the consequences that our children would face. Addie always said that love was stronger than hate and that we would get through anything that life threw at us. I thought about those words over and over as tears welled up in my eyes. The tears slowly increased and I buried my head into my pillow so Agnes and Addie would not hear my cries. I was powerless to defend my family from this pain. I felt her pain as though it were my own. I knew that Addie felt the same pain even though she did not show it. It was a pain that she didn't have to experience as a child growing up, but one which she married into.

On another occasion when Agnes brought a Caucasian date home to meet us, the boy looked at me, turned around and walked out.[545] After this incident I decided it was my turn to counsel Agnes. I knocked on her bedroom door but she didn't answer. The door was unlocked so I entered the room. Agnes was lying on her bed with her face buried into her pillow. I sat on her bed and rubbed her back. Agnes turned over and cried: *"I will never bring another boy home again dad. I can't deal with this anymore."* I hugged Agnes tightly. *"I'm so sorry baby girl. I wish there was something I could do to protect you. You are going to meet people in life that are mean and rude and you are going to meet people that will never understand or accept your parent's marriage." "I know daddy."* Agnes replied. *"I love you and mom so much. It's just that sometimes it feels so unfair the way people treat us. Sometimes I feel like giving up."* I looked into Agnes eyes. Her pain was my pain. *"Baby, life is going to bring you many challenges. You will grow as a person from each experience. I wish I could transform your pain to me but unfortunately I cannot. I can tell you one thing though. You are not going to give up. Many years ago your Dad was called a quitter. Do you know what I did? I swore that I would never be called a quitter again. I fought to make people believe in me. You are a Jennette. You're not a quitter. You're a fighter."* We embraced again. As mixed children, Agnes and Joie suffered from not fitting into any peer groups. I am sure they also suffered from terrible racial slurs that they never spoke of.

---

[545] Interview with JoAnn Flannery-Mostaccio Joe Jennette's great-niece.

My limousine business was thriving at this time, and so was my boxing gym. This helped me to block out my personal problems. I had many young, hungry fighters who trained under me. Whenever I saw that a kid wasn't cut out for the sport, I would give him the straight dope. One such kid was Charlie Gellman, or Chuck Halper, his ring name. Charlie came into my gym with Franklin, my brother Marshall's son. Franklin and Charlie had played football together for Emerson High School. Charlie trained hard and gave as good as he got in sparring. Charlie was Jewish and he started boxing to help his family pay for food. His father was a carpenter who struggled to find work. His dad couldn't get into the carpenters' union because of anti-Semitism. When Charlie fought he took a lot of heavy shots and I could tell he had no realistic chance to make a living at the sport. He was very intelligent and was wasting that intelligence in boxing. He was 24-years-old when I handed him the hammer and nail. The hammer and nail represented that it was time to hang the gloves up. I told Charlie: *"Look. You've reached a point where you're a good club fighter and you can become a journeyman fighter. You'll never be a champ because you're not that good."*[546] Charlie appreciated my honesty. He wound up making me very proud. Charlie received a doctorate in business administration and became the director of three New York area hospitals including the Long Island Jewish Hospital. He helped many ex-fighters who had health or financial problems, all free of charge. Charlie, when interviewed years later, commented on my gym: *"Great fighters used to come through that gym. Every once in a while Jack Johnson would come in or Sam Langford. There was Charlie Phil Rosenberg and Jimmy Braddock. Joe Jeannette was my trainer and he told me, 'I'll let you fight up to a point and then I'm going to stop you. You're not going to be a champ. But you are smart enough to make it in the world on your own.' I wasn't going to argue with the great Joe Jeannette. I learned all about his career at the gym. He never got a title shot, but as far as I could tell he wasn't bitter about it. He was a quiet man and didn't talk much about that part of his career."*[547]

On September 12, 1928 I boxed in the first of several exhibition contests against Sam Langford. The exhibitions took place in Nova Scotia over a two week period. Some of the towns we fought in were Kentville, Bridgeton, and Digby. I participated in the exhibitions to help Sam earn some money. The events were sold out and many fans had to be turned away at the doors.[548]

On July 18, 1929, Jimmy Braddock fought for the light heavyweight championship against Tommy Loughran. The fight took place in New York. Loughran outboxed Jimmy and won the decision. Afterwards, when asked about the fight, Jimmy responded: *"Loughran? I didn't see no Loughran."*

---

[546] *When Boxing Was A Jewish Sport* by Allen Bodner pg. 150.
[547] *When Boxing Was A Jewish Sport* by Allen Bodner pg. 150.
[548] *Halifax Herald* September 11 & 14, 1928.

Where was Loughran? I was supposed to fight that guy tonight."[549] Jimmy suffered through tough times after that loss. He was considered washed up by insiders of the fight game. He went back to working on the docks in Hoboken. He would lose nineteen out of his next thirty bouts.

On Tuesday, October 29, 1929, the stock market crashed. The effects of the crash were felt around the world. No one could find work. Millionaires became bankrupt overnight. We were lucky to survive on my savings from the limousine business and what little I made from gym dues. Many of the kids could not afford the twenty-five cent dues during this time and I let them train in the gym for free.[550] Addie would yell at me for being such a poor businessman, but what could I do. The kids just didn't have any money. I could see myself in them.

The situation became so severe that our church, St. Michael's, located on 18th Street, lent out small plots of land on their large property to families in need. The families grew vegetables on the plots.[551] The church also purchased cows and chickens to help supply area residents with eggs and milk. The people in the area were so desperate that they prayed all day in church for relief. The local police had to keep the crowds moving as Novenas were performed by the church every hour. On some days over twenty thousand people flocked to the church to pray for relief. The Novenas were prayed to Saint Gabriel, who is the Patron Saint of Mercy. The Masses were held in Latin. St. Michael's Church was enormous, like a giant canyon, and the priest's voice would echo down from his pulpit like it was a voice from heaven.[552]

My limousine business suffered, as did every other business. First we scoured through the sofa and chairs for any spare change we could find to buy bread or milk. When that ran out there were times when Addie went to the church, where the priests gave her milk and eggs from the cows and chickens that they raised.

Jack Johnson was also feeling the economic slide. He wound up working at Herbert's Museum on 42nd Street in New York City for beer and food money. The museum had a ten-cent entrance fee. Johnson was one of five acts. The other four were a fat lady, a sword swallower, a tattooed man, and the main attraction was fleas. Jack would stand on his stage and answer any questions that the crowd would ask. Some of the questions he was asked were: *Who was the greatest fighter that ever lived? "Jack Johnson." Who was the best man you ever fought? "That's a hard question to answer. I fought and beat so many good ones. But I would have to say Joe Jeannette or Sam McVea."*
What's the most important thing for a fighter to know? "How to hold his feet. His

---

[549] *Champions of the Ring* by Gerald Suster pg.145-46.
[550] Conversation with Nick "Whizzer" Mastorelli; former gym member.
[551] "Lest We Forget" by Reverend Clement W. Buckley, C.P.
[552] "Lest We Forget" by Reverend Clement W. Buckley, C.P.

stance, in other words. Unless he uses his legs properly, he can't possibly be a good fighter. The right foot is the pivot around which all proper boxing maneuvers revolve.[553]

Jack visited me many times while he was living in New York. He would complain about how humiliating it was having to perform in a circus act. Of course, Jack would also bring up how Dan McKetrick beat him out of his purse against Frank Moran. The money was still frozen in a French bank.[554]

In March 1931, an article came out in the *Irish Weekly Times* written by Georges Carpentier. In the article, Georges talked with disdain about the "public policy" in London preventing a mixed bout between Al Brown, the Panamanian Negro, and a white opponent. He explained: *"There is no bar to colour in France. And curiously enough, it was a black boxer who had much to do with popularizing boxing in my country, Joe Jeannette, whom I was pleased to employ as my principal sparring partner during my preparation for my battle with Dempsey. Jeannette was one of the first fighters of renown to invade Paris, and from him did I add considerably to my store of knowledge. Among the many letters that reach me are requests by would-be fighters to give some idea of the different exercises most likely to win success.*

"It was Joe Jeannette who first taught me what an amazing thing training is and the benefits that come from thoroughness. To me he was a revelation. It was more than a year before I fought him (and then he was the winner) when I obtained permission to see him in his gymnasium. At that time I had not even dreamed that I should be thought good enough to fight such a master.

"When I entered his workshop he was walking on his hands. 'For why do you do such a thing?' I inquired. 'Wal, my boy,' he drawled, 'I'll tell you. By turning yourself upside down you so employ and test your brain centres that when you are hit on the jaw your head is the less likely to go spinning round. No man alive can keep his feet if he is hit properly and heavily on the point; but if you will follow this particular exercise, which means that I shoot my feet in the air and walk round on my hands, you become less susceptible to that kind of drunkenness which is induced by a clip on the jaw.'

"Jeannette was no student in the everyday understanding of the term; but of all fighters, white or black, I do not remember one who broke more completely from training methods of a stereotyped kind, and nor one who showed greater intelligence in the practice of physical culture. To win a high position, whether a fight is pending or not, a man must always be in training- mentally and physically... He must always be searching for new ideas. To attempt something new is the surest way to keep fresh both in mind and body and escape a seizure of that most harmful, heart destroying thing called staleness."[555]

In September 1931, a tragedy struck our family that no one could have foreseen. My brother Marshall's son Franklin was a terrific athlete, and he excelled at football. He played for Emerson High School in Union City in 1927. My brother's family moved to West New York in 1928. West New York bordered Union City to the north. Franklin played semi-pro football

---

[553] *The Heavyweight Championship* by Stanley Weston pg. 70.
[554] *The Heavyweight Championship* by Stanley Weston pg. 82.
[555] *Irish Weekly Times* March 31, 1930.

after high school. When he was only 23-years-old he suffered a serious spinal cord injury on the football field that paralyzed him from the neck down. Franklin was rushed to the Jersey City Medical Center, where he lingered for months. On Sunday, November 4, 1931, Franklin died from complications due to his injuries. My entire family was devastated. We had heard many stories from family members of how colored people were not given the same treatment as whites in hospitals, that they were given rooms in basements or by boiler rooms. I would have to say this was not the case with Franklin, as he was given the best treatment possible. The tragedy did have one silver lining. Addie and Katherine finally began talking again after twenty-one years. They sat together watching over Franklin every day, hoping to see some sign that he was going to get better. The mourning of Franklin brought the entire family closer together.

Harry Wills, the great black heavyweight that came after Langford, Johnson, McVea and I, came out with an autobiography. In the book he talked of the old fearsome foursome: *Jack Johnson was the meanest of the lot. Jack was a smart fellow in many ways, but in others he showed no sense at all. He got so stuck on himself he had the idea everyone should fall down and worship him. Johnson always wanted to show off. He wanted to attract attention all the time, and he didn't care much how he did it. As long as he made people talk about him he was happy, and he never stopped to think that he was doing himself more harm than good.*

"If you were a young fellow trying to get along, Johnson would not show you anything. He would rather show you up instead. Take the way he treated me when he was training to fight Jim Flynn at Las Vegas. I was a young fellow then who didn't know much, but anxious to get somewhere.

"Jack Curley, who was promoting the match and looking after Johnson, offered me a job as sparring partner. I was glad to take it because I needed the money and thought I might learn something from the champion. There was a big crowd looking on the day we put on the gloves. From the start, Johnson tried to make me look silly so he could laugh at me in front of the crowd. Remember, at this time, although I was broke, I had something of a reputation, earned through hard fighting, and a boxer's reputation is his only asset. Anyone but Johnson would have thought of that and acted accordingly. All Johnson could think of was his desire to make me look foolish.

"Of course I expected to be hit and hit hard. I would not have minded that, for I was strong and tough, and it is all in the game. But when Johnson stopped straight boxing and tried to make me look bad, I got kind of sore. Johnson was very proud of his strength. He thought there was no one in the ring his equal in that respect or in any other, for that matter. One of his favorite tricks was to grab your arms, waltz you around and laugh, and then suddenly let you go and uppercut you.

"Well, after he tried that on me a few times, laughing and kidding with the crowd at my expense, I decided I'd see which was the stronger of the two. The next time he grabbed my arms to shove them back I set myself and threw him across the ring. That wiped the grin off his face in a hurry, for the crowd began to laugh at him instead of with him, something that makes a big difference to these babies who like to show off. Having lost his goat,

Johnson began to slug. That was playing right into my hands, for I was tougher and a harder hitter. After mixing it for a few moments he began to get the worst of it so he clinched and held on, meanwhile trying to laugh it off.

"That was the only time I boxed with Johnson. He told Curley to pay me off and let me go. He didn't want anyone in his camp he could not handle as he pleased. That incident is typical of Johnson's whole career. He never cared how he hurt other people's feelings as long as he could make himself look big. Showing off was the cause of all his troubles. At the same time I would like to say right here that if Johnson did not act right when he won the title he was made to pay dearly. Although he could have avoided the trouble that came his way, he was not treated fairly, either. I think that all intelligent persons will agree with me that neither Johnson nor the people that undertook to run him out of boxing have any reason to be proud of the way they acted."[556]

Wills spoke of Langford, McVea and I: *"Talk about hitting! Well, I met some hard punchers in my time, and all I can say is that the hardest blows any of them ever landed on me were like a slap in the face from a woman compared with those bone crushing wallops of Langford's. They seemed to go right through you.*

"When Sam hit you in the body you'd kind of look around half expecting to see his glove sticking out of your back. When he hit you on the chin-well, when that happened you didn't think at all until they brought you back to life again.

"Sam McVey was a good fighter, but he was not a good fellow like Jeannette or even Langford. Sam had a mean streak in him and he liked to boast. He used a lot of tricks that were unfair. He also had a left hook that was the best I ever saw. Langford could not whip over that blow with more speed or accuracy and there was plenty of shock to it."[557]

In 1928 a nineteen year old kid named Stanley Poreda walked into the gym. Stanley had come to my gym merely to lose weight. Every time he sparred he told his opponent to take it easy. I never paid any attention to Stanley because I didn't think he was serious about boxing. I'll let Stanley explain how that changed: *"One day I went in to work four rounds with a fellow they called 'the Dutchman,' who was a heavyweight fighter around the small Jersey clubs. We were supposed to take it easy but 'the Dutchman' had different ideas. He belted me all over the place for two rounds. Then I got mad and went after him. I didn't care if he was a fighter, he wasn't going to get away with it. To my surprise, and no doubt to his, I knocked him down several times and finally Jeannette stopped it. That was the first time Jeannette paid any attention to me. 'Boy,' he said, 'If you've got the guts you might be a pretty good fighter.' And he started to show me a few things."[558]*

Stanley, of Jersey City, was six-foot one-inches tall. He became a serious boxing pupil and turned into a decent prospect. Poreda's first boxing match was in early 1928 against Ridgefield's Charlie Wepner. Both fighters turned professional without any amateur fights but Wepner was much more

---

[556] *Baltimore Afro-American* June 13, 1931 pg. 14.
[557] *Baltimore Afro-American* June 13, 1931 pg. 14.
[558] *New York Sun* March 11, 1931.

experienced then Stanley having spent more years in the gym prior to his pro debut.[559] The match was held in Grantwood N.J. Poreda earned a draw and that was something to be proud of in light of his greenness and Wepner's experience.[560] Poreda amassed a professional record of 21-3 with 10 knockouts. He was quickly climbing the ranks and I was hopeful that he might gain a shot at the world title in the near future. On January 15, 1932 Stanley fought club fighter Salvatore Ruggirello. Ruggirello held a 19-23 record and he was supposed to be a relatively safe fight for Stanley. Poreda wound up getting knocked out in the fifth round. He was knocked down a total of five times when referee "Gunboat" Smith decided to call a halt to the contest. Ruggirello had sixteen knockouts going into the bout and Stanley should have taken his power more seriously.

During the bout a reporter spoke with "Babe" Ruth who was ringside for the fight. The "Babe" decided not to keep our training sessions a secret any longer. The following article titled "Close One for Ruth! Babe recalls with shudder he trained for fight with Gunner in 1918" was printed on January 22nd: *Babe Ruth, the man who won't take the $70,000, shuddered along with 10,000 others when Stanley Poreda was knocked out the other night, but not at the same thing. It so happened that Gunboat Smith refereed the match between Poreda and Salvatore Ruggirello, and Joe Jeanette, a great Negro heavyweight of other days, was Poreda's chief second. "Those two guys tried to make a fighter out of me once." Ruth told Artie McGovern. "That is, Jeanette tried to make the fighter and Smith was all set to finish the job, when I was playing with the Red Sox and didn't know any better. Jeanette trained me for two months for a fight with the Gunner, but I got smart at the last minute. What happened to Poreda tonight wouldn't have been a circumstance to what the Gunner would have done to me."*[561]

Although Poreda never won the heavyweight title he would go on to defeat some of the top heavyweights in boxing including Ernie Schaaf, Primo Carnera, and Tommy Loughran. Poreda once remarked: *"Joe Jeannette is a great teacher. If I don't get to the top it will not be… because I haven't been schooled right."*[562]

On July 8, 1932, the gym was abuzz over the rumor that Jimmy Braddock had been arrested for assaulting two police officers. It turned out that the rumor was true. Apparently Jimmy's brother Alfred and two other men tried to gain access to a woman's home at around four in the morning, and when they were denied entry they proceeded to break several windows to her residence. All three men were arrested. When Jimmy found out about the arrest of his brother he went down to the police station to get his brother released. When the police refused to release his brother, Jimmy

---

[559] Conversation with Linda & Chuck Wepner.
[560] *The Arena* August 1931.
[561] Untitled New York Article January 22, 1932.
[562] *New York Sun* March 11, 1931

gave Police Captain Louis Bachmann a broken nose and Patrolman Robert Murphy a black eye. Jimmy was arrested for assault and battery.[563] Braddock had lost four out of his last five bouts leading up to the arrest and his boxing career was in a tailspin, as he went from being a prospect to an opponent.

On March 30, 1933, the town of Union City rededicated Jeanette Street, which was located a block north of my home, in my honor. It was a very proud moment for my family and I.

In May, Dan McKetrick recalled to sports reporter Edward O'Neil a bout between myself and John Lester Johnson: *"Joe loved a bit of rest before an engagement," Dan McKetrick explained, "and this night, in the midst of one of his frequent tours, he was trying to get it, in the cold and drafty dressing room of a sporting club in Utica, N.Y." Joe was fighting John Lester Johnson, who as McKetrick explains, was a "gabby Negro," but a pretty good fighter. He broke a couple of Jack Dempsey's ribs one night.*

"Jeannette had shifted to ring clothes and was stretched out under overcoats and blankets on a rubbing slab, trying to keep warm and get his customary nap at the same time. Johnson was dressing in the next room. John Lester spied Jeannette stretched out, eyes just closing. 'Harya there, Jeannettey,' he called loudly, 'Harya feeling tonight?' Joe came up with a start and looked around. 'All right,' he growled. 'How're you?' And back he laid. 'Oh, I'm fine,' chatted John Lester, dancing around. 'Nice place they got here. I feel grand.'

"Jeannette tossed and tried to get his nap. Johnson talked and talked. 'Boy,' said Johnson, expansively near time for the call for the main bout, 'Ah wish you'd been with me tonight. Ah sure had some of the most delicious fricasseed chicken ah ever did see. Thick gravy. Tender meat. Swellest thing ah ever did taste.'

"Jeannette gave up. Nothing would shut John Lester up. Joe growled, threatened. Johnson never heard. They went into the ring, Jeannette probably the maddest Negro in the world at that moment. The bell rang and Joe stormed from his corner. Savagely, he fainted once, twice, tangled John Lester all up, then smote him the mightiest left hook he ever threw into a man's stomach. He leered down on Johnson's prostrate form, then moved away. Over his shoulder he said just this: 'There's one chicken 'ats fricaseed.'"[564]

---

[563] *Hartford Courant* July 8, 1932.
[564] *Baton Rouge La. Morning Advocate* May 7, 1933.

Joe Jennette's boxing gym circa 1920s, West Hoboken N.J.

Heavyweight contender Stanley Poreda training with "the old master" Joe Jennette, 1929.

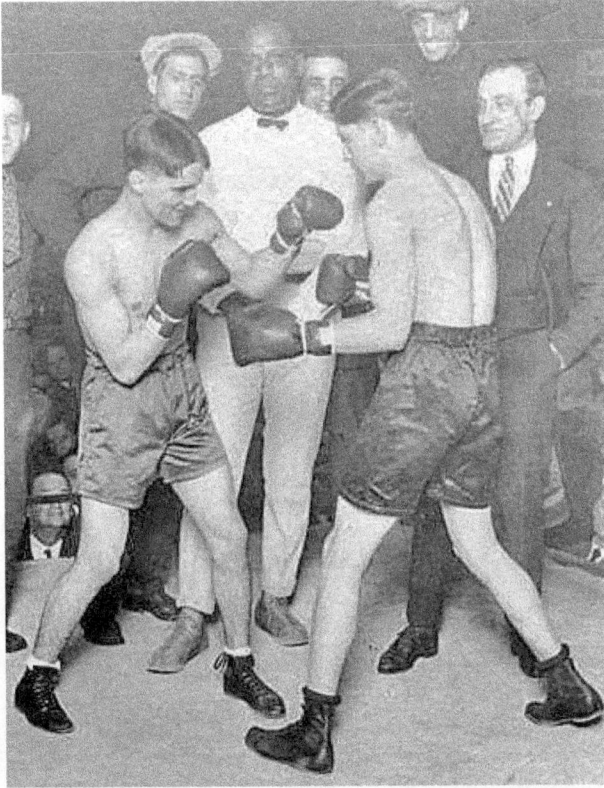

Joe Jennette refereeing a professional boxing contest between
George Woods and Freddie Huber, Jersey City, February 19, 1929.

Interior of Joe Jennette's gym, basketball court on right, circa 1930s.

Joe Jennette poses in his gym with F. Wiedeman.

Joe Jennette's gym. Jennette on right, while F. Wiedeman on left hits a punching bag.

Joe Jennette & his boxing team pose in gym, circa 1930s.

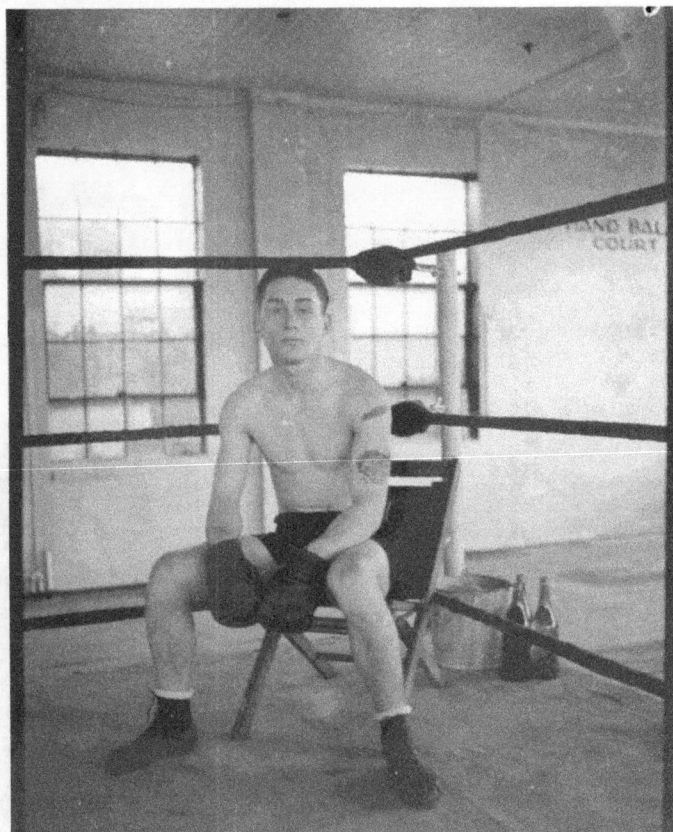

Lightweight Allie Rowan poses in Jennette's gym.
Handball court is on right, circa 1930.

Jennette siblings L to R: Joe, Daniel, Marshall, Agnes, Annie, Grace, Marcella, & mother Sabina, circa 1930.

Jennette family, Standing L to R: Grace, Marshall, Joe, Daniel, & Marcella. Seated L to R: Annie, Agnes, & mother Sabina, circa 1930.

Joe Jennette with mother Sabina.

Unkown, Joe, & Daniel Jennette.

Heavyweight prospect Frank Poreda poses in Jennette's gym.

St. Michael the Archangel Church & Monastery burning on May 31, 1934, Union City N.J.

Firefighters combating St. Michael's fire.

Fighters Trained by Jennette

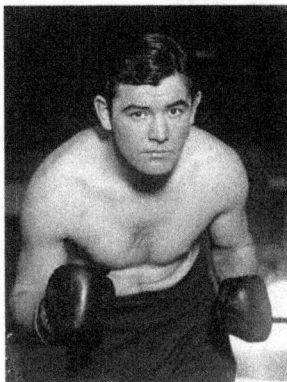

Jimmy Braddock
Heavyweight Champion

Jack Sharkey
Heavyweight Champion

Georges Carpentier
Light-Heavyweight Champion

Jim Stewart
Heavyweight Contender

Stanley Poreda
Heavyweight Contender

Carl Morris
Heavyweight Contender

Tom Kennedy
Heavyweight Contender

Jim Barry
Heavyweight Contender

Bobby Brady
Featherweight Contender

Joe Jennette Trading Cards

Felix Potin

Ogden's

Cope's

Surbrug's

Cohen, Weenen's, & Co.

Will's

Mecca

Philadelphia Caramel Co.

Turkey Red

Chapter 22
The Bulldog and the Brown Bomber 1934-37

On Thursday, May 31, 1934, my Union City neighborhood was shaken by a major fire. The St. Michael's Church and Monastery became engulfed in flames. I was working on one of my limos in the garage when I heard voices screaming in the street. When I stepped out of my garage I saw people staring into the sky. I turned to look up and the sky was covered in thick black and grey smoke. There were people running in all directions. Some people were screaming that members of the German Nazi party had ignited a bomb. In April, local Nazi party sympathizers had marched from Verein Hall, the local German social club, to the steps of city hall in support of Hitler's Nationalist party. It turned out that the fire was accidentally started by construction workers. During the fire, trolley cars and buses were halted or rerouted away from the area. The sounds of the fire trucks' clanging bells and roaring sirens filled the air. A woman ran past me screaming: *"St. Michael's is burning! St. Michael's is burning!"*

St. Michael's was burning? It couldn't be. I ran, along with Addie and hundreds of others to get a closer look. St. Michael's was five blocks south and two block east of our home. When we turned the corner of 22nd street the huge dome roof of the Church was engulfed in flames. We stood and watched as the thick wooden beams cracked and exploded under the pressure of the severe heat. Fire trucks responded from as far away as Manhattan. They raced to the scene by ferry boats and through the Holland Tunnel. An enormous thunderous roar shattered the air as the dome of the roof collapsed into the church.

The attached Monastery was also completely engulfed. The Monastery was built in 1864 and the Church was erected in 1875. Over the years, the Church was the spiritual home to many Catholic immigrants of German, Italian, and Irish descent. My family worshiped at the church since 1906. The Church and its accompanying Monastery were used as a provincial house, seminary, residence for priests and brothers, and a center for Novena devotions. We stood and watched the building burn along with many others, deeply saddened. I thought back to memories of the church and of how it helped us through the depression. Many people wept openly. The Monastery and Church would be rebuilt by area residents. The Monastery's ceilings were originally plastered by the George W. Cranwell contracting firm in 1864. Cranwell's son's George and James regularly utilized my limousine service. The wealthy construction company owners, who also built William Peter's first brewery building, paid me extra to bodyguard them when I was contracted to chauffeur for them.[565]

---

[565] Information from Brian & Margaret Barrett; Cranwell descendants.

On August 26, 1934, I had a full schedule. So busy I forgot it was my birthday. Addie reminded me and she asked me to close the gym early. We were relaxing at home when she walked over to the gym area and called me to help her. She said she spotted a spider and didn't want to touch it. I walked through the archway from the house to the gym. The lights were off. I reached for the switch and a loud roar went up: *"Surprise!"*

Addie had planned a surprise party for my 55th birthday. I hadn't suspected a thing. Among the guests who attended were Sam Cohen, the manager of the Hudson Theater, Allie Ridgeway, George Lynch, Mr. and Mrs. Freddie Huber, "Irish" Bobby Brady, Bill Reppenhagen, Stanley Poreda, my brother Marshall and his wife Katherine, and my children Joie and Agnes. Telegrams were sent by Governor A. Harry Moore and Jersey City Mayor Jim Hague, as well as others. The entertainment was provided by Albert Watchman, Hugo Lehrinda, and Bert Scanlon.[566] It was a wonderful party. I was blessed to have so many friends.

My mother Sabina had moved to Bridgeton, Connecticut along with my brother Daniel and my sister Agnes Jennette-Roberts. My mother died at the age of 81 in 1934. My brothers, my sisters, and I all took the loss very hard. We were a close knit family due to my mother's devoted nurturing.

On September 29, an article was published by Alvin Moses. In the article he quoted the deceased Sam McVea on the state of black fighters in boxing: *"For more than 15 years colored boxers as a group have remained wholly and solely in the coffee and cake class. Leading white boxers have side-tracked them on excuses that failed to make sense, resorting finally to the time worn color line when all other arguments seemed to ground upon the rocks. While I'm not and never will be sponsor of colored fighters meeting each other only, as throughout the South, I do feel that something should be done by our sportsmen, who possess sufficient finance, to eradicate existing conditions in the fight racket for our boys.*

"In the Italian, Jewish and Irish sections, you will find fight clubs and gymnasiums in which 95 percent of the principals are their own race members. Those boys become what promoters style 'club fighters' and graduate from those gyms and fight clubs to 'big time' as a shot in Madison Square Garden is generally termed. I contend that there is no reason under the sun why four or five of our men couldn't float a boxing club that would give weekly employment to hundreds of boys whose present earning capacity is virtually nil.

"The golden age of boxing among our boys would return overnight and a half dozen of our wealthy men with a real voice in boxing activities would gain us the national and local respect we stand so sorely in need of. The amateurs are chock full of good boys who make possible the easy life of certain officials while enriching the treasury of papers like the Daily News, Chicago Tribune, et al. I train any number of these lads and know that sometimes the diamond-studded trinkets they receive for taking a brutal whipping more often than not find their way to the pawn shop. What price glory! Lads of our own flesh

---

[566] *New York Amsterdam News* September 1, 1934.

and blood born here- hundreds from the West Indies and elsewhere- systematically being exploited- and what are we doing about it? Not a darn thing.

"Since retiring from the game I have been associated with the Manhattan Gymnasium in the capacity of instructor. No finer training spot for our boxers can be found in Greater New York. Unless something is done to perk up that beaten complex our fighters have with no other prospect in sight than the opportunity to become human punching bags around training camps, the next quarter century will find scarcely any good boxers of color."[567]

In October 1933, Jimmy Braddock visited me for advice on his right hand. He had broken it several times, most recently in a September 25 no-decision bout. He was afraid to unload it in fights. I told him not to throw the right at all for at least six months. If that meant staying away from the boxing gym so be it. Jimmy followed my advice and stopped boxing. He returned to training in March of 1934 and he felt no pain in his hand when he used it. Jimmy was not training in my gym or in any other gym at the time of his comeback. I didn't know it at the time, but he could not afford to pay the quarter dues, so he was training in a cloak room of a tavern.[568] If he had told me about his financial problems I would have let him train in my gym for free. That was Jimmy. He was a very proud man.

From 1934 to 1935, after his hand healed, Braddock went on an unbelievable winning streak. He knocked off several high ranking contenders when he was supposed to have been washed up. On June 14, Jimmy upset Corn Griffin, knocking him out in three rounds in Queens. He followed the knockout with wins over John Henry Lewis and Art Lasky. The three wins put Jimmy in line for a title shot against Max Baer. On June 13, 1935, Jimmy faced Baer for the heavyweight title in Long Island City, New York. I felt like a part of me was in the ring with Braddock that night. When the fight was over and Jimmy's hand was raised, I jumped out of my ringside seat with joy. Jimmy walked over to where I was seated and shook his glove at me. He didn't have to say a word, as his facial expressions said it all.

Several weeks after his victory, he stopped by my gym to talk. He explained to me the feelings he had felt the night he won the title. He told me that he felt that I was in the ring with him, especially whenever he started doubting himself. I told him to make the most money he could from the title and wear the crown well. I reminded him what a great honor and privilege it was to be champion. I also asked him if he remembered when we spoke years earlier about the "color line." He said he had.

Early in 1934, an amateur light heavyweight fighter named Gene Mickens caught my eye. I took over as his trainer. He lived in nearby Weehawken, NJ, and he reminded me of myself with his speed and power. I worked with

---

[567] *Baltimore Afro-American* September 29, 1934.
[568] *Relief to Royalty* by Lud.

Mickens on his technique. He reeled off six straight wins, including a major upset over favored Sammy Slaughter on May 13, 1935 at Laurel Gardens in Newark, NJ. Mickens, a late substitute, had a record of 6-1 going into the fight. He won an eight round decision over Slaughter, who was a veteran with a record of 42-19-5. I spoke to a U.P. reporter named Jack Cuddy after the Slaughter fight: *"Bout a year now I been makin' Gene Mickens into Joe Jeannette. An las' night Ah knowed Ah had done it. Seemed like when Gene stepped out theah against Slaughter, it was me answering the bell. He looked like Ah used to. Ah teached him and trained him and rubbed him- an' prayed over him. Ah transpired myself right into him. Ah was nevah champion in the old days but Ah'm on mah way to the title now- in Mickens. Light heavy title maybe heavyweight.'*[569]

After my quotes came out in the paper, Addie was furious. I did not speak like the reporter had written. He purposely made it seem like I was uneducated. I was aware that some reporters did this when quoting blacks. Many reporters did it to Jack Johnson. I would never let Cuddy interview me again. Two fights later Mickens would lose a decision to "Two Ton" Tony Galento. Mickens would never reach contender status, ending his career in 1945 with a record of 21-18 with 6 knockouts.

In May 1935, a reporter asked Jack Blackburn, the great old fighter, how his charge Joe Louis would fare against Jack Johnson. Blackburn replied: *"Louis would whip Johnson for sure. We wouldn't be a bit afraid to take him on. Louis reminds me more of Joe Jeannette than any other fighter I ever saw. He's just as cool, just as tough, and can punch like old Joe in his prime.'*[570]

In September 1935, Lud Shahbazian a *Hudson Dispatch* reporter ascended the stairs of my boxing gym to interview me: *'Joe Jeannette, Uncrowned Champ, Noted for Clean Record in Long Ring Career.' The years have rested easily on the shoulders of Joe Jeannette, one of the greatest Hudson County Negro heavyweight boxers and in his prime known as the uncrowned heavyweight champion of the world. He was New Jersey's only serious threat to the heavyweight championship until Jimmy Braddock came along to actually win the title.*

In his gymnasium on Summit Avenue, Union City, the other day Joe was reminiscing about the many fights he had taken part in and of the greats of the ring he met and defeated, both black and white. Joe is not the easiest man to talk to, especially about himself as he is as reluctant to talk of his own prowess in the 'squared circle' now as he was 25 years ago when he used his fists to do his talking and to establish a reputation that made many of the 'white hopes' draw the color line.

Although he fought Sam McVey 49 rounds in Paris in 1909 to emerge the victor when McVey could not come up for the 50th round, he declares the hardest fights he ever had were with Sam Langford, the Boston Tar Baby. Seven times these men met in the ring and Jeannette was the only one to score a knockout. But even that did not establish who was the superior as many boxing experts still are at odds as to which one was the greater.

[569] *Washington Post* May 15, 1935.
[570] *Chicago Defender* May 25, 1935.

The question most lively in the minds of boxing enthusiasts today is what chance Max Baer will have against the newest Negro threat on the boxing horizon, Joe Louis. Joe Jeannette seems to think that Baer will have little if any chance. When questioned as to Louis' ability to take punishment, which sports writers have been striving to have answered for the past year, Joe smiled and said, "I will tell you a story which will and will not answer the question. A few years after I entered the ring I went to Philadelphia in quest of a match with Jack Blackburn, who is as present the trainer of Louis, and who in his prime was one of the cleverest men ever to draw on a glove. The same question was asked about Blackburn then as is asked about Louis today. Can he take it?"

"The match was finally made," continued Jeannette, "although I had yet to gain any recognition as a serious threat to the heavyweight boxing situation. However, a number of New York boxing experts came to Philadelphia several weeks before the bout with one purpose in mind, to find out how Blackburn would stand up under punishment, as they knew I could hit hard enough to put him through the acid test."

"The match never came off, however. Word got to Blackburn's manager that the 'trial horse' could hit like a 'trip hammer' and box as good as Blackburn, so the contest was called off. So you see," said Joe, "they never found out whether or not Blackburn could take it and I think they will never know whether Louis can take it or not, for the simple reason that there is no man clever enough to subject him to any degree of punishment."

To look at Jeannette today one would never think he is a veteran of more than 300 ring battles. There is hardly a scar on his face. He has no cauliflower ears, the trademark of all boxers. His hands are sound, his mind is active and alert- his carriage straight and he is a gentleman in the fullest sense of the word. Wherever Joe Jeannette went he always left a good impression.

Willie Lewis, a famous American boxer of a decade ago, who trained Joe for his famous match with Sam McVey, in a magazine article recently had this to say about Jeannette; "The reason why Louis' name excites me is because the toughest whitest Negro I ever knew was that other Joe, Jeannette. For 15 years I fought them all, big and little black and white. I met over a dozen champions but there is one man among all those whom I have gone into ring battles against or seconded, too, whom above all others, I will take off my hat. That is the good old black-faced, soft spoken, hard fisted, straight-acting Joe Jeannette."

"There never was a fighter who fought more grueling battles, never a ring man who went through a more arduous ring campaign than Joe Jeannette. There never was a fighter who showed more iron endurance, more rawhide stamina and bulldog courage than Joe Jeannette displayed in that great 49 round battle with Sam McVey in Paris. I saw it and I should know, in my mind that was the greatest bout in ring history."

When Joe was in his heyday he was a picture of physical perfection. Colored a dark brown he was as lithe as a cat- was 185 pounds of chained lightning- could hit with the force of a battering ram and could flit about like a lightweight. The only physical defect left by his years of boxing is the loss of his hair. "That was not caused by the onrushing years," said Joe, "but from training too fine for a bout with Georges Carpentier, the Orchid Man, who fell several years later beneath the pounding fists of Jack Dempsey."

In order to get the bout with the Frenchman Joe had to weigh-in within several pounds *of Carpentier and $1,000 forfeit money was posted. Jeannette had to dry out for a week before the bout came off and his only meal each day was three glasses of tomato juice. When he entered the ring he was too finely drawn and his skin dried out, and although badly weakened managed to win the decision easily. However, soon after, his hair began to fall out and in a few months he was almost bald.*

Whenever a Negro fighter enters the ring, for some unknown reason there seems to be a certain amount of humor that arises among the fans. However, Jeannette very seldom gave the fans a chance for a laugh as he was all business and did his work as quickly and with as little pain as possible, both to himself and his opponent. Despite that, Joe was always willing to take a joke and give grounds for one if the occasion arose. At one stage of his career he had a sparring partner by the name of Battling Brooks, a huge Negro, who, according to Joe, did more damage to the air, than to his opponent.

Like all sparring partners Brooks got the idea that he was better than the man he was training with and finally talked himself into believing he was Jeannette's master. Joe did not want to put a short finish to an unpromising career but Brooks kept asking for it by going around telling how he had floored Jeannette in several practice bouts. Joe, realizing Brooks should be taught a lesson, finally agreed to a match in Perth Amboy, the match-maker being Joe McNulty.

The bout was a six round affair and Joe toyed with his bigger opponent for the first three rounds with Brooks beginning to think he was really showing the master up. When the gong sounded for the fourth round Jeannette walked slowly to the center of the ring and offered to shake hands with Brooks. A sickly pallor came over Brooks' face. "This ain't the last round Joe," he said with quaking knees. "It is for you," said Joe. And with that there was a swish of brown leather through the air and Battling Brooks was rendered a minus quantity for the balance of the evening.

Joe has only one regret and that the fact that he was born too soon. "The largest purse I ever collected was $3,000," he said, "and it certainly makes me feel as though I wasted a lot of time when I read about the million dollar gates." But Joe is happy with his wife and family and has one accomplishment which can never be taken away from him- a reputation that many white men would envy, a book of memories and experiences cemented together by years of honest dealing with his fellowmen.[571]

My son Joie had formed a six piece wedding band.[572] Whenever someone called for a wedding limousine we offered the bands services. In October of 1935 Joie brought home Bill Kelly, one of his band members. Agnes and Kelly immediately hit it off and started dating.

In 1936, the City of Union City received a grant from the Federal Works Progress Administration Project, which was awarded as part of President Roosevelt's New Deal. The grant was to build a new stadium on the site of the former Consolidated Brewery. The site was currently being used as a public playground. The location was a block south of my house, spanning Summit Ave. and Hudson Boulevard, between 22nd and 26th Streets. The

[571] *Hudson Dispatch* September 1935.
[572] Interview with Denise Del Priore-Villano.

stadium was going to be modeled after the Coliseum and arenas of Greece. The construction helped to bring much needed employment to the area, adding over one hundred thirty jobs. The site would also house the annual Thanksgiving football game between city rivals Emerson and Union Hill High Schools. They had been playing each other every Thanksgiving Day since 1919. A boxer named Walker Smith would later fight in the stadium as an amateur and a pro. He would be known to the world as "Sugar" Ray Robinson.

On June 19, 1936, Joe Louis met German heavyweight Max Schmeling. I had brought my heavyweight Phil Johnson down to Louis' training camp in Lakewood N.J. to spar with Louis a week before the bout. Jack Johnson had tried to become a part of Louis' camp, but Joe's managers rejected his offer. Johnson was bitter about this. When asked by reporters what he thought of Louis, Johnson stated: *"Louis holds his left too low, is off balance, and does not land properly. He is a mechanical fighter who won't know what to do when his plan of battle is upset. Any fighter who circles to his left can beat him."*[573] Johnson's words were cast aside as bitterness from not being hired to train Louis. However, Jack's words would become prophetic as Max Schmeling exposed Louis' weakness and knocked him out.

On Sunday, October 18, 1936, our son Joie got married. Addie and I were thrilled. We were not able to have a church wedding ourselves so we prepared for our son's wedding like it was the wedding that we never had. Joie was marrying his sweetheart Angelina Rufino, of Hoboken N.J.

Angelina, or Angie, was the oldest of six children. She was born on November 23, 1910. Her brothers' names are Frank, Julius, Salvatore, and Louis. Her sister's name is Frances. Angie's father, Raffaele Rufino, died in 1933 when the truck he was driving fell off of the viaduct leading from Hoboken to Union City. A local newspaper wrote of the incident: *Rufino, west bound on the viaduct had reached the wings and was halted there by a red light. He applied his brakes as the truck began to roll back, but they failed to check the truck, which was rapidly gaining momentum. Rufino apparently tried to stop it by backing into the curb but he miscalculated the half-swing he gave the wheel and the truck's wheels hit the curbing flush, mounted the comparatively slight obstacle offered by the curb and went through the guard rail.*[574] Eyewitnesses stated that it appeared as though Raffaele, after realizing that the truck was going over the side, tried to jump out of the cab but it was too late. He plunged seventy-five feet. Angie's mother, Katherina Guiseppe-Rufino, died within a year of her husband from an illness. Angie struggled to keep her family together after the sudden deaths of her parents.

Angie wanted her brother Frank, who was born a year after Angie, to walk her down the aisle. Frank was against his sister marrying interracially and

---

[573] *Unforgivable Blackness* by Geoffrey Ward pg. 441.
[574] *Jersey Observer* 1933.

fought with her for weeks leading up to the wedding. Frank finally gave in and escorted Angie down the aisle.

The wedding was held at Angie's Church, St. Ann's of Hoboken. The Roman Catholic Church, located at 704 Jefferson Street, opened its doors in 1906. The church had sponsored the popular St. Anne's feast annually since 1910. Members of the church also tried to talk Angie out of the marriage. I had my employees drive both families to the church in my limousines. When we arrived at the church we noticed a line of approximately twelve women standing at both sides of the stairs leading to the entrance of the church. We were so excited and thrilled. It looked as though the women were conducting some type of Italian marriage ritual.

We exited the limousines and began our walk into the church. It appeared strange to me that all the women were dressed in black gowns with matching veils. As we passed, the women began spitting on the floor in front and behind us.[575] It was a terrible situation. Addie held her composure for our son's sake though there were tears in her eyes. My son and his bride held their heads up high and ignored the women. Other invited guests were not so restrained, though, and the police had to be called to remove the protesters. Addie's sister Mary screamed at the women: *"You call yourselves Christians. You're nothing but hypocrites. You're spitting on your own souls!"* Angie's brother Frank, to everyone's surprise, was more visibly upset with the protesters then anyone. He cursed and screamed at the women until they were escorted away by the police. Frank and Joie would become close friends after the incident.

We later discovered that the women had organized to protest the interracial marriage of my son and his bride. I thought back to France in 1909 when I was sparring in a courtyard with Marc Gaucher. There was a large crowd watching. When I started getting the better of Gaucher the women in the crowd started spitting and cursing at me.[576] Joie and Angie acted as though the incident didn't affect them but I'm sure it did. They changed their church from St. Anne's to St. Lawrence R.C. Church in Weehawken.

Two years and nine days after winning the heavyweight championship, Jimmy Braddock defended it. The top contender was Max Schmeling from Germany. Schmeling had defeated Joe Louis by stunning knockout a year earlier. Nazi Germany had offered Jimmy a large sum of money to box Max in Germany. Jimmy turned the offer down. Instead, he was the first white boxer in twenty-two years to give a black heavyweight a shot at the world's title. I was very proud of Jimmy. He never did forget our conversations. There were several reasons behind Jimmy's decision to fight Louis instead of Schmeling. Jimmy did not want the heavyweight title to leave the United

---

[575] Interview with Denise Del Priore-Villano.
[576] Information written on a photo of Jennette sparring in France.

States. His favorite fighter was John L. Sullivan, and like the great John L., Jimmy wanted to lose his title to an American. Joe Gould struck a deal whereby Jimmy would get ten percent of the heavyweight champion's future earnings for ten years if he lost the bout. Jimmy also wanted to give a black man a shot at the title. He knew from all our conversations how much suffering I had gone through not getting my title shot.

The local gyms were full of talk about the upcoming battle between Jimmy Braddock and Joe Louis. Was Louis the real thing? Was Braddock washed up? In June, I was working with one of my boxers, heavyweight Phil Johnson. Phil had sparred with Louis for his match with Max Baer. I was working with Phil on his footwork when Addie came upstairs and told me someone wanted to talk to me. I told her I was busy training Phil. Phil Johnson's son Harold would follow his father's footsteps and also become a boxer. Addie left. When she came back she said the gentleman said he would wait until I was done. I looked out of the window and saw a brand new sparkling white four-door Packard touring sedan parked outside, with several well-dressed men standing around it. My curiosity was aroused.

I told Phil to keep hitting the bag and work on shifting his weight with his punches. I proceeded downstairs to see who these well-dressed men were, and more importantly, what they wanted. I stepped out onto the street and I immediately recognized Jack Blackburn. We hugged each other and exchanged pleasantries. Blackburn said that Joe Louis wanted to speak with me. Blackburn called out: *"Hey Chappie, come over here."* Louis walked towards me from the car. I was caught completely off guard. This was an awkward moment. Jimmy's opponent was at my gym. After collecting myself I invited Louis and Blackburn into my home.

I led them into the kitchen, where we drank coffee and ate Addie's homemade crumb cake. We sat and talked. Louis said he had heard stories about my career from Blackburn. I pulled my scrapbook from the bookcase and Louis looked it over while we talked. He told me he felt awful that I never received a shot at the heavyweight title. I laughed and told him I wish I could have had a shot at some of the money the young boxers were now making.

Louis told me he was aware of what I went through as a fighter and he said that if he won the title he would do his best to make me and all colored boxers proud. I told him I was impressed that he understood the importance of the title. I was most impressed that he understood the importance of the title to our race and how the champion's actions while wearing the crown affected all of black America. Louis told me he had heard people say that if I had won the title before Johnson everything would have been different. We would not have suffered all the setbacks we did. I told him maybe Jack did not act the best as champion, but he was in a very difficult situation and it is not easy to judge someone when we are not in their shoes. I almost couldn't believe I was defending Jack Johnson. I guess the years had softened me up.

Blackburn broke into the conversation and said he told Chappie how much Louis reminded him of me when I was boxing. I thanked Jack for his compliment. I told Louis to make sure he saved his money, and I reminded him that his actions should he win would be representing much more than himself. I reminded Louis why we had to wait so long to get another title shot. He thanked me again and then he asked me about Braddock. I told him Jimmy was a nice, hard-working boy and a good family man. Louis said that if he won he wanted me to give Braddock a message. He wanted me to tell him "thank you" for the opportunity. After we finished talking, Louis stood up and turned to leave. He turned back to me with a smile and said that he had one more question. He wanted to know who I thought would win and who I was rooting for. I laughed at him and told him that after competing in close to four hundred boxing matches, I can honestly say I want the winner to be the one who trains and fights the hardest for the title. As for whom I am rooting for, I told him I was rooting for both boxers to leave the ring as healthy as they enter it. The only thing you can do, I told Louis, is your best, and I believe that if you do that, good things will follow. Louis smiled at me and said: *"You should have been a politician, Mr. Jennette."*

On June 22, 1937, in Chicago's Comiskey Park, Joe Louis and Jimmy Braddock fought for the title. Jimmy knocked Louis down in the first round with his vaunted right hand. Unfortunately for Jimmy, Louis got back up. For the next eight rounds Louis gave Jimmy a terrible beating. Jimmy needed between thirty and fifty stitches to close up all the cuts on his face. The end came in the eighth round, when Louis knocked Jimmy out. Jimmy could have quit on his stool and no one would have questioned him. When Gould asked Jimmy between the seventh and eighth rounds if he wanted the fight stopped, Jimmy responded: *"I want to go out like a champion. I want to be carried out."*

Louis became the second black heavyweight champion in boxing history. After the fight, Jimmy stated to a reporter: *"I was nothing and then I was heavy weight champion of the world. All I had was guts and gumption, a spot of skill, some craft and an ability to take punishment. If I did it, you have a chance and you can do it too."*[577] Louis and Braddock maintained a close relationship after the match.

In 1937, Addie's sister Mary and her husband Oswald lost their farm in North Bergen. It was a combination of the high taxes and having to purchase new pasteurizing equipment that caused the loss. The family moved upstate to Pleasant Valley, New York, where they opened another farm with hogs and cows. We visited them several times a year.

I enjoyed going up to the farm. Addie's nieces and nephews would come around me to play. I was known as the "tickler." I would tell the kids to

---

[577] *Champions of the Ring* by Gerald Suster pgs. 148-9.

look up at the birdie and then tickle them under their chins. Addie was called *Tante* (German for Aunt) and I was called *Unkie*. The kids, Oswald, Joseph, and Agnes, never noticed that their Aunt and Uncle were from a mixed marriage. To them we were just *Tante* and *Unkie*. In the late 1940s, I would play the same tickling game with Agnes Hartlieb-Flannery's daughter's JoAnn, Mary, and Suzie. The girls loved to play with my stumped finger.[578]

Near the end of 1937 my daughter Agnes and Bill Kelly decided to marry. Agnes and Bill did not want a repeat of what occurred at Joie's wedding so they decided to get married at city hall. After the wedding we held a small reception at the Top Hat restaurant on Hudson Boulevard. Ada and I were thrilled for Agnes. Not long after the marriage Agnes and Bill started experiencing difficulties due to Bill's drinking and staying out late. Agnes eventually decided to leave Bill. She moved to Florida to start a new life. Ada and I did not want her to move away but we understood she needed a fresh start.

---

[578] Interview with JoAnn Flannery-Mostaccio Joe Jennette's great-niece.

Joe Jennette Jr. & Angelina Rufino-Jennette on their wedding day, October 18, 1936.

L to R: Vincent James Del Priore, Unknown female, Joe Jennette Jr., Angelina Jennette, Julius Rufino, Unknown female, Unknown male, Unknown female, & Samuel Rufino. Joe & Angelina Jennette's wedding photo October 18, 1936.

St. Anne's Church, 704 Jefferson Street, Hoboken N.J. Front steps where Joe Jr. & Angelina Jennette were confronted by parishioners opposed to interracial marriage.

Agnes Jennette relaxing at the beach, circa 1930s.

From L to R; Gus Lesnevich, Johnny Dundee, Joe Jennette, Harry Balogh, James Braddock, & Sam Taub at Our Lady of Victories Church amateur boxing show, Jersey City N.J., circa 1943.

Amateur boxing show at St. Peter & Paul's in Hoboken N.J. 1938, L to R; Joe Shugrue, Joe Jennette, Frankie Burns, Frankie Nelson, Jimmy Braddock, and Gus Lesnevich.

Jimmy Braddock's testimonial dinner at the Top Hat in Union City February 24, 1938; seated from left Mae Braddock, Jimmy Braddock, Joe Louis & Marva Louis. Standing L to R; Joe Jennette, Frankie Burns, & Joe Shugrue.

Joe Jennette leaning on one of his limousines outside of his gym with
unknown Naval officer, circa 1940s.

Joe Jennette Junior in Navy, 1943.

Joe Jennette with niece Agnes Von Atzingen, JoAnn Mostaccio's mother.

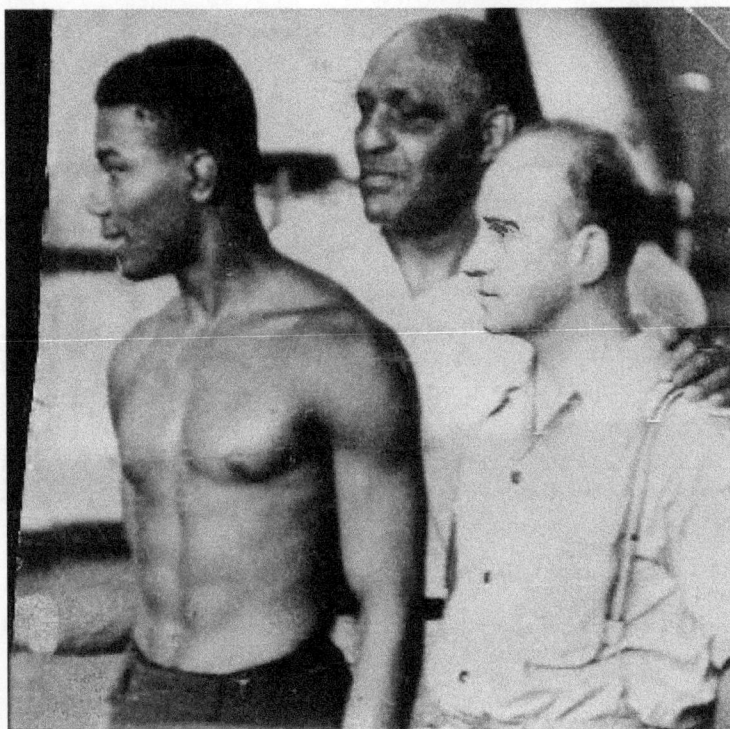

Joe Jennette working corner of an amateur prospect, circa 1940s.

Chapter 23
1938 to 1958

On January 30, 1938, nine days after defeating Britain's Tommy Farr by ten round decision, Jimmy Braddock announced his retirement from boxing.[579] On February 24th at the Top Hat Hotel and Restaurant in Union City a testimonial dinner was held in Jimmy's honor. Three years prior, at the same restaurant, Jimmy was honored for winning the heavyweight championship of the world. Five hundred guests were on hand to honor Braddock. The guests included myself along with Jimmy's wife Mae and his manager Joe Gould. Also in attendance were Lew Diamond, Tony Galento, Joe Shugrue, Frankie Burns, and Tommy Farr. Heavyweight champion Joe Louis and his wife Marva stopped by to join in the celebration; they were accompanied by his managers, Julian Black and John Roxborough, as well as his trainer Joe Blackburn.[580] Louis had defended his title just one day prior with a third round knockout over Nathan Mann at Madison Square Garden. In April Jimmy opened a restaurant at 49th Street and 7th Avenue in New York City called Inn Braddock's Corner.[581]

In 1935 Nat Fleischer, editor-in-chief of *The Ring* magazine, wrote the first of a four book series on black boxers. The series was called *Black Dynamite*. The fourth book in the series focused on myself along with Jack Johnson, Sam Langford, and Sam McVea. Mr. Fleischer wrote me in April 1938 asking for information, photographs, or newspaper clippings on my boxing career for his book. Unfortunately, I did not have much info to send him. My most prized possessions were my scrapbook of newspaper clippings and photographs from my fighting days and the trophies and medals I had won. I was not going to part with those possessions for anyone. I did have a wrist watch I was presented with after a fight years earlier that I sent him. I knew that Nat collected watches.

I never fought amateur. When I go to amateur shows I enjoy watching the boxers competing solely for the pride of victory. When I started boxing, I wanted to prove to myself that I was tough enough to compete in boxing. After conquering that step, I wanted to prove to the boxing world that I could climb to the elite level of the sport. After years of boxing for the coin, however, we all fall victim to the business side of the sport. The passion starts to fade and the primary goal becomes the size of the purse. Watching the pure passion and love of the sport that exudes from competing amateurs brought back feelings I hadn't felt in years. It was exhilarating.

It is hard to believe that so many years have passed since my fighting days.

---

[579] *Omaha World Herald* February 2, 1938.
[580] *Hudson Dispatch* February 25-26, 1938.
[581] *Trenton Evening Times* April 12, 1938.

Most of the current boxers have never heard of me, besides the fact that I run a boxing gym. Running the gym is getting more and more difficult, everyday going through the motions. I had given up on finding a boxer with the talent to reach the top of the heavyweight division. Every kid who walked into the gym had the same sparkling energy to be a champion. Unfortunately that spark faded quickly when they put on the mittens and were rewarded with their first headache. It is almost comical to see a kid walk into the gym with the confidence to say: *I am going to be champion of the world.* Only to have that cockiness sucked out of him in a few weeks, either by the punches to the head or the rigorous training regimen.

On December 8, 1941, the United States officially entered World War II after Japan bombed Pearl Harbor. Soon after, my son Joie enlisted in the Navy.

In early January 1942 I was interviewed on NBC radio. Alvin Moses wrote an article on the interview: *There was something hauntingly proper about Nat Fleischer, editor of The Ring boxing magazine, chiding ring-warrior Joe Jeanette for a display of modesty during a recent radio chat in a New York studio. With few exceptions, the truly great Negro figures in sports have felt the urge to be bashful about their red-blooded achievements when their interrogators were white. No doubt this is due largely to the fact that they so seldom receive invitation to chat informally over a hookup as wide in its jurisdiction as NBC where Sam Taub and Bill Stern officiate for the Adam Hat cooperation. Sam Taub, colorful Jewish fight-announcer, invited Jeanette to appear on the program with other leading figures in the boxing firmament, and Sam is enough to make… Beatrice Kay (Gay 90's fame), blush like a schoolgirl. Taub has one distinction which we say without malice rates him on parity with still another member of his racial group, Harry Balogh, in this connection. Both are "million-a-minute" word specialists. They would count that evening lost which saw them dispense a subject with a few hundred pointed words when they could easily conjure up a few thousand unnecessary split-infinitives.*

Such was the odd position of Hoboken Joe Jeanette, called the "iron man" by a contemporary writer of forty years ago when he was a holy terror with boxing gloves on. Without his gloves, the roominess of an 18 foot ring, and the traditional referee to break him out of wordy clinches or bromides, with loquacious Samuel, perhaps modesty was the order of the day.

Taub asked Joe to tell him the details of the fight with McVey that went 49 rounds before Jeanette was declared the winner. "How many times were you knocked down, Joe?" queried Sam. "Well," drawled the brown brawler, "my manager Dan McKetrick told me I was on the floor 27 times." "How many times did you put Sam McVey on the deck?" persisted Taub. "Never knocked him down once," answered Jeanette. Back and forth flowed the conversation, Jeanette venturing to say that the writing experts were in error in claiming the fight went only 49 rounds. "McVey came out to face me at the start of the 50th round," said Joe, "and then collapsed on his face. This was a finish fight, you know, but had it been scheduled for a 40-round affair, like a lot of fights were signed for in those days, McVey would have been way out in front on points scored."

Then up stepped the bookish Fleischer, "Joe, I want to set you right on something you failed to tell the radio audience, and my friend Sam Taub. If you'll drop into my office one morning next week, I will show you a clipping from the Paris Herald, as well as the Times, which claims you knocked down McVey eleven times, and that you were floored by McVey 31 times." Without benefit of television, one could imagine the look of amazement on Jeanette's face as he seemed to grunt, ugh. Doubtless that throaty stoical grunt represented the Indian part of Joe for numerous white writers down through the years have set up the claim that his complexion and features were as much that of the American Indian as those of Joe Gans were Arabic, tsk, tsk, tsk.

Jeanette wouldn't prosecute that point further. Despite the weight of this seemingly irrefutable evidence by Fleischer, the brave Negro heavyweight stuck to his belief that he never once knocked McVey off his feet. Most reliable sports authorities will take issue with Fleischer on this point, as well as the total number of knockdowns scored by Jeanette's Negro opponent, who hailed from Oxnard, Cal. Our research on the matter reveals a report of the fight carried in an issue of the Police Gazette, (Fleischer's once identified with sporting manual), under date of July 1935. Let us see together, dear readers, just what actually was written about this imbroglio that was contested on April 17, 1909... "One of the most terrific battles that ever took place in the history of pugilism was the one between Joe Jeanette and Sam McVey. The battle was to a finish and never were two fighters put to a severer test, and never did fighters show greater courage and stamina than did McVey and Jeanette in this grueling battle which went 49 rounds before a winner was decided."

Skipping over a lot of incidents which space does not permit us to record, we come to one part of the Taub-Fleischer-Jeanette interview which appears to sustain the giant Negro's contention somewhat. The writer continues, "McVey appeared to have every physical advantage over Jeanette, but in one important particular: McVey did not overmatch Jeanette in courage. Twenty-six times during the 49 rounds of the fight, McVey sent Jeanette to the floor with smashes that would have put away any ordinary fighter."

And then speaking of the 49th round finish the writer graphically writes: "about half-way in the 49th round Jeanette got a left drive into the stomach of McVey, and like a flash, crossed his right over to the point of McVey's chin. Down went the powerful McVey and he was unable to rise before the fatal 10 seconds were counted over him. Toward the end of the year, McVey tried to wipe out the defeat, but not in a finish bout. Instead, the pair battled to a 30-round draw." No mention was made of Jeanette scoring a single knockdown over McVey- but we do not doubt that he did- at least once, for he could hit with the best when the spirit moved him.[582]

On May 21, 1942 at the Manhattan Odd Fellows Temple, the Reveille Club of New York held a testimonial dinner for heavyweight champion Joe Louis. Louis was serving as a private in the Army. I was asked to speak at the event. I praised Louis for the way that he carried himself inside, as well as outside of the ring. Louis had just lost his long-time trainer, Jack

---

[582] *Atlanta Daily World* January 15, 1942

Blackburn, who died on April 24. I turned to Louis and told him that he made all of us proud, especially "Chappie." Louis and Blackburn had affectionately called each other "Chappie" when they were together. The Reveille Club was started by twenty-three Negro veterans of World War I. It was the first testimonial dinner accorded Louis by members of his own race.[583]

In May 1945, Jack Johnson was interviewed on interracial marriage. In the article titled "Does Interracial Marriage Succeed," Johnson stated: *"Some folks say that an interracial couple can't be happy after they are married, that they come from different backgrounds and will not be able to get along. But I can honestly say that I have been happily married to my present wife for twenty years. And all the people I know who have married into the other races seem to be happy together. Maybe it's because interracial love has to be twice as strong before a couple will say 'I do.' They know that when they do say 'I do,' they really have to mean it; that they face a fight from the start with only their love to hold them together. I know what that means because I feel that I would fight the world for my wife, and I am sure that my wife would do the same for me. To any couples like my wife and me, I say: As long as you are together and in love, then the world and life are happy for you. Today the world no longer demands the high price I paid for getting married to the woman I love so much.'*[584]

On August 14, 1945, World War II officially ended with the surrender of Japan. The day was called "The Victory over Japan Day," or "V-J Day." Everyone was so happy that the war was finally over. Joie would finally be coming home. Some people walked up the stone steps of St. Michaels' church, which was rebuilt after the fire, on their knees as a sign of thanks. All during the war, busloads of worshipers arrived daily at the church to partake in Novenas to pray for an end to the fighting.

I snapped out of my daydream and back into reality. It is November 27, 1945, and I am sitting in the dressing room at the Henry Hudson Hotel, waiting to spar my old nemesis Jack Johnson. If only someone could have pulled this off thirty-five years ago, I might not be just letters in a name on the great Jack Johnson's fight ledger. Most boxing history books do not even mention Sam Langford, Sam McVea, or myself, because we never became world champions. The truth is we never had the opportunity to be world champions.

I have to admit I admired the way Jack would not be denied his title opportunity. I also feel sad that he did not use this great opportunity to give other colored boxers the same opportunity. Yes, it is true that champions try to take matches with the least risk and the highest reward, but it is also true that Johnson once stated: *"I want to be the only black heavyweight champion."*

I have to wonder if some of his antics were purposely committed to prevent other blacks from attaining the title, or if they were just ploys to

[583] *Canton Repository* May 22, 1942
[584] *Negro Digest* May 1945; "Does Interracial Marriage Succeed."

help him find the easiest fights possible for the most money. My relationship with Jack was a strange one over the years. We were friends and fierce competitors all at once. We were both from the same world of professional boxing. We both shared the personal pain of racism directed at us for our color and for our choice of wives. Sam Langford and I celebrated with Jack in New York City after he won the heavyweight title. We felt as though it was a victory and an opportunity for all of us.

Our November 1945 exhibition started out with photo shots of Jack and I, along with the promoter and the referee Harry Wills. Wills was another great black boxer who never received a title shot. Some of the names in attendance included Damon Runyon, Frankie Genaro, Joe DiMaggio, Johnny Dundee, Joe Batty, Mickey Walker, "Knockout" Brown, "Soldier" Bartfield, "Young" Otto, Abe Attell and hundreds of others. After the photos, Jack and I clowned our way through the first round, as those in attendance laughed and cheered us on. When the bell rang for the second round we started off at the same pace until Jack unloaded with a hard straight right hand that I barely slipped. I stepped in with a heavy left hook to the body followed by a right to the head. Jack stepped in with a left hook-right cross combo. The crowd fell silent as they got a glimpse of the fighting spirit of two legendary warriors who were turning back the clock. The third round was even more heated. I was up for a fight and Jack knew it. In one of the clinches Jack whispered to me: *"Take it easy on the old man."* I shot back: *"You started it with that right hand old man."*

I dipped and ripped a right uppercut up the middle of his chest. He barely leaned back out of the way. When the bell rang ending the exhibition, the crowd stood and cheered for several minutes. The *Philadelphia Tribune* described the event: *It seemed that every newsreel company in town was on hand. They had been told in front that Jack Johnson and Joe Jeannette were going to fight an exhibition and such an exhibition was big enough, it was figured, to swamp the place with writers and photographers, which was done.*

The exhibition was just that to a certain extent in which Johnson and Jeannette clowned playfully, swung at Wills, the referee, and grimaced at the crowd. After the first round, however, the feel of the sixteen ounce gloves got good to both and the crowd was treated to some scientific boxing not seen in a ring since the day Wills and Sam Langford hung up their gloves for good.

The two ancients circled each other as warily as when they were fighting such greats as Tommy Burns, James Jeffries, Sam Langford and others. They sparred for openings and the sound of the heavy gloves on head and body was just as convincing as a real main event at Madison Square Garden. Through it all, the crowd looked on intently, sensing that it was getting a freebie on one of the best sports shows of the times.[585]

It had been twenty-three years since I last fought in a boxing ring. After

---

[585] *Philadelphia Tribune* December 15, 1945.

our exhibition, we went back to the dressing room to get changed. It would be the last time that I put on fighting trucks. It would also be the last time I saw Jack Johnson.

When we finished changing into street clothes and exited the dressing room, we were met by two totally different crowds. Jack was met by the same crowd of boxing hangers-on that had hounded him in his career. Cigar-smoking hustlers, drunkards, gamblers, and boxing groupies, both men and women alike, with their phony personalities, awaited him. Waiting for me outside the dressing room was my wife Addie, my son Joie, his wife Angie, and my daughter Agnes. My old boxing pals Joe Shugrue, Ownie McCabe ("Young" Rector), Frankie Nelson, and "Babe" Orlando were also there to support me. They were all beaming with pride and came running over to hug me. It was at this moment that I realized that it was I, not Jack, who was the lucky one. It was I all along who was the winner. I might not have had the opportunity at the big payday and the heavyweight championship, but I had something you could never win in the ring. I had a wife and children who loved me dearly, and I them. There isn't a championship belt in the world that can bring that type of happiness. I also learned something else that day. I was proud of my heritage and my skin color. I had accomplished things in my lifetime that most people, of any race, could only dream of. I had a lot to owe to my race and my heritage for these accomplishments. No longer would I let the ignorant people of the world determine how I would feel about myself. My entire life I had been made to feel uncomfortable because I was of mixed race. Subconsciously I let it affect every part of my life. I made myself a promise that I would never again let other people dictate how I felt about myself.

Several newspapers ran stories after my exhibition bout with Jack Johnson. I walked to purchase the papers at a local newspaper stand the morning after the show. When I returned home, I grabbed my old dusty scrapbook from the bookshelf and brought it into the kitchen where I laid it on the table. I grabbed the scissors from a kitchen drawer and sat down to cut out the articles. When I started cutting I noticed my hands were shaking. This was not from the exhibition. I had noticed my hands were shaking for several weeks. I didn't want to scare Addie, so I didn't tell her. I would mention it to the doctor on my next visit. I called Addie into the kitchen and asked her to cut the articles out for me. Addie had always cut straighter then I did. After she was done, I pasted the articles into the scrapbook and set it back up on the shelf.

Agnes had come all the way up from Hollywood, Florida for the event. She officially divorced her husband Bill Kelly in 1945. Agnes moved back home and worked as a seamstress. She managed a dress shop in Union

City.[586] Agnes was very skilled at sewing. She never used a pattern when she sewed. She would create all her dresses by eye.[587]

On June 10, 1946, Jack Johnson died in an automobile accident while heading to New York from Texas. Johnson was driving a Lincoln Zephyr that was given to him by Henry Ford. Ford liked Jack, and he also liked the publicity his company received whenever Jack was stopped for speeding in one of Ford's cars. Johnson and his companion, Fred Cook, had just stopped at a diner outside of Raleigh, North Carolina. In the diner they were told that blacks had to eat in the back. Johnson and Cook were starving so they ate. When Jack left the diner he was enraged. He entered his car and took off at a high rate of speed.[588] Johnson lost control on a sharp turn, crossed the center white line, and slammed into a telephone pole. A newspaper headline mockingly stated that Jack: *"Crossed the white line for the last time."*

I cried the night that Jack Johnson died. At that moment, once again, I realized that our lives paralleled each other much more than they differed. We both felt the same pain in the ring, as well as outside of it. Of the four great black heavyweight boxers of our era, only Sam Langford and I were left. Jack was buried as he wished, next to his second wife Etta Duryea. I thought back to when Jack and I sat on that bench in Paris and how he told me how much he loved and missed Etta. Jack's wife Irene Pineau-Johnson spoke at his funeral, she said: *"I loved him because of his courage. He faced the world unafraid. There wasn't anyone or anything he feared."*[589] That statement was certainly true. After Jack retired from boxing he stormed a KKK rally all by himself. He told the gathering that they should practice love and kindness, not hate. The Klansmen were stunned. They stood frozen like statues as Jack spoke, and they were still motionless as Jack walked out of the rally.[590]

In 1948, President Harry Truman ordered the desegregation of the armed forces and Jackie Robinson broke the color barrier in professional baseball.[591] On May 18, 1949, my good friend and stable-mate Willie Lewis died of cancer. He had been fighting the disease for several years. In July of 1949, I suffered a debilitating stroke.[592] I could not walk without help and I could not speak properly. I was to live the remainder of my life confined to a chair in my home. I rented the gym space to the West Hudson County Sporting Club and my son Joie took over the limousine business.

On August 26, 1949 I celebrated my 70th birthday. Hudson Dispatch reporter John G. Connolly wrote the following article: *Soft spoken and mild-*

---

[586] *Afro American* January 25, 1947.
[587] Interview with JoAnn Flannery-Mostaccio Joe Jennette's great-niece.
[588] *Unforgivable Blackness* by Geoffrey C. Ward pg. 447.
[589] *Unforgivable Blackness* by Geoffrey C. Ward pg. 448.
[590] *Champions of the Ring* by Gerald Suster pg. 72.
[591] *Interracial Intimacies* by Randall Kennedy pg. 266.
[592] *Washington Afro-American* July 8, 1958.

mannered Joe Jennette, one of the classiest heavyweights in the early 1900's, will relax in his home, 2616 Summit Avenue, Union City, tomorrow- his 70th birthday- and recall with pardonable pride his fistic accomplishments of four decades ago when he was the toast of American and European boxing circles.

His neat book of clippings is the only link Joe has with the past when he took on the best, including Sam Langford, Jack Johnson, Georges Carpentier and Sam McVea, for he has little or no interest in the boxing game of today.

"It isn't the same anymore," said the fistic marvel of his time. "We fought with all we had in those years. Trouble today is that the fight goes where the money lays on too many occasions. No sir, the fight game just isn't the same."

To meet the tall Negro in his gas station in Union City is a revelation for anyone who thinks that all fighters show the scars of battle. Joe was more than a fighter, he was a master boxer, and because of his agility and sharpness, he carries no trace of the blows struck by the Johnsons, Langfords and the rest.

"With Louis gone," reflected Jennette, "the heavyweight ranks are now devoid of any battler who can be tabbed great. Louis could have fought in any generation and gone to the top. That man had class."

Why is the fight game in such a sad state? Joe has the answer to that question. "Fighters want to come up to the big money too fast... they're lazy... don't want to get the necessary experience that will keep them on top."

When Jennette was forced to close his little gymnasium atop his garage awhile back, that was the signal, as far as he was concerned, that the youth of today has lost sight of the fact that one must work for anything. There were years when the gym flourished and so did the fight game. Things fell off gradually. Boys didn't want to spend the long afternoons sweating in the Jennette gym. Joe closed it with a tear.

Today he spends most of his time working around his garage and arranging for his limousines to be hired for weddings and funerals. He's contented and is looking forward to many more years as a Union City businessman.

Joe has to be prodded a bit before he'll talk about the days when he rated headlines here and abroad. He smiles when he shows clippings from French newspapers in which he is called "champion de mond" (champion of the world) by virtue of his slashing 49-round victory over Sam McVea, the European heavyweight titleholder.

For a fellow who fought Sam Langford, the "Tar Baby," 18 times; McVea four times and champion Jack Johnson seven times, Jennette is quite modest. That's his way.

"Langford was the boy who gave me my toughest battle," smiled Jennette. "I was handicapped from the third round on in one of our battles in 1910 when Langford floored me with a terrific smash in the middle of the face. He broke my nose and I bled as though I had been slashed with a knife. He never stopped peppering me with blows to the face for the rest of the night."

Jennette claims that but for Jack Johnson he may well have gone on to become heavyweight champ.

"Langford and myself were boxing at a time when, due to Johnson being champ, colored boxers had a hard time securing matches with white men. Public sentiment was against mixed fights and we had to battle among ourselves.

397

"I fought Johnson seven times before he whipped Jeffries for the title. Jack was a soft touch compared to 'Tar Baby' Langford."

Jennette was born in the Homestead section of North Bergen and, other than his trips to Europe and about this country when fighting, has always made his home in North Hudson.

Although he talks much about his fights with Langford, Joe gets the biggest kick out of telling the story of his three-hour battle to a finish with McVea, Europe's best.

The Union City Negro had defeated McVea in a 20-rounder in Europe but the decision was reversed by the frightened referee when the partial home crowd almost started a riot. Jennette demanded McVea meet him in a fight to the finish and the bout was arranged.

A slashing affair, the likes of which the sporting pubic never sees today, found the two men pounding away at each other for more than three hours. McVea finally collapsed in the 49th round. When revived he came over to Jennette and said: "Joe, that was the finish."

He laughs heartily when asked to recall the time he fought three men in one night in London. "They managed to get three husky English longshoremen to fight me that night," Joe explained. "I took care of the first two in short order- too quickly in fact. The third was in the ring getting instructions when he decided prizefighting was not his thing. He ran from the ring."

In all, Jennette has had a full life and has no axe to grind with the world like many people have.[593]

On July 18, 1951, "Jersey" Joe Walcott won the world's heavyweight championship in his fifth try. He defeated Ezzard Charles by knockout in Pittsburgh, Pennsylvania. After his victory a testimonial dinner was held on his behalf. I was invited to attend and speak at the event but my deteriorating health prevented me from doing so. My dear friend, sportswriter Lud Shahbazian, offered to speak on my behalf. Lud spoke of my career and how Jack Johnson completely ignored me after he became champion, refusing to even say hello to me in public for over four years. At the end of Lud's speech he turned to Walcott and softly spoke: *"I just want Joe Walcott to realize where he wouldn't have been if Joe Louis had been like Jack Johnson.*[594] *At this very moment a man sits in his home, confined to a chair. He should have been heavyweight champion of the world but fate denied him that privilege. He gave his heart and soul to this sport but was betrayed by both the champion that refused to fight him and the public who refused to demand that he be given a title opportunity. Wear your crown proudly as I know you will Joe, and remember the fighting spirit of that other Jersey Joe wears it with you."*

In 1954, we sold our home but kept the business and gym. Addie and I moved down the block to stay with my son and his wife Angie in their two-

---

[593] *Hudson Dispatch* August 25, 1949.
[594] Notes from Lud Shahbazian's speech at Joe Walcott testimonial courtesy of Gregory Speciale.

family home. For many days afterwards, I would sit and stare out of the window and watch the cars and people pass me by. I would listen to our parakeets as they whistled throughout the day. One day I watched as a coal delivery truck pulled up out front and the driver got out to make a coal delivery. In the truck there was a small boy about eight-years-old. I watched as the boy opened the door to the truck, jumped out, and climbed up into the back of the coal truck with a small toy shovel. The man started setting up to shovel the coal down the chute. The boy was in the back playing and his face and clothes were getting covered with soot. A woman came out of her house and started screaming at the man. I opened the window so I could hear more clearly. The woman was screaming: *"How dare you use that small boy to shovel coal. I should report you to the police right now!"*

The man was obviously flustered and red-faced. He tried to explain that the child was his son and school was closed and the boy wanted to come out to work with him. The woman kept screaming and threatening him as she went back into the house. The man turned to the boy and I could hear him yell to him: *"Look what kind of trouble you got me into."*[595]

After the delivery was made the man picked his boy out of the back of the truck and they drove off. I stood there by the window thinking for several minutes. A breeze came through the window and I closed my eyes in reflection. I could see my seconds waving towels to refresh me as I sat on a stool in between rounds. I could smell the fresh irises, gourdons, and lilies. I could hear the faint melody of "Yankee Doodle Boy" being sung behind me by Willie Lewis and the French women shouting: *"En Garde! En Garde!"* I burst out in laughter. What a life I had lived. From a horse farrier's son, to a coal-truck driver, to a professional boxer fighting all over the United States and Europe, to having my own limousine business. It all went by so fast.

Sam Langford was by far the toughest man I ever fought. He had the hardest, shortest, crispest, punches I ever felt. Jack Johnson was the best defensive counter-puncher and boxer and he used his reach better than anyone. The big difference in Jack's game and Langford's was Sam would come in to overwhelm you with force, while Jack would let you beat yourself by over-committing or making mistakes.

Sam loved life. He was always joking before, after, and even during his fights. He loved to smoke cigars and have his drink. But most of all Sam loved to eat. Of all the boxers I faced and had the opportunity to watch, I admired Sam Langford the most. He was fearless and he had so much confidence in his abilities.

In May 1935, Sam had a second eye operation and he regained partial sight in his right eye. Unfortunately, in November he was struck by a car

---

[595] Conversation with Joseph Louis Botti.

and suffered internal injuries. His eye-sight was gone again. In December of the same year, New York Mayor Fiorello LaGuardia gave Sam a job for the city.

In January 1944, Sam was discovered living in one room in a rundown hotel on 139th street in New York City. He was alone, blind, and penniless. Sam was discovered by writer Al Laney, who was writing a newpaper story on Langford's life.[596]

Sam was inducted into *The Ring* magazine's boxing hall of fame in 1955. He was the first non-champion to receive the honor. Sam lived out his last days in a nursing home in the Boston Area. There were several fundraisers held for Sam, and the money they raised allowed him to stay in the private home.

Sam did not regret anything. He enjoyed life to the fullest. He was proud of his professional boxing career and his record in the sport. He was the consummate professional. One cannot attain the level of fighting that Sam did without having a passion of the highest degree. Sam died on January 12, 1956 at the age of 72. With the passing of each of my rivals I felt a little part of me left this world with them. The tears I cried for Jack Johnson paled in comparison to the tears I shed for Sam.

On March 11, 1956 *Newark Star Ledger* reporter Art Lea Mond wrote an article on my career: *...When we dropped at the Jennette place we talked with Joe's wife, the pleasant Adelaide Jennette. She said, "Joe's not very well these days. Visitors make him nervous and flash bulbs make him worse. In January we had a little celebration in honor of our Golden Wedding Anniversary. He enjoyed having his son Joe and daughter, Agnes, and a few friends on hand but he tired quickly." This was the gracious lady who had been with her man through thick and thin, through good times and bad. Did she recall the largest amount her husband ever received for a fight? "It was $3,000. That terrific 49-round fight with Sam McVey at the Cirque de Paris in Paris. No, I didn't see it but we lived a short distance away, heard it. I had the children with me and I could hear the cheers and groans through that long affair. Finally Dan came to the house (that was manager Dan McKetrick) and I learned Joe had knocked Sam out in the 49th round. Hard to forget that fight." You know what Jennette received for one of his numerous fights with Jack Johnson? Sixty-count them-dollars. Yep...[597]*

On May 17, 1958, I was honored by the Veteran Boxers Association, Ring 14 of Hudson County, as its man of the year. I was too ill to attend, so my son Joie and my daughter Agnes attended on my behalf. Agnes gave a heartfelt speech on what a great father I was to her and Joie. She also spoke of how proud I was of my boxing career and how I cherished the photos and newspaper clippings in my scrapbook. Agnes said: *"All you have to do is mention boxing to my Dad and a spark lights up in his eyes. He will pull out that old dusty scrapbook which he loves so much, and he'll start telling stories of his great battles*

---

[596] *Sam Langford: Boxing's Greatest Uncrowned Champion* by Clay Moyle.
[597] *Newark-Star Ledger* March 11, 1956.

with Sam Langford, Jack Johnson, and Sam McVea. Even today, when he has a guest over, though Dad cannot walk very well, he will just call out to my Mom and point to the bookshelf. She knows exactly what book Dad wants. He is so proud of his boxing career and we are so proud of him." Agnes also spoke of how thankful I was to be honored by the V.B.A. I was told there wasn't a dry eye in the room after Agnes' speech.

Joe Jr. in sailor uniform.

Joe Jennette & unknown child.

Joe Jr. in front of Jennette's garage.

Angie & Joe Jennette Jr.

Joe Jennette at beach.

Joe Jennette, November 27, 1945.

Joe Jennette & Jack Johnson boxing an exhibition at Henry Hudson Hotel, N.Y.C.,
November 27, 1945. Harry Wills referee.

Family & friends gather at holiday dinner at Joe Jennette's home. Joe Jennette sitting with wife Ada at rear of table with Angie & Joe Jr. Standing behind them. Jean & Jules Rufino sitting left of Jennette.

L to R: Joe, Ada, & Ada's family members.

Joe Jennette on left, Ada third from left, & friends at Christmas.

L to R: Unknown, Agnes, Joe, Angie, and Ada Jennette.

Joe Jr. & Angie Rufino-Jennette.

Bill Kelly & Agnes Jennette-Kelly.

Angie Rufino-Jennette, Denise Del Priore-Villano, & Joe Jennette Jr.
celebrate Denise's second birthday, circa 1952.

Joe Jennette with wife Ada's relatives, circa 1950s.

Say Goodbye to a Great Sparmate

Hudson County fistic greats of yester-
year gather about the bier of Joe Jen-
nette last night at Leber Funeral Home,
Union City. On the left are Joe Shugrue,
Lt. Ownie McCabe of Boulevard Police
(Young Rector), and Frankie Nelson, while
on the right are Joe Jennette Jr. and Babe
Orlando.

Joe Jennette is laid to rest at Leber Funeral Home Union City N.J. July, 3rd, 1958.
L to R: Joe Shugrue, Ownie McCabe, Frankie Nelson, Joe Jennette Jr. & Babe Orlando.

Agnes Jennette-Gibbs, circa 1970s.

Agnes Jennette-Gibbs with second husband Wendell Gibbs, circa 1970s.

L to R: JoAnn Flannery-Mostaccio, Agnes Hartlieb-Flannery, Mary Von Atzingen-Hartlieb, and Agnes Jennette-Gibbs, circa 1975.

Angelina & Joe Jennette Jr., circa 1980s.

Unveiling of Union City's first historical marker L to R: Henry Hascup, Commissioner Mauriuri Martinetti, Henry Munker, Commissioners Lucio Fernandez & Chris Irizarry.

Sabrina Jennette & family pose by historical marker, April 17, 2009. From L to R; Tyler Fox, Maia Fox, Latasha Jennette, Laila Fox, Leila Fox, & Sabrina Jennette.

Joe Jennette historical marker ceremony L to R; Gregory Speciale, Joe Botti, Sabrina Jennette (Joe Jennette's great-niece), & Henry Hascup, Union City N.J., April 17, 2009.

L to R; Union City Commissioner's Chris Irizarry & Mauriuri Martinetti, Denise Del Priore-Villano (Angie Jennette's niece), Commissioner Lucio Fernandez & Joe Botti. Villano receives her proclaimation at historical marker ceremony.

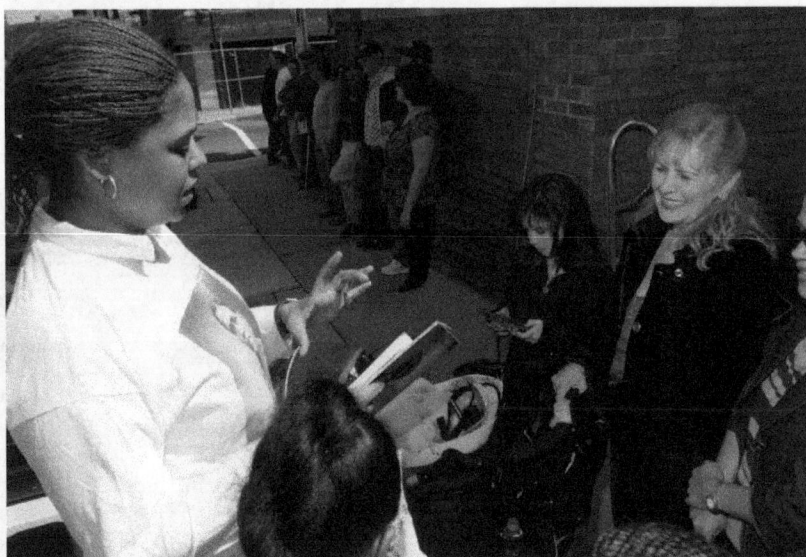

Sabrina Jennette speaks with this author's family members at the historical marker ceremony, from right Michelle Botti, Patricia Caputo, & Jenna Botti.

Photos of Joe Jennette's missing scrapbook

Chapter 24
Death and Rediscovery of a Forgotten Man

On July 2, 1958, Joe Jennette was taken to North Hudson Hospital in Weehawken, New Jersey, where he died after a long battle with heart disease. Jennette was buried in Fairview Cemetery in Fairview, New Jersey.

A month prior, on June 2, 1958, Richard Loving, a Caucasian male, married Mildred Jeter, an African-American female, in Washington D.C. The couple was unable to marry in their home state of Virginia because interracial marriages were illegal there. The marriage would bring to the forefront state laws that banned interracial marriages, and eventually led to a landmark civil rights decision by the U.S. Supreme Court, which ruled that it was unconstitutional for states to bar interracial marriages.

Upon Jennette's death, the great Hudson County sportswriter Lud wrote the following article: *Boxers of Yesteryear in Tribute to Jennette as 'Great Fighter'*

"He was a great fighter. His record shows that. Anybody who stood up to the likes of Jack Johnson and Sam Langford as he did- and as often as he did- had to be a great fighter." "It's a shame he never got a chance at the heavyweight championship." "Once Jack Johnson won the heavyweight title he wanted no part of Joe Jennette. It wasn't that way when Johnson was hungry."

Those were the sentiments heard over and over again last night at Leber Funeral Home on Hudson Blvd., Union City, where the former greats of Hudson County fistdom turned out to pay final respects to Joe Jennette, great Negro heavyweight of yesteryear, who died Wednesday night at North Hudson Hospital.

Lying there in the eternal silence that is death, the onetime giant who had taken on all comers in his day, looked as huge and formidable as ever, as the buddies of his boxing days, men who had tangled with him in exhibition bouts and in gymnasium training sessions filled by the Frankie Nelsons, the Frankie Burnses, the Joe Shugrues, the Ownie McCabes and the Phil Kealeys were there. So were ex-pugilists of more recent times- such as Jimmy Francis and Babe Orlando and Al Roth and Battling Walker and Steve Charlock.

And so were civic personalities such as Abel Bozzo and Will Leeger, Sam Zuccaro and Fred Buccaro, principal of Robert Waters School which is just one block away from the Jennette residence, who learned his boxing so well under Jennette that he later won a college boxing championship while at Syracuse University.

Nelson Recalls Bouts. Nelson, head of Ring 14 of Veteran Boxers of America, which on May 17 last honored Jennette with the club's award of the year, shook his head sadly as he recalled how often he and Jennette boxed in Hoboken as well as other places for Liberty Bond Drives of World War 1: "A group of us went out 3 and 4 nights a week," Nelson related. "Usually I boxed Jennette, while Frankie Burns tangled with Young Rector and Babe Orlando squared off against the late Johnny Duff. We boxed quite often for Hoboken Knights of Columbus Council 159. The next night we'd be in Camp Dix or somewhere else. Of course, our bouts were exhibitions," Nelson related, "but Joe was so big and heavy that even his light taps jolted you."

"You can say that again," said Shugrue, who was one of the few men to stop Benny Leonard and was known internationally along with Jennette. *"I refereed a bout of Jennette's at the old Oakland and I happened to go in to break a clinch when he happened to let a right go. Well,"* said Joe, *"the place he happened to hit me hurt for days. I can still feel it, I think."*

Injured Left Arm. The men who had boxed and sparred with Jennette over the 2 decades during which the Union Cityite fought on both sides of the Atlantic Ocean discovered something about him last night that they had never known while Joe was alive. Almost without exception every one of the ex-boxers who discussed Jennette's career felt Jennette had been handicapped through his career by an injured left arm.

Said Babe Orlando, who sparred with him often in the 20's at Jennette's Summit Ave. gym: *"He never boxed you straight-away. He always came at you sideways, so to speak. And he had a short left that when he hit you, you felt like you had been jolted by a pole. He kind of whipped and snapped the left at you, actually jabbing you with the back of his hand. He was the only fighter I knew who jabbed that way."*

Al Benedict of the famous old West Hoboken family, one of Jennette's few local opponents (even though their meeting took place in Joplin, Mo.) had what seemed a logical explanation for this. Contacted by the Hudson Dispatch at his home in Lakewood, Benedict said *"Jennette's left arm wasn't really short. It seemed that way because he couldn't straighten it out fully. He had hurt it early in his career and that's why he jabbed the way he did."*

It remained for Jennette's family to correct a wrong impression. *"It wasn't his left arm that he injured,"* said his wife, Adelaide, and her daughter, Mrs. Agnes Kelly. *"It was his right arm. And I should know,"* said Mrs. Jennette, *"because I always had to alter the right sleeve on his shirts. I think that because he couldn't go all out with the right, he just had to perfect his left that much more. But everybody thought his left arm was injured because of the way he held it."*[598]

Joe Junior took over the 18-car limousine and gas station business after his father's death in 1958.[599] The boxing gym, which had been rented out to the West Hudson County Sporting Club upon his father taking ill, was closed down. Joe Junior refused to have children, because he did not want his offspring to endure the suffering he had experienced while growing up as an interracial child.[600] Joe Junior and his wife Angie would tell family and friends that they were unable to have children because of a medical issue.

In 1960 Agnes Jennette-Kelly married Wendell Gibbs. Agnes and her new husband moved to Pleasantville N.J. Adelaide Jennette moved to Pleasantville with her daughter.

After closing the limousine business in the 1960s, Joe Junior worked as a custodian for the Union City Board of Education, assigned to Hudson

---

[598] *Hudson Dispatch* July 3, 1958.
[599] *Afro American* January 25, 1947.
[600] Interview with JoAnn Flannery-Mostaccio & Denise Del Priore-Villano.

Elementary School. Although segregation officially ended in 1964, sixteen states still had anti-miscegenation laws on their books until all of these laws were overturned by the Supreme Court on June 12, 1967.[601] In *Loving v. Virginia*, the United States Supreme Court pronounced anti-miscegenation laws incompatible with America's fundamental constitutional precepts.[602]

On February 1, 1968 Adelaide Jennette died in Pleasantville N.J. She was 81 years old. In February of the same year, Joe Jennette was inducted into *The Ring* magazine's hall of fame along with "Sugar" Ray Robinson. On June 15, 1969, Jennette was inducted into the New Jersey Boxing Hall of Fame.

In the early 1980s, Joe Junior's home was burglarized. All of Joe Jennette's trophies and medals were taken, never to be seen again. Joe Junior lived his entire life in Union City N.J. Joe Junior's niece Denise Del Priore-Villano described her Uncle as: *"a kind man, loving and very religious. He loved his nieces and nephews and was a great musician. He loved music. He also loved his father and was sad about how he was such a great boxer and how racism held him back. Aunt Angie was also kind and loved to cook and bake, her apple pie was the best. Aunt Angie was also very proud of her father-in-law and would always talk about his career."*

Agnes Jennette-Gibbs was honored as Ms. Senior Citizen of Atlantic County in 1983. On May 1, 1985, Agnes Jennette-Gibbs' second husband Wendell Gibbs passed away.

In 1991, Agnes was recognized by President George H. W. Bush in a National Association of Counties "County Point of Light" presentation. She played piano for entertainers who performed in Atlantic County area nursing homes. Agnes played organ for Our Lady of Residence senior citizen home in Pleasantville for twenty-eight years and devoted much of her time making crafts for the home's gift shop. Joe Jennette Jr. died in 1993 with his wife Angie by his side. Joe's sister Agnes Jennette-Gibbs died on February 24, 1995.[603] Agnes, like her brother Joe, bore no children. She would tell family and friends that she was unable to bear children due to a medical issue.

In 1996, two Union Hill High School student reporters named Mike Suarez and Kevin Penton researched Jennette and found that his daughter-in-law, Angie Jennette, was still living in Union City. They visited Angie and she joyously recounted stories of her father-in-law with them. She trustingly lent Penton and Suarez Jennette's scrapbook. In their article for Union Hill High School's *Hiller Times*, Penton and Suarez wrote: *Mrs. Jennette is the proud owner of probably the most extensive archival collection dealing with Joe Jennette in the world. Included are posters, numerous photographs, and a scrapbook beyond belief. Its yellowed sheets contain about 100 pages of newspaper clippings and photographs from the*

601 *Mixed Messages* by Fred & Anita Prinzing pg. 101.
602 *Interracial Intimacies* by Randall Kennedy pg. 243.
603 *Press of Atlantic City* February 27, 1995.

first quarter of the century, detailing Jennette's life to the finest detail.[604]

On June 15, 1997, Joe Jennette was inducted into the International Boxing Hall of Fame in Canastota, New York, along with "Sugar" Ray Leonard.

Angelina "Angie" Jennette, Joe Junior's wife, died on January 13, 1999. When Angie's niece, Denise Del Priore-Villano, cleaned out her apartment, she found only a painting of Joe Jennette and several family photographs. The scrapbook was nowhere to be found. Villano states that in the months leading up to her Aunt Angie's death, Angie would often tell Denise to: *"get the scrapbook back from that Union Hill High School boy,"* but Villano states her aunt never told her the boy's name. Penton, when interviewed by this author, said he had lent the scrapbook to a boxing collector named Ben Hawes of Washington State in the summer of 1996. A year prior, Mr. Hawes had paid a researcher to trace Joe Jennette's heritage, which included any living relatives. Mr. Hawes then used that information to contact Angie Jennette via telephone. He discovered that Jennette had kept a scrapbook and that it had been borrowed by Penton and Suarez. Angie Jennette gave Mr. Hawes Kevin Penton's phone number. After speaking with Penton, Hawes states that he and his father planned to visit Penton to look at the scrapbook while on their annual trip to New Jersey in June.[605]

Hawes stated to this author that on June 11, 1996, he visited Penton's home. Hawes took some photographs of the pages in the book, but had to leave because his father was waiting in the car for him. Hawes said he left and returned to Washington State, but he and Penton agreed to speak in the future about Hawes possibly borrowing the book. Hawes stated that Penton agreed to ship the scrapbook to Hawes in Washington State. Penton stated to this author that Angie Jennette was unaware that he lent her scrapbook to Mr. Hawes.[606] Hawes stated that he was in possession of the scrapbook for about three to five months and photocopied nearly the entire book. Hawes said he shipped the scrapbook back to Penton in August of 1996. Mr. Hawes provided this author with a copy of a shipping receipt. Hawes stated he has not seen the scrapbook since shipping it back to Penton.

In a letter to this author, Hawes stated: *"I have not had possession of the scrapbook nor any idea of its whereabouts after I mailed it back to Kevin. I assumed it was returned to the family. I was fortunate, through persistence and luck, to have had possession of the scrapbook for a period of time. It is unfortunate and frankly very sad that the scrapbook is missing. It was/is a wonderful piece of boxing, human, and American history.*[607] Penton stated to this author that he returned the

---

[604] *Union Hill Times* "Joe Jeannette: The Forgotten Hero" by Penton & Suarez February, 1996 pg. 7.
[605] Letter from Ben Hawes to Joe Botti February 15, 2011.
[606] Conversation with Kevin Penton
[607] Letter from Ben Hawes to Joe Botti February 15, 2011.

scrapbook to Angie in September of 1996.[608]

As of the writing of this book, the scrapbook's whereabouts are unknown. It should be noted that Mr. Hawes sent this author several newspaper articles and photographs that were copied from the scrapbook. The articles were helpful in giving a more complete view of Joe Jennette.

In 1982, at the age of sixteen, I walked into a boxing gym in Bayonne, N.J., and was hooked for life. I was led to the gym by a conversation at the Ringside Bar and Grill, which is owned by Mario Costa. The bartender that night was Bob Rooney Sr., who happened to run the Bayonne PAL boxing program. Two of the patrons were my friend John Greeley's father John Greeley Sr., and Donald Maiorino. Greeley Sr. and Maiorino encouraged John and I to give boxing a try, so we headed down to the PAL to learn boxing from Rooney and his co-trainer Sal Alessi. I boxed in the gym on and off for the next few years.

I stopped training in 1987, after I suffered major head trauma in a car accident. In 1989, I heard a commotion outside of my apartment window at 5th Street and New York Avenue in Union City. I opened the window and saw some kids fist fighting in the street. I broke up the fight and told the kids if they thought they were really tough they should head to a local boxing gym. The kids told me there were no boxing gyms in the area. One of the kids said his brother knew me and knew I boxed before and that I should teach them. I gave in to their pleas and pulled out some old boxing gloves and started giving lessons in the basement of the two-family home.

Before long, I was bringing area kids to local amateur boxing competitions. I had a N.J. Golden Gloves finalist in 1991, Marco "Tony" Otero. One of my Junior Olympic boxers, Leon Felipe Ramirez, went to the 1991 Golden Glove finals show with a small cut over one of his eyes. Pro boxer Ricky Meyers was at the show and he asked Ramirez if the cut was from a punch. Ramirez replied that the cut was not from a punch. He said he suffered the injury when he slipped a punch and his eye struck the cinderblock wall in the basement where we trained. Word spread that we were sparring in a basement without a ring and the president of the New Jersey Golden Gloves, Dan Shannon, donated a boxing ring to us.

I went to a local city commission meeting and asked then Mayor Robert Menendez and Commissioner Bruce D. Walter for help. Walter was the grandson of Cesar Walter, who was the Hudson County boxing inspector who weighed-in Harry Wills and Luis Firpo at Joe Jennette's gym back in 1924. The Mayor and commissioners helped us find a location. In 1992, we opened the first Union City Boxing Club gym at 906 Palisade Avenue in Union City, in the basement of the Doric Temple building. My passion for the sport of boxing had returned. In 1993, '94, and '95, the Union City

---

[608] E-mail from Kevin Penton to Joe Botti February 21, 2011.

Boxing Club won the first place team trophy in the New Jersey Golden Gloves Tournament. In 1993 we won the division-two trophy and in 1994 and '95 we won the division-one trophy. In 1994 and '95 we had a combined twelve Golden-Glove champions. On September 16, 1994, the Union City Boxing Club promoted the first female amateur boxing contest in the history of New Jersey. The bout was held at Edison Elementary School in Union City. Both boxers, Melissa DeLaCruz and Angela Rivera, were members of the Union City Boxing Club. DeLaCruz won the three-round bout by decision.

In 1997, I became a police officer in Union City. A few months after I was hired, then Chief Paul Hanak told me there was a street rededication being held for a boxer named Joe Jennette. I had never heard of Jennette and felt funny about going to the event on duty. I didn't go to the ceremony. I regret that decision to this day. I missed an opportunity to speak with Jennette's daughter-in-law Angie. The Mayor of Union City at the time did not even know the street was named after a man. He thought Jeannette Street was dedicated to a woman.[609]

The rededication was being held because Jennette had been inducted into the International Boxing Hall of Fame. The event was attended by Angie Jennette, Paul Venti, a legendary boxing judge, and N.J. Boxing Hall of Fame President and historian Henry Hascup.

In 2007, I was in the process of moving the gym from 906 Palisade Avenue to 410 27th Street, the location of the old Public Service car barn where Jennette had trained a hundred years prior. I was researching information to put in the flyer I was creating for the re-opening event. I came across a web site that had a blog about Union City Boxer Joe Jennette, and I responded by inquiring about the boxer. The blog was created by Tom Hartlieb, who is a great nephew of Adelaide Jennette. Tom's grandmother Mary was Adelaide's sister. From that blog, I met Sabrina Jennette. Her great-grandfather was Marshall Jennette, Joe's brother. I also met Gregory Speciale, who operates the joejennette.com website. Through Greg I met JoAnn Flannery-Mostaccio, Mary Hartlieb's granddaughter. Together we compelled Union City to correct the spelling of the street named in Joe Jennette's honor from Jeannette to its proper spelling, Jennette.

On April 17, 2009, Gregory Speciale, Sabrina Jennette, Henry Munker, Commissioner Lucio Fernandez, Mayor Brian Stack and I organized the placing of an historical marker at the site of Jennette's home and gym, 2612-16 Summit Avenue, Union City. Two weeks before the ceremony I was speaking with a friend in the neighborhood named Donald Terhune. Don told me a man he recently met, named Joe Villano, had asked him if

---

[609] Conversations with Henry Hascup, NJ Boxing Hall of Fame President.

Don had ever heard of Joe Jennette because Joe's wife Denise was related to Jennette. Denise's Aunt Angie was Joe Junior's wife. I was shocked when Don told me about the chance encounter. I told Don that we were holding a historical marker ceremony for Joe Jennette in two weeks. I met Joe and Denise and invited them and their relatives to the ceremony.

In many ways it appeared as though an outside force had brought Sabrina, Greg, Denise, JoAnn, and I together, like pieces of a puzzle, just in time for the historical marker ceremony. JoAnn was unable to attend the ceremony due to a family illness. The proudest moment of Joe Jennette's career was his 49-round finish fight against Sam McVea. It seemed as though he had willed all of his living relatives, as well as his biggest fans, to be there to celebrate the event with him. Even a former Jennette gym member, Nick "Whizzer" Mastorelli, was on hand to honor his old coach. In the February 1996 article written for the *Hiller Times*, Suarez and Penton wrote: *Sadly, if nothing else is done, especially in his hometown, in a few years the memory of Joe Jennette will be gone for eternity.*[610]

They can rest assured that his name will indeed live on, as since the article was written, a short film on his epic battle with Sam McVea, *Joe Jennette-The Boxer Who Refused To Quit*, was released in 2008, the improper spelling of the street named after him was corrected in 2008, and a historical marker was placed at his home and gym in 2009. At the time, no known video footage of Jennette existed. Since that time, several videos of Jennette have been unearthed, including his exhibition bout against Jack Johnson at the War Bond Rally in 1945 and Jennette's 1913 fight against Sam Langford in Paris.

When Joe Louis came on the scene in the 1930s, he was schooled on how to react after knocking out a white man. He was told not to celebrate or to lift his chin up, but to walk to a neutral corner humbly. He was also told not to be seen in public with white women, as this might reignite memories of the Jack Johnson reign. As great a champion as Jack Johnson was, his out-of-the-ring actions at that most sensitive time in our nation's history created many setbacks for African-American athletes in the United States. One must wonder if Joe Jennette, instead of Johnson, had been the first African-American world's heavyweight champion, would things have progressed differently for the African-American athlete or for African-Americans in general? Jennette was humble and reserved. He was not boastful inside or outside of the ring, and he was a loving family man.

Would Langford or Jennette have beaten Johnson if given an opportunity while he was champion? We will never know the answer to this question. One thing is certain. From 1915 until 1937, many great black boxers were denied an opportunity to fight for the heavyweight championship.

It is also a fact that many Americans did rally around Jack Johnson to

---

[610] *Hiller Times* 'Joe Jeannette: The Forgotten Hero by Kevin Penton & Mike Suarez February 1996 pg. 6.

bring the heavyweight championship back to America in 1908, and thirty years later, they once again rallied around an African-American boxer, Joe Louis, when he fought the German boxer Max Schmeling. Louis would go on to use his status as heavyweight champion to break many barriers for African-Americans in the United States.

Joe and Adelaide Jennette were very private people, but I am sure that if they were alive today, they would echo the sentiments of Barbara Douglas, a wife of an interracial marriage, when she said she had: *"experienced great happiness in marriage and that interracial marriages were not automatically destined for failure."*[611]

They would also agree, I'm sure, with Fred & Anita Prinzing's theory on the primary motivation for interracial marriage. The primary motivator, they stated: *"is love."*[612]

The following Jewish proverb was taken from Prinzings' book:
It was an ancient rabbi who asked his students how they could tell when night had ended and the day was on its way back.
"Could it be when you see an animal in the distance and can tell whether it is a sheep or a dog?"
"No," answered the rabbi.
"Could it be when you look at a tree in the distance and can tell whether it is a fig tree or a peach tree?"
"No," answered the rabbi.
"Well then, when is it?" the students demanded.
"It is when you look at the face of any woman or man and see that she or he is your brother or sister. Because if you cannot do this then no matter what time it is, it is still night."[613]

Sam Langford called Joe Jennette the gamest boxer he ever met. Jack Johnson called Jennette the toughest man he ever faced. A reporter once called the era of Jack Johnson, Sam Langford, Sam McVea, and Joe Jennette, the "pier six heavyweight era." Nat Fleischer called the four heavyweights "Black Dynamite," and Gregory Speciale called them the "Fearsome Foursome." Whatever term you choose when referencing them, they were the class of the heavyweight division, and whether or not the world was ready for them, they were ready and able to fight for equality and opportunity.

Johnson regarded Sam McVea and Joe Jennette as being the greatest men he ever fought.[614] Nat Fleischer, who some argue is the greatest boxing historian of all time, said: *"Jack Johnson often remarked to me that the man who gave him one of the toughest battles he ever had, was Joe Jeannette, and Joe was then only*

[611] *Marriage Beyond Black & White* by Barbara & David Douglas pg. 11.
[612] *Mixed Messages* By Fred & Anita Prinzing pg. 57.
[613] *Mixed Messages* By Fred & Anita Prinzing pgs. 148-9.
[614] *Champions of the Ring* by Gerald Suster pg. 56.

a novice.'[615] Johnson stated: *"Joe Jeannette is a tough fighting proposition. I'm not afraid to face him in a ring, but I would much rather fight Sam Langford or Sam McVey.'*[616] Johnson also stated: *"Jeannette is the toughest man I ever fought and the hardest to hurt. Why the more I hit that man the stronger he got. No wonder he beat Sam McVea in a finish battle.'*[617] Sam Langford always said Jennette gave him the: *"toughest fights.'*[618] Langford stated: *"Joe Jeannette, to my way of thinking, was the toughest man in the ring.'*[619] It was believed Langford "carried" many of his opponents because so many boxers feared his power and ferociousness. Joe Woodman, Langford's manager, when asked of the legitimacy of the Langford-Jennette battles, insisted that every fight between Jennette and Langford was: *"on the level.'*[620]

Gregory Speciale spoke at the historical marker ceremony on April 17, 2009, and had this to say of Jennette: *"This great man wasn't only a great fighter, but he just might have been the greatest all-around athlete that ever lived."*

Sabrina Jennette, Joe Jennette's great-niece, also spoke at the event: *"I remember as a little girl hearing stories of Uncle Joe from my grandfather, but, not knowing much, as he passed away seven years before I was born. However, in recent years, I have gotten to know him not just as Uncle Joe but as Joe Jennette, 'the boxer who refused to quit.' It is such an honor to be the relative of such a great man."*

Denise Del Priore-Villano commented on her great-uncle and his family: *"Joe Jennette Sr. used to bounce me on his knee; he loved children and I always felt welcomed in his home. I am sure that now they are looking down from heaven with big smiles on their faces to see what is now happening."*

JoAnn Flannery-Mostaccio, Joe Jennette's great-niece, commented on her great-uncle: *"Unkie was such a loved member of my family. When I was a kid he was so much fun, he enjoyed playing with us, and didn't mind us crawling all over him. When he was in the hospital dying, my house became very quiet, there was such sadness hanging over all of us. I can still feel the sadness. I remember my mother running to the phone every time it rang, just waiting for that call to say Unkie had passed away. We had a party line so she had to count the rings, to know whether it was a call for her. Then when the call did come in, I remember all the crying that went on, with my mother and my grandmother, just as sad as we had ever seen them."*

Below is a copy of my speech from the historical marker event:

"My family has had deep roots in Union City for over one hundred years. I have been active in boxing for over twenty-seven years. Yet until recently I knew close to nothing about Joe Jennette, until meeting Gregory Speciale and Sabrina Jennette close to two years ago. With their help and the assistance of Mayor Brian Stack, Commissioner Lucio

[615] *Black Dynamite "Fighting Furies"* by Nat Fleischer pg. 191.
[616] *Kalamazoo Gazette* August 21, 1912.
[617] *Jersey Journal* September 30, 1910.
[618] *Hudson Dispatch* January 13, 1956.
[619] *Telegram* April 23, 1911.
[620] *Pittsburgh Courier* May 7, 1927.

Fernandez and Henry Munker, today became not just a dream but a reality.

"I had no idea that one of the greatest boxers to ever lace on a pair of gloves lived right here in this very home. Not only did he beat all of the best boxers of his era, including Jack Johnson, Sam Langford, Sam McVea, and Georges Carpentier, he also ran a very successful boxing gym here, from 1924 until 1949.

"In this very building, James J. Braddock, the Cinderella Man, learned how to polish his skills as a professional boxer. Other famous boxers who walked up those stairs included Harry Wills and 'Two Ton' Tony Galento. Everyone who ever met Joe Jennette said he was the nicest, friendliest person you would want to meet.

"Jennette volunteered to box in many war-bond fundraisers during both the First and Second World Wars. Today is the one hundred year anniversary of Jennette's epic, three and a quarter hour, forty-nine round fight against Sam McVea. The bout was the longest boxing match of the twentieth century.

"I can stand here and state how Joe Jennette was cheated out of a title shot that he overwhelmingly deserved, but he would not have wanted that. He was proud of his career and his achievements, which included two African-American world titles. Although Joe never had the world championship belt strapped around his waist, he truly was a champion. A newspaper reporter stated many years ago that Joe Jennette was 'a champion in everything but name.' Mr. Jennette was also a great family man. He was in an interracial marriage at a time when it was dangerous and in most states illegal. The fact that he chose to live and raise his children in this community is a great testament to our town. Union City has always been a place where people of all walks of life can live and work towards their own American Dream.

"Joe Jennette was denied a title shot because of racial overtones of the great white hope era, and there was a string of twenty-two years, from 1915 until 1937, that African-American boxers were denied a shot at the heavyweight title. I don't think it was a coincidence that the first heavyweight to give an African-American boxer a shot at the title trained right here under Joe Jennette. That boxer's name was James J. Braddock, 'The Cinderella Man,' and the boxer he gave that opportunity to was Joe Louis. ...

"Joe Jennette would often let children in the area train in his gym whether they could afford the dues or not... I know that Joe Jennette had a great smile on his face when he saw that boxing remained available for the kids of Union City. Many boxing magazines have said that if Jennette had been born at another time he would have died a famous man. Today we are here to assure that his memory is not forgotten." (April 17, 2009)

Sample of boxers who were trained by Joe Jennette:

Stanley Poreda
Lou Lombardi
Jimmy Braddock
Allie Ridgeway
Carl Morris
Phil Johnson

Bobby Brady
Barry Carlton
Jack Sharkey
Jerry White
Gene Mickens
Jim Stewart

Young Zazarino
Frankie Carlton
Herman Heller
Billy White
Jim Barry
Tom Kennedy

Jack DeMave
Joey Costa
Ralph Lenny
Georges Carpentier
Frank Moran

Sample of boxers who conditioned themselves at Jennette's gym:

Tony Galento
Babe Orlando
Jimmy Carter
Steve Dudas
Johnny Hayes
Fast Black
George Deschner
Carmen Roman
Joey Ross
Johnny Daly
Young Zaccone
Joe Pepperted
Kid Troubles
Eddie Bergan
Babe Seiger
Buckey Keys
Pat Sullivan
Al Roth
Ray Rovelli
Italian Joe Gans
Ray Shara
Chuck Connors
Charl. Phil Rosenberg

Billy Vidabeck
Lew Snyder
Tony Melore
Freddie Huber
Vic DeMave
Dixie Diamond
Dodo Jackson
Andy Lake
Bobby Burns
Johnny Yarns
Battling Manno
Busty Grimes
Sammy Lowskey
Johnny Duff
Sam Rubin
Mickey Taylor
Eddie Mooney
Lou Rosenfeld
Phil Roselli
Al Dell
Allie Todisco
Tommy Fay
Allie Rowan

Joe Borrell
Harold Mays
Barry Martone
Jimmy Francis
Sailor Morse
Danny Lewis
Frank Poreda
Jack Hubbell
Jackie McCoy
John Drummie
Puggy Cospito
Christ Karchi
Johnny Lowskey
Yg. Von Derlin
Frankie Nelson
Joe Braddock
Tommy Brady
Jimmy Delmont
George Scott
Mickey Dell
Andy DeVodi
Al Settle

Jeff Smith
Steve Cheloc
Johnny Howard
Bobby Michaels
Dom Pascali
Oscar Sokolow
Frank Roman
Micky Lewis
Bart Garrigan
Billy Plaum
Tony Cal
Jimmy Sullivan
Joe Erb
Joey Seiger
Young Rector
Al Braddock
Charlie Krikorian
Joe Malone
Willie Shaw
Tommy Dell
Pip Damis
Tony Greb

Union City Boxing Club members pose for photo, circa 2013. The gym is located in the same "car barn" where Joe Jennette trained in 1912. Standing L to R: Carlos Osorio, Juan "The Beast" Rodriguez, Jason "Monstruo" Escalera & Joe Botti. Kneeling L to R: Herkin "Bebo" De La Rosa & Deandre "Dynamite D" Guzman.

Final resting place of Joe & Adelaide Jennette, Fairview Cemetery, Fairview N.J.

Lud Shahbazian sketch of Joe Jennette circa, 1935.

Bibliography

Books, Journals, & Compositions

The Art of Boxing   Georges Carpentier
New York   1926

Benjamin Cardoza Meets Gunslinger Bat Masterson   William H. Manz
St. John's University 2004

Beyond The Ring   Jeffrey T. Sammons
Illinois   1988

Beyond the Whiteness of Whiteness   Jane Lazarre
Durham   1996

The Big Black Fire   Robert H. DeCoy
Los Angeles 1969

The Big Fights   Harold Meyers
New York   1950

Bill Sterns Favorite Boxing Stories   Bill Sterns
New York   1948

Black Champion   Finis Farr
Connecticut 1964

Blackface   Ken
Padgett

Broadway: The American Musical 2004   American Decades
1998

Carpentier   Georges Carpentier
London   1958

Champions of the Ring   Gerald Suster
London   1992

Crossing The Line   McNamara, Tempenis, & Walton
Connecticut 1999

Dumb Dan   Dan Morgan
New York   1953

The Fight Game   James & Frank Butler
London   1954

Fighting Furies   Nat Fleischer
New York   1939

The Fireside Book of Boxing   W.C. Heinz
New York   1961

The Heavyweight Champions
New York   1970   Stanley Weston

Jack Johnson is a Dandy
New York   1969   Jack Johnson

Jass.com Bert Williams & George Walker   Thomas L. Morgan

La Boxe   Pierre Lafitte
Paris   1914

Love In Black & White   Mark & Gail Mathabane
New York   1992

The Odds Against Me   John Scarne
New York   1966

Interracial Intimacies   Randall Kennedy
New York   2003

Unforgivable Blackness   Geoffrey C. Ward
New York   2004

La Marseillaise   Claude Joseph Rouget de Lisle
1792

Lest We Forget   Rev. Clement W. Buckley,
C.P.

Lost Sounds: Blacks & the Birth of the Recording Industry 1890-1919   Tim
Brooks

Marriage Beyond Black & White   David & Barbara Douglas
Illinois   2002

Memories   Harry Preston
London   1928

Mixed Messages   Fred & Anita Prinzing
Chicago   1991

My Lord, What a Morning   William Waring Cuney
1910

Negro   Nancy Cunard
New York   1970

Nobody   Bert Williams & Alex Rogers
1905

Palookas & Plutocrats   Henry W. Clune

Paris Noir   Tyler Stovall
New York   1996

426

Relief to Royalty Union City 1936	Ludwig Shahbazian
Seconds Out London 1924	Fred Dartnell
Shake Hands & Come Out Fighting London 1953	L.A.G. Strong
Sweet Adeline (You're the Flower of my Heart) 1903	Richard H. Gerard & Harry Armstrong
Sweet Peggy O'Neil	Irish Folk Ballad
Thirty Years a Boxing Referee London 1915	Eugene Corri
Thrilling Fights London 1946	Norman Hurst
100 Greatest Boxers of All Time New York 1984	Bert Randolph Sugar
Visible Men: African American Boxers Duke Univ. Press 2009	Theresa Runstedtler
Waltz Me Around Again, Willie 1906	Will D. Cobb & Ren Shields
The Yankee Doodle Boy 1904	George M. Cohen
Yesternow: A Tribute to Jack Johnson	Miles Davis

Newspapers & Magazines

Amsterdam Evening Recorder	*New Journal & Guide*
Anaconda Standard	*New Orleans Item*
Atlanta Constitution	*New York Age*
Auburn Citizen	*New York Amsterdam News*
Augusta Chronicle	*New York Clipper*
Baltimore Afro-American	*New York Herald*
Baltimore Sun	*New York Press*
Baton Rouge La. Morning Advocate	*New York Sun*
Beaumont Journal	*New York Morning Telegraph*
Big Book of Boxing	*New York Times*
Boxing	*New York Tribune*
Brooklyn NY Daily Eagle	*Oklahoma Daily Reader*
Boston Daily Globe	*Omaha World Herald*
Boston Herald	*Oswego Daily Times*
Boston Journal	*Philadelphia Tribune*
Capitol Plains Dealer	*Pittsburgh Courier*
Canton Repository	*Plain Dealer*
Chicago Daily Tribune	*Plainsboro Dealer*
Chicago Defender	*Post Standard Syracuse NY*

Cincinnati Enquirer
Cleveland Plain Dealer
Dallas Morning News
Detroit Free Press
Denver Post
Elmira Gazette
Elmira NY Telegram
Evening Journal Jersey City
Evening Telegram NY
The Freeman
Harrisburg Patriot
The Hartford Courant
Hudson Dispatch
Hudson Reporter
Idaho Statesman
Illinois State Register
Indiana Star
Indianapolis Freeman
International News Service
The Irish Weekly Times
Ithaca Daily News
Jersey Journal
Kalgoorlie Western Argus
Kalamazoo Gazette
L'Auto
La Boxe & Les Boxeur
La Vie au Grand Air
Le Monde Illustre
Le Plein Air
Le Sport Universal Illustre
Lexington Herald
Long Island Star-Journal
Los Angeles Times
Macon Telegraph
Millbrook Round Table
The Milwaukee Journal
Mirror of Life and Sport
National Police Gazette
Negro Digest
Newark-Star Ledger

Pro Quest Historical Newspapers
The Register
Ring Magazine
Schenectady Gazette
Seattle Daily Times
Seattle Sunday Times
Springfield Daily News
Springfield Daily Republican
Springfield Union
St. Louis Post-Dispatch
Syracuse Herald
Syracuse Journal
Syracuse NY Daily Journal
The Telegram
Trenton Evening Times
Union Hill Times
Utica Daily Press
Washington Afro-American
Washington Post
Washington D.C. Evening Star
Watertown Daily Times
Weekly Irish Times

Joe Jennette's Statistics

157 bouts, 79 won, 9 lost, 6 draws, 62 no-decisions, 1 no-contest, 66 K.O.'s.[621]
Date of Birth: August 26, 1879, New Durham, North Bergen, N.J.
Date of Death: July 2, 1958, Weehawken N.J.
Residence: Union City N.J.
Tale of the Tape:
Height: 5 ft. 9 1/2 in. Wing Span 75 1/2 in. Chest at Rest 42.1 in.
Waist 33 in. Biceps Lengthened 13 1/2 in. Biceps Folded 15.1 in.
Forearm 12.6 in. Thigh 24.6 in. Calf 15.6 in.
(Above Measurements taken April 1909 Paris, France)

A compilation of Jennette's record against his four leading opponents; excluding newspaper decisions:

Jack Johnson   1-1-1   (4 no-decisions)

Year	Official Result	Rounds	Location	Source
1905				
05-09	No Decision	3	Philadelphia, Pa.	*Philadelphia Inquirer*
11-25	Win D.Q.	2	Philadelphia, Pa.	*Boston Globe*
12-02	No Decision	6	Philadelphia, Pa.	*Philadelphia Inquirer*
1906				
01-16	No Decision	3	New York, N.Y.	*Evening Journal,* Jersey City
03-14	Loss Points	15	Baltimore, MD.	*Baltimore Sun*
09-20	No Decision	6	Philadelphia, Pa.	*National Police Gazette*
11-26	Draw Points	10	Portland, Maine	*Boston Herald*

Sam McVea   1-1-2   (1 no-decision)

Year	Official Result	Rounds	Location	Source
1907				
04-15	No Decision	10	New York, N.Y.	*New York Times*
1909				
02-20	Loss Points	20	Paris, France	*La Vie au Grand Air,* Paris
04-17	Win Retirement	49	Paris, France	*La Vie au Grand Air,* Paris
12-11	Draw Points	30	Paris, France	*La Vie au Grand Air,* Paris
1915				
04-27	Draw Points	12	Boston, Ma.	*Springfield Union,* Massachusetts

Battling Jim Johnson 1-0-1   (7 no-decisions, 1 no-contest)

Year	Official Result	Rounds	Location	Source
1912				
07-19	No Decision	6	Philadelphia, Pa.	*Boston Daily Globe*
10-30	No Decision	10	New York, N.Y.	*Washington Post*
1913				
01-01	No Decision	10	Brooklyn, N.Y.	*Cleveland Gazette*
01-21	Win DQ	15	Providence, R.I.	*Rockford Republic,* Illinois
1914				
07-01	No Decision	10	New York, N.Y.	*Albuquerque Journal*
07-15	No Decision	10	New York, N.Y.	*Montgomery Advertiser*
08-05	No Decision	10	New York, N.Y.	*New York Times*
11-10	Draw Points	12	Boston, Mass.	*Boston Daily Globe*

---

[621]Source-International Boxing Hall Of Fame

1915

05-10	No Decision	10	Montreal, Canada	*St. Albans Messenger*, Vermont

1918

08-20	No Contest	8	Newark, N.J.	Unverified

Sam Langford   2-5-2   (5 no-decisions)

Year	Official Result	Rounds	Location	Source
1905				
12-25	Win T.K.O.	8	Lawrence, Mass.	*Boston Globe*
1906				
04-05	Loss Points	15	Chelsea, Mass.	*Boston Globe*
1907				
01-11	Draw	12	Lawrence, Mass.	*Boston Globe*
1908				
03-03	Draw	12	Boston, Mass.	*Boston Globe*
09-01	No Decision	6	New York, N.Y.	*Philadelphia Inquirer*
1910				
09-06	Loss Points	15	Boston, Mass.	*Boston Globe*
1911				
01-10	Loss Points	12	Boston, Mass.	*Boston Globe*
09-05	No Decision	10	New York, N.Y.	*New York Times*
1913				
10-03	No Decision	10	New York, N.Y.	*New York Times*
12-20	Loss Points	20	Paris, France	*La Vie au Grand Air*, Paris
1914				
10-01	No Decision	10	New York, N.Y.	*Philadelphia Record*
1915				
04-13	Win Points	12	Boston, Mass.	*Boston Globe*
1916				
05-12	Loss K.O.	7	Syracuse, N.Y.	*Post Standard* Syracuse, N.Y.
1917				
09-14	No Decision	12	Toledo, OH	*Philadelphia Record*

Joe Jennette's Unofficial Boxing Record

1904

Date	Opponent	Result	Location
11-11	Morris Harris	Loss NWS 6	Philadelphia, Pa.

1905

Date	Opponent	Result	Location
03-02	Morris Harris	Loss NWS 6	Philadelphia, Pa.
04-20	Black Bill	K.O.-Loss 2 of 6	Philadelphia, Pa.
05-09	Jack Johnson	Draw 3	Philadelphia, Pa.
06-08	Black Bill	Win NWS 6	Philadelphia, Pa.
07-06	George Cole	Loss NWS 6	Philadelphia, Pa.
08-28	George Cole	N.C. 6	Philadelphia, Pa.
10-07	Pat O'Rourke	K.O.-Win 2 of 6	North Bergen, N.J.
10-11	Black Bill	K.O.-Win 7 of 10	Wilmington, Del.
10-26	Jim Jeffords	Win NWS 6	Philadelphia, Pa
10-28	George Cole	Win NWS 6	Philadelphia, Pa.
11-02	Black Bill	Draw 6	Wilmington, Del.
11-25	Jack Johnson	Win D.Q. 2 of 6	Philadelphia, Pa.
12-02	Jack Johnson	Loss NWS 6	Philadelphia, Pa.
12-21	Walter Johnson	N.C.-3	New York, N.Y
12-25	Sam Langford	K.O. Win 8 of 12	Lawrence, Mass.

1906

Date	Opponent	Result	Location
01-16	Jack Johnson	Loss NWS	New York, N.Y.
03-14	Jack Johnson	Loss 15pts	Baltimore, MD.
04-05	Sam Langford	Loss 15pts	Chelsea, Mass.
09-06	Black Bill	Win KO 4 of 6	Philadelphia, Pa.
09-20	Jack Johnson	Loss NWS 6	Philadelphia, Pa.
11-26	Jack Johnson	Draw 10pts	Portland, Maine

1907

Date	Opponent	Result	Location
01-11	Sam Langford	Draw 12	Lawrence, Mass.
02-11	Jim Jeffords	Win KO 7 of 10	Portland, Maine
03-08	Yg. Peter Jackson	Win NWS 6	Philadelphia, Pa.
04-15	Sam McVea	Win NWS 10	New York, N.Y.
06-11	Morris Harris	Win TKO 4	New York, N.Y.

1908

Date	Opponent	Result	Location
01-13	Joe Phillips	Win KO 3 of 6	New York, N.Y.
01-27	Jim Jeffords	Win KO 2 of 6	New York, N.Y.
02-17	George Cole	Win TKO 4 of 6	New York, N.Y.
03-03	Sam Langford	Draw 12	Boston, Mass.
03-09	Sam Campbell	Win TKO 6	New York, N.Y
05-08	Jim Barry	N.C. 6	New York, N.Y.
09-01	Sam Langford	Loss NWS 6	New York, N.Y.
09-15	Sandy Ferguson	Win 12 Pts	Boston, Mass.
12-07	Morris Harris	Win NWS 6	Philadelphia, Pa.

1909

Date	Opponent	Result	Location
01-23	Big Ben Taylor	Win KO 3	Paris, France
02-06	Charley Croxon	Win TKO 2	Paris, France
02-20	Sam McVea	Loss 20 Pts	Paris, France
04-17	Sam McVea	Win Rtd 49	Paris, France
05-01	Jack Scales	Win KO 1	Paris, France
05-22	Sandy Ferguson	Win 20 Pts	Paris, France
05-27	Harry Sherring	Win TKO 4	London, U.K.
05-27	Trooper Cooke	Win TKO 2	London, U.K.
06-22	Sandy Ferguson	Loss 12 Pts	Boston, Mass.
08-27	Sandy Ferguson	Win TKO 8 OF 10	Bronx, N.Y.
09-18	Al Kubiak	Loss NWS 6 of 6	Philadelphia, Pa.
10-30	Al Kubiak	Win KO 10 of 20	Paris, France

431

11-13	Sid Russell	Win 15 Pts	Paris, France
12-11	Sam McVea	Draw 30 Pts	Paris, France

1910

05-24	Andy Morris	Win TKO 3 of 12	Boston, Mass.
06-03	Jim Smith	Win NWS 10	New York, N.Y.
07-01	Morris Harris	Draw NWS 10	New York, N.Y
09-06	Sam Langford	Loss 15 Pts	Boston, Mass.
09-30	Morris Harris	Win NWS 10	New York, N.Y.
11-10	Black Bill	Win KO 5 of 10	New York, N.Y.
12-27	Jeff Clark	Draw 10	Newark, N.J.

1911

01-10	Sam Langford	Loss 12 pts	Boston, Mass.
02-08	Jim Barry	Draw 6	Philadelphia,
03-16	Jim Barry	Win NWS 10	New York, N.Y.
04-20	Al Kubiak	Win KO 9 of 10	New York, N.Y.
07-25	Al Kubiak	Win KO 3 of 10	New York, N.Y.
08-01	Tony Ross	Draw NWS 10	New York, N.Y.
08-23	Dummy Maxson	Win KO 1	Bronx, N.Y.
08-29	Porky Dan Flynn	Win NWS 10	Bronx, N.Y.
09-05	Sam Langford	Loss NWS 10	New York, N.Y.
11-30	Bill Watkins	Win KO 1	Albany, N.Y.
12-07	Jewey Smith	Win KO 3	New York, N.Y.
12-11	Yg. Jack Johnson	Win KO 4 of 8	Memphis, Tenn.
12-15	Nat Dewey	Win 8 pts	Chattanooga, Tenn.
12-18	Al Mitchell	Win KO 4	Memphis, Tenn.
12-21	Tpka Jack Johnson	Win KO 3	New Orleans, La.
12-26	Jack Twin Sullivan	Win NWS 10	Buffalo, N.Y.

1912

01-19	Griff Jones	Win KO 3	Utica, N.Y.
02-19	Chuck Carleton	Win NWS 3	Philadelphia, Pa.
02-19	Morris Harris	Win NWS 3	Philadelphia, Pa.
02-27	Andy Morris	Win TKO 6 of 15	New Haven, Conn.
03-13	Nat Dewey	Win TKO 7of 10	New York, N.Y.
04-01	Griff Jones	Win TKO 4 of 10	New York, N.Y.
04-04	Black Bill	Win KO 3 of 12	Lewiston, Ma.
05-24	George Rodel	Win KO 11 of 15	Plymouth, Devon, U.K
06-15	Black Bill	Win DQ 6 of 10	Brooklyn, N.Y.
07-15	Mickey McDonough	Win TKO 2	New Bedford, Mass.
07-15	Jeff Madden	Win WKO 4	New Bedford, Mass.
07-19	Battling Jim Johnson	Draw NWS 6	Philadelphia, Pa.
08-09	Yg. Hank Griffin	Win KO 3	Scranton, Pa.
08-19	Jeff Madden	Win TKO 2 of 10	New York, N.Y.
08-20	Battling Brooks	Win TKO 2	Newark, N.J.
08-20	Bill Tate	Win KO 2 of 6	Newark, N.J.
08-30	Griff Jones	Win KO 2 of 10	Queens, N.Y.
09-02	Jeff Clark	Loss NWS 6	Pittsburgh, Pa.
09-09	Tony Ross	Win DQ 7 of 10	New York, N.Y.
10-30	Battling Jim Johnson	Win NWS 10 of 10	New York, N.Y.
11-27	George Christian	Win KO 8	Columbus, OH.
12-06	Chuck Carleton	Win TKO 2 of 10	New York, N.Y.

1913

01-01	Battling Jim Johnson	Win NWS 10	Brooklyn, N.Y.
01-17	Jeff Clark	Win NWS 10	Joplin, Mo.
01-21	Battling Jim Johnson	Win DQ 15	Providence, R.I.
01-24	Chuck Carleton	Win KO 1 of 6	Easton, P.A.
02-02	Jack Thompson	Loss Pts	?????????
02-10	Jack Reed	Win TKO 2	Hazleton, P.A.
03-17	Jack Reed	Win TKO 3	Queens, N.Y.
04-16	George Cotton	Win TKO 4	Philadelphia, Pa.

432

05-21	Black Bill	Win NWS 10	Brooklyn, N.Y.
06-23	Jeff Clark	NC 7 of 8	Memphis, Tenn.
06-27	Al Benedict	Win TKO 3	Joplin, Mo.
07-01	Harry Wills	Draw 10 pts	Orleans LA.
07-04	Nat Dewey	Win 10 pts	Savannah, GA.
07-22	John Lester Johnson	Win NWS 10	New York, N.Y.
10-03	Sam Langford	Draw NWS 10	New York, N.Y.
12-20	Sam Langford	Loss 20 pts	Paris, France

1914

02-21	Alf Langford	Win KO 7	Paris, France
03-21	Georges Carpentier	Win 15 pts	Paris, France
04-08	Andrew Johnson	Win KO 4	Merseyside, U.K.
05-02	Kid Jackson	Win KO 7	Paris, France
05-04	Colin Bell	Win 20 pts	London, U.K.
06-09	Harry Wills	Draw NWS 10	New Orleans, LA.
06-16	Silas Green	Win TKO 3	Brooklyn, N.Y.
07-01	Battling Jim Johnson	Win NWS 10	New York, N.Y.
07-15	Battling Jim Johnson	Draw NWS 10	New York, N.Y.
08-01	Black Bill	Win TKO 9 of 10	Brooklyn, N.Y.
08-05	Battling Jim Johnson	Win NWS 10	New York, N.Y.
08-11	Bill Tate	Win TKO 6 of 10	Rockaway, N.Y.
09-12	Jim Kruger	Win KO 2	Martins Ferry, Ohio
10-01	Sam Langford	Win NWS 10	New York, N.Y.
11-10	Battling Jim Johnson	Draw 12 pts	Boston, Mass.
12-14	Bill Tate	Win NWS 10	Brooklyn, N.Y.

1915

01-11	John Lester Johnson	Win NWS 10	New York, N.Y.
02-01	Bill Tate	Win KO 2	New York, N.Y.
02-26	Larry Williams	Win KO 5of 10	Montreal, Quebec, Can.
03-19	Cleve Hawkins	Win NWS 10	Montreal, Quebec, Can.
04-09	Arthur Pelkey	Win TKO 8 of 10	Montreal, Quebec, Can.
04-13	Sam Langford	Win 12 pts	Boston, Mass.
04-19	Battling Brooks	Win KO 4	New York, N.Y.
04-27	Sam McVea	Draw 12 pts	Boston, Ma.
05-10	Battling Jim Johnson	Loss NWS 10	Montreal, Quebec, Can.
05-14	Battling Brooks	Win KO 5	New York, N.Y.
07-02	Bill Watkins	Win NWS 10	New York, N.Y.

1916

02-25	Silas Green	Win KO 6	Montreal, Quebec, Can.
03-24	George Cotton	Win KO 2	New York, N.Y.
05-12	Sam Langford	Loss KO 7 of 10	Syracuse, N.Y.
08-04	Porky Dan Flynn	Win NWS 10	Rochester, N.Y.
08-17	Jim Smith	Win TKO 5 of 10	Queens, N.Y.
08-19	Jack Driscoll	Win KO 3	Brooklyn N.Y.
09-04	Jack Hubbard	Win KO 5 of 10	Watertown, N.Y.
12-04	Tony Ross	Win KO 3 of 10	Arlington, PA.

1917

07-06	Tango Kid	Win KO 6	Brooklyn, N.Y.
07-20	Andre Anderson	Win NWS 10	Brooklyn, N.Y.
09-14	Sam Langford	Loss NWS 12	Toledo, OH
09-17	Gabe Gulart	NC ND 10	New York, N.Y.
12-19	George Christian	Win NWS 6	Philadelphia, Pa.

1918

04-15	Jack Thompson	Draw NWS 6	Philadelphia, Pa.
07-19	Kid Norfolk	Win NWS 8	Jersey City, N.J.
08-20	Battling Jim Johnson	NC ND 8	Newark, N.J.
10-11	Kid Norfolk	Win NWS 8	West Hoboken, N.J.
11-22	Jim Coffey	NC ND 4	New Haven, Conn.

| 12-02 | Andy Schmader | Win NWS 8 | West Hoboken, N.J. |
| 12-08 | Andy Schmader | NC ND 8 | Jersey City, N.J. |

1919

02-10	Tom Cowler	Win NWS 8	Jersey City, N.J.
05-01	Clay Turner	Win NWS 8	Jersey City, N.J.
05-23	Tom Cowler	Win NWS 10	Buffalo, N.Y.
10-20	Harry Wills	Loss NWS 8	Jersey City, N.J.
11-11	Bartley Madden	Win DQ 4 of 8	Bayonne, N.J.

1922

| 06-01 | Harry Gibson | Draw 6 | Orange, N.J. |

Index

413

www.ingramcontent.com/pod-product-compliance
Lightning Source LLC
Chambersburg PA
CBHW030935150426
42812CB00064B/2884/J